Wilhelm Lübke

History of Art

Vol. 2

Wilhelm Lübke

History of Art
Vol. 2

ISBN/EAN: 9783743413429

Manufactured in Europe, USA, Canada, Australia, Japa

Cover: Foto ©Thomas Meinert / pixelio.de

Manufactured and distributed by brebook publishing software (www.brebook.com)

Wilhelm Lübke

History of Art

HISTORY OF ART

VOL. II.

LONDON : PRINTED BY
SPOTTISWOODE AND CO., NEW-STREET SQUARE
AND PARLIAMENT STREET

HISTORY OF ART

BY

DR. WILHELM LÜBKE

PROFESSOR OF THE HISTORY OF ART

TRANSLATED BY F. E. BUNNÈTT

IN TWO VOLUMES

VOL. II.

LONDON: SMITH, ELDER AND CO.

1868

CONTENTS

OF

THE SECOND VOLUME.

———•◦•———

CHAPTER IV. GOTHIC STYLE.   PAGE

  1. Character of the Gothic Epoch
  2. Gothic Architecture—   3
    a. The System
    b. Extension—   7
      France   .   .   . 17
      Netherlands .   .   . 23
      Germany   .   .   . 26
      England and Scandinavia   . 37
      Italy 44
      Spain and Portugal   .   . 51
  3. Gothic Sculpture and Painting—
    a. Subject and Form   .
    b. Historical Development—   54
      The North   .   .   . 57
      Italy 81

•

FOURTH BOOK.

THE ART OF MODERN TIMES.

CHAPTER I. GENERAL CHARACTERISTICS OF MODERN ART 101

CHAPTER II. MODERN ARCHITECTURE.

  a. In Italy 111
    First Period. Early Renaissance .   .   . 112
    Second Period. High Renaissance   .   . 121
    Third Period. Bizarre Style   .   . 133

PAGE

b. Other Lands		135
France		136
Spain		137
Netherlands		139
England.		140
Germany		141

CHAPTER III.   PLASTIC ART OF ITALY IN THE FIFTEENTH CENTURY.

1. Sculpture		144
a. The Schools of Tuscany		144
b. The Schools of Upper and Lower Italy		153
2. Painting		158
a. The Tuscan School		158
b. The Schools of Upper Italy		171
c. The Umbrian School		181
d. The Neapolitan School		189

CHAPTER IV.   THE PLASTIC ART OF ITALY IN THE SIXTEENTH CENTURY.

1. Sculpture		191
a. Florentine Artists		193
b. Masters of Upper Italy		205
c. Imitators of Michael Angelo		209
2. Painting		211
a. Leonardo da Vinci and his School		212
b. Michael Angelo and his Followers		227
c. Other Florentine Masters		237
d. Raphael and his School		244
e. Correggio and his School		267
f. The Venetian School		274

CHAPTER V.   NORTHERN PLASTIC ART IN THE FIFTEENTH AND SIXTEENTH CENTURIES.

1. Sculpture		295
a. In Germany		297
Wood Carving		297
Stone Carving		302
Bronze Works		309
b. In France, Spain, and England		317
2. Painting		322
a. The Netherland Schools		326
b. The German Schools		342
c. French and Spanish Painters		363

Chapter. VI. PLASTIC ART IN THE SEVENTEENTH AND
            EIGHTEENTH CENTURIES.

PAGE

1. Sculpture 366
2. Painting 372
    a. Italian Historical Painting 373
    b. Spanish Painting 381
    c. Dutch Historical Painting 386
    d. German, French, and English Painting . . 396
    e. Northern Genre-Painting 399
    f. Landscape, Animal Painting, Flower Painting, and Still Life . 406
        In Italy 407
        In the Netherlands 411

Chapter VII. ART IN THE NINETEENTH CENTURY . . 418

    Architecture 421
    Sculpture 426
    Painting 433

LIST OF ILLUSTRATIONS

IN

THE SECOND VOLUME.

—•◦•—

NO.   PAGE

245. System of the Cathedral at Amiens   10
246. Ground-plan of the Cathedral at Amiens 10
247. Cross springer from Cologne Cathedral 13
248. Window tracery 13
249. Finial. Church at Herrenburg . 15
250. Window from the S. Chapelle at Paris 15
251. Façade of the Cathedral of Rheims 19
252. Cathedral of Beauvais. Interior . 20
253. S. Maclou at Rouen. Exterior . 21
254. Halle at Ypres. Exterior . . 24
255. Town Hall at Oudenarde. Exterior 25
256. Church of St. Catharine at Oppenheim. Exterior . . . 28
257. Marienkirche at Mühlhausen. Interior 30
258. Frauenkirche at Esslingen . . 31
259. Gable of S. Stephan at Vienna . 32
260. Townhall at Münster . . . 34
261. Artushof at Dantzig. Interior . 36
262. Interior System of Wells Cathedral 38
263. Interior System of Worcester Cathedral 38
264. Cathedral of Salisbury. Façade . 40
265. Cathedral of Exeter. Window and column 41
266. Cathedral of York. Pillar . . 42
267. From Henry VII.'s Chapel at Westminster 42
268. Cathedral at Drontheim . . 43
269. Cathedral at Siena . . . 46

NO.   PAGE

270. S. Petronio at Bologna. Ground-plan 48
271. Certosa at Pavia. Interior . . 49
272. From the Palazzo Buonsignori at Siena 50
273. Cathedral of Burgos. Exterior . 52
274. Cathedral of Toledo. Interior . 53
275. Christ from the Cathedral of Amiens 59
276. Relief from the Cathedral at Rheims 60
277. Apostle from the S. Chapelle at Paris 61
278. Statues from the Minster at Strassburg 62
279. Statue from the Schönen Brunnen at Nuremberg 63
280. Relief from the Frauenkirche at Esslingen 64
281. Tomb Relief from Mainz Cathedral 67
282. Angel from a tomb at Schwerin . 69
283. Head of a bishop from the same tomb 69
284. Glass painting from Königsfelden 73
285. Miniature of Wilhelm von Orange 75
286. From a Bible at Stuttgart . . 76
287. The Imhof Altar-piece at Nuremberg 78
288. S. Ursula from Cologne Cathedral 80
289. Relief from the Cathedral at Orvieto 83
290. Relief by Andrea Pisano, Baptist, at Florence 85
291. From Giotto's paintings, in S. M. dell' Arena. Padua . . . 88
292. From Orcagna's? Triumph of Death 92
293. Crowning of the Virgin by Fiesole 95

NO.		PAGE
294.	Painting from the Incoronata at Naples	97
295.	Capella Pazzi at Florence	114
296.	Palazzo Strozzi at Florence. Exterior	116
297.	Court of the Pal. Gondi at Florence	117
298.	Pal. Vendramin Calergi at Venice	119
299.	S. Maria della Grazie at Milan	120
300.	Court of the Cancellaria at Rome	125
301.	Court of the Pal. Massimi at Rome	126
302.	St. Peter's at Rome. Section	130
303.	Court of Pal. Sauli in Genoa	133
304.	Palazzo Pesaro at Venice	134
305.	Façade of the Louvre at Paris	138
306.	Chapel in the Cathedral of Toledo	140
307.	Portal of the Otto-Heinrichsbau at Heidelberg	142
308.	Relief by Ghiberti, Baptistry at Florence	147
309.	Madonna of Luca della Robbia	149
310.	Relief by Donatello, S. Antonio, at Padua	151
311.	Relief by Bened. da Majano, S. Croce at Florence	153
312.	Relief by Tullio Lombardo, S. Antonio at Padua	156
313.	From Masaccio's Frescos, S. M. del Carmine in Florence	160
314.	Fresco painting by Fra Fil. Lippi	162
315.	Fresco painting by Filippino Lippi	164
316.	Fresco painting by Benozzo Gozzoli	166
317.	Fresco painting by Domenico Ghirlandajo	167
318.	From Signorelli's Last Judgment	169
319.	Christ mourned by Angels, Mantegna	174
320.	Coronation of the Virgin by Borognone	177
321.	Christ by Giov. Bellini	180
322.	Madonna by Pietro Perugino	184
323.	Madonna by Francesco Francia	189
324.	Baptism of Christ by Andrea Sansovino	195
325.	Moses by Michael Angelo	200
326.	Slave by Michael Angelo	201
327.	Tomb of Giuliano de' Medici by Michael Angelo	202
328.	Riccio's Candelabra in S. Antonio at Padua	207
329.	Jacopo Sansovino's Bronze Door in S. Marco at Venice	208
330.	From Lionardo da Vinci's Last Supper	216
331.	Holy Family after Lionardo da Vinci	218
332.	Lionardo's Vierge in Bas-relief	220
333.	S. Catharine by Soddoma	223
334.	Head of Roxana by Soddoma	225
335.	Michael Angelo's Cartoon of Pisa	229
336.	Sibyl by Michael Angelo	230
337.	Prophet by Michael Angelo	230
338.	Creation of Light by Michael Angelo	231
339.	Group of the Ancestors of Mary by Michael Angelo	232
340.	Raising of Lazarus by Seb. del Piombo	235
341.	Descent from the Cross by Fra Bartolommeo	239
342.	Madonna by Andrea del Sarto	242
343.	Raphael's Sposalizio	247
344.	From Raphael's Tapestries	254
345.	Decorations from the Loggie of the Vatican	256
346.	From Raphael's Frescoes of the Farnesina	257
347.	Madonna della Sedia by Raphael	259
348.	Transfiguration	263
349.	From Giul. Romano's Frescoes in the Villa Lante	265
350.	Madonna della Scodella, Correggio	270
351.	Magdalene by Correggio	272
352.	The Concert by Giorgione	276
353.	The Daughters of Palma Vecchio	278
354.	Peter Martyr by Titian	280
355.	Madonna with saints by Titian	282
356.	Venus by Titian	285
357.	Holy Family by Moretto	287
358.	Allegory by Tintoretto	290
359.	From Paul Veronese's Adoration of the Kings	292
360.	From Rosenkranz by Veit Stoss	301
361.	Jörg Syrlin's Portrait, Ulm	302
362.	Statues from the church at Stuttgart	304
363.	From the Seven Stages of Adam Krafft	305
364.	Relief by Adam Krafft on the Nuremberg Public Scales	307
365.	Peter Vischer's Tomb of S. Sebald	311
366.	Mermaids from the Tomb of S. Sebald	313
367.	Relief from the Tomb of S. Sebald	313
368.	Apostles from the Tomb of S. Sebald	314
369.	The Anchorites by Hubert van Eyck	329
370.	The Annunciation by Hubert van Eyck	330
371.	Sibyl and Augustus by Rogier van der Weyden	334

NO.		PAGE
372.	From the church of S. Ursula by Memling	336
373.	The Two Misers by Quintin Messys	338
374.	Christ and the Tempter, after Lucas van Leyden . . .	340
375.	Christ on the Cross by Martin Schongauer . . .	343
376.	The Handkerchief of Veronica by Zeitblom	345
377.	The Deriding of Christ by Hans Holbein	348
378.	Madonna of the Burgomaster Meier by Holbein	349
379.	Holbein's Madonna of Solothurn .	350
380.	Meeting of Saul and Samuel by Holbein	351
381.	From Holbein's Dance of Death .	354
382.	Crowning of the Virgin by Dürer .	361
383.	Knight, Death, and Devil by Dürer	364
384.	Group from a painting by Cranach	366
385.	Apollo and Daphne by Bernini .	371
386.	Statue from the church at Stuttgart	372

NO.		PAGE
387.	Equestrian Statue of the great Elector by Schlüter . . .	374
388.	Venus and Mars by Annibale Caracci	379
389.	S. Cecilia by Domenichino . .	380
390.	Magdalene by Guido Reni . .	382
391.	False Players by Caravaggio .	383
392.	Female portrait by Velasquez .	387
393.	St. John by Murillo . . .	388
394.	Rubens' Raising of Lazarus . .	390
395.	Group of Children by Rubens .	394
396.	The Children of Charles I. by Van Dyck	396
397.	Rape of Ganymede by Rembrandt	398
398.	The Raising of Lazarus by Rembrandt	399
399.	Moses at the Spring by Nicolas Poussin	402
400.	Genre picture by Teniers . .	405
401.	Genre picture by Ger. Dow . .	408
402.	Landscape by Claude Lorraine .	414
403.	Landscape by Jac. Ruysdael . .	418

THIRD BOOK.

THE ART OF THE MIDDLE AGES.

Continued.

OUTLINES

OF

THE HISTORY OF ART.

————o◦⦂◉⦂◦o————

CHAPTER IV.

GOTHIC STYLE.

———

I. CHARACTER OF THE GOTHIC EPOCH.

In the last epoch of the Romanesque style, we have seen an intellectual movement preparing and ever more developing, an effort to rise from the strict circle of tradition to newer and freer forms. After the Germanic mind had assimilated with Christian tradition and antique laws, its own independence began to develope itself more boldly, and to find expression in original forms. It is true that for a time the strictness of hierarchical tradition fettered these freer movements, and priestly law, in the garment of the antique, governed all intimations of life. But once awakened and sensible of its own power, the Germanic spirit of liberty was no longer to be shackled ; it broke asunder the strict rules of tradition, and gave a new direction to life and to art.

This revolution first becomes apparent in the beginning of the thirteenth century ; but it did not spread everywhere with equal decision and rapidity. So long as it was necessary to imbue the

B 2

Germanic mind with Christian and antique tradition, Germany—
which, moreover, under the rule of powerful emperors, stood at
the head of European affairs—took precedence of other lands
both in civilisation and art. But now, when the consequence of
this union was to be reaped, when individual perception was
rescued from hierarchical bann, France—and especially the Germanic north-east portion of the land—took the lead. The connection with Italy had here never been so hearty and thorough
as in Germany, and therefore the link with antique tradition was
freer. Chivalry had developed itself here more rapidly than
elsewhere. The easily excited feeling, at that time peculiar to
this nation, had drawn it especially to take enthusiastic part in
the crusades; and in the middle of the thirteenth century, King
Lewis the Saint undertook a crusade of his own accord. Thus
the mighty social revolution, which these visionary expeditions
called forth in the life, habits, and views of the West, appear
especially striking in France. · The wonders of the remote East,
the adventurous character of the expedition, and the mixture
with foreign nations—all this shattered the old conceptions, and
created a new circle of ideas. The old severe period had passed
away for ever, and a new epoch began, marked by brilliant and
varied movements. Added to this, Germany at this time was
passing through that long period of distraction and confusion,
which began with the decline of the Hohenstauffen power, a
period conducive, indeed, to the prosperity of cities and citizens,
but which for ever broke the European power of the empire;
while, on the other hand, in France the domestic power of a
kingdom rising from an insignificant germ was more and more
strengthened by wise policy, and spread unceasingly from the
north over the entire country. All these forces combined to
place France at this epoch at the height of the movement in
civilisation, and to procure, after a short struggle with transmitted forms, an entirely new garb for the new spirit; while
elsewhere, as in Germany and Italy, a similar though more
moderate mental movement was satisfied with a richer and more
splendid remodelling of the Romanesque.

This new spirit—this freer movement—may be clearly perceived in the various branches of civilised life. Its vaguely divined but enthusiastically pursued aim was the deliverance of the individual from hierarchical fetters; only, it is true, in the limited measure commensurate with the religious views of the middle ages. It was not an opposition to the Church that was desired, although there was now less recoil than formerly at a rebellion, in case of need, against the highest verdict of the Pope. The age was more devout, more religious, than the former one; but the powerfully awakened feelings were no longer satisfied with the strict universality of the priestly dogma —they desired to grasp more deeply and to feel more excitingly the truths of religion, and to give expression to their own sentiments. In the sphere of the Church itself, school divinity rose to the utmost importance, attracting the most brilliant and the boldest minds, and leading to a profound penetration of religious dogmas. It is very significant of the state of feeling at this period, that the worship of the Virgin Mary ever gained ground with greater power and depth, and religion assumed the character of a sacred love. This tendency was, however, closely connected with the reverence of the female sex, which had reached a great height, and which went hand in hand with the advance of chivalric feeling. As if in a holy rapture, the knight was occupied, in the poems of the period, entirely with thoughts of his mistress, and a perfect fascination seemed to hold him fettered. These sentiments, however, are so far removed from the basis of reality, that feeling becomes lost in the most subtile ideality, and infallibly soon falls a victim to conventional show.

Still, in the fulness of youthful ardour, and in all the grace of fresh enthusiasm, this feeling is wafted to us in poetry. Nothing can more triumphantly proclaim the newly awakened life of this period than the revival of national poetry. Hitherto the Latin tongue, although strangely ossified and degenerated, had universally prevailed as the one means of intellectual expression. Historians and poets had alone in it been able to declare their ideas, and national languages were condemned to inglorious silence. Suddenly the national mind seems to have remembered its own existence. Bards boldly touched the strings, and inspired the long-despised mother tongue to express the sublimest thoughts and the deepest feelings; the Provençal troubadours resounded their enthusiastic songs; and the German chivalric epic, slowly following the French model, displayed in Wolfram von Eschenbach the wondrous perfection and highest expression of the poetry of that day.

Art could not escape the influence of this mighty impulse. High as its significance had been in the Romanesque epoch, it now assumed a still more important position. If in the earlier period it had arrived at higher perfection by withdrawing from one-sided monastic culture, it now obtained a still deeper and more vigorous life as the national mind pervaded it, and the excited feelings of the laity strove to find expression in it. Architecture first acquired a new and bold organisation, in the wonderful structure of which the most subtile combination triumphs; while at the same time the lifelike effect of the whole, the free uprising and delicate construction, with its display of countless elegant forms, affords a powerfully poetical expression of the excited feelings of the mind. In the plastic arts the solemn Romanesque style was entirely abandoned, and the calm sublimity of antique figures gave place to a lofty inspiration and to a depth of true feeling. A tender youthful life pervades every work, wafting towards us, as it were, the presentiment of a fresh spring.

This movement became conspicuous in France at the end of the twelfth century; and in the early years of the thirteenth century it reached such a complete and decided form, that it soon spread with great rapidity over the countries on all sides. As, however, the idealism of this entire epoch was too one-sided in its delicacy, and was too far removed from reality in its enthusiastic elevation, it could not long remain on its bold height. As scholastic divinity was soon transformed into subtlety, as the expression of the tenderest love withered away into conventional court-like form, so, in the sphere of art, architecture, sculpture, and painting alike evidence, even in the fourteenth century, that striving after external formalism, which is wont to cause the decline of an idealistic art sooner than of any other. From 1350 these critical symptoms visibly increase; and with the fifteenth century occurs that mighty reaction of realism and of the antique which puts an end to the mediæval forms.

2. GOTHIC ARCHITECTURE.

a. *The System.*

The same effort which called forth, in the Romanesque epoch, such important changes in architecture, produced a style of building, which is connected with that of the earlier epoch in its ground-plan, but in its construction, as well as in its artistic stamp, gains a thoroughly new and original importance. Buildings of this style were ignominiously called 'Gothic' in an age of one-sided views, because it was thought that only rude barbarians like the old Goths could have produced such works. Recently, however, this Gothic style has been raised to honour, and may with justice bear the old name, as the repeatedly attempted designations of 'German, old German, or pointed style' do not fully and rightly denote the nature of the matter.

If we inquire as to the origin of this style, which might appear to have been a mere caprice compared with the varied and brilliant development of the Romanesque style, we discover at last that it was produced neither by motives of worship nor expediency, but that it owes its origin alone to a striving after an ethical artistic ideal. The strongly awakened national mind yearned to express itself with greater freedom and independence in every sphere of life; it struggled everywhere after a lively expression of that which is felt within, and the result of this in architecture was a new style. That this style bore the character of freedom, lightness, and boldness, of slenderness and sublimity to a peculiar extent, was a necessary consequence.

One of the most important aids in this revolution was afforded by the pointed arch. This form in itself is not new to us. We have seen it in Egypt as early as the ninth century, and we have

found it almost universally employed among the Mohammedans.
We traced it from thence, passing to the Normans in Sicily; but
we found it also, in all probability as an original conception, in
the tunnel-vaulted churches of Southern France. That, in the
course of the crusades, the frequent acquaintance with Oriental
buildings procured constant adoption for the pointed arch in
Europe is very probable, as in the later part of the twelfth century, after the reign of Frederic I., it is found more and more in
use in German-Romanesque buildings. But all these examples
are of a decorative or isolated character; nowhere but in the
Gothic building do we find the pointed arch made the fundamental law of the construction, and vaulted roof, arcades,
windows, and niches all executed with its assistance.[1] It is
consequently one of the main merits of this style that it has
recognised this form, which was formerly used at will, in its
constructive importance, and has made it the central point of its
system.

This importance, however, is of a twofold kind. The pointed
arch, either in its more or less lancet-like or blunted elevation,
gave different height to the separate arches, or—which was more
important—carried up the arches of various span to the same
height. Hence the necessity vanished for quadripartite arrangement which had marked the Romanesque style; hence the broad
vaulting of the higher and broader aisles ceased, and the central
aisle could now have the same number of arches as the side
aisle—the arrangement of the ground-plan was freer and more
animated, and the whole effect of the interior was more lively.
The pointed arch also, from the smaller tension of its different
parts, lessened the side thrust, producing a pressure rather downwards than towards the side. With this another important
innovation was connected. The cross springers were not merely
constructed of strong quarry stones, but the diagonal lines of the
vault had similar cross ribs, and thus a firm scaffolding was
obtained, in which the calottes were inserted, as light and thin as

[1] Wherever it appears in German transition-architecture, it is in consequence of a
reaction of the Gothic style.

possible, as though merely designed to fill up the space at will. There was no longer the massive vaulted roof of the Romanesque period, which exercised a side pressure on all points with equal weight, and therefore required everywhere equally strong counter-forts in strong masses of wall. It was only necessary to secure the different points of support; it was only necessary to furnish the wall with a strong counterfort just where the springers of the arches and the ribs of the roof met the pillars, in order that the parts between might be treated as spaces to be lightly filled up or perforated with windows.

This innovation produced a revolution to which architecture owes the perfect alteration of its physiognomy; for buttresses now arose at the points to be supported, and between them were placed broad and high windows, which supplied the interior with an effect of light hitherto unimagined and totally changed its character. But they did not stop at these fundamental features. As the buildings constructed had generally three aisles, the side aisles being far lower than the central aisle, they could not immediately obtain a sufficient counterfort for the vaulting of the latter, endangered as it was by its double height and breadth. One or two flying arches were, therefore, thrown across from those points of the wall of the central aisle, which required to be strengthened, to the wall surrounding the side aisle; the whole of the side pressure thus fell upon the out-side wall, which was supported by massive buttresses. (Fig. 245.) The principle of construction already existing in the tunnel-vaulted churches in the south of France was thus transformed into a new system. The advantages afforded by supports of this kind soon allured to a much more splendid development of the design, the lofty central aisle being enclosed by two lower side aisles on each side, thus returning to the five-aisled basilica. In this case, buttresses were carried above the middle row of pillars, and these buttresses received the flying arches of the central aisle, and allowed a second similar arch to be spanned to the outer wall; indeed, as occasionally two arches were raised one above another, four flying arches were employed to render the one point secure. But even in these important features of construction, it is plain to perceive that the Gothic style did not emanate from a practical point of view, nor from any need of constructive efficiency; but, impelled by its æsthetic principle, it passed beyond what was necessary to an extent which no style of architecture either before or after has even remotely desired.

In this manner the plan of the Gothic church fashioned itself

Fig. 245. System of the Cathedral at Amiens.

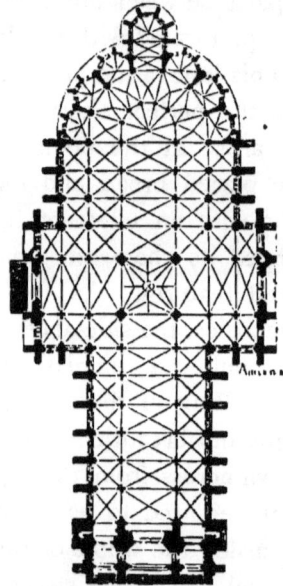

Fig. 246. Ground-plan of the Cathedral at Amiens.

once more on the ground-plan of the old basilica, but with the modification of the cross-vaulting of the Romanesque building. Choir, transept, and nave, with a considerable tower, form now, as before, the fundamental features of the church structure; but all these characteristic features are increased to the utmost extent, and raised into a richly organised and effective design. The richest design was adopted for the choir—that, namely, created by the Romanesque style—the choir of Southern France, furnished with surrounding aisle and chapels; only, instead of the semicircular apsis, a polygonal termination was introduced, in which generally there were an uneven number of sides, so that the central point fell upon a wall, and not in an angle. The octagon and the dodecagon are the favourite forms, and from these the choir receives a form of five or seven sides. In a corresponding manner the aisles are attached to the main building, and the small chapels are similarly attached to the aisles. (Fig. 246.) The transept in this richer style has likewise usually three aisles, and frequently has large portals at the side walls, while the nave constantly consists of five aisles. Thus the rich construction of the most important early Christian basilicas was again attained—indeed, essentially surpassed; but the spacious effect was met by a diametrically opposite effect, the airy breadth being limited in the same proportion as the height was raised: it may be sufficient to mention, in proof of this, that in S. Paolo in Rome the breadth of the central nave is about 80 feet with a height of 110 feet; while in the cathedral at Cologne, with a breadth of only 45 feet, it rises 140 feet high. The triumph, however, of the Gothic style is, that it transformed the old stiff framework of the basilica into flowing architectural life, and into a complete and consistent organisation.

This ground-plan of Gothic architecture received a perfectly new expression in the execution of the different parts. The last reminiscences of antique forms were set aside, and the Germanic mind stamped upon every member and every small detail, its own independent laws of form. The pillars which separated the aisles were generally formed by a round stem, against which, as supporters of the ribs and springers, a number of three-quarter columns stood. Usually four stronger columns corresponded with the transverse and longitudinal springers, and a similar number of weaker ones met the cross rib-work. Sometimes, between the separate columns, the stem of the pillar was hollowed out by a fluting, and thus a sharper effect of light and shade was obtained. The columns were connected with each other and with the stem of the pillar by a polygonal base, and were marked in the ground-plan as one member. This basis

was divided for the several columns into just as many special
bases, likewise polygonal in form, and connected with each other
and with the stem of the pillar by fine riband-like members, in
which the form of the Attic base frequently appeared. In a
similar manner, the fine and distinctly constructed cornice of the
capital was carried round the whole pillar; but only the capitals
of the columns were, as a rule, covered with ornaments. These
ornaments were far removed from the plastic richness and variety
of Romanesque detail ; only two light wreaths of leaves were
carried round the cup-like form, so that between them the
substance of the capital was plainly visible and they appeared
only lightly fastened to it. The formal character of this ornament
was also thoroughly new, for, far removed from the conventional
leafwork of the Romanesque style, the Germanic love of nature
revelled in the abundance of its native flora, and portrayed
with graceful variety sometimes the leaf of the oak, sometimes
that of the thistle or the ivy, the vine, the rose, the holly, and
other native plants, with an effective adherence to nature.
Animal and human forms, as well as the rich fantastic creations
of the Romanesque period, were almost wholly excluded.

The more lively organisation of the pillars corresponded both
with the construction of the arcades, and with that of the
springers and rib-work of the roof. The stiff rectangular form
of the former age was at first softened by fluting with alternate
rounding, and soon was developed in a manner corresponding
with the new style. It still consisted only of deep flutings,
alternating with roundings, and with a projecting member of a
pear or heart-shaped outline, which seems to have arisen from
the tapering of the round member, and constitutes one of the
specific elements of Gothic architecture. We find it usually
alone on the cross rib-work; in the cross springers, and still
more in the wide arches of the arcades, it appears variously
combined with other forms. (Fig. 247.)

The windows, also, are extremely important in the formation
of the Gothic style. In the last Romanesque epoch, a richer
light and a freer perforation of the walls had been sought for by

forming the windows in groups. The Gothic style here, also, profited by the final results of this plan. It broke the surface of the wall with one large window placed between two pillars, this window being divided in a vertical direction by stone bars (mullions). (Cf. Fig. 248.) These bars, which were divided like the columns into stronger and weaker, were connected together at the upper end by pointed arches, and comprised within the large arch of the window. In the openings thus arising, circles or other suitable geometric forms were inserted as stone tracery; and these,

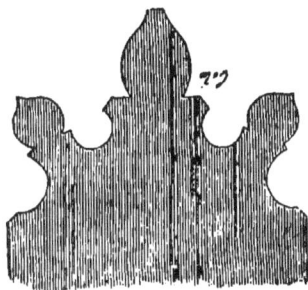

Fig. 247. Cross Springer from the Choir of the Cathedral at Cologne.

again, were filled with trefoils, quatrefoils, or still richer forms. (Fig. 248.) These divisions and tracery at first assumed a circular form, but speedily adopted the true Gothic fluted profile; while the mullions, which were at first finished like slender columns with bases and capitals, subsequently passed directly into the stone tracery above. The broad magnificent windows, filled with lustrous glass paintings, form a splendid element of the Gothic style, and were executed with ever new and charming variety.

Fig. 248. Window-work of the developed Gothic Style.

Below the windows of the upper nave, triforiums, such as had been familiar to the Romanesque style, were introduced; now, however, enlivened with richer geometric tracery, and forming a part of the window structure. The general effect of the interior was increased by the lofty bold vaulting, the slender

delicately constructed pillars, and the broad magnificent windows; the latter even, covering as they did almost the whole
surface of the walls with their glass painting, took the place
of the wall painting which had been before so eagerly cultivated. Compared with the Romanesque buildings, the effect of
the interior is more free, airy, bold, and elegant; the mind feels
itself drawn upwards by these aspiring pillars and bold vaulting,
and recognises in these solemn courts, illuminated as they are
by mystic light, the inspiration of an epoch full of fresh youthful
faith.

The buttress especially prevails in the exterior. The buttresses are massively designed, but taper considerably, gradated
by various bands of entablature, and partly connected with the
rest of the building. Their surfaces are enlivened by geometric
tracery, or by niches with figures placed within them. The point
is formed by a slender pyramidal tower (named Finial in architectural language), which is composed of a slender pointed roof.
(Fig. 249.) Sometimes, instead of this, baldachins with statues
crown the top of the buttress. No less rich is the form of these
buttresses, the upper end of which slopes obliquely down, containing inside the pipes for the outlet of the water, which is
emptied, far from the building, through the mouth of some fantastic animal. The upper edge of the buttress is generally elegantly crowned by small stone flowers, in knots or bunches,
which are also to be found on the top of the finials. The mass
of the buttress is gracefully broken by rosettes or tracery work.

The whole surface between the buttresses is filled up by
broad windows, which have a projecting gable as their upper
termination to shelter the more delicate parts from the wind.
The upper edge of this gable is ornamented with knobs, the
point is crowned by a cruciform plant, and the surface is enlivened with tracery work, of a simple kind at first (Fig. 250),
but subsequently of greater richness.

This infinitely rich abundance of plastic detail, extending,
filigree-like, over all parts, dissolving the fixed outline into a
number of airy members, and making the mass of stone fade, as

it were, into countless flowers, affords a rich and striking effect, in combination with the rich windows, with the strong deep fluting and sharply projecting members of the roof-cornice, as well as the open-work galleries extending over it, which form a passage round the entire building. What a contrast to the calm solemn masses of the Romanesque style, only broken by

Fig. 249. Finial (Collegiate Church at Herrenburg).

Fig. 250. From the Ste. Chapelle at Paris.

small windows, and constructed with moderate lisenes, friezes, and cornices, and exhibiting the solemn character of noble reserve! Here, on the other hand, everything presses forward, everything strives after outward manifestation, each member desires to live out its separate existence with gladness and strength ; so that, amid all this rivalry of projecting and aspiring details, the total effect is decidedly endangered. In the choir, especially, where the polygonal sides, with their aisles and chapels, rise on high with all their masses and forms intersecting and crowding against each other, a want of rest and distinctness is produced, which may, indeed, excite the fancy, but cannot satisfy the sense for beauty.

More calm, on the other hand, is the effect of the façade with its mighty towers, which likewise exhibit the law of pyramidal aspiration, of restless growth, and a gradual tapering and diminishing of form. Provided at each corner with strong buttresses, between which the surface of the wall is perforated with large and richly constructed windows, their upper termination is formed by a slender, boldly aspiring cupola, which, completely perforated by the devices of the style, is composed of eight stone ribs and geometric tracery, and in its light filigree-like appearance victoriously exhibits the triumph of mind over matter, and of the æsthetic principle over all that may be called expedient and practical.

The portals occupy an important position, not merely as regards the façade, but the exterior of the building in general. More slender and wider than at an earlier period, they are usually divided by a central stone post, and in the construction of their walls they manifest a rich variety of forms, carrying out with greater freedom and splendour all that had been begun in the Romanesque period. They are composed of a number of sharply cut, strongly projecting, and deeply hollowed forms; and in the deeper flutings, statues of saints are placed on slender columns with graceful pedestals, while in the archivolts, single sitting figures or small groups are to be seen in rows above each other, enclosed by consoles and baldachins. As, however, the arrangement of these groups with their base corresponds with the radius of the respective circle, it acquires an air of constraint and unnaturalness. The arched panel is also adorned with representations in relief, usually placed in different rows above each other, and effecting rather an external division of the space than an organised construction. These portals, however, from their rich abundance of ornament, as well as from the profound symbolic character of their sculpture, produce an effect of brilliant splendour and imaginative power.

Such are essentially the main features of the system, which, indeed, is not developed universally with the same richness and consistency, and which also affords considerable scope for national peculiarities.   The style maintains its pure beauty and harmony until about the year 1350.   From thenceforth a restless fermentation begins in architectural taste, which loosens the harmonious connection, wrests decoration from its union with construction, and ends with the complete degeneracy and dissolution of the style.   The peculiar character of this process of development we shall enter into more closely on our consideration of the separate local groups.

b. *Outward Extension.*

FRANCE.[1]

Of no former style can the place and period of its birth be shown with the same accuracy as of the Gothic.   Paris and its immediate neighbourhood were its cradle, and the territory of north-east France saw the first stages of its development.   It was the ingenious combination of northern French architecture which blended together into a new style the different elements hitherto scattered through the various schools of France—the rich choir of the Burgundian buildings, the flying arch of the south, and the cross-vaulting of Normandy.   Even in the middle of the twelfth century, when the rest of the West was strongly Romanesque in its architecture, a new choir arose in the church of St. Denis, near Paris (consecrated in 1144), under the brilliant and powerful rule of the art-loving Abbé Suger; and this choir, in spite of subsequent transformations, undoubtedly for the first time presents a complete buttress system, the perfect pointed arch, and the rich finish of surrounding aisles and chapels.   It is true the aisles and chapels were still formed in a semicircle, and in the detail also the Romanesque forms were retained in all buildings until the thirteenth century; but the idea of the construction and composition was new—in one word, it was the Gothic.

[1] *Denkm. d. Kunst.*   Pl. 50 and 51.   Cf. also the works quoted on p. 415, note 1.

A series of churches, both in the immediate vicinity and in
more distant parts, soon followed this system, at first exhibiting
various attempts and innovations, with Romanesque elements of
detail, but subsequently evidencing advance and extension of
the system.   The beautiful church of St. Remy, at Rheims, and
the mighty cathedrals of Laon and Paris, belong to this number.
The two latter have much affinity with each other in design and
execution : they have the heavy round pillar, galleries extending
over the side aisles, and above these an especial triforium, as
well as the broad hexapartite vaulting which marked an earlier
epoch.   At the same time, the façade structure in both is grandly
and heavily developed, and adopts the great wheel window of
the Romanesque epoch as the main element of the central
building, which henceforth was to experience a richer and more
brilliant development under the influence of Gothic tracery.
The grand cathedral of Bourges, begun at about the same time,
is of a similar character.

With the beginning of the thirteenth century, the results of
the preceding period were more strictly adhered to, the plan of the
interior reached its freest and most distinct completion, and the
structure acquired that airy lightness, that imposing boldness of
proportions, which henceforth was to render the Gothic style
victorious throughout the whole Western world.   The earliest of
these works, the cathedral of Chartres, the choir and aisles of
which were newly restored after a fire, between the years 1195
and 1260, has the heaviness of the Romanesque style, in
the form of its windows and buttresses, as well as in the development of the choir.   Freer, bolder, and lighter is the cathedral of Rheims, which was begun in 1212, and was completed, in
the course of the century, by Robert de Couci, and the façade of
which (Fig. 251) affords the most magnificent example of a
complete early Gothic building.   But the sum of all preceding
efforts is comprised in the grandest manner in the cathedral of
Amiens, built between 1220 and 1288, because here for the first
time the principle of the Gothic style is triumphantly carried
into the smallest detail, and in its ground-plan and structure (cf.

Figs. 245 and 246) it affords a model, the influence of which speedily appears in the most important buildings of the West. The pillars here gradually acquire that slender clustered form, the capitals are adorned with elegant leafwork, the heavy galleries are set aside, but triforiums and windows supply their place with brilliant splendour, and in the ground-plan of the choir, with its

Fig. 251. Façade of the Cathedral at Rheims.

seven chapels, the polygonal design is employed in a normal manner. While the central aisle here attains a breadth of 42 feet and a height of 132 feet, the cathedral of Beauvais, which was commenced soon after, with its central aisle of 45 feet in breadth and a height of 146 feet, surpasses all proportions hitherto attained in such a bold manner, that in 1284, twelve years after its completion, the choir fell in, and was obliged to be remodelled in its transformation. The system of the Gothic style was now established, and was employed everywhere with splendid success. The time of Louis the Saint, about the middle of the thirteenth century, witnessed the noblest and most distinct perfection of the style; and the palace chapel erected by this king, the so-called

Fig. 252.   Interior of the Cathedral of Beauvais.

Ste. Chapelle at Paris, built by Peter of Montereau between 1243 and 1251, is the most costly gem of this classic period of the Gothic style. (Fig. 250.) The zeal for building, which had reached its highest pitch, called forth the splendid restoration of most of the cathedrals throughout the entire country. In the early part of the century, the cathedral of Troyes, begun in 1208, was recommenced; the mighty cathedral of Rouen rose in Nor-

mandy between 1200 and 1280; the most splendid choir in the
Gothic style was added to the noble Romanesque nave of the
cathedral of Le Mans; and the smaller cathedral of Tours

Fig. 253.   Exterior of S. Maclou, at Rouen.

appeared as an elegant imitation of the church of Amiens.
Further south, this style advanced victoriously, exhibiting in the
cathedrals of Auxerre, Lyon, Clermont-Ferrand, Limoges, and
in the choir of the cathedral of Narbonne, important evidences

of its henceforth almost uncontested supremacy.   In French-
Switzerland its influence was perceived in the cathedral of
Geneva, and still more in the noble, severe, early Gothic cathedral of Lausanne.   Nevertheless, in the south of France, a
more simple plan was adopted with one broad nave and chapels
built within it, as in the grand cathedral of Alby, slowly executed
about 1282.

The fourteenth century, exhausted and distracted by the
fatal wars with England, witnessed in France a less rich advance
in architecture, although there was even now no lack of partial
renovations and restorations of older buildings.   Not merely
were the older cathedrals in course of construction continued, but
the bold and almost exaggerated slenderness and elegant lightness of the system, which had reached its highest point of perfection, was expressed with noble grace in churches such as
S. Ouen at Rouen (about 1318), and the unfinished S. Urbain at
Troyes.   On the other hand, from the beginning of the fifteenth
century, a magnificently rich revival of the Gothic style appeared,
designated by the French with the name of the Flamboyant
style.   It indulged in the preponderance of splendid decoration,
which at the same time went hand in hand with a playful capricious transformation of the forms of detail.   The tracery of the
windows was especially affected by it, being now composed of
flame-like curves.   The arches also assumed a form curved outwardly, too slender in parts, and too much depressed in others,
and splendid but somewhat cold tracery work covered the
exterior.   Normandy especially is rich in unusually elegant
works of this kind, among them St. Maclou at Rouen is conspicuous for the splendour and richness of its finish.   This concluding epoch also witnessed a rich advance in the decoration of
private buildings, as is evidenced by the Palais de Justice at
Rouen, the castle Meillant, and the House of Jacques Cœur at
Bourges.

THE NETHERLANDS.[1]

The Netherland territory, enclosed by France and Germany, exhibits in its architectural works a distinct reflection of the influence and artistic position of these two great countries. In the Romanesque epoch, when Germany stood at the head of Europe, and took the lead in the art movement, the Netherland buildings chiefly bore the character of the neighbouring Rhine lands. In the Gothic epoch, when the influence of France asserted its victorious sway, this influence was most striking in the weaker neighbouring land. The architecture of the Netherlands follows henceforth the early Gothic style of France, and adheres for a long time to this primitive mode of expression.

Among the more important buildings is the cathedral of St. Gudula at Brussels, a building of a grave character and mighty proportions; also the cathedral of Utrecht, likewise executed on a French ground-plan; and the cathedral of Antwerp, which belongs to a later epoch, having been begun in 1352, and not completed till the fifteenth century—a building grand and spacious in design, subsequently even enlarged to seven aisles, and without a parallel in the picturesqueness and beauty of its perspective. In Holland, the style is flat, even in the more important buildings, owing to the adoption of brick and the constant employment of wooden ceilings instead of stone vaulting.

Far greater importance has been reached in the Netherlands, especially in Belgium, in secular architecture. The towns of Flanders had at that time obtained a degree of power and importance by commerce and navigation, with which throughout the entire West only the great free cities of Italy could compete. Wealth and civil power were grandly expressed in the secular buildings of these cities. The designs are large and spacious, far surpassing all material necessity. The essential part of their decorative form is borrowed from the church architecture of the time, yet in such a manner that, in its application and

[1] *Denkm. d. Kunst.* Pl. 5. Schayes, *Histoire de l'Architecture en Belgique.* 4 vols. 8vo. Brussels, 1849, et seq.

composition, the secular character of the building is plainly recognised.   Thus there are not merely town halls, but guildhalls,
and various other buildings designed for civil purposes.   Projecting towers rise generally at the corners of the buildings, and

Fig. 254.   Hall at Ypres.

the centre is frequently crowned by a mighty bell-tower, the
so-called Beffroi.
     The resources at the disposal of the rich guilds of these
mighty cities for these public aims is evidenced, among others, by
the hall of the clothmakers at Ypres, executed between 1200 and
1364, and now used as a town hall. (Fig. 254.)   The building,

which is of considerable dimensions, rises two stories high, with
noble pointed windows. It is finished with rich battlements,
and at each corner with a small and slender projecting tower, the
centre being commanded by a massive beffroi, the corners of
which terminate in four graceful turrets. A similar design is

Fig. 255. Town Hall at Oudenarde.

exhibited in the hall at Bruges, which was begun in 1284, but
was not completed till later. This secular architecture reaches
its utmost perfection in the council hall at Bruges, begun in the
year 1377, and which, with its slender pointed windows, its rich

and baldachin-covered statues, its splendid battlements, and small projecting towers at the corners and in the centre, exhibits a completeness of structure as rich as it is distinct. At a later epoch, this style reached its grandest development in the town hall at Brussels, built between 1401 and 1455, which was followed in the latter part of the fifteenth century by the still more magnificent town hall at Louvain, and by that at Oudenarde (Fig. 255), which was not built until the sixteenth century, and occupied the years from 1527 to 1530.

GERMANY.[1]

Germany seems at first to have been more opposed than most other countries to the Gothic style. Its adherence to the transmitted Romanesque style suffered it only gradually to perceive the advantages of an architecture springing up on a foreign soil; and this did not take place, as we have seen, until the new mode of building had exercised a transforming influence upon architectural works in the so-called transition style. Even then Gothic buildings were isolated, and Romanesque tradition maintained its position far into the thirteenth century, producing a series of splendid works. Yet on this account, Gothic architecture was here to acquire a more distinct and regular development than elsewhere.

Among the first buildings which betray in Germany the tendencies of the Gothic style, is the choir of the cathedral at Magdeburg,[2] begun about the year 1208, which possesses the polygonal aisle and series of chapels after the French model, but is yet throughout interwoven with Romanesque detail. (The nave belongs to the fourteenth century, and the façade with its two stately towers was not completed till 1520.) The first pure Gothic buildings of Germany show, however, an originality in the adoption of the style, a freedom in the transforma-

---

[1] *Denkm. d. Kunst.* Pl. 53-56. Cf. the works mentioned in the Romanesque style.

[2] *Denkm. d. Kunst.* Pl. 53. Fig. 5. Pl. 54 A. Clemens, Mellin, and Rosenthal, *Der Dom zu Magdeburg.* Fol. 1830.

tion of the fundamental form, and a delicacy in the execution of the detail, all of which brilliantly display the creative power of the German masters. This is especially the case with the Liebfrauen church at Treves,[1] built between 1227 and 1244, in which the formerly favourite central building is splendidly enlivened by the Gothic system, and especially by the ingenious application of the French series of chapels. In a no less original manner, but far more important as regards the further development of the style, the same architectural tendency is evidenced in the church of S. Elizabeth at Marburg[2] (1235 to 1283), which in its choir and transepts returns to the earlier Rhenish design of a polygonal termination, and which affords in its nave the important example of the first Gothic church with three aisles of equal height, although the windows are arranged over each other in two rows.

German Gothic architecture completely follows its French models in its famous work, the cathedral of Cologne,[3] which was begun in 1248, and which in its entire choir, with its aisles and chapels, is almost identical with that of the cathedral of Amiens. But in the distinct and regular construction of the whole, in the noble completeness of its abundant ornament, the German style here reaches a stage of independent perfection. After the choir had been consecrated in the year 1322, the completion of the transepts and nave was slowly continued, and in the latter the highest amount of imposing space was again reached, as it was formed with five aisles. The central aisle is 44 feet in breadth, and the main dome rises 140 feet high. The entire length of the mighty building amounts externally to 532 feet. The whole was to have been finished by two colossal towers, with slender open-work spires, which remained unfinished, and the original sketch of which exhibits a style bordering on exaggeration.

[1] Schmidt, *Baudenkmale von Trier.*
[2] *Denkm. d. Kunst.* Pl. 53. Figs. 6 and 7. Moller's *Denkm. deutscher Baukunst.*
[3] *Denkm. d. Kunst.* Pl. 54, 54 A, 54 B. Cf. the splendid work by Boisserée, *Der Dom zu Köln.* Stuttgart, 1823.

Farther up the river, in the middle Rhine country, the elegant church of S. Katharine at Oppenheim [1] (1262 to 1317) is a
far more original work (Fig. 256), and is distinguished by the
splendid decoration of the exterior.   In the course of the thirteenth century the somewhat heavy nave of the minster of Freiburg was built,[2] to which, however, is added the noblest specimen

Fig. 256.   View of the Church of S. Katharine at Oppenheim.

of an open-work spire in the west tower, projecting in front of
the façade.   The minster also at Strasburg,[3] with its broad and
splendid nave, completed in 1275, possesses a certain solemn
strictness of proportion ; but it affords in its façade, which was
commenced by Erwin von Steinbach in 1277, a remarkable

[1] F. H. Müller, *Die Katharinenkirche zu Oppenheim.*   Darmstadt, 1823.
[2] *Denkm. d. Kunst.*   Pl. 53.   Figs. 1–4.   Moller's *Denkmale.*
[3] *Denkm. d. Kunst.*   Pl. 53.   Fig. 8.

specimen of the blending of the German and French style. The beautiful wheel window, as well as the strong emphasising of the horizontal members, belong to the French style, while the German is represented by the distinct arrangement of the two bold towers, only the northern one of which, reaching a height of 468 feet, was completed by Johann Hültz of Cologne in the year 1439.

In Southern Germany the cathedral at Ratisbon,[1] begun in the year 1275 by Andreas Egl, represents the German-Gothic style in a peculiarly noble and distinct manner. The richer French choir is set aside, and in its place each of the three aisles has an independent polygonal termination, in which we recognise a reaction of the more simple German design, which henceforth may be regarded as the favourite form in Germany. On the other hand, the choir of the unfinished cathedral at Prague, which was begun in 1343 by Matthias v. Arras, and was continued in 1385 by Peter Arler of Gmünd, evidences a complete return to the French ground-plan.

Most of the buildings we have mentioned, although begun in the thirteenth century, were not completed in their magnificence until the following century, or even later. Altogether, in the fourteenth century, Germany witnessed another period of prosperity, and a second time took the lead in artistic matters, governing by its architecture, which had now become completely imbued with the vigour of the national life, almost the whole European world as far as Italy and Spain. In the thirteenth century, the nave of the cathedral at Halberstadt[2] was commenced; the choir, however, which was not added until 1327, retains the surrounding aisle, though it rejects the chapels, with the exception of one on the east side. The whole building is one of the most beautiful specimens of distinct, moderate, and yet elegant German-Gothic. Among the South German buildings, one of the most imposing designs is the five-aisled cathedral at Ulm,[3]

---

[1] *Denkm. d. Kunst.* Pl. 55. Fig. 3. Popp and Bülau, *Die Architektur des Mittelalters in Regensburg.* Fol. 1834.

[2] Lucanus, *Der Dom zu Halberstadt.* Fol. 1837.

[3] *Denkm. d. Kunst.* Pl. 55. Figs. 4 and 5.

which was begun in 1377, and the somewhat sober construction
of which is counterbalanced by its mighty dimensions. The
unfinished tower was intended for a bold open-work spire.

Fig. 257.   Interior of the Marienkirche at Mühlhausen.

From this period the preponderance of secular power is
accompanied by a decline of nobler architectural feeling; architecture acquires a somewhat mechanical expression, the details
are not free from artificial work and caprice, and in the vaulting
we observe the playful forms of network and stars. The
windows were filled with twisted tracery, and the divisions of

the pillars were less compact, indeed, occasionally even the capital was omitted, and the divisions of the pillars, travelling in all directions, radiated in the ribs of the vaulting. The dimensions are, however, often considerable, although without any finer beauty of proportion. This is compensated for by the rich decoration of the details, the portals or pulpits, the sacramentshäuschen (the receptacle for the sacred elements of the communion), the lectorium, and such-like parts, often exhibiting an admirable richness of fancy. With this also is connected the increase of the more sober form of the hall church, which, since the fourteenth century, prevailed more and more in Germany. This form is principally to be found in Westphalia and Saxony, where the Liebfrauen and Lamberti churches at Münster,[1] the Wiesenkirche at Soest, and the five-aisled Marienkirche at Mühlhausen (Fig. 257), and the cathedrals of

Fig. 528. Façade of the Frauenkirche at Esslingen.

Minden and Meissen [2] (the former belonging entirely to the thir-

---

[1] W. Lübke, *Die Mittelalterliche Kunst in Westfalen.*
[2] *Denkm. d. Kunst.* Pl. 55. Figs. 1 and 2. Schwechten, *Der Dom zu Meissen.* Fol. Berlin, 1823.

teenth century), represent this style of building in a noble manner. The hall churches appear but rarely in South Germany. One of the most elegant examples, the Frauenkirche at Esslingen,[1] is distinguished by richly adorned portals, and by a graceful open-work spire. (Fig. 258.) The Frauenkirche at Nuremberg, built between 1355 and 1361, is an especially interesting specimen owing to its rich façade. S. Sebald possesses a choir, which in its surrounding aisle, equally wide at all parts, exhibits this form in an imposing manner, applied to the polygonal ground-plan; and this example is followed by the choir of S. Lorenzo,[2] built between 1439 and 1477, the nave of which is a noble work of the thirteenth century, with a façade remarkable for its unusually richly decorated portal and splendid wheel window. Farther, in one of the grandest German structures, the church of St. Stephen at Vienna,[3] there is at least an approximation to the hall form, as the central circle is somewhat higher than the side aisles, but

Fig. 259. Gable of S. Stephan at Vienna.

is without windows. The choir, which was begun in the fourteenth century, exhibits, on the contrary, three aisles of equal height, terminating with polygonal apsides. The heaviness of

---

[1] Heideloff, *Die Kunst des Mittelalters in Schwaben.*
[2] *Denkm. d. Kunst.* Pl. 55. Fig. 6.
[3] Ibid. Pl. 55. Figs. 7-9. Tschischka, *Der S. Stephansdom in Wien.* Fol. Vienna, 1853.

the colossal roof is, however, lessened externally by an unusually splendid gable covered with open geometric tracery (Fig. 259); and in the pyramidal gigantic tower, which rises 435 feet high, and which was begun by Wenzla and was completed in 1433, Gothic architecture possesses one of its most magnificent works.

The final epoch, beginning with the fifteenth century, exhibits numerous hall designs, especially in the Saxon districts. The churches of this kind are for the most part light and spacious, free and bold in their aspiring members, but infected in their details with all the degeneracy of this half-temperate, half-fantastic style. There is a restless winding, bending, flourishing, and intersecting of the members which—as, for example, in the north portal of the cathedral at Merseburg, the nave of which was consecrated in 1517—may be regarded as a specimen of genuine Gothic absurdity. Another and no less wild extravagance is to be seen when architecture forgets itself so entirely, in a rude adherence to nature, that it loses sight of the ideal laws of form, on which its entire creation rests, and in slavish imitation represents whole trees and branches in stone, with various whimsical caricatures of nature. Thus it is on the portal of the monastery church of Chemnitz, which likewise belongs to this concluding epoch. Other buildings of the same epoch are the Peter-Paulskirche at Görlitz (1423–1497), which is especially light, bold, and free; and the Liebfrauenkirche at Halle, built between 1530 and 1554, and many others.

In the North German coast lands, brick building[1] appears as a special transformation of the Gothic style, and, adhering to its former tendency, expresses its nature by coarse massive design, strong pillars, and by a rich and graceful decoration of the surface. It may be conjectured in general that the earlier buildings were more technically complete, distinct, and solid; while from the middle of the fourteenth century, and still more with the beginning of the following century, a certain pervading roughness increases in corresponding proportion with luxuriantly rich

[1] *Denkm. d. Kunst.* Pl. 56.

decoration of the surface. We must also remark, that these buildings remain unplastered both within and without, exhibiting the serious, strongly effective colour of the stone.

Some churches follow the plan of the high central aisle, and

Fig. 260. Town Hall at Münster.

even have the richly constructed French choir at its termination, only that the system of supports is considerably simplified, and the magnificence of the ground-plan is also essentially modified. The main work in this style is the Marienkirche at Lübeck, begun in 1276 : it is a building of grand proportions, severe and serious in its general effect. Of a similar character is the Cistercian church at Dobberan, completed in 1368—a noble structure, light and slender in its effect. Closely allied with it in style, though more mighty in its masses, is the cathedral at Schwerin, and no less so the colossal Marien churches at Rostock and Wismar. In Pomerania, also, the same style is exhibited in many buildings of importance, such as the Marien churches at Stargard and at Stralsund (completed in 1460). The cathedral at Havelberg, the restored cathedral and Elizabeth church at Breslau, exhibit the same style in a simplified form.

Far greater is the number of hall churches, in which, especially at a later period, magnificent effect is obtained by splendid surface decoration, with variegated polished stones in the most graceful patterns. This style is exhibited with extraordinary richness and nobleness of form in the Marienkirche at Prenzlau (1325–1340). It appears in noble moderation in the cathedral and Marienkirche at Stendal, in gigantic proportions in the Marienkirche at Colberg, still more grandly, but without all detail, in the immense Marienkirche at Dantzic; and in contrast with this, in the superabundant display of magnificence and in the rich surface decoration of the church of St. Catharine at Brandenburg, which was begun in 1401 by Heinrich Brunsberg of Stettin. Lastly, South Germany possesses in the Frauenkirche at Munich (1468–1488), and in the Martinskirche at Landshut, which was completed in 1473, similar brick buildings conspicuous from their colossal form.

Secular architecture did not attain in Germany to the richness and grandeur of that of the cities of Flanders, but yet there is no lack of varied, and often noble forms. Building in hewn stone appears in many stately town halls, above all that at Brunswick, which is distinguished by its peculiar design and graceful arcades in two galleries—that at Münster, which exhibits a slender gable, distinctly constructed, and adorned with windows and statues. (Fig. 260.) Private houses of stone are to be found at Münster, Kuttenberg, and Nuremberg, at which place the

Nassau house is remarkable for its simple design and graceful polygonal projection. Among castles, we may distinguish the fortress of Karlstein in Bohemia, built by Charles IV., and the magnificent Albrechtsburg at Meissen. Specimens of a finished framework building are exhibited in the town hall at Hanover, and in the elegant town hall at Wernigerode, and others.

The advance made in secular architecture, in the countries in which brick buildings appear, is very considerable. At Tanger-

Fig. 261. Hall of the Artushof at Dantzic.

münde, there is one of the most splendid town halls, with a gable richly decorated with open-work tracery; and Stendal possesses in its Uenglinger Thor, a city gate combining great boldness and graceful elegance. Above all, however, in magnificence are the secular buildings in the Prussian lands of the Teutonic order. The Artushof at Dantzic—the old hall of assembly of the merchants —is one of the most distinguished works of this kind. The vaults rest on slender granite columns, the ribs rising on all sides like palm leaves, and giving the vaulting an elegant fan-form, a favourite style in other Prussian lands of the Teutonic order. (Fig. 261.) The highest triumph attained by this architecture is exhibited in the principal castle of the Teutonic order, the proud Marienburg, which combines in its central castle, with a completeness as grand as it is artistic, the dwelling of the grand master, with its magnificent refectory—the fine refectory of the order—and various other designs.

ENGLAND AND SCANDINAVIA.

For the second time England[1] received a new style of architecture from France; but she knew now better than before how to transform the style into an independent one of her own, so that English-Gothic art presents a striking contrast to that of the Continent. Even the design of the ground-plan underwent considerable simplification. Not merely was the nave formed with only three aisles, thus obtaining an unusual length, but the alteration appears principally in the plan of the choir, which returned to sober and moderate proportions; for not only the surrounding aisle and chapels were omitted, almost without exception, but the choir usually terminated coldly and simply in a straight line with the side aisles, obtaining only an addition in the lady chapel placed at the east, but not enriched by it. At the same time the choir was often formed of equal length with the nave, so that the whole building extended to an unusual length, only broken by the two transepts frequently introduced. Added to this, the height of these buildings was extremely small, and the cross vaults rested for the most part on consoles against the walls, above or below the triforiums, without regard to the system of pillars, so that the vertical development was rendered only subordinate. The cathedrals of Wells (Fig. 262) and of Worcester (Fig. 263) afford examples of this arrangement—the former an incompact structure; the latter at least attempting to produce an outward connection between the supports of the vault and the arcades. We here perceive the English aversion

---

[1] *Denkm d. Kunst.* Cf. also the works quoted on page 425.

to the vaulted structure, which is not even now conceived in its organic consistency; and this aversion was still more conspicuous at an earlier period. The exterior acquires a similar simplification, the buttresses being limited to what is indispensably necessary, and the flying arches frequently completely omitted. Thus

Fig. 262. Interior System of the Cathedral of Wells.

Fig. 263. Interior System of the Cathedral of Worcester.

here also a strict horizontal form preponderates, rendered still more decided by the flat roof, which is concealed behind high battlements. Two stately towers usually rise by the façade, and to these a third massive quadrangular tower over the larger transept is almost always added; but these towers rarely have slender spires, and are generally finished with battlements and small corner finials.

The first introduction of the Gothic style into England took place in the year 1174, when a French architect, Wilhelm von Sens, was summoned to conduct the rebuilding of the cathedral of Canterbury after the fire: the semicircular choir, with its surrounding aisle, the whole construction and details, correspond for the most part with the early Gothic style, interwoven with vestiges of the Romanesque, which prevailed at this period in the north of France. In the following period, Westminster Abbey, the choir of which was built between 1245 and 1269, displays the complete French cathedral design with its polygonal choir, surrounding aisle and chapels, and its rich system of supports. The new principle was now soon generally adopted in England, but it received such a specific transformation that the architectural works of the thirteenth century are not unjustly designated as belonging to the early English style. Starting with the universal ground-plan previously described, this style arrived at greater simplicity of form, though betraying a rich life in the detail. As the pillars of the nave stand without regard to the vaulting, they resolve themselves into a stack of slender column shafts, which column shafts often loosely surround the stem of the pillar. The construction of the arcade arches corresponds with them in richness of profile. Above them there is always a triforium, either consisting of a row of separate lancet arches, or of groups of lancet arches opening between slender columns. The windows do not yet generally exhibit the Gothic geometric tracery, but consist for the most part of two or three narrow lancet windows grouped together. The simple cross vault of the nave rests upon columns, which are placed on consoles against the upper wall, and only rarely are continued to the arcade arches, and even then without regard to the pillars.

Among the most important buildings of this epoch is the cathedral of Salisbury (1220 to 1258), which is executed in the same consistent form throughout, and is a work of noble grace, purely and distinctly expressing the English style in its choir with two transepts and its elegant lady chapel, partially introduced within the building. The façade, which is flanked by two slender towers, is especially magnificent. (Fig. 264.) The proportions are also remarkable for English architecture, for, with a length of 430 feet, the central aisle is only 33 feet broad and

78 feet high. Similar proportions and distinctness of execution
in the style of the English early Gothic are also shown in the
minster of Beverley; likewise in the choir of the cathedral of
Worcester, which was consecrated in 1218, with its stack of
columns, grouped lancet windows, sober triforiums, and cross

Fig. 264. Façade of the Cathedral of Salisbury.

vaults: the nave was added subsequently. The transepts and
nave of Wells Cathedral were likewise constructed in strict adherence to this primitive style, between 1214 and 1239; also
the broad vast façade, with its two towers and unusually rich
figure ornaments, which was erected in 1242: the choir, on the
other hand, was added in the fourteenth century. To the same
style also belongs the choir of Ely Cathedral, built between
1235 and 1252, which contains a peculiarity of design in a large

octagon, executed about the year 1322, calling to mind the Italian domical buildings, and in which the stone vaulting is merely imitated in wood. Lincoln Cathedral is also of great importance; its mighty structure, measuring 524 feet in external length, having been likewise executed in the thirteenth century. This style is, lastly, very magnificently displayed in Lichfield Cathedral, the nave and transepts of which belong to this period, while the eastern parts were executed later. The two west towers here, and the great tower over the square, have extremely high and slender spires.

Fig. 265. Cathedral of Exeter. Window and Pillar.

The fourteenth century witnessed also in English architecture that richer mode of execution, aiming at more brilliant detail, which appeared universally prevalent at that time, and which led in England to the so-called *Decorated Style.* This is perceived especially in the adoption of luxuriant, though perhaps not organic, geometric tracery in the windows, and in a graceful result of network and stars, which we find constantly used. One of the most splendid works of this period is Exeter Cathedral, the main parts of which were consistently constructed between 1327 and 1360. Graceful stacks of pillars, rich geometric tracery for the windows, and elegant starred vaults, combined with an unusual construction of buttresses on the exterior, give the building a lively and graceful stamp. No less important is York Cathedral, the choir of which belongs to the first half of

the fourteenth century and the nave to the second half of the
century : it is likewise a building of magnificent effect and grand

Fig. 266.   Cathedral at York.
Pillar.

design.   The same stage of development
is represented by the abbey church of Mel-
rose, now a picturesque ruin ; while the
nave of Winchester Cathedral, restored
about 1393, with its slender, skilfully constructed pillars, its blind gallery instead of
a triforium, and rich network vaults, forms
the transition to the following epoch.

Towards the beginning of the fifteenth century, this style
passed completely into the perpendicular, which with its increased
richness still adopted an element of geometric work, and in the
window tracery exhibited a lattice-like perpendicular bar work,

Fig. 267.   From Henry the Seventh's Chapel at Westminster.

and covered every surface with geometric network. Added to this,
about the year 1450, we find the adoption of an ugly, flattened,
shallow arch, curved in the middle, the so-called Tudor arch, and
the arches of arcades and vaults are fantastically covered with rich
decorative points and teeth ; indeed, the completion of the vault
is so full of ornament that the keystones hang down like pegs,
and the vaults therefore seem partly to hover freely, while vast
geometric tracery covers the surface between the ribs, and the

richest kind of fan vaulting becomes increasingly prevalent. This style reaches its utmost splendour in Henry the Seventh's Chapel, which was added to the choir of Westminster Cathedral between 1502 and 1520. All the surfaces of the walls and vaults are overspread with an exuberant profusion of rich detail, so much so that the seriousness of the architecture is lost in a charming play of enchanting fancy. This later style is no less charmingly displayed in the wooden springers of the ceiling, which, from the national preference for wooden structure, frequently even in the last century had taken the place of stone vaulting, and at this period was much more constantly employed, especially in chapter

Fig. 268. Cathedral at Drontheim.

halls, and castle halls, and in the colleges connected with universities. Even in the principal spaces, such as the central aisle, the choir, and transepts of the churches, such wooden ceilings appear instead of vaults ; as, for instance, in St. Mary's Church at Oxford, built in the second half of the fifteenth century, and in the churches at Lavenham and Melford and many others. The wooden construction of the roof is at the same time rich and

gracefully finished in all its parts, and the geometric work borrowed from stone buildings frequently plays a brilliant part in
the decoration.   This is displayed in an especially elegant
manner in the chapter house of the cathedral of Exeter, in the
great hall of the palace at Eltham, and many other works.

Among the Gothic buildings of Scandinavia,[1] the grand
cathedral of Drontheim, the principal parts of which belong to
the thirteenth century, stands foremost. In the form of the
ground-plan, and in the treatment of the detail, the influence of
English early Gothic is unmistakable, but in the decorative
effect it is enriched by many northern elements, and reaches an
extreme magnificence. The design of an octagonal domical
building, with surrounding aisles attached to the choir, possesses
great perspective beauty, and manifests especial nobleness of
execution. (Fig. 268.) The cathedral of Upsala in Sweden,
alleged to have been begun in 1287 by a French architect named
Etienne de Bonneuil, belongs to the series of brick buildings,
formed with a rich choir-plan after the French form.

ITALY.[2]

Gothic architecture was adopted in Italy equally independently as it had been in England, and no less originally than in
England was it remodelled in harmony with the national ideas
and needs.   But a most peculiar relation to the Gothic resulted
from the prevalent taste of the people, inclining, as it did, to
antique traditions.   Even in the Romanesque epoch, the vaulted
design had only been adopted to a limited extent, while the
greater part of the land remained faithful to the simple flat-roofed
basilica.   How then could an entirely foreign style break the
fetters of such strong tradition ?   Nevertheless, the general tendency of the time was here also so powerful, that even in the
thirteenth century many churches were constructed in the Gothic
style.   Yet only in rare exceptions did they adhere to the

[1] A. v. Minutoli,'*Der Dom zu Drontheim, &c.*
[2] *Denkm. d. Kunst.* Pl. 57 and 58. Cf. the works quoted on p. 403.

northern ground-plan. In the first place, it was the pointed arch which was taken from the Gothic, but which was essentially employed to satisfy the preference for vast space of proportionate width. The central aisle, too, was raised only a little above the side aisles, and small, for the most part circular, windows were introduced into the upper walls, so that the principal light came from the high windows of the side aisles. Thus they were far removed from the slender and aspiring tendency of the northern Gothic, and still farther from the effort to break up the calm surfaces, and to resolve the whole into a mass of slender, supporting, and resisting members. They had before delighted so much in extensive wall paintings that they could not deprive these of their necessary surfaces. Hence they only introduced small narrow windows, which, owing to the brightness of the southern sky, admitted sufficient light into the interior. By this means they obtained spaces of a grand span, which were vaulted freely and widely, and often produced a wonderfully harmonious and solemnly calm effect.

The exterior, like the interior, dispensed with the rich complicated composition of the northern Gothic. As the central aisle only moderately rose above the side aisles, and the mild climate and the custom of the country favoured flat roofs, the buttress system was limited to a small extent, the flying arches were for the most part omitted, and the buttresses appeared more in the character of Romanesque lisenes. Thus the calm effect of surface, with but slight projection of the main divisions, appears prevalent here, analogous with the antique and Romanesque mode. The building was adorned with a brilliant decoration of varied plates of marble, entirely in the spirit of the earlier epoch. Altogether, Romanesque laws remained in force in every respect, both as regards the design of the whole, as exhibited in the favourite dome over the transepts and the façade executed as an independent decorated work, and also as regards the detail of the forms; the pointed arch, with its other Gothic marks, such as the knobs, finials, &c., exhibiting a mixture of the round arch and other Romanesque elements. Thus

Gothic architecture in Italy never arrives at an organised and consistently developed whole, but only at a remodelling of the former style by increased decoration. Yet in the interior, these buildings possess an independent artistic importance from their grand spaciousness, in their exterior, from their distinctness of

Fig. 269. View of the Cathedral at Siena.

form, and in the whole, from the noble splendour of their decoration and paintings.

Gothic architecture was first introduced into Italy by a German master, Jacob, in the church of S. Francesco at Assisi, which was built between 1228 and 1253. Its position on a rising ground necessitated the arrangement of a lower church with circular arches, over which rises the upper church, executed in strict Gothic form, with one aisle and transepts. The narrow windows leave bare considerable surfaces of wall, which are covered with paintings. This spacious design becomes full of grand effect in the cathedral of Florence, which was commenced in 1294 by Arnolfo di Cambio (erroneously called Arnolfo di Lapo). Here, too, the aim at space is apparent, and is exhibited with great boldness in the quadratic vaults of the central aisle, which are about 60 feet broad. But this tendency here falls into a one-sided extreme, the unfavourable effect of which is increased by the extremely scanty lighting. The colossal octagonal dome, with its three transepts studded with chapels, was not finished till a later period. A splendid marble façade was added to the building in the year 1334 by the painter Giotto; but it was not completed, and it was subsequently removed. The same great master executed the bell-tower by the side of the façade, the noble construction and rich marble decoration of which produce a rare artistic harmony.

The same idea of the combination of the domical building with the nave design is conceived in an original manner in the cathedral of Siena, built in the thirteenth century, without the hexagonal dome, however, being placed in distinct relation to the three aisles. The interior possesses lively perspective charm, although the alternation of white and black marble is somewhat too unquiet. The exterior (Fig. 269) is rendered especially important by the façade, with its rich coloured decoration, executed about 1284. But it was first in the cathedral of Orvieto, begun in the year 1290, under the architect Lorenzo Maitani, that this façade construction attained its highest perfection, displaying just as much lavish splendour of plastic marble ornament and grand mosaic painting as it exhibited distinct and harmonious organisation. The interior, on the contrary, shows a retrograde to the flat-roofed basilica. The famous Campo Santo at Pisa, completed by Giovanni Pisano in 1283, is among the noblest works of Italian Gothic architecture.

Milan cathedral, begun in 1386, in the plan of which a German master named Heinrich von Gmünd participated, belongs to the late period of the Gothic epoch.   In this mighty structure, entirely constructed of white marble, we cannot fail to see a decided adoption of the German ground-plan.   The five-aisled nave, the three-aisled transepts, the extraordinarily close position

Fig. 270.   Ground-plan of S. Petronio at Bologna.

of the pillars, and the construction of a choir aisle, are all characteristic of this tendency ; while the Italian feeling prevails in its height, and a threefold gradation takes place from the central aisle to the extreme side aisle.   Great, however, as is the poetical effect of the interior, enchanting as is the dazzling marble magnificence of the exterior, yet higher architectural demands are but little satisfied.   Utterly different is it to a second gigantic building of this epoch, which—after the plan of the church of S. Petronio in Bologna, begun in 1390 by Antonio Vincenzi—adapts the Gothic forms to Italian requirements. In the system of the nave (Fig. 271) we plainly see a return to the principle followed in the cathedral of Florence; but by the addition of two chapel aisles the building obtains a richness of perspective vistas, which makes us doubly regret that the colossal plan was only partially executed. A five-aisled transept, with a mighty octagonal dome in the centre, was to have been added to it, and the choir was to have been formed in harmony with the nave, and finished with a surrounding aisle and a series of chapels. The whole length was designed at 640 feet, and the breadth of the dome was to have been equal to that of the Florentine cathedral. The nave is now poorly finished with a large semicircular niche.

Fig. 271. Church of Certosa, near Pavia.

Lastly, the church of Certosa, near Pavia (Fig. 271), built about the year 1396, is among the noblest structures, in which the Italian love of space found free and beautiful expression in the Gothic system.

The secular architecture of Italy produced a number of important works. Florentine palace architecture—the most important productions of which are the Palazzo Vecchio and the Bargello—possesses a character of powerful defiance and gloomy fortress-like sternness. On the other hand, Florentine secular architecture exhibited in the Loggia de' Lanzi, built about the year 1376, a rare distinctness and great beauty of proportion; while at the same time the circular arch was again employed. Palace architecture in Siena attains to a consistent and noble construction with a great intermixture of brick, as is evidenced, for instance, in the magnificent Palazzo Pubblico, and a number of fine private palaces, among others the Palazzo Buonsignori. (Fig. 272.) Among the open halls in various cities, the Loggia de' Mercanti (the Exchange) at Bologna exhibits the elegant style of the fourteenth century, executed in rich brick architecture. Free, light, and graceful, and bearing an expression of luxurious life, are the palaces of Venice, the façades of which are broken almost entirely by elegant loggie; thus expressing direct relation to canal life, and compensating for the want of court yard. A

Fig. 272. From the Palazzo Buonsignori at Siena.

rich and elegant palace is the splendid Cà Doro; the Palazzo Foscari, Pisani, and others are also graceful and attractive. This style acquires an expression of grand dignity in the palace of the Doge, begun about the middle of the fourteenth century, the lower and upper colonnades of which are, in their way, the most magnificent in the world.

In the early period of the fifteenth century, the Gothic style in Italy was supplanted by the revival of the antique (the Renais·sance), and could only produce isolated works, the character of which is essentially modified by the intermixture of antique elements.

SPAIN AND PORTUGAL.

The Gothic style probably first made its way into Spain[1] from the adjacent country of France. The imaginative mind of the people, which, in the former epoch, had produced a blending of their own architecture with Moorish forms, was thus, as it were, already prepared for similar admixtures of style. Hence, the earliest Gothic buildings combine not only much of the rich Romanesque style of the country, but also even some of the luxuriant decorative elements of Moorish architecture. An especially brilliant style seems to have been thus produced. Although, from insufficient investigations and facts, we are not yet accurately informed with regard to the stages passed through in this course of development, yet Spanish-Gothic art in its complete form presents to us striking characteristics. The strict constructive system and rich ground-plan are here conceived with taste and understanding; but, nevertheless, in the structure itself a gradation of the comparative heights is adopted, similar to the Italian Gothic. The façade is constantly constructed after the northern manner. There is even no lack of open-work spires, although in the later epoch German influence here also preponderates; but, at the same time, with equal predilection, the dome is retained over the transept, and the ornament combines the rich abundance of Gothic forms with the luxuriant and playful decoration of Moorish architecture. Thus buildings appear here which, in grandeur of design and splendour of execution, may be reckoned among the most important works of the entire middle ages.

The Gothic style appears to have been first adopted in Spain in the cathedral of Burgos, which was founded in the year 1221. It is a mighty structure, having a polygonal choir with a surrounding aisle and chapels, indicating just as distinctly in its

[1] *Denkm. d. Kunst.* Pl. 58. Cf. the works on vol. i. p. 428.

ground-plan a French model as its details are interwoven with
Moorish reminiscences. The façade, on the other hand, with its
open-work spire (Fig. 273), is a work of the German master
Johann v. Köln, between the years 1442 and 1456. Still more
grand in design and bold in execution, is the cathedral of Toledo,
commenced in the year 1227, by a Spanish architect named Pedro
Perez, which endeavoured to surpass that of Burgos. The proportions are still more considerable—the whole building is de-

Fig. 273. Exterior View of the Cathedral of Burgos.

signed with five aisles and with a polygonal choir (Fig. 274),
round which the side aisles are carried like choir aisles with small
chapels; an arrangement which likewise appears in a French
work, the cathedral of Bourges. The central aisle rises about
140 feet high; but the side aisles are, like many Italian buildings,'

gradated in height, so that the inner one is considerably above the outer aisles. Here, also, magnificent decoration—in which various Moorish ideas are intermingled—gives the interior an extremely rich effect. Still more decidedly apparent is French influence in the noble cathedral of Leon, the design of which bears most affinity with the cathedral of Rheims. Begun about the middle of the thirteenth century, this splendid structure is distinguished

Fig. 274. Interior of the Cathedral of Toledo.

by the nobleness of its forms and the bold slenderness of its proportions, as well as by its broad and high windows.

In subsequent Spanish works, foreign influences are modified in favour of forms more in harmony with national customs and the southern climate. The height is less bold, but a rich dome is generally placed over the centre of the transept, as had been the case in the Romanesque epoch ; the windows become smaller, the wall surfaces larger, and the breadth of the main spaces, as in Italy, is often very considerable, so that an effect similar to that of the Italian buildings is frequently produced. The cathedral of Valencia, begun about the year 1262, is distinguished by a splendid dome-tower, but in all essential parts it is a creation of the fourteenth century. Among the most important buildings, executed in a genuinely national spirit, is the cathedral of Barcelona; an imposing work with a rich aisle, with chapels running round the choir, and a broad central aisle 42 feet wide with side aisles, along which is placed a row of chapels at regular intervals. The idea of these designs, which are very frequent in Catalonia, recalls to mind Italian buildings, such as S. Petronio at Bologna, and the Certosa near Pavia. Large quadratic vaults with still bolder spans mark S. Maria del Mar; but the mightiest vaults of the whole Gothic epoch seem to be in the cathedral of Palma, the central aisle of which measured 71 feet in breadth, and the entire nave was 190 feet wide. The cathedral of Gerona is also very grand; a three-aisled choir with surrounding chapels is annexed to a one-aisled nave, 73 feet broad, with its accompanying series of chapels.

Subsequent buildings for the most part set aside the richer French choir, and give a more simple arrangement to the ground-plan generally. Among these structures, the cathedral of Seville (begun in 1403) is one of the most imposing works. The height of its five aisles is gradated, after the model of the cathedral of Toledo. The transept is rendered prominent by a dome.

In Portugal, the church of the monastery of Batalha,[1] begun in 1383, is famous as a building distinguished by distinct arrangement and consistency of style. Still more sensibly do we here feel the lack of special investigation with regard to the architecture of the country.

3. GOTHIC SCULPTURE AND PAINTING.

a. *Subject and Form.*

While architectural productions gradually pass from the Romanesque style to the Gothic, and many transition stages bring about this change, so that both these movements, different as they are, flow almost imperceptibly one into another, a

---

[1] *Denkm. d. Kunst.* Pl. 58. Figs. 5 and 6. Murphy, *Plans, &c. of the Church of Batal.* Fol. London, 1795. Cf. also Fournier's *Briefe in C. v. Lützow's Zeitschrift f. Bild. K.*

perfectly similar process takes place in the plastic arts. Their subjects and their tasks remain essentially the same as in the former epoch ; the sphere of representation is indeed somewhat widened and enriched, but in its main features it remains the same, and even the more general relations which connected art with religion scarcely suffered any perceptible alteration. Nevertheless a movement is observable through the whole circle of the plastic arts, the productions of which still adhere to Romanesque forms and antique tradition, and splendid examples of which we find in Germany and Italy until far into the thirteenth century. Yet this pure antique stamp of the antique, noble as it may be, no longer satisfied the excited feeling of the awakened national mind. An animated striving, similar to that which we have seen in our considerations upon architecture, long laboured at the remodelling of the old forms ; and about the middle of the thirteenth century a new style had resulted, which was indeed in every respect different from that which Romanesque art could have produced. Scarcely, however, had this form reached its perfection, than it spread as rapidly and uncontrollably as Gothic architecture had done over the whole Christian world of the West, and was adopted with one accord by all ; thus affording testimony of how completely it expressed the feeling of the age. The whole of the fourteenth century adhered universally to the new style of art, which on this very account soon again became conventional, and often degenerated into external mannerism, just as the tender homage of the Minnesingers was speedily transformed into courtly etiquette.

This new style did not arise because there was anything new to bring forward, but because the old was conceived with new feeling, and suitable expression for this feeling was desired. The deeply excited mind of man desired to breathe out in forms his personal interest in sacred things, and in the great doctrine of redemption. Ardent enthusiasm, fervent longing, and extravagant devotion were to be expressed by chisel and painting, and were thus expressed in reality. Figures lost the stately dignity, the stamp of exalted repose which linked them with the antique; they were represented as slender and flexible, tender in form, with a fanciful inclination of the head; they bent the whole body forward with a movement, which placed the centre of gravity on one side, letting the other recede, as though the figure were following the slightest vibration of feeling; they expressed these emotions of the mind by a touch of smiling graciousness, which almost without exception illuminated the features.

This expression, thus bordering on the sentimental, was increased by the predilection for forming youthful figures; and a sharper contrast can scarcely be imagined than between this tender blooming youth and the aged and morose creations of Byzantine art. Manly energy and bold defiance are alien to this style; and even the masculine figures have an expression of almost womanly sweetness, so that they seem like a living reflection of the age of Minnesingers, of Mariolatry, and of reverence for women. The drapery flows full and rich down to the feet in soft and beautiful folds over the slender and delicate limbs. Although in its main features it still betrays the form of antique costume, it has so far modified it in harmony with the new national characteristics that it appears to be wholly different. The actual costume of the period had preceded the work of the artist, and as the eye had become more susceptible of the impressions of the external world, the altered form of costume was also reflected in the artist's creations. Indeed, a circumstance apparently so insignificant, as that the linen stuff, formerly worn by preference, should have given way to the use of fine woollen material, was not without influence in the transition from a stiff lifeless parallel arrangement of the folds to a soft and varied arrangement of the drapery.

But, however much true feeling separates the figures of this epoch from the former, in their regard to the architectural whole not only does the same strict law prevail, but it is even heightened. Although a new feeling animates the figures, although the individual seeks to express in them himself and his own sentiments, yet the separate production claims no importance in itself; it appears throughout in the background and in architectural framework, whether it be really or apparently specially produced for this end. Hence these figures, in spite of all individual feeling, were fettered in the grand universal ideas which they served to express, and in their bearing alone were brought more distinctly and more closely home to the feelings of men.

In one respect, however, architecture effected an essential transformation in the works of the plastic arts, while she opened a wider field to sculpture in her rich plastic constructions ; but at the same time almost entirely suppressed wall painting by the complete breaking-up of the surfaces of the walls into windows, assigning in its stead to painting on glass an extensive sphere of activity, which, indeed, could never make any freer advance, owing to the extraordinary technical restraint of this style. Italian art alone knew how to preserve this important scope, and thus in this very epoch to lay the foundation for its subsequent grand results.

When the noble enthusiasm and ideal elevation of life abated, art also soon followed its example. The stricter law of architecture earlier relaxed ; but in the plastic arts, the movement that had once passed into the general consciousness and into the very fibres of humanity lasted tolerably long. Even up to the fifteenth century it maintained a tolerable purity, and indeed exhibited increased power and depth of feeling. Then, however, a new spirit, that of realism, forced its way into the world, brought about a complete transformation of artistic conceptions, and produced an entirely new style in the plastic arts, which, with a mighty revolution, began a new epoch.

b. *Historical Development.*

IN THE NORTH.

In plastic art;[1] which was now most closely connected with architecture, France stands at the head of the movement. The new cathedrals required sculptured ornament, such as no earlier

[1] *Denkm. d. Kunst.* Pl. 59 and 60 A. Cf. W. Lübke, *Geschichte der Plastik.* Leipzig, 1863.

epoch had known to the same extent. The side walls of the portals, the door posts, the arches, and the tympanon itself, but still more the favourite horizontal galleries of the French Gothic style, which terminated the main story of the façade, were furnished to a great extent with sculptured ornament. If we consider the size of these buildings, if we remember that three portals were generally attached to the façade, added to which splendid entrances were frequently formed at the façades of the transepts, we can readily conceive that plastic art was here afforded a scope such as it had enjoyed at no previous epoch. Thus the necessity and the capability increased for the composition of those profoundly symbolic representations, which speak to us like a Divina Commedia hewn in stone. The Fall, the Redemption, the Resurrection, and, as the highest conclusion, the enthroned Judge of the world, separating the good from the wicked, is the ever-repeated train of thought in these grand cyclical works—to the fundamental idea of which, with rich allusions, are attached the saints of the local traditions with their special legends. Thus the mind of the people was raised from their familiar sacred stories to the universal truths affecting the whole of humanity. Added to this, there were often nearer allusions to human life itself, to the round of its labours, representing the changeful passing of days and years; and this also was exhibited in indissoluble connection with the divine system of the world.

In the first place, we find a series of these works, which, like the buildings of the period, occupy a characteristic transition place between the Romanesque and the Gothic style. The sculptures on the façade of the cathedral of Paris are important in design, although much injured and retouched. On the north portal, the representation begins with the life of Mary; and here already we see how the strict traditional style was developing into flowing life and noble grace both in the expression and in the form of the heads. The main portal, with its richly-arranged representation of the Last Judgment, has suffered most from destruction and alteration; the plastic ornament of the southern side portal for the most part belongs to an earlier epoch. On the other hand, the sculptures on the façades of the transepts, which were executed in the second half of the thirteenth century, exhibit complete emancipation from the old stiff types, and the noblest and most distinct perfection of style. A similar train of ideas as that on the main façade of Notre-Dame at Paris is to

be found grandly executed on the three portals of the façade of the cathedral of Amiens,[1] where, likewise, the history of Mary and of a local saint form the subject of the representations on the side portals, while the main portal contains the solemn delineation of the Last Judgment. A lively idea is given of nobleness of style, especially of finely executed drapery, in the colossal figure of the Redeemer, which is on the central portal pillar (Fig. 275); Evil overcome by Him is represented at his feet in the form of a lion and dragon. Still more extensive are the plastic works which adorn the portals at the transepts of the cathedral of Chartres.[2] Nearly two thousand larger and smaller figures are distributed in strict architectural arrangement, comprising, with their rich historical and symbolic connection, the whole doctrine of Redemption, as well as the entire encyclopedic knowledge of the day. Here, too, the style is solemnly elevated, still bearing some affinity with the severe seriousness of the earlier epoch. On the other hand, we see the plastic ability of the period rising to almost perfect freedom and grace in the numerous splendid portal sculptures of the main façade of the cathedral of Rheims,[3] which again follow the

Fig. 275. Christ, from the Cathedral of Amiens.

[1] *Denkm. d. Kunst.* Pl. 60 A. Fig. 2.   [2] Ibid. Pl. 59. Fig. 6, and Pl. 60 A.
[3] Ibid. Pl. 60 A, 3-6.

same train of ideas, and in the main portal contain a representation of the Last Judgment, the different parts of which show corresponding variety of artistic treatment. In the tympanon, the Judge of the world is enthroned, severely and solemnly; on the central pillar is the noble and mild figure of the Redeemer in the act of blessing, one of the most perfect productions of the art of the middle ages; on both sides of the entrance the apostles are depicted, full of power and striking characterisation; lastly, the sitting figures of the saints are gracefully executed on the tympanon (Fig. 276), and, in naïve and natural attitudes, we see the naked figures of the rising ones leaving their graves.

Fig. 276. Figures in Relief from the Cathedral at Rheims.

If we consider the truly immeasurable abundance of this world of figures, only the most important of which we have mentioned, and which were all produced in the course of the thirteenth century, we cannot but be astonished at the energy and creative power of this epoch, the youthful freshness of which is perhaps tested by nothing so brilliantly as by the combined creations of architecture and sculpture. The second half of the century, especially the time of Louis the Saint, reaches a height which not unjustly may be compared with the age of Pericles. And even in purity and classic nobleness of style, the entire middle ages have nothing to show which can stand by the side of the noblest of these works. The masters of the sculptures at Rheims have reached a perfection of style which calls to mind the noblest antique, only that independent feeling is expressed with warmth and gentleness. On the other hand, the latter appears to a one-sided degree in the sculptures in the Ste. Chapelle in Paris, where the figures of the apostles (Fig. 277), from their peculiar attitude, their inclined bearing, and the expression of the head, almost approach the sentimental, but which are still kept in moderation by the free and grand conception of the whole, and especially by the distinct and noble arrangement of the drapery. After the 13th century had thus vented itself in these splendid creations, both sculpture and architecture considerably abated in France during the fourteenth century, and the more isolated works which proceed from this epoch begin already to incline to a conventional conception. In Germany,[1] on the other hand, artistic power began to awake at this period to new productions, attractive from their variety and pleasing grace, if not from the grandeur of their designs. As early as the thirteenth century, many plastic decorative works can be pointed out, which had adopted the new style established in France. Even in works such as the before-mentioned sculptures of Wechselburg and Freiberg (vol. i. p. 444), the new movement is plainly to be perceived, while adhering to the Romanesque conception. Similar creations, only exhibiting this new principle still more apparently, are to be found in the statues at the south portal of the east façade of the cathedral at Bamberg, as well as in the interior of the church at the sides of the east choir. This young and vigorous age ventures even upon equestrian statues,

Fig. 277. Figure of an Apostle from the Ste. Chapelle at Paris.

[1] *Denkm. d. Kunst.* Pl. 59.

in its fresh feeling of the importance of the individual, as is evidenced in the lifelike equestrian statue of King Conrad II. in the cathedral at Bamberg, and the statue of the Emperor Otto the Great in the market-place at Magdeburg. A series of sculptures in the cathedral at Naumburg are among the most excellent works of this style. On the other hand, only rarely, as in the cathedrals at Strasburg (Fig. 278), and at Freiburg, do we

Fig. 278. Statues from the Minster at Strasburg.

find that more extensive and profound plastic decoration which belongs to the French cathedrals.

In the fourteenth century, sculpture in Germany exhibited attractive variety ; and although it never rose to the production of grand cyclical compositions, which were no longer admissible owing to the almost exclusively architectural ornament of the churches, yet in many isolated works there is a great depth of feeling, and we may often also perceive great delicacy of execution.   A high value in this respect belongs to the statues of Christ, His mother, and His apostles, on the pillars of the choir of

Fig. 279. Judas Maccabæus, from the beautiful Spring at Nuremberg.

the cathedral at Cologne,[1] the completion of which, however, falls after 1350. Noble freedom and beauty is expressed in the drapery, while they exhibit that gently inclined bearing and elevated attitude, which becomes almost universal, even to mannerism, in the works of this epoch.   They are, moreover, peculiarly interesting, from their excellent polychromatic execution.   To a somewhat later period belong the sculptures of the southern portal of the façade and the reliefs of the high altar, which are worked in white marble on a back ground of dark marble.   Much that is interesting is preserved in other Rhenish churches.

Nuremberg seems to have displayed especial influence and activity.[2]   The rich sculptures on the magnificent façade of S. Lorenzo stand just between the thirteenth and fourteenth centuries.   The main portal contains the statue of the Madonna on its central pillar.   On both sides are the apostles and prophets; in the tympanon above there are scenes from the life and sufferings of Christ ; and, finally, the representation of the Last Judgment, with its mass of figures.   About the middle of the fourteenth century, Sebald Schonhofer was a renowned and active artist, who elevated this style in his works to a peculiarly pure and noble expression.   Hitherto the execution of the 'Schöner

---

[1] *Denkm. d. Kunst.* Pl. 59. Figs. 3 and 4.

[2] R. v. Rettberg, *Nürnberg's Kunstleben, &c.* Stuttgart, 1854.

Brunnen,' or Beautiful Fountains, has been erroneously ascribed
to him (1385 to 1396), the arrangement and selection of which
afford evidence of the secular ideas of the period. Sixteen
statues are placed on the eight pillars under graceful baldachins.
In the first place the seven electors, then three Christian heroes,
three Jewish, and three heathen heroes—namely, Clodwig, Charlemagne, and Godfrey de Bouillon ; Joshua, Judas Maccabæus,

Fig. 28c. Last Judgment, from the Frauenkirche at Esslingen.

and David; Hector, Alexander the Great, and Julius Cæsar.
Higher up are Moses and the seven prophets ; and besides them
various heads of men and animals, water pipes, and such like
things. Another work of the same period, which may apparently
with more justice be imputed to Schonhofer, is the sculpture on
the porch and main portal of the Frauenkirche, the central point
of which is formed by the history of Mary and her glorification.
The sculptures on the south and north portal (the so-called

'bridal door') of the church of S. Sebald occupy a lesser position, and belong to the end of the century.

Swabia seems in the early part of the fifteenth century to have been rich in the production of plastic work. Abundant appropriation for this work was found in the decoration of the Frauenkirche at Esslingen,[1] the buttresses and portals of which exhibit a considerable number of sculptures. On the main portal of the south side there is a representation of the Last Judgment, which is executed with original freshness, and is not without various naïve touches. It also deserves notice on account of the whole architectural design. The figures have still an ideal stamp, but with this is combined a striving after an energetic natural conception, which invests the whole with a more healthy and vigorous character. Added to this, the figures are less slender in form. (Fig. 280.) Far richer and more important are the plastic works with which the stately cross church at Gmünd was adorned, about the year 1410.[2] The main portal of the church at Thann in Alsace exhibits splendid sculptured ornament.

A remarkable artistic position is occupied by the numerous works of the school of sculpture at Tournay, the productions of which, beginning with the middle of the fourteenth century, may be traced far into the fifteenth. They are for the most part tomb monuments, representations in relief, which, emanating from mediæval sentiments, combine with them a delicate detail of nature, and thus prepare the way for the subsequently brilliant tendency of Flemish realism. These monuments are for the most part in the possession of a private individual; others still have their old position in the various churches of the town. These were followed by the works of a sculptor named Claux Sluter, who was much employed at the Burgundian and French courts, and whose name plainly shows German or Dutch descent. The Mosesbrunnen[3] in the Carthusian house at Dijon, executed by him in the year 1397, is a work of a bold and free style, also

---

[1] Heideloff, *Schwäbische Denkmäler.*
[2] Cf. Lübke's *Geschichte der Plastik.* Pl. 398, et seq.
[3] Du Sommérard, *L'Art du moyen Âge.* Cap. v. Pl. 1.

exhibiting the germs of a more delicate and natural conception. This is evidenced with surprising distinctness in the monument of Philip the Bold, now placed in the Museum at Dijon, and likewise executed by the same master about the year 1404. We here find that energetic naturalness of representation, which, twenty years later, was introduced by Hubert van Eyck, as a new and victorious principle in painting.

England also took part in the plastic efforts of this epoch, although her architecture is but little designed for sculptured ornament. A splendid exception to this is afforded by the façade of Wells Cathedral, which exhibits an extensive cycle of sculptured works, executed in the strict and noble style of the thirteenth century, and containing the fundamental ideas of the Christian doctrines from the Creation to the Last Judgment, from the beginning to the end of time. More free and graceful is the style of the likewise numerous reliefs, which decorate the triangles of the arches in the triforium gallery of Lincoln cathedral : noble angel forms in lively motion, and excellently filling up the space.

Far more important in the history of English sculpture are the monuments,[1] in which the important facts of the life of the departed were conceived, and were represented with delicate taste. They are for the most part plates of reliefs, on which the form of the deceased is exhibited in all the vigour of life, generally with legs crossed over each other, and early manifesting a touch of pure style and close adherence to nature. Numerous works of this kind are to be found in the cathedrals and in other churches of the country. Several are in the Temple Church in London : especially interesting, on account of its striking characterisation, is the monument of Duke Robert of Normandy, the eldest son of William the Conqueror, in Gloucester Cathedral.

In other lands the monuments have not this preponderating importance, yet they afford essential points in the history of the development of art. For the most part they are only grave-

---

[1] *Denkm. d. Kunst.* Pl. 60 A. Stothard, *The Monumental Effigies of Great Britain.* London, 1817.

stones, which, if they are inserted in the floor of the church, exhibit very shallow relief, or are even merely traced over with a hollowed sketch, the lines of which are generally filled up with colour. Besides these, however, the stones were placed upright

Fig. 281. Monument of Archbishop Peter of Aspelt in Mainz Cathedral.

against the walls, and in this case a stronger relief was admissible. Excellent specimens of these are to be found in France, in the vault of St. Denis; in Germany, among many others, in the

church of St. Elizabeth at Marburg, in the cathedral of Mainz[1]
(Fig. 281), and especially in the cathedral at Cologne, where
many sarcophagus-like monuments exhibit a freer development
of plastic art; above all the beautiful monument of the Archbishop Frederic of Saarwerden, who died in the year 1414 A.D.,
one of the noblest and most perfect works of its kind. Similar in execution and rich in polychromatic work is the monument of Duke Henry IV. (1290), in the cross church at
Breslau.

Bronze work appears at this epoch principally used for baptismal fonts, chandeliers, reading desks, and other similar church
furniture; but not unfrequently it is also applied to monuments.
A splendid work of this kind is, for example, the monument of
King Henry III. of England and his Queen Eleonora in Westminster Abbey, cast by William Torell about the year 1290, and
full of characteristic life; also the monument of the Black Prince
in Canterbury Cathedral, executed about 1376, in the late period
of the Gothic style. Among the German works, one of the most
remarkable is the monument of Archbishop Conrad von Hoch-
staden in the cathedral at Cologne. In North Germany,
Flanders, and France, and also in the Scandinavian north, there
are a number of bronze grave plates, on which the figure of the
deceased is merely engraved with a strongly hollowed outline,
surrounded by graceful devices, enlivened with angels, apostles,
and saints, making music. We perceive successive stages of
development in many North German plates, the earliest of which
is a double plate in the cathedral at Schwerin with the representation of two bishops (about 1347); next follows a double plate,
in the cathedral of Lübeck (about 1350[2]); further there is a plate
in the Nikolaikirche at Stralsund (about 1357); and, lastly, the
noblest and most splendid of all is the larger double plate in
the cathedral at Schwerin (about 1375). The style of the ornament, of the little figures, of the gracious angels who are

---

[1] See excellent Photographic Representations in the splendid Work by H. Emden,
Der dom zu Mainz.

[2] Milde, *Denkmäler bildender Kunst in Lübeck.* Fol. Lübeck, 1843-47.

seated among vine tendrils, making music (Fig. 282), is here full
of sweetness and grace, while the figures of the two bishops
stand out in grand dignity and lifelike characterisation. (Fig.
283.)

Carving in ivory was also much employed, at this epoch, for
small portable altars or boxes, and other matters of secular use,
upon which graceful representations from the Minnesingers are
executed in elegant reliefs.

Still more extensively are precious metals employed for costly

Fig. 282. Angel from a Tomb at
Schwerin.

Fig. 283. Head of a Bishop from a Tomb
at Schwerin.

relic-cases, representing elegant and richly finished Gothic
churches, with buttresses and arches, with finials, open-work
gables, and slender spires ; but especially the various vessels for
divine service — the chalices, censers, and monstrances—were
formed in the most splendid manner, and adorned with all the
ornament of this luxuriant style.

Lastly, we must mention the numerous sculptures in wood,
which were more and more universally adopted in Germany

since the fourteenth century, and were specially employed for the decoration of altars. They are for the most part adapted to give us important information with regard to the use of colours, the polychromatic finish of mediæval sculpture. Not merely did the middle ages delight in the most extensive use of colour in these carvings in wood, but also on the stone images which are to be found on monuments or in the interior of the churches as architectural ornament. It was partly the deep feeling that struggled for expression in these works, which needed the tender blending of colour to temper the severity of the form into a softness full of soul, and partly the polychromatic style of the architecture; and the varied light, which streamed in through the painted windows, required that the same principle should be carried out on all other works designed for ornament. Thus we see the extensive altar shrines, which were often closed with double folds, entirely filled with statues and reliefs, the latter carved in wood, with perspective shading like paintings, standing out from a richly designed gold ground, and surrounded with graceful ornamental frames, and sheltered with baldachins. The little figures themselves, also, executed for the most part in a small size, are covered with magnificent gilded and damasked drapery, the edges and reverse side of which are resplendent with glittering colours, especially azure and red. The naked parts, especially the head, were painted after nature in the tenderest manner, and the gilded hair alone indicated artistic formality. The architectural frames were harmoniously executed in gold, blue, and red, evidencing by alternation and combination of colours a masterly and practised skill.

These costly carved altars, in which the mediæval sculpture of the north obtains one of its most brilliant triumphs, do not appear, it seems, until the fourteenth century, and were executed with increasing predilection until the end of mediæval art. In many German churches we find splendid specimens of this kind, which, to a great extent, have still preserved their old polychromatic ornament. Of these works we will only mention the altar at Tribsees, in Pomerania, which has an original but somewhat rude representation of the Last Supper. The great mass of similar works in carved wood will be alluded to on our consideration of a subsequent epoch.

While the Gothic style thus favoured the development of the plastic art, *painting*[1] was not only not advanced by the new movement, but it was even decidedly retarded. While architecture, as we have seen, robbed it of the more extensive surfaces, wall painting fell into disuse throughout the whole north, and was only rarely and exceptionally employed. The great future, which seemed in store for this art during the sway of the Romanesque style, now seemed irreparably lost, and the northern nations purchased the satisfaction of expressing themselves in the Gothic style, with the utter loss for centuries of the ability to represent their highest ideas in extensive creations by means of that art which seemed rightly designed to express them. Painting saw itself, therefore, in the north almost entirely thrown upon the productions of more insignificant art, and even in the altar paintings its sphere was considerably limited by the predilection for carved works. Thus, henceforth, in northern painting there was a certain idyllic limitation, a preponderating emphasis given to tenderness of feeling, and the taste of the artist was restrained within narrow limits.

Among the best known Gothic wall paintings, those in the apsis of the church at Brauweiler, which belong to the early period, and especially those on the vaults and walls of the former chapel at Ramersdorf, near Bonn, possess simple beauty; the latter, moreover, is one of the rare specimens of a complete cycle, finishing with the Last Judgment. Others are to be found in the choir of Cologne Cathedral, in the church of S. Thomas at Soest; and a complete series of biblical scenes are in the monastery church at Wienhausen, besides important remains on the vaults of the Marienkirche at Colberg, in the cathedral at Marienwerder, and in the church of St. Vitus at Mühlhausen on

---

[1] *Denkm. d. Kunst.* Pl. 60.

the Neckar. The Emperor Charles IV. seemed to give a more influential position to wall painting; but his predilection for material splendour urged him to bestow a preference on mosaic work, which was not favourable to a freer development of the art. The grand representation of the Last Judgment, on the south side of the cathedral at Prague, is of this kind, as well as a portion of the paintings in the Wenzelskapelle of the same cathedral, and the church and two chapels belonging to the castle of Karlstein in Bohemia. In France, the great wall painting of the Last Judgment, in S. Philibert at Tournus, is a remarkable work; and the recently discovered paintings of the church at Gorkum, in Holland, may be mentioned as belonging to the early period.

The loss experienced by wall painting, as regards artistic powers and means, was bestowed predominantly upon glass painting. While in the former epoch, the simple Romanesque windows had been adorned with glass paintings, how much stronger must the inclination to this mode of ornament have been now aroused, when in the broad and high Gothic windows, space and opportunity was afforded for comprehensive representations. The simplest style was, when the richly designed and tapestry-like window was terminated with single figures like a splendid border. But complete scenes of biblical and legendary subjects were also distributed over the vast surfaces, though always in a framework which frequently exhibited most beautifully the Gothic form. But not merely the architectural division of the whole, the intersection of the framework, but still more the heavy, inconvenient, mosaic-like arrangement imposed so many limitations on this branch of art, that its works can only produce effect by the wondrous glow and harmonious splendour of the colours, and by the just conception and execution of single figures. How imperatively, however, the strictest architectural rule is necessary in these works may be seen in the productions of the later epoch, which sought to cast aside these conditions, and strove after a freedom of composition which is denied to these works. Glass painting especially flourished, in the thirteenth century, in those parts of France in which the Gothic style had arisen and progressed.   Most of these cathedrals, above all those of Chartres, Rheims, Rouen, Bourges, Tours, and Le Mans, afford splendid specimens of it.   Equally so does the Ste. Chapelle at Paris.   Glass paintings of the thirteenth century are rare in Germany; and not till the fourteenth century does this art there rise to a perfection, evidence of which is furnished by

Fig. 284.   Glass Painting from Königsfelden.

numerous works far into the fifteenth century.   Among the noblest of these may be numbered the windows in the choir of Cologne Cathedral,[1] in the minsters of Freiburg and Strasburg, in the cathedral at Ratisbon, in the church of S. Catharine at Oppenheim, in the Marthakirche at Nuremberg, in the Dionysius kirche at Esslingen, and others.   Among the works of the fourteenth century the glass windows of the monastery church

[1] See a coloured Illustration in the *Denkm. d. Kunst.*   Pl. 54 B.

at Königsfelden in Switzerland occupy a distinguished place. (Fig. 284.)[1]　In England the glass paintings of York Cathedral, and in Spain those of the cathedrals of Toledo and Leon, are much famed.

In miniature painting also, in the early period of Gothic art, France took the lead of all other countries.　In the art of 'illuminating,' as it was called in Paris, the French masters were widely famed.　This artistic work went hand in hand with the scientific life which at that time rendered the Paris University the first in the world, and by its numerous productions it acquired a uniformly finished style, solid technical skill, and elegant perfection.　The Gothic style afforded a fixed architectural basis, and the glass painting exerted an evident influence upon the mode of representation, so that even unessential externals, such as strong black outlines, were transferred to it.　A psalter in the Library at Paris, alleged to have been executed for Louis the Saint, and richly adorned with miniatures, is especially worthy of remark.　It contains numerous scenes from the Old Testament, simply and distinctly portrayed with deep harmonious colours on a gold ground, enclosed in a frame of strict Gothic architecture.　Here, however, as in most other French works of this kind, the technical execution is regarded at the expense of intellectual freshness and finer feeling.

The case is different with the German miniatures,[2] which at this period are particularly devoted to the illustration of secular poems, especially those of the Minnesingers, and for the most part in their lightly shaded drawings in pen and ink betray a freshness of feeling and a naïve originality, which harmonise well with the tender poetic feeling of the poems.　One of the most attractive specimens of this kind is a manuscript of Tristan von Gottfried of Strasburg, now in the Library at Munich, and which seems to have been executed before the middle of the thirteenth century.　The understanding of the physical organi-

---

[1] This illustration, from a drawing of Herr Gräter's, I owe to the Antiquarian Society in Zurich, which is preparing a publication of the whole.
[2] See Fr. Kugler's *Kleinen Schriften, &c.* Vol. I. and II.

sation is still deficient, but a just feeling is expressed in the
attitudes ; and there is a childlike naïveté in the expression of the
heads. The figures are left free of colour on a coloured ground,
though the drapery is shaded. Still more decidedly do the pictures in the manuscripts of the Minnesingers partake of the
character of the Gothic style—thus, for instance, the Wien-
gartner Manuscript in the Royal Library at Stuttgart, belong-

Fig. 285. Miniature Picture from William of Orange.

ing to the latter half of the thirteenth century ; the numerous
pictures of the Manesian manuscript in the Library at Paris ;
and the manuscripts of William of Orange in the Library at
Cassel in the year 1334, which exhibit lightly sketched figures
gracefully placed on a gold or tapestry-like background.

Wherever, on the other hand, sacred events had to be delineated in bibles, psalters, or gospels, free artistic humour indulged
itself, in peopling the gay branchwork extending along the edge of
the leaves with wonderful and playful creations of the imagination,
in which free merry fancy and ingenuity often rose to the most
charming play of humour. Most clever designs of this kind are
to be found in a manuscript in the Museum at Berlin ; others,
no less original, are in a bible of the fourteenth century in the

public Library at Stuttgart. (Fig. 286.) In Bohemia also, in the course of the thirteenth century, a similar style of miniature painting appeared, numerous specimens of which, full of life and originality, are afforded by a bible with prints in the library of Prince Lobkowitz at Prague.

Lastly, in panel painting Germany surpasses all other northern lands, especially after the middle of the fourteenth century, when this style of art was practised with much success.[1] These panel pictures were occasionally used as covers to altar shrines, the principal representation of which often consisted of a wood carving, but constantly the main part of the altar was a painting which was enclosed by two movable folding pieces, likewise painted both inside and out. When the altar was closed, the

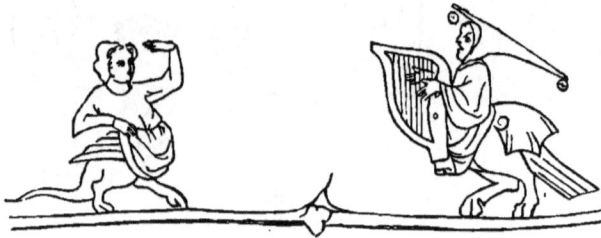

Fig. 286.   Drawings round the Edges of a Bible in Stuttgart.

outside generally exhibited some simple figures, as, for example, the Annunciation, or saints held in especial honour. When the altar was opened, the great central panel, together with the two inner sides of the folds, presented either in series of separate scenes a whole cycle, such as the life of Mary or the Passion, or the central piece contained one larger representation, to which were added smaller ones on the folds. The pictures on the wooden panels, which for this purpose received a fine grounding in chalk, were *in tempera*—i.e. executed with a tenacious cement, white of egg, or such like. This material favoured a fine and carefully detailed execution. The colours are for the most part tender, light, and toned down by constant gilding. More and

[1] Hotho, *Die Malerschule Hubert's van Eyck, &c.* 1 vol.

more we find an inclination to imitate in the drapery the costume of the time, with its rich magnificence, and its jewels of gold, pearls, and precious stones. Yet the representations still stand out from a figured gold ground, thus excluding all idea of nature, and giving the whole an ideal character.

Much as in these works the general tendency of the age, with its soft expression of feeling and its spirituality, predominates, yet after 1350, combined with this characteristic, there appear peculiar styles and independent schools, the earliest of which distinguishes itself in Bohemia under the rule of the art-loving Emperor Charles IV. We have already mentioned the numerous wall paintings in Prague and Karlstein. Panel pictures are also to be found here, as well as in the galleries of Prague and Vienna. Nicholaus Wurmser of Strasburg and two Prague artists, Kundze and Theoderich, are famous as the masters who executed these works. The prevailing character of their works is great softness, inclining almost to indistinctness in the forms, but producing great fervour and tenderness of expression. The colouring is extraordinarily delicately shaded; the forms, however, are for the most part broad and even clumsy, the nose being extremely thick and round, the lips full, the eyes large, and with an expression rather of openness than depth; at the same time the attitude of the figures is awkward, and is rendered more so by the high shoulders and short neck. The church at Mühlhausen, on the Neckar, founded in the year 1385 by a citizen of Prague, contains many wall paintings and panel paintings belonging to the later period of this school.[1]

The Nuremberg school,[2] which reached its prime in the middle of the fourteenth century, is still more important. Painting here appears under the decided influence of the great sculptor Sebald Schonhofer and his associates, and by strict delineation and decided form endeavoured to rival the sister art, while at the same time, by the aid of deep colouring, the true picturesque effect was retained. The figures are gracefully slender, and,

---

[1] Heideloff, *Die Mittelalterliche Kunst in Schwaben.*
[2] Von Rettberg, *Kunstleben Nürnbergs.*

although conventional, are occasionally free in attitude, and the
heads exhibit tender expressive feeling.   One of the most important works is the Imhoff altar, from the Lorenzo church, now
in the citadel, the principal painting of which represents the
Crowning of the Virgin. (Fig. 287.)   The noble flow of the dra-

Fig. 287. The Imhoff Altar-piece at Nuremberg.

pery, the hearty expression, the grace of the figures, combined
with distinctness of form, exhibit much affinity with the sculptures of Schonhofer, so that the origin of the work may be supposed to be about 1361, before the end of the century.   The
later works are remarkable for somewhat stout physical proportions.   Thus we find it in the Tucher high altar of the Frauenkirche, belonging to the year 1385, which contains the Annunciation, the Crucifixion, and the Resurrection, and on the folding

leaves the birth of Christ and the two princes of the apostles. The Volkamer altar, in the choir of S. Lorenzo, belongs to the beginning of the fifteenth century; its representations are taken from the life of Christ, and from the legends of S. Theokar; the Haller altar, also, in S. Sebald, represents the crucified Saviour between Mary and John and various saints.

Later than the former, but all the more noble and pure in its development, is the Cologne school. Probably it also was trained by the plastic works, which evidence great elegance here in the beginning of the fourteenth century; but from earlier times there seems to have been much activity in painting, and the productions in this sphere of art belong to the most important of their time and kind. The tender deep feeling, which is stamped on the figures of the Gothic style, were nowhere expressed in painting with so much life, depth, and devotion as here. Hence these Cologne masters are the purest representatives in their pictures of this tender and feeling style; hence they exercised the most decided influence upon the adjacent territories, and far into North Germany, in consequence of which, however, greater conventionality stamps their style. Like the Prague school, that of Cologne starts with a tender conception and soft execution, but it combines with this a delicate feeling for noble forms, for grace of demeanour, and for depth of expression. A soft blending of the light and yet full-bodied colouring, and a childlike purity and sweetness, diffused over the better works of this school a charm of piety and religious fervour, such as is known by no other school in so pure and perfect a manner. It must be admitted that there are limits here also, and that the female and youthful figures, and this again in their humility and devotion, form the strong point of these painters, who succeed but ill in the portrayal of strength and manliness, and not at all in the delineation of passion; but these are truly the barriers of the time, whose positive side, whose truth and beauty, all the more serenely shine forth.

The most important works of the Cologne school are connected with the names of two masters, corresponding with the two principal epochs. Meister Wilhelm (von Herle?), whom the Limburg chronicle of the year 1380 extols as 'the best painter in the German lands,' is the earlier of the two. Pure

Fig. 288. S. Ursula, from a Picture in Cologne Cathedral.

childlike innocence, tenderness of feeling, and sweetness of expression, prevail in his gracefully slender figures, combined with a blending of colour which elevates the earthly into heavenly glory: 'the soul is quite alive, the body scarcely so.'[1] The heads have a delicate oval; the nose is long and thin, the mouth small, full, and lovely, the brow high and pure; the eyes, placed somewhat obliquely, have a soft dovelike expression. Among the principal works of this master, we must mention the Klaren-altar, now in the Johanniskapelle of the cathedral at Cologne, containing numerous representations from scenes of the child-hood and passion of Christ.

The second master is Stephan (Lochner), whose name has been preserved for us by the travelling manual of Albert Dürer, and with whom we associate the noblest work which the painting of the middle ages could produce—the famous cathedral painting, executed in the year 1426, formerly in the chapel of the town hall, and now preserved in one of the choir chapels of Cologne Cathedral.[2] The principal panel represents the Adoration of the Kings; on the folding panels within, St. Gereon with his followers, and St. Ursula with her attendants (Fig. 288), are portrayed, the two principal saints of the city; outside is the Annunciation. Meister Stephan treads in the footsteps of his predecessor. He is filled with the same depth of devotion and innocence, and ex-hibits them in the same noble figures; but by stronger modelling, deeper colouring, and by the introduction of the much orna-mented dress of the period, he imparts to them a higher degree of reality, without, however, losing the tender ideal tone, which hovers, like a spiritualising ether, round all genuine mediæval forms. Thus in these wonderful works, the art of that period attained an unsurpassed excellence.

ITALY.

Plastic art in Italy strove after and attained, more than in the previous epoch, a position independent of architecture. While the Gothic style here fashioned its strict system with greater freedom, it did not exercise such unlimited despotic sway over

---

[1] Hotho's *Malerschule Hubert's van Eyck, &c.* p. 239.
[2] *Denkm. d. Kunst.* Pl. 60. Cf. the excellent Engraving by P. Massau.

plastic art, and self-confidence had been even earlier so far
awakened in various masters, that they had not surrendered their
works so entirely under the dominion of architecture.   Added to
this, many of the most important masters were engaged at the
same time in all three arts, or at least in painting and architecture, and from this there resulted a juster weighing of the
limits and privileges of the separate arts.   When plastic art was
combined with architecture, it was in an unconstrained manner,
according to preponderating picturesque laws of arrangement.
Rich space for painting was, moreover, attended to in the whole
organisation of buildings, so that in the vast wall surfaces and
vault compartments this art could indulge in that grand freedom
of conception and composition which, in course of time, must
have given it a decided superiority over northern painting.

In sculpture,[1] the new advance was chiefly brought about by
Giovanni Pisano, the son of the great Nicola. Born about 1245 (he
died about 1321), he at first took an active part in the execution
of his father's later works, especially the pulpit in the cathedral
at Siena.   If in these works, he was conscious of a newly
awakened life of feeling, in contrast to the calmer beauty of the
antique conceptions of Nicola, this feeling burst forth still more
strongly and decidedly in Giovanni's own creations.   Though
this revolution may have been caused by the general temperament of the time, yet the presence of numerous German sculptors may not have been without its influence. But Giovanni did
not adopt the new style with that tender fervour and mildness
which were generally prevalent in the north.   He knew how to
heighten his greater freedom and life into an expression of the
deepest excitement and dramatic passion, and he combined with
this a rare abundance of ingenious ideas in composition.

Among the earlier works of this master, we must mention,
above all, the high altar in the cathedral at Arezzo (about 1286);
an extremely rich work, representing in an abundance of reliefs
and small statues, executed in a noble flowing style, full of life
and action, the legends of the Virgin and other saints, as well as

[1] *Denkm. d. Kunst.*   Pl. 61 and 63.

the figures of the apostles, prophets, and angels. Another of his earlier works, which he executed with many pupils and associates, are the extensive sculptures on the façade of the cathedral at Orvieto,[1] the execution of which belongs to the close of the thirteenth century. Not in architectural framework, as in the northern cathedrals, but in free, picturesque arrangement, partly surrounded by elegant branchwork, these representations are spread in strong relief over the four great wall surfaces between the portals and by the side of them. We find, in profound connection, the whole doctrine, from the Fall of Man to the Redemption and the Last Judgment, depicted with great life. Many things still remind of Nicola's style; others proclaim

Fig. 289. Cain and Abel. Relief from the Cathedral at Orvieto.

in their lively dramatic conception the advance of the later school. (Fig. 289.)

Still more powerful, passionate, but at the same time not more free from overloading, is the pulpit in S. Andrea at Pistoja, completed in 1301 ; like earlier similar works, it rests on splendid marble columns supported by lions, and the triangular spaces between the arches and the breastwork are adorned with an abundance of excellent reliefs and statuettes. We see the Birth of Christ, the Adoration of the Kings, the Murder of the Inno-

---

[1] Engravings of these have been published by Gruner.

cents, the Crucifixion, and the Last Judgment, all restless, overloaded, natural to violence and ugliness, but powerfully affecting
and full of strong life, the separate figures free and noble in
attitude, and not without some remnant of the antique.

After the year 1304, he executed the monument of Pope
Benedict XI. in S. Domenico at Perugia; and in 1311 the pulpit
of the cathedral at Pisa, which was, however, subsequently destroyed, and now only exists in fragments. Perfect in beauty
and truly regal in grace is the statue of the Madonna and Child,
which he executed for a portal on the south side of the cathedral
of Florence: it is a work full of nobleness and grandeur,
although without that depth of feeling which marks the Gothic
art of the North.

A great number of pupils and imitators followed Giovanni's
style; numerous altars, pulpits, and monuments testify throughout Italy to the pervading influence of this master, whom we
may call the parent of an epoch. At this time the focus of
artistic activity was formed by Florence, whose great master Giotto
(1276–1336), with his universal gifts, knew how to advance the
plastic art also by his active influence. He himself designed
the plastic ornament, and even partly undertook its execution,
for the façade and clock tower of the cathedral of Florence
which he had himself constructed. On the beautiful clock tower,
in rows of small reliefs, the various stages of the development of
man are represented with great cleverness and profound arrangement. From the creation of the first man, through all the conditions of the simplest natural life, through the victorious struggle
with the elementary powers, to the height of an existence purified by art and science, and safe under the maternal guardianship
of the Church, this rich cycle is depicted with perfect distinctness,
in simple and true plastic touches.

Under Giotto's influence, Andrea Pisano next arrived at independent and masterly power (1270 to 1345). Under Giotto's
guidance, he was engaged in the execution of the reliefs on the
clock tower; but his own master-work is preserved to us in the
southern bronze gate of the baptistry at Florence, executed in

the year 1330, and one of the most perfect works of this kind. In twenty-eight gracefully framed compartments, arranged in a strictly architectural manner, the events of the life of John the Baptist, together with representations of the Virtues, are executed in an unsurpassably simple and strict relief style. With two or three figures, and the smallest appliances, each incident is distinctly expressed; at the same time the forms have a light flowing attitude and movement. (Fig. 290.) Florentine sculpture

Fig. 290. Relief from the south Portal of the Baptistry at Florence, by Andrea Pisano.

at this period comprises, lastly, one of the most important masters, who likewise accomplished great things in all three arts —namely, Andrea di Cione, best known under the name of Orcagna (–1376). His master-work as a sculptor is in the splendid tabernacle of the main altar of Or San Micchele, at Florence (executed in the year 1359), perhaps the most magnificent decorative work in the world. Richly covered with variegated mosaic patterns, it comprises an abundance of reliefs, with representations from the life of the Virgin, single figures of the prophets, saints, and angels, which for the most part display the Gothic mode of feeling, combined with lofty grace and noble simplicity. The beautiful medallion reliefs on the Loggia de' Lanzi, built after his death, have, from archival researches, been recently denied as his works.

In the other parts of Italy, also, from Venice to Naples, the plastic arts were much cultivated at this period; many names of artists are mentioned, and many extensive and magnificent works were executed. Naples alone possesses in its churches, above all, in Sta. Chiara and S. Giovanni a Carbonara, a number of splendid monuments of the princes of the house of Anjou; yet these do not on the whole attain to the life and delicacy of the Pisan school.

Still more than plastic art, painting [1] was also at this period the favourite art of the Italians, an art to which the greatest creative minds applied themselves with especial energy. The productions of the earlier epochs in this sphere of art were only beginnings, from which the wonders of Italian art now rose with ever greater excellence. Not limited, as in the North, by narrow altar panels and the clumsy rules of glass painting, painting could express, on the vast wall surfaces and vault compartments which Italian architecture conceded to her, the whole extent and depth of the Christian ideas; in the most comprehensive themes the eye could take in the whole subject, the art could learn to develope itself freely and boldly, and could evidence with power that in the highest sense it was the Christian art. And when we rapidly survey the importance to which this art had now risen in Italy, we forget the want of consistency of its Gothic architecture, which alone prepared the way for this development.

The principal scene of this art perfection is Tuscany, where, in two great local schools, painting advanced in different styles. It was especially the Florentine masters, who conceived life with

[1] *Denkm. d. Kunst.* Pl. 62 and 63.

unbiassed eye, and combined with these fresh views a profound representation of the sacred legends. These artists were most interested in historical delineations, such as are afforded by the life of Christ, of the Virgin, and saints ; yet compositions also appear of mysterious symbolic import, executed with an abundance of lifelike traits, the idea of which was frequently suggested by Dante's wonderful poem. The great Giotto, whom we have already mentioned as an architect and a sculptor, is the first and mightiest master of this period, whose activity throughout the whole of Italy, from the Venetian to the Neapolitan territories, is evidenced by grand compositions, and whose overwhelming influence long left its impress upon the Italian art of his age. His intellectual power is only fully exhibited in comprehensive representations. He ever aimed at decision in his style, at convincing distinctness in his delineation of events, at energetic characterisation and strong dramatic life. These excellences belong to his works in an unsurpassable manner, and are combined with a precision in the construction and arrangement of large compositions and extensive series of paintings. With these mighty characteristics, the perfection of the single form is indifferent to him, and even beauty is superfluous. The type of his heads is extremely uniform, and of a grand though not attractive outline. We cannot fail to perceive a remnant of the long slender Byzantine faces and figures, but the mental expression appears entirely new and fresh, and is full of power. He succeeded but ill in expressing the more passionate emotions, such as anger, hate, and horror. On these occasions the features are easily distorted to grimace ; but in the general bearing and action, the figures express every feeling with unsurpassable truth, and both agitation and fervour are exhibited with thrilling power.

There are three principal works which display his greatness and importance. At the age of twenty-seven (1303), he produced the almost boundless cycle of paintings in the church of S. Maria dell'Arena at Padua. It is a long one-aisled building, roofed with tunnel vaults, the whole walls and vaults of which he adorned with paintings, containing the history of Christ and of the Virgin, the Last Judgment being depicted on the entrance wall. Giotto shows himself here, throughout the work, to be the mightiest artist of all ages. All that was conventional before he freed from its fetters; he grasped the matter at its innermost substance, and entered into the very heart of the incident. Agitating, fervent, touching, giving every emotion of the mind its full expression, he portrays the highest ideas in the simplest manner. Lacking accurate anatomical knowledge, it is ever merely the general intimation with which he works; and the same in colouring, which is executed in light tints with little

Fig. 291. From Giotto's Paintings in S. Maria dell' Arena, at Padua.

shade; but even so it is of striking power and irresistible effect. At the same time he gives surprising glimpses of actual life, and knows how to introduce even genre-like ideas, and to execute his work with such grandeur that they in nowise affect the sacred, noble, and historical subject, but only exhibit it more clearly.

Of this kind are the scenes in which Joachim, in deep distress, comes to the shepherds in the field, when, on returning, full of happy emotion, he embraces his wife, and other such-like scenes. Many exhibit violent expression of passion. Thus, for instance, John, who is on the point of throwing himself, with outstretched arms, on the body of his beloved Master. (Fig. 291.) An equally important cycle is afforded by the paintings on the central vault of the lower church of S. Francesco at Assisi. The four vaults contain grand symbolic creations, representing the three religious vows of Poverty, Chastity, and Obedience, and the Glorification of St. Francis. The master has here imparted a breath of life and freshness to the dry allegory by lifelike poetical associations, and has also in a grand manner proved his skill in a noble and harmonious arrangement of the space.

The porch of St. Peter's in Rome has a large mosaic picture, executed after a design of Giotto, representing the vessel of Peter—that is, according to the traditionary symbol, the Church of Christ—on the storm-tossed sea. While demons are agitating the violent storm, Christ walks helpingly and comfortingly forward on the waves, and holds out His hand to the already sinking Peter.

Of Giotto's few panel paintings, we must mention a cycle of twenty-six small pictures, which he had painted for the screen of the sacristy of Sta. Croce in Florence, which are now for the most part in the academy in the same city. The small miniature-like representations, the subject of which is the life of Christ and St. Francis, evidence the same distinctness and all the power of living narration.

How completely Giotto ruled the painting of his time is to be perceived in the extraordinary number of creations, especially wall pictures, which have been preserved in the churches of Florence and other parts of Tuscany. The chapels, chapter houses, and sacristies of the great churches belonging to the religious orders—for instance, Sta. Croce, Sta. Maria Novella, Sta. Maria del Carmine at Florence, S. Francesco, and the Campo Santo at Pisa—are rich in works of this kind, which often exhibit Giotto's style in their comprehensive application, and frequently in their talented execution. Among the pupils whose names are known to us, Taddeo Gaddi (Life of the Virgin in S. Croce), Spinello Aretino (from Arezzo), and Niccolo di Pietro (the two latter about 1390), are the most important.

One of the mightiest followers of Giotto, and bearing great mental affinity with him, is Orcagna, whom we have already met

with as an important architect and sculptor. A rich abundance
of his creations are preserved in the Capella Strozzi in Sta. Maria
Novella at Florence. On the wall of the window there is a large
representation of the Last Judgment : above in solemn dignity
is the enthroned Judge of the world, surrounded on both sides
by angels, who are hovering down with trumpets and instruments
of torture. The Madonna and John the Baptist are kneeling in
the mild and humble attitude of intercession; in two rows on
each side, seated on clouds, are the strong energetic forms of the
apostles ; below are the rising figures, bands of the saints and
the faithful, light forms on a dark-blue ground, rich in beauty,
although the expression of character preponderates. More important still is the representation of Paradise on the left wall.
Above, Christ is enthroned by the side of the Madonna under a
Gothic baldachin, surrounded by angels. The whole of the remaining space is filled with rows of saints on each side. The
arrangement is still generally stiff, and without picturesque grouping ; but the grand beauty of the heads, the rich free characterisation of the figures, and the inexhaustible abundance of the
noblest forms of drapery are truly enchanting. No picture
throughout the whole Gothic epoch combines so much rich
beauty. The colouring is light, distinct, and warm, the counte-
nances have a gentle oval—noble youthful features, fine profile,
and careful modelling. In the execution of the figures we find a
remarkable advance made beyond Giotto; and this is also evidenced in the altar panel of this chapel, which, according to its
inscription, was painted by Orcagna in 1357. It represents
Christ, surrounded by angels, solemnly enthroned, holding out
the key to the kneeling Peter with His left hand, while with the
right He extends the book to Thomas Aquinas, who is also
kneeling, and who is presented by the Madonna ; a commis-
sioned glorification of the Dominican order, out of which nothing
but a solemn dignified representation was to be made. Another
altar piece of this master's, consisting of numerous divisions, and
formerly in S. Pietro Maggiore in Florence, is now in the National
Gallery in London. The central piece contains a crowning of

the Virgin, rich in figures : she is constrained in attitude, but the head is beautiful, and the drapery magnificent.

But the manner in which this master knew how to compose his works, and the mighty grasp with which he caught the living expression, are evidenced in his great representation of the Last Judgment, in the Campo Santo at Pisa, and still more strikingly in his ' Triumph of Death.'[1] If in other great works of this kind the painter had to follow ecclesiastical tradition, here the great master represents in a free and bold form the perishableness of all earthly things, and shows us death as the inexorable annihilator of all that is beautiful, blooming, and noble. On the right, on a flowery turf, surrounded by luxurious orange groves from which cupids are hovering down, we see a company of ladies and knights, in the festive costume of the period, the men with falcons on their hands, the ladies with their lapdogs. In confidential talk they listen to song and stringed instruments, so that one could fancy oneself transported to the merry society of the Decameron of Boccaccio. But, unforeboded, the mighty decree rushes through the air, and death appears in the form of a fearful woman with streaming black hair, and powerfully uplifted scythe raised for the fatal stroke. Close by, as if lying in sheaves, is a rich harvest of dead, princes and nobles of the world, whose souls have been carried away by descending angels and devils. While these happy ones without misgiving fall a prey to death, a group of sick, crippled, and miserable in vain stretch out their arms in entreaty to the angel of death, for whom they yearn as their only deliverer. (Fig. 292.) High rocks rise on the left, and a hunting party of nobles and ladies are galloping out from the defiles ; but suddenly the horses start, uneasiness seizes the pack, and the joyful train stand as if enchanted, for close before their merry company three graves open, showing the half-mouldered bodies of noble princes. A grey hermit is standing by, and pointing out to the proud of this

---

[1] Crowe and Cavalcaselle and others refuse him these works; and they differ essentially with regard to that in S. Maria Novella, without being able definitely to assign it to another master.

world the fearful picture of the nothingness of all earthly things.
Up the mountain side, there are other holy men, who, far from
the tumult of the world, in pious solitude, lead a life of renunciation.   Good and bad spirits are disputing in the air for the
souls of the departed : the saved ones are borne upwards on the
right to blessedness by hovering angels; the condemned are
hurled on the left by fantastic demons into the fiery abyss of a
flaming mountain.   Never perhaps has the triumph of death

Fig. 292.   Group of Beggars from the Triumph of Death, alleged to be by Orcagna.

over all creation been portrayed with such poetic power.   The
execution is careless, and does not attain to the calm beauty and
value of the paintings of S. Maria Novella; but the mind of a
great master is unmistakable.   Here, as in S. Maria Novella,
a representation of Hades by Bernardo Orcagna, the brother of
Andrea, is added to the picture of the Last Judgment; but,
although that in the Campo Santo is distinguished by a certain
demon-like vastness and unearthliness, that in S. Maria Novella

is only an unsuccessful attempt to imitate the wonderful divisions and circles of the poor souls in Dante's ' Inferno.'

The school of Siena is essentially different. Its efforts aim less at a lifelike conception of existence, than at a portrayal of the inner life of feeling. By careful devotion to the separate form, it reaches a tender perfection of the figures, and a sweet and feeling beauty of expression, which render it more suited for altar-pieces than for extensive frescoes. Throughout we can here trace an inner affinity with northern art. The principal master of this school is Simone di Martino, usually, though erroneously, denominated Simone Memmi (1276–1344). His rare pictures—for instance, a Madonna with Saints, in the Academy of Siena, and two Madonnas in the Museum at Berlin —breathe a deep fervour and beauty of mind; wherever, on the other hand, he attempts larger works, as in the wall painting of the Madonna as Queen of Heaven, in the Palazzo Pubblico at Siena, he appears constrained and weak. Among the other Sienese masters, we must mention Lippo Memmi, whose altar paintings display a similar style with those of Simone. Far from a vigorous and richly pulsating life, the school ended in an idyllic repose, and allowed the great changes which befel Italian art in the course of the fifteenth century to pass unnoticed by, and ossified at last into lifeless repetition of customary forms.

With the beginning of the fifteenth century, there appeared a new and independent development of Italian painting, which aimed more universally at a powerful conception of nature, at a more radical study of form, and at more complete perfection of colouring and of perspective. While, however, most of the painters of this epoch followed this new realistic style, and thus established the sway of modern art, one master, living secluded in a monastery, remained true to the tradition and conceptions of the middle ages, and knew how to infuse a new life into them by the incomparable fervour and beauty of his feeling. Fra Giovanni Angelico,[1] called *da Fiesole*, from the place of his birth

---

[1] *Denkm. d. Kunst.* Pl. 67.

(1387–1455), stands uniquely prominent, like some late opened
and wondrous blossom of an almost unknown period, in the
midst of the stirrings of a new life.   The inspired fervour of the
Christian mind, the angelic purity and beauty of the soul, have
never been so gloriously portrayed in plastic art as they are in
his works.   The tender breath of an almost supernaturally ideal
life plays round his creations, and smiles from the rosy features
of the youthful heads, or is wafted to us like heavenly peace
from the dignified figures of his aged men.   The expression of
humility, of a cheerfulness resting in God, the calm sabbatic rest
of those who are devoted in true love to the Most High, forms
the range of his representations.   The varied emotion, the
changeful course of life, the energy of action and passion, are
absent from his works.   His sphere is closely limited : it is as it
were a continuation of that after which the Sienese strove; but
within its limits it attains to great perfection, and at the same
time imparts a high degree of finish to the whole, by rich colouring, by imperishable freshness and beauty of the˙ tints, and
tender modelling, by an unsurpassable nobleness in the fall of
the folds, and by a solemn tone of feeling and distinct grouping.
With all this is combined a loving, miniature-like delicacy of
execution.   Numerous panel pictures, for the most part of
small dimensions, testify to the harmonious beauty of his art ;
the larger figures not unusually, on the other hand, lack sufficient energy of life.   An abundance of smaller works are to be
found in the academy at Florence, among them an exquisite Life
of Our Lord, from which we have taken a Crowning of the
Virgin. (Fig. 293.)   Christ is represented sitting on the clouds
with His mother.   While with both His hands He gently places
the crown on her bended head, she crosses her hands humbly
and timidly over her breast, and seems in the expression of profound humility scarcely to understand her glorification.   The
garments of both the figures fall with rich beauty of folds, and
complete the incomparable harmony which pervades the whole.
The same subject is similarly treated in a picture in the Museum
of the Louvre.

One of his most splendid works is a miniature altar in the sacristy of S. M. Novella, in Florence, the three compartments of which contain the Annunciation, the Adoration of the Three Kings, and again the Crowning of the Virgin : it is of the greatest beauty, warmth, and tenderness; the figures are beautifully

Fig. 293. Crowning of the Virgin Mary, by Fiesole.

rounded and excellently draped, the Madonna in the deepest humility, and Christ in glorious majesty.   The monastery of S. Marco in Florence, to which he belonged as a brother, contains a series of the noblest of his wall paintings : in the chapter house there is a representation of Christ on the Cross, lamented by His adherents and the representatives of the Church : it is a work of great depth, beauty, and dignity of feeling.   Besides this, in many of the cells, there are various pictures full of the most spiritual fervour; thus, for instance, the Resurrection, and Christ appearing to Mary in the Garden after the Resurrection.   The sublimest of all his works is on the vaulting of the chapel of the Madonna di S. Brizio, in the cathedral of Orvieto : it portrays Christ as judge of the world, mighty, grand, and—remarkably enough—with that bold movement of the hand for the rejection of the condemned which Michael Angelo subsequently so powerfully adopted in his Last Judgment : by his side are beautiful choirs of angels, and angels with trumpets; also the prophets, who form a wonderfully constructed group of magnificent figures. Lastly, in his extreme old age (1447), he produced the representations from the life of St. Stephen and St. Laurentius, in the chapel of Pope Nicholas in the Vatican, and proved himself here also to be an able artist in his distinct and charming conception of life.

In the other parts of Italy numerous able artists appeared between 1350 and 1450, some of whom were affected by Giotto's influence, while others modified the general style of the period in a more independent manner. The most important among them are, Aldighiero da Zevio,[1] who, about the year 1370, decorated the chapel of S. Felice in S. Antonio, at Padua, with wall paintings; Jacopo d'Avanzo, who completed these works, and painted the chapel of S. Giorgio, near S. Antonio : both of these artists display in their works a lively conception and richly-finished colouring. At the same period, in Venice, a striving after softly blended colouring is apparent in the pictures of Antonio Vivarini and Giovanni Alamano (thus a German). Lastly, in the neighbourhood of Ancona, there appeared Gentile da Fabriano (about 1450), whose conceptions show great similarity with those of Fiesole in their tenderness and fervour. No less rich than that master in religious ardour and devotion, he surpasses him in his fresh and naïve views of actual life. A cheerful and noble feeling is expressed in his paintings, a number of the most excellent of which have unfortunately perished. Among the works still existing, the first place is occupied by an Adoration of the Kings, a work rich in figures and poetically conceived, executed in the year 1423, and now in the academy of Florence. In the Brera Gallery, in Milan, there is an exquisite Crowning of the Virgin ; the Museum at Berlin possesses an Adoration of the Kings, which exhibits his mode of art no less

---

[1] E. Förster, *Wandgemälde in der S. Georgenkapelle zu Padua.* Fol. Berlin, 1841.

charmingly, and there is a beautiful enthroned Madonna at Herr
O. Mündler's in Paris.

In Naples, a cycle of wall paintings, rich in idea, on the
vaults of the little church of S. Maria Incoronata, a work which

Fig. 294. Extreme Unction. Painting in the Incoronata at Naples.

was earlier universally ascribed to Giotto, evidences the hand of
an artist influenced by that great master. They contain a representation of the seven sacraments, and an allegorical glorification
of the Church. (Fig. 294.) The unknown but excellent master
has throughout in a few significant touches portrayed his sub-

ject in some distinct incident, which is expressed with great power and characterisation in an abundance of lifelike and striking features. The Sacrament of Penance is especially touching, that of the Holy Communion is full of happy devotion, and all are executed with few figures, and with an excellent adaptation to the space. Lastly, Colantonio del Fiore (–1444) stands at the close of mediæval art, and forms a link with the style of the following epoch. Yet few authentic works from his hand have come down to our own day, and these few are, moreover, scarcely to be discerned owing to their injured condition. Recently, even his existence has been questioned.

If we compare the works produced during the Gothic epoch in Italy with the productions in the North, it is not to be denied that in the lands on this side the Alps the artistic ideal was absolutely architectural, in favour of which plastic art, and still more painting, was compelled to relinquish its independent development. In Italy, on the contrary, the highest architectural ideal was abandoned in favour of a general development of all three arts, which advanced hand in hand with equal rights, and were cultivated in noble freedom one with another. If painting at length arrived at the highest results of all, this arose from an inner necessity which lay in the nature of this art, and which, as we have before stated, made it a true Christian art, the proclaimer of the ideas of Christianity.

FOURTH BOOK.

—◆—

THE ART OF MODERN TIMES.

CHAPTER I.

IF Christianity had called all men to liberty, this mission had been repressed in the mediæval church by the superior power of the hierarchy. This priestly rule had been a beneficent necessity in the barbarous ages. Under its protection the young germ of Germanic culture had been strengthened, and had burst forth with vigour to unfold gloriously in the free sunshine. Thus we have seen, in the course of the middle ages, absolute hierarchical power disappearing, and a chivalric and civil state of society struggling to disengage itself from the old fetters; yet ecclesiastical laws ruled unimpaired in the minds of men, and art received the dogmas of religion in the spirit of universal tradition.

But the yearning for freedom and for independency of will, which, in contrast to the dull subjection of the East, was given to the Western world as a precious heritage in the path of life, awakened after a short slumber to still bolder struggles. Even in the middle ages there were not lacking signs which announced this fresh dawn of day. We have seen at its first gleams the strict organisation of Gothic architecture, this purest offspring of the mediæval mind, relaxing and indulging in a capricious play with decorative forms; but we have traced at the same time, in the works of sculptors and painters, the deep longing to evidence by individual expression the wonders of the mind divine. The breath of a deeply agitated mental life began to elevate the strict typical forms. So long as the individual was fettered by the ban of civil bodies and guilds, he could not rise to independence and freedom of views; when, however, the individual boldly rested

on himself, the decaying barriers crumbled to pieces, and the
end of the middle ages was unavoidable.

It is no matter of chance if a series of great events came to
the help of this strongly pulsating struggle—events the influence
of which, combined with the advance of new ideas, completely
changed the whole condition of Europe, opening a new world to
the Western nations, and affording them an unforeboded extent
of opinions and views. It was a world-wide dispensation that,
about the middle of the fifteenth century, by the invention of
printing, free course was given to thought, which was borne
from land to land, from one people to another, and a common
bond knit all minds, in spite of narrow national limits; it was a
world-wide dispensation that, about the same time, the conquest
of Constantinople by the Turks carried a stream of Greek culture
to the West, bringing rich nutriment to the already awakened
taste for the antique ; and that, lastly, even before the end of the
century, the discovery of a new quarter of the world wonderfully
enlarged the knowledge of the home of the human race, over-
threw with one blow the old views, and not merely opened new
kingdoms to the inquiring mind, but also to the roaming fancy.
While the Old World itself seemed to burst its fetters, and new
immeasurable territories seemed to open beyond the long
imagined boundaries, how could the views and laws of the
middle ages still maintain their right ? All the narrow circles in
which the world had so long moved began to waver, and with
the internal dissolution a general revolution of the outward life
was also continually carried on. The city republics of the middle
ages fell powerless to pieces before the impulse to form greater
political combinations and more extensive territories. The idea
of the modern state began to be formed and to be realised, and
sovereign power arose out of the ruins of mediæval charters and
commonwealths.

But within this mighty ferment, amid all this struggle of
power, craft, and boldness in this remarkable epoch, one thing
asserted itself victoriously, and this was the self-conscious, free
individual, and the power of individual genius. The revived

and deep study of antiquity strengthened this power, and introduced a period of higher culture, which put an end to the learning of the guilds of the middle ages, and united all who aspired to soar above the narrow limits of national life into one great bond. With youthful enthusiasm the most distinguished men pressed to the study of classic literature, searched in the libraries of monasteries for forgotten writings of the Greeks and Romans, and shared their costly treasures with each other ; at first by manuscript copies, and afterwards by the newly invented art of printing. Fostered by these studies, a new idea of life and of the world began to spread abroad, and the ossified scholasticism and dogmatism of the middle ages sank back into nothing before · the torch of human culture. Even the Church could not exclude herself from the newly advancing spirit ; even the Vatican opened its gates to it, and the vicegerent of Christ emulated secular princes and nobles in the protecting nurture of re-awakened heathen antiquity.

But while in the south this new culture was almost entirely formal, in the German north it prepared the way for that deeper and more serious revolution which insisted upon a renovation of religious life. This current of reform had already found ardent advocates in Italy, but it had been repressed there by force. With the whole power and moral energy of conviction, it now broke forth in Germany, and accomplished in the Reformation the victorious liberation of the conscience from hierarchical fetters, and thus a complete sundering from the middle ages. Indeed, this religious revolution reacted even upon the old Catholic Church. Wherever she came into direct contact with Protestantism, she experienced a regeneration which was likewise tantamount to a remodelling, and only when she persisted in traditional exclusiveness did she stagnate, as she does even at the present day, in mediæval dulness.

This revolution of the entire life must have exercised a powerful influence upon the development of art, and must have advanced it in many respects. The common basis henceforth in all branches of art is the sway of individual fancy over tradition.

In the middle ages, the creations of art had no independent importance; their figures were only symbols for the universal ideas which the Church afforded. Custom determined the matter, the conception, and the treatment; and as the artistic work was identified with its ecclesiastical aim, the name of the artist engaged in its creation vanished. We have seen how in Italy the consciousness of artistic individuality was first roused when the freer and more independent importance of art hurried onwards into new channels and vast perspective scope. Now for the first time the results of this effort were obtained, and the final consequences were reaped. Art would not separate itself from a religious import, far rather, perhaps with greater emphasis than before, men still built, chiselled, and painted for ecclesiastical objects. But the artist held a freer position with regard to tradition. He manufactured the sacred legends, the tenor of the Christian creed, after his own manner, drew from the depths of his innermost soul new animation for his subject, and from a loving study of nature and the ancient works of art, he gathered a new mode of treatment, the lifelike characteristics of which, hidden within the efforts of the former epoch as in a tender bud, now first burst forth into full blossom. Nature no longer appeared hostile or mysterious to these artists. They watched her whole beauty, they sought to exhaust it by deep study, and to impart a power of reality to their figures, of which the middle ages had not ventured to think. The study of anatomy and perspective, the finer observation of light and its effects, and the consequent perfection of colour to the most delicate shades, were the results of these efforts. Once the artist had placed himself creatively in the midst of life, every other man became to him a subject of serious and loving representation. The symbolising idealism of the middle ages had died away: realism unfolded its banner, and made its conquering march through the world.

In addition to all this, the mind now was ready to take a lively individual interest in the subjects represented; it no longer treated ecclesiastical subjects for their own sake, but for the sake of the free artistic idea which they afforded for the eye, and the deep and genuinely human truth and beauty they presented for the heart. These works of art were no longer created to supply an ecclesiastical need, but to satisfy a mighty impulse of the mind, and a personal desire for beautiful and important productions. No wonder if these creations now laid claim to acceptance for their own sake, when they proclaimed the eternal element in the human breast, not at the command of the Church, but at the bidding of that inner voice, and thus stood forth as revelations of the divine.

But the sister arts did not pursue their new aim either in the same manner or in one common course. The fate of the different arts is henceforth sundered from each other, thus attesting the individualistic character of this epoch, and the diverse efforts of the art of the north and south are now truly exhibited in their ultimate consequences. Henceforth, in our considerations, we have to separate architecture from sculpture and painting, and Italian art from that not Italian. It is true there comes at first a golden period, when in Italy works arose, under the direction of great masters, in which all the arts were combined into an harmonious effect ; soon, however, the dissolution of the old connection began, and, separate from each other, the different arts sought their especial paths, sculpture and painting forsook the framework of architecture, and strove to establish a new and independent existence. This fact has been constantly deplored ; and it is not to be denied that it has its strongly-dark side, and that a too exclusive culture of the two plastic arts could not take place but at the expense of a more grave monumental style. But here, also, an historical necessity was fulfilled which we must endeavour to comprehend. And when we reflect how long the plastic arts have borne the fetters of architecture, how long they were bound to subordinate service by virtue of the sovereign sway of their mistress, we shall indeed not grudge the liberated arts the happiness of now being able to follow their own laws, which urged them to perfection within their own especial sphere.

Thus we can understand that that art in which the general

thoughts and sentiments of the age were especially expressed, must recede henceforth behind those arts which reflect the individual life and feeling. Architecture went her own way and sought in antique works a new law for her forms. There was indeed a transition epoch, in which both in ecclesiastical and secular buildings a blending with the established forms of the middle ages was attempted; but this path was soon decidedly left, mediæval tradition was absolutely set aside, and a link was formed with a far older tradition—namely, that of the antique world. While the classic forms now no longer appeared as the necessary expression of organised life, but rather clothed the architectural body, as it were, with a noble covering, by this looser connection, modern architecture gained the freedom of harmoniously fulfilling all the requirements of existence. The plastic arts, and among these, again, painting, hold indeed a more independent position. In Italy, where during the whole Gothic epoch extensive monumental painting succeeded in maintaining its old right intact, the thoughtful depth of the great cycle paintings, in which even now the universal Christian ideas were treated, was combined with that deep power of natural delineation, that touching fulness of individual life, which exercised a totally different charm upon the eyes and minds of men, educated and uneducated, than ever had been produced by the more unfinished works of the middle ages. No longer what the Church prescribed, but what the individual artist felt as true and divine within his own soul, became a subject for representation; and no longer because the work of art contained those well-known sacred stories, but because it comprised a world of independently conceived beauty, did it become a matter of value and admiration.

That painting, however, now took the lead more than ever in art, and more than ever engaged the creative power, is explained by the whole tendency of the age. Even in the middle ages it showed itself predominantly the true Christian art, and plastic art withdrew into the second rank. The aim of sculpture is the representation of the perfect beauty of the human body. This task had been already fulfilled in Greek art with a perfection which admits of no imaginable increase. The striving after ideal beauty necessitates, however, at the same time an inclination to a general type, for special individual features are only obtained by deviation from the rule, and general beauty is multiplied by the predominance of characteristic traits. While in antique sculpture the conception of beauty was composed of various forms, just as perfect light divides into a rich series of colours; yet these are always embodiments of species, of universal ideas, of common distinctions of age and sex, and never of separate individuals. Added to this, the full beauty of the body is only to be attained by the representation of the whole naked figure, and at the most a drapery like the antique, which rather betrays the form than conceals it, may be combined with the true object of plastic art. In the same proportion, however, as the general beauty of the form is especially emphasised, the deeper signification and more thoughtful expression of the countenance recedes, and the head must be lowered to that amount of characterisation which can be combined with the perfect development of the whole figure. The more antique views harmonised with these conditions, the more decidedly was the Christian conception opposed to them. When physical beauty was regarded as indifferent, or indeed pernicious and hazardous, when all the value of appearance was placed in its devotion to the highest aims, when the spiritual and inner life of the mind held the first place, then plastic art necessarily languished; and even when in the middle ages, as with Nicola Pisano, antique beauty sought again to establish itself under the cloak of Christian subjects, the purport of the representation soon reacted so strongly against the obtruded form that this was soon cast aside as an empty shell.

When, with the epoch of renaissance, the antique style was adopted more deeply, seriously, and extensively as a standard model, it might have been imagined for a moment that a new golden age for sculpture had now arrived. It does indeed at first make a brilliant start, and produces works of thoroughly

original beauty, to which the antique had served as a light, but
the nature of which was, notwithstanding, completely independent.
But this delusion did not long last, and even in the happiest
epoch of revived sculpture it never altogether reaches the
importance of the painting of the same period; indeed, the very
excellences which commend their works to us are—characteristically enough—rather belonging to painting than to sculpture.
No wonder when we consider that it was the individual life, the
characteristic peculiarity of the separate figure, the lively expression of the deeply agitated subject, evidenced by means of the
movements of the physical form, which filled the artist's mind
and claimed all his creative powers in its representation. To
this passionate impulse the whole mediæval tradition had to
give way, the sacred figures had to leave the abstract ideal background of ancient art, to clothe themselves not unfrequently in
the gay costume of the age, and to stand out in the free surroundings of nature, and in the streets and squares of the
fifteenth century. So satisfied was this generation with its own
existence, that the saints of the Old and New Testament, and
of the legends, had to purchase the right of existence for the
most part by being masked in the costume of the present. And
even when, imbued with the antique style, an ideal drapery was
adopted, it was not considered discordant with it to bring it
into immediate contact with the costume of the period. This
tendency urged sculpture, as it were, to by-ways which lay far
removed from its true open path—namely, into a preponderating
emphasising of characteristic features, and into an execution of
reliefs, which from their abundance of figures, and from their
landscape and architectural background, were like paintings
transferred to stone.

We thus see clearly that the characteristics of the period point
incessantly to painting. Painting is and remains henceforth the
principal art of the modern epoch. It does not strive after the
perfect beauty of the human form ; it gives in general only a
deluding appearance of reality; but while, on the one side, it
renounces all that is so important, it gains, on the other hand, a

no less essential compensation. Through the newly devised means of perspective, and by the advance in colouring, it could display in rich groups an abundance of figures—it could release these figures from the ideal gold ground of mediæval art, and could transport them into the midst of the smiling beauty of nature, in a green landscape under a blue sky, or in splendid halls in the extensive vista of a highly decorated architecture, and could represent with fresh feeling the sacred stories of old in the gay attire of the age. With youthful energy it adopts all the power and depth of characterisation, all the passionate agitation of the moment, all the free manifestation of individual life; and with its true-hearted earnestness, its loving profoundness, it knows so well how to enchant and to fascinate, that we can no longer remember any anachronism, and can bathe with joyful gratitude in the inexhaustible fountain of life which gushes forth in these works.

Now, as ever, the mental impulse of the age created the means necessary for its own fulfilment. Even in Giotto's time, the fresco, with its clear and light colouring, its free bold execution, its lasting and solid technical work, seems to have supplanted the old tempera paintings for wall pictures. Henceforth it alone prevailed in the execution of grand monumental representations. A still more important invention was that of oil painting, introduced into Flanders by the brothers Van Eyck, and diffused with rapidity over all the art schools of Europe—an invention which, from its power, brilliancy, and delicate glow, afforded unsurpassable technical advantages to realistic efforts, and the cultivation of which was subsequently to lead to wholly new art tendencies, to new effects, and to new aims. Other inventions must here be mentioned also—namely, those of copper-plate and wood-cut, which disseminated artistic conceptions by mechanical multiplication, and thus contributed to a quicker interchange and more manifold association of the various masters and schools.

But not merely the means of painting, but the sphere of representation was infinitely enlarged. Since there was no longer a desire to paint what was religious, but what was humanly beautiful and important, the general human side was not only taken in religious subjects,' but even the mythological and legendary world was conquered anew for art. In the conception and execution of these subjects, individual fancy could have free and independent action. Soon secular historical painting appeared ; genre painting and landscape painting followed, and even wider was the sphere which painting made its own ; so that at last the whole life of nature and every expression of human activity and circumstance were estimated by artistic fancy in proportion as they could be considered by the light of the eternal, the true, and the beautiful, and could be glorified by art.

In what manner, however, in the course of time, the new principles gradually assumed a more distinct form, were more and more acknowledged, and in conception and treatment received this final completion, will be shown in the following historical examinations. As, however, Italy first decidedly opened a way for the modern spirit of art, and preceded the rest of the world by grand strides, Italian art will throughout occupy the first place in our considerations.

CHAPTER II.

a. *Italy.*[1]

WE have seen how throughout the middle ages the antique style may be traced in the productions of Italian art, and how even the Gothic style was obliged to accept a kind of equal balance with it. In the heart of the land, the old centre of Roman dominion, it was never wholly uprooted by the influence of Christianity, and, although in barbarous degeneracy, its forms maintained in Rome an uninterrupted existence. Just as deeply as the spirit of antique art lay in the genius of the people, just so forcibly did the monuments, even in their mutilation, proclaim its imperishable beauty. Regardlessly as the love of building and of feud had, each in its own manner, offered violence to the treasure of antique monuments, yet there were still sufficient of those splendid works preserved to remain a matter of admiration and study to thoughtful artists. Nevertheless, it needed the pioneering efforts of Petrarca and his pupils and associates in literary work to open the way, even to artists, to the full appreciation of the antique. About the year 1420, the Renaissance begins its course of development, at first still adhering to mediæval forms and elements of construction, and in its further advance so exclusively following antique constructions and forms of detail, that a new architectural creation was called forth, and mediæval tradition was completely set aside.

[1] Quatremère de Quincy, *Histoire de la Vie et des Ouvrages des plus célèbres Architectes.* 2 vols. Paris, 1830. J. Burckhardt's *Cicerone and Illustration of Ital. Ren. in vol. iv. of Kugler's Gesch. d. Baukunst.* Stuttgart, 1866. Grandjean de Montigny et Famin, *Architecture Toscane.* Fol. Paris, 1846. P. Létarouilly, *Édifices de Rome moderne.* Fol. Paris, 1840. Percier et Fontaine, *Choix des plus célèbres Maisons de Plaisance à Rome.* Fol. Paris, 1809 and 1824. Cicognara, *Le Fabbriche più cospicue di Venezia.* Fol. 1820. Gauthier, *Les plus beaux Édifices de la Ville de Gènes.* Fol. 1818. F. Cassina, *Le Fabbriche di Milano.* Fol. 1847.

FIRST PERIOD.—EARLY RENAISSANCE.[1]

(1420–1500.)

The fifteenth century is the period of that transition which endeavoured to reconcile previous architectural traditions with antique forms. In church architecture there was a partial return to the flat-roofed basilica, occasionally even to that constructed with cross vaults; nevertheless, there was an effort to characterise this system of structure by antique organisation. In large domical buildings, the various results of bold mediæval art were not disdained, and we find the effort after vast and beautiful spaces as the fundamental idea pervading all the epochs of Italian architecture. In secular buildings, the leading features of the mediæval façade were adopted—such, for instance, as the principle of the window placed between small slender columns, a principle as efficient in construction as it was graceful. Even now, the main charm of the new mode of building lay in secular architecture, especially in palaces, which arose out of the mediæval fortress, just as the art-ennobled princely life of this epoch was developed from the warlike, defiant, feudal, and chivalric life of the former period. Thus the palace courts were finished with equal richness and beauty, being surrounded with open arcades, which were frequently repeated in the upper gallery. Whether slender columns or strong pillars were employed for their support, the antique forms were here also used in preference to the mediæval.

These antique forms were, however, employed with some caprice. They imitated faithfully, it is true, all that was to be seen of antique works, without, however, having a clear idea of the fundamental proportions, nor divining the more delicate relations of the members with each other. They disposed of the forms, therefore, for the most part superficially and at random; and the less they perceived their strict regularity, the more freely could they give themselves up to a charming fantastic style,

[1] *Denkm. d. Kunst.* Pl. 64.

which at this period of new youthful enthusiasm filled all minds, and seduced the artists frequently into superabundant decoration. Just as certainly as these works possess an excess of a playful and overloaded character, just as certainly as they present many weak points to the strict architectural critic, just so certainly do they stand, in freshness, naïveté, abundance of imagination, and graceful finish of form, as high above the contemporaneous decoration of the late Gothic, as free artistic feeling does above the petty formality of mechanical rule. Hence it is these very works of the early Renaissance style which for the most part exercise that irresistible power of attraction which is the beautiful prerogative of enthusiastic youth.

Florence, long the cradle of art, was also the birthplace of the Renaissance, and the great master, Filippo Brunellesco (1377–1446), was its father. It is said that Brunellesco passed many years of his life in Rome engaged in studying, measuring, and drawing the Roman buildings; that he gave his attention especially to the grand architectural productions of the antique; but also that he knew how to estimate the merits of the mediæval buildings of his native country, was evidenced when, after long delay and difficulty, after struggles and contrarieties, the work was consigned to him, the execution of which he had made the task of his life—namely, the completion of the dome of Florence Cathedral. Arnolfo's gigantic idea had remained unfinished for more than a century and a half, till in the year 1420 the Signoria of Florence convened an assembly of architects from all countries, and Brunellesco, with his distinct and well-weighed plan, bore away the palm. Taking the baptistry of his native city as his model, Brunellesco constructed the dome with a double vaulting, but with the mighty diameter of 130 feet, without employing a centering, with its mighty drum rising high above the eight massive pillars, ascending in bold elliptical outline to a height of 280 feet, and crowned at length by a lantern, which rises 50 feet higher. Thus arose one of the boldest master-works of all ages, in the execution of which it is not the master's smallest praise that he knew how to keep in harmony with the existing forms, especially the pointed arch ; and considering the merit of this building, which extended far into after-times, forming an epoch of its own, we gladly excuse the faulty construction of the drum and the feeble introduction of light. The heavy effect of the interior is, moreover, principally occasioned by the dark frescoes, with which the vaulted roof unfortunately was subsequently covered.

In what manner Brunellesco conceived ecclesiastical build-

Fig. 295.　Capella Pazzi at Florence.

ings, when he could proceed independently from the beginning, is evidenced by the beautiful church of S. Lorenzo, in Florence (about 1425), in which he again raised the flat-roofed columned basilica to honour, and produced an important effect by distinctness of arrangement and grand development of the space. The side aisles are vaulted and are deepened by chapel niches, the transept is marked by a small dome, the details of the column and pilaster are formed strictly after the antique Corinthian style. Unfortunately, however, in order to make the arcades appear more slender, the columns are again burdened by the protuberating entablature of Roman architecture, and a doubtful example is thus given to succeeding times. The church of S. Spirito, in Florence, which was executed after his plan, was constructed in a similar manner.[1] But that he was also capable of expressing grace and elegance is shown in the Capella Pazzi, in the courts of S. Croce, in the plan of which he most beautifully followed the Greek cross, with tunnel-vaulted transepts and a light dome over the central space. The porch, too, with its vaults ornamented with coloured terra cotta, by Luca della Robbia, is very charming. (Fig. 295.) No less fine are the slender colonnades of the Foundling Hospital of the Innocenti, where the arches rise immediately from the columns. The Badia of Fiesole are constructed with noble simplicity and rural cheerfulness, and are appropriately grouped with a simple church, refectory, and colonnade.

No less great, and perhaps still more successful, was Brunellesco in secular architecture, for in the Palazzo Pitti he exhibited a model for Florentine palaces which has never since been surpassed in elegance and majesty of effect. In a gigantic freestone structure, which a race of giants seem to have raised, he gave an artistic form for the first time to the so-called Rustic style, the solid character of which disdains all decoration, and finds its balance by broad and circular-arched windows.

His successor, Michelozzo Michelozzi, followed this model in the equally vast Palazzo Riccardi, built by Cosimo Medici; but the rustication is more delicately gradated, the windows have a graceful mediæval division by columns, and the whole building is effectively finished by a main cornice with consoles—too heavy, it must be admitted—but executed after Roman models. The court is surrounded by a beautiful colonnade, in which the

---

[1] *Denkm. d. Kunst.* Pl. 64. Figs. 1 and 2.

Corinthian columns are immediately connected with the arches in mediæval fashion, a style to which the Florentines subsequently adhered. This palace architecture reached its noblest perfection in the Palazzo Strozzi, begun in 1489 by Benedetto da Majano, which, in the most beautiful proportions, combines the delicate construction of the rustic style, the noble division of the stories, and the elegant columns of the windows in perfect harmony, and is unsurpassably finished by the famous cornice

Fig. 296. Palazzo Strozzi, at Florence.

executed by Simone Cronaca. (Fig. 296.) A smaller building, in which the serious majesty of the palace is blended with the well-proportioned grace of the dwelling-house, is the Palazzo Gondi, erected about 1490 by Giuliano da S. Gallo, and rendered attractive by a charming colonnade, with its fountains and flights of steps. (Fig. 297.) The adjacent city of Siena also follows this Florentine style in its stately Pal. Piccolomini, built in 1460, in its smaller Pal. Spannocchi, with its mighty cornice enlivened by medallion heads, in the Pal. Nerucci, and in the Pal. del Magnifico. The neighbouring Pienza also (the birthplace of

Pius II.), which was raised to ephemeral importance by Pius II. (Æneas Sylvius Piccolomini), still possesses, as memorials of its fleeting magnificence, the cathedral, the episcopal palace, the grand Pal. Piccolomini, with its colonnades and loggie, and many smaller buildings.

We find a more scholastic and more strictly consistent adoption of the antique in the works of the versatile Leo Battista

Fig. 297. Court of the Pal. Gondi at Florence.

Alberti (1404–1472). In the Palazzo Rucellai, at Florence, he followed, it is true, the existing form of palace architecture, but he endeavoured to combine with it a massive construction of pilasters. In the façade of S. Maria Novella he introduced the unfortunate invention of volute-like members, which reconcile the breadth of the lower story with the more slender superstructure, and which henceforth were to play a grand part in the ecclesiastical façades of the Renaissance style. In S. Francesco, at Rimini,[1] he gave the façade the decoration of an antique triumphal gate, finishing the side aisles with half gables. Lastly, in Florence, he made a wonderful attempt, in the choir of Sta. Annunziata, to annex to the nave, after the model of the basilica, a dome with adjoining apsides, by which means he neither arrived at a picturesque or harmonious combination.

Further south, the new style advanced only in a sporadic manner, and was introduced by Florentine architects. Rome possesses in its Palazzo di Venezia, built by Bernardo di Lorenzo, a mighty work of this epoch, and in the larger, but still unfinished, court it exhibits the first example of a pillared building executed after the model of the Colosseum. In Naples, as in Rome, we find at first only foreign architects. A Milanese, Pietro di Martino, built, about the year 1443, the gracefully decorated triumphal arch of King Alfonso;[2] and the Florentine, Giuliano da Majano, erected, about 1484, the simple noble marble structure of the Porta Capuana.

The buildings of Venice produce an entirely opposite effect. The Renaissance style seems to have been brought here by Lombard architects; but the rich City of the Lagunes imparted to it that cheerful fantastic element which had prevailed in her former palace structures, adding to it a splendid coating of marble, in which varied colour was combined with elegant plastic ornament. The arrangement of the façades retained the same picturesque loggie which had resulted at an earlier period from the locality, and from its connection with the water; and only the expression of the whole was altered into a more classic and antique style, although the forms were indeed more capriciously dealt with than in Central Italy. This tendency prevailed for a long time, so that the early Renaissance is here continued into the sixteenth century.

The master-work of this epoch is the Palazzo Vendramin Calergi, built by Pietro Lombardo in 1481; constructed below with pilasters, and in the two upper stories with columns, and

---

[1] *Denkm. d. Kunst.* Pl. 64. [2] Ibid. Fig. 8.

finished with a rich frieze and cornice, the windows having a division column and geometric tracery. Among the other buildings of this epoch, the palace-like houses of fraternities, the so-called Scuole, occupy a distinguished place; thus, for example, the Scuola di S. Marco, of the year 1485, and the magnificent Scuola di S. Rocco, which belongs to the sixteenth century, and was profusely decorated with variegated marble panels and luxuriant plastic ornament. Lastly, in the last few years of the fifteenth century, the uniquely grand court of Venice, that of the

Fig. 298. Vendramin Calergi, at Venice.

ducal palace, was executed in splendid material, but with a somewhat monotonous construction: the magnificent gigantic staircase was completed by Antonio Rizzo in 1498.

In Lombardy, the façade of the Certosa at Pavia, begun by Ambrogio Borgognone in 1473, is among the most splendid productions of this epoch. Coated with marble, and covered from the socle with a lavish abundance of reliefs, medallions, statues in niches, and the like, the architectural forms are lost in a wanton play of plastic decoration; and, strangely enough, this most lively of all church façades belongs to the most silent of orders. Milan

and its neighbourhood contain attractive examples of the earlier
works of Bramante, whom we shall meet with again as one of
the principal masters of the following period. He built the
choir and the transept of S. Maria delle Grazie, vaulting the
principal space with a vast dome, and finishing it on three sides
with semicircular niches. The exterior (Fig. 299) is gracefully
decorated with rich details in burnt stone. In the elegant dome
of the sacristy of Madonna di S. Satiro, he displays perfect grace

Fig. 299. S. Maria delle Grazie, at Milan.

and the utmost nobleness of decoration. Antonio Filarete
opened the way for the splendid brick decoration of these
countries in the Ospedale Grande, built about 1456, the incomparably splendid façade of which, with its pointed windows, discovers in its construction and ornament the spirit of dawning

Renaissance. The most brilliant advance in brick building is, however, to be found in the numerous palaces at Bologna, which have for the most part an open arcade in the lower story, an elegant column dividing the windows, the façade crowned with a splendid console, and which even in their inner courts exhibit grace of design and elegance of execution. The Pal. Bevilacqua has the most beautiful court yard, and the Pal. Fava and Gualandi display elegantly finished façades. This style was also transferred to the adjacent Ferrara, where the unfinished and ruinous Pal. Scrofa presents one of the most imposing and beautiful secular works of the early period. The Pal. de' Diamanti, built in the year 1493, is executed, on the other hand, entirely in diamond-cut blocks, with which the delicate pilasters do not harmonise. The Pal. del Consiglio, in Padua, built by the Ferrarese master, Biagio Rossetti, is conspicuous for its open hall and nobly constructed upper story coated with marble ; the Pal. del Consiglio, in Verona, is a noble work of the famous architect Fra Giocondo, who carried the Renaissance style to France ; in Brescia the grandly designed and splendidly executed Pal. Communale, with its open hall in the ground floor and the splendid construction of the' upper story, is one of the most remarkable works of this epoch; and the little church of S. Maria de' Miracoli, with its profusely decorated façade. A complete example of the extensive designs for princely residences is afforded by the noble palace of Urbino,[1] begun in 1468 by a Dalmatian named Luciano Laurana, and completed by Baccio Pintelli, with its elegant colonnade and numerous richly adorned apartments : it is a model of artistic and noble secular architecture.

SECOND PERIOD : HIGH RENAISSANCE.[2]
(1500–1580.)

So long as the new style of architecture had its principal seat in Florence, it preserved that free transition character, which

[1] Cf. F. Arnold, *Der Palast von Urbino.* Fol. Leipzig.
[2] *Denkm. d. Kunst.* Pl. 71.

resulted from the blending of mediæval and antique forms. About the year 1500 its scene was changed, and with it the fate of Renaissance. The art-loving Pope Julius II. drew the greatest masters of modern times to his court, and Rome henceforth became the central point of art. A period of twenty years was formed into a second Periclean epoch, in which once more all the arts in harmonious concurrence produced works of the highest importance and of imperishable beauty. It was an inner necessity with architecture that on this classic soil it should itself become classic. There began a deeper and more thorough study of the antique remains, they sought to investigate more strictly its laws and relations, and the discovery of Vitruvius facilitated the abstraction of a fixed canon of forms. Henceforth the antique members were more purely formed and more distinctly used ; and, instead of the former naïve love for rich decoration, there appeared a noble moderation and a deeper relation of the forms to the organisation of the whole. Nevertheless the antique world of forms was and remained only an external and freely selected garment, which was introduced from free choice, not from internal necessity. The true architectural idea, the beautiful distribution of the spaces, the grand design of the whole, belonged just as exclusively to the new architects as the requirements which gave rise to the architectural design belonged to the new age. More than ever, Italian taste now celebrated its highest triumph in noble, free, and beautifully arranged spaces. In palaces and churches free scope was allowed to the artists ; and it is all the more evidence of noble moderation that the masters themselves knew the limits of beauty and regularity.

Now also the Renaissance style produced its grandest works in secular architecture. It knew how to give the appropriate individual form to each required part, and worthily to express in its palaces the noble ease of a free and highly cultivated existence. The stories of the façades were defined by cornices ; they were happily balanced in their proportions to each other, and were besides divided by a light pilaster work of the various antique styles. Windows and portals abandoned likewise the mediæval forms, and were framed in the antique style : sometimes they were crowned with small gables. In the courts, the pillared style was gladly employed, the model for which was found in the Colosseum and other similar Roman buildings ; yet we also meet with light columned courts. In both cases, as in the pilasters of the façade; the various classic styles were employed after the antique model ; thus exhibiting a transition from the heavy and simple to the lighter and richer forms in the Doric, Ionic, and Corinthian styles. The decoration of the inner spaces was likewise effected, according to the antique model, by a system of sculpture and painting combined ; and these works reach a pitch of incomparable beauty.

Less favourable was the development of church architecture. It is true here also there were not wanting productions of the first rank, works of grand artistic power ; but the unqualified return to the heavy massive system of the pillars and tunnel-vaults of the Romans, which were merely ornamentally covered with antique forms, was a retrograde movement compared with the productions of the middle ages, both as regards construction, and also as regards the idea expressed by the splendid Roman forms, which was opposed to those of Christian feeling. In the ground-plan the adoption of a nave or central design was left to the free discretion of the artist; yet in all cases they sought to combine with the building the design of a mighty dome, which, after Brunellesco's model, remained now a principal point in ecclesiastical architecture. The façades were usually formed in the earlier period with two stories of pilasters, which corresponded with the inner construction of the building ; but generally the ugly volute members were required to connect the two stories. The wish here also to display few and grand main forms soon gave rise to those colossal pieces of decoration, which, with their columns and broad antique gables, present a clumsy imitation of antique temple façades, an ugly contrast with which is formed by the insignificant windows and portals.

In the historical consideration of this period, we may divide it into two epochs, the limits of which may be dated about 1540.

About this time, a somewhat colder intellectual element began to prevail in architecture, which, it is true, still appears pure and correct in detail, but at the same time exhibits a certain emphasising of the principal members ; half-columns are used instead of the moderate pilasters, and the desire for stronger effect is evident in the rest of the detail.   It is the transition to the concluding period, the bizarre style, which forcibly extricated itself from the strict laws of architecture.

The great founder of the Roman school is the before-mentioned Bramante, whose real name was Donato Lazzari of Urbino (1444–1514).   In his Milanese buildings we find the youthful love of decoration belonging to the early period; but in Rome he began and established the strict, simple, and noble manner of a riper epoch.   His principal work in secular archi-tecture is the palace of the Cancelleria, which, together with the church of S. Lorenzo in Damaso, also executed by him, is finished with a single mighty façade.   The building, which is formed of beautiful travertine, has a delicate rusticated construc-tion, the lower story is simple and plain, and the two upper stories are constructed with rows of pilasters in pairs, standing on stylobates, and supporting a perfectly antique entablature, to which a cornice with consoles is added as a termination to the whole.   The windows on the ground floor are small and qua-drangular, in the principal story they are round-arched, but with antique framework and crowning ; in the upper story, to which a half-story (mezzanina) is added, they are again small and quadrangular.   Singularly beautiful are the noble proportions and the harmonious construction of the whole, while the most delicate and modest style is observed in the details.   The court yard, with its colonnade in three stories (Fig. 300), is the noblest and most beautiful work of the whole Renaissance style.[1] The same system of façade, with a few well-judged deviations, was repeated by Bramante in the Palazzo Giraud.[2]   In the Vatican Palace, he built the Cortile of S. Damaso, rendered so

----

[1] *Denkm. d. Kunst.*   Pl. 71.   Fig. 2.   [2] Ibid. Fig. 1.

famous by Raphael's Loggie, and which, with its slender and noble pillared halls, produces an extremely grand effect. Lastly, he conducted for a time the building of St. Peter, of which we shall speak later.

The decided influence which Bramante exercised over his contemporaries is to be traced in a series of important creations

Fig. 300. Court of the Cancelleria in Rome.

by similar able masters. One of the most distinguished is Baldassare Peruzzi (1481–1537), who constructed many smaller buildings in Siena, of a modest but truly artistic effect. His noblest work in Rome is the Villa Farnesina,[1] rendered famous by Raphael's wall and ceiling paintings, and one of the most graceful buildings of this period. Enclosed between two projecting wings, is an open pillared-hall, on the vaulting of which Raphael painted the story of Cupid and Pysche. While the spaces in the interior are gracefully arranged, and are beautiful in their proportions, the exterior, with its scanty means and insignificant material, presents a nobleness of construction from a row of noble Doric pilasters; and with this is combined an

[1] *Denkm. d. Kunst.* Pl. 71. Fig. 3.

expression of cheerfulness and festiveness, arising from a frieze
of genii with garlands. The Palazzo Massimi, with its picturesque portico and an elegant court, is also his work. (Fig.
301.)

Next follows Raphael (1483–1520), who proclaimed himself

Fig. 301. Court of the Pal. Massimi at Rome.

an architect of importance, not merely in the architectural backgrounds of his frescoes, but also, in the Palazzo Pandolfini, in
Florence,[1] he stands among the masters of the age as the
executor of a noble work of art. The rustication at the angles,
and the framework of the windows formed by pilasters or
columns, which support a triangular or round gable, appear for

[1] *Denkm. d. Kunst.* Pl. 71. Fig. 4.

the first time in this and other buildings of the same period. Raphael was also for some time engaged in the building of St. Peter. One of the grandest palaces in Rome, the Palazzo Farnese, built by Antonio da Sangallo the younger, exhibits in its colossal façade a similar style, the effect of which, however, is somewhat heavy owing to the crowded position of the windows. The principal entrance leads to a spacious vestibule with Doric columns, tunnel-vaults, and wall-niches, then to a mighty quadrangular court, with strongly developed pillared arcades, which Michael Angelo added, together with the grandly effective cornice of the façade. A smaller vestibule opened towards an imposing loggia at the back of the building, which, being repeated in the upper stories, gave this façade also a grand effect. Lastly, among Bramante's followers, we must mention Giulio Romano, whose principal work in Rome, the Villa Madama, exhibits even in its shameful ruin evident traces of its former beauty. After the year 1526, Giulio conducted the buildings of Duke Gonzaga at Mantua; among them the Palazzo del Te is conspicuous more for its extensive frescoes than for its somewhat severe and cold architecture.

Besides the Roman school, the Venetian school at this period was almost the only one which preserved an independent style; and this was guided almost exclusively by the extensive and brilliant works of the Florentine Jacopo Tatti, surnamed Sansovino (1479–1570). He, too, adopted the more severe treatment of the antique forms; combining with them, however, a stronger construction, a greater luxuriance of decoration, and a freer and more picturesque arrangement, in which we cannot fail to perceive a reaction of the decorative splendour of early Renaissance. He produced his master-work in 1536, in the Library of San Marco,[1] by which he succeeded in worthily rivalling the splendid structures of the earlier epoch. The façade is small; but a powerful effect is produced by a strong construction of Doric columns below, and Ionic columns above,

---

[1] *Denkm. d. Kunst.* Pl. 71. Fig. 11.

between which open arcades extend along both stories, below resting on pillars, and above on ornamental columns. This effect is increased to the utmost by the rich plastic ornament on the triangles left by the arches, on the keystones and the friezes, and obtains a lively finish in the breastwork of the roof, on which are placed statues and obelisks. For a long time, this unsurpassably magnificent building was the model for Venetian architecture, and was subsequently imitated by Vincenzo Scamozzi in the Procuratie Nuove, built by him in the year 1532. Another splendid building of Sansovino is the Palazzo Corner, begun in the year 1532; while he subsequently adopted a ruder and more simple style in the Zecca and the Fabbriche Nuove.

Other cities in Italy, in this brilliant epoch, also vied with each other in buildings, upon which is stamped the impress of noble dignity and high artistic freedom. Verona possessed her Michele Sanmicheli (1484–1559), whose powers are evidenced in the simple graceful circular building of the Madonna di Campagna, the palaces Bevilacqua, Canossa, and Pompei, as well as in the city gates, Porta Nuova, P. Stuppa, and P. San Zenone, which are constructed in a rude fortress-like character. The mighty Pal. Grimani, in Venice, is also his work. Another Veronese master, Gio. Maria Falconetto (1458–1534), built the Pal. Giustiniani, in Padua, with its luxurious court yard and charming summer-houses, as well as many of the gates of the city. At the same time, Andrea Riccio, surnamed Briosco, who was famous as a master of decorative plastic art, executed in 1520 the grand building of S. Giustina, in which the many-domed system of S. Antonio (and of S. Marco, in Venice) is transported into the severe forms of classic architecture, and produces an effect of mighty space.

A turning point occurs in the history of architecture with the appearance of the mighty mind of Michael Angelo Buonarroti (1475–1564), who produced incomparable works in all three arts, and for a long period almost monopolised all creative power. Impelled by a powerful subjective impulse, he burst asunder the laws of architectural work, composed only on a large scale, aimed at strong general effect, and cared little for the formation of the detail. Among his earlier buildings are the unfinished façade of San Lorenzo at Florence, and the somewhat insignificant funeral chapel of the Medici, built in the same church in 1529, and which acquires greater importance from its sculptures. In Rome, besides the works already mentioned in the Palazzo Farnese, he executed the design of the Capitol with its buildings—a work incomparable in its picturesque charm—the strange and insignificant Porta Pia, one of his latest works, and, above all, he completed the dome of St. Peter.[1] In the year 1506, the rebuilding of the church had been begun in grand dimensions by Bramante. It was to rise in the form of a Greek cross, with a grand dome, and with semicircular terminations to the transepts and the choir. After Bramante, Raphael undertook the building, for which he designed the plan of an extensive nave. Soon after, the building came into Peruzzi's hands, who added smaller domes at the four corners. At length, in the year 1546, Michael Angelo undertook the building, at the age of seventy-two, for nothing but 'the honour of God,' projected a new plan, in which he returned to Bramante's original idea of a Greek cross, and executed with vigour the choir, the four mighty main pillars with their arches, and the drum of the dome above them. For the dome itself he sketched ample plans, and formed a large model, according to which the giant structure was to be finished after his death. As, in the proportions of 140 feet in diameter and 405 feet in height, he surpassed the great Florentine model of Brunellesco, he surpassed it still more by admirable artistic development and construction. By the great pendentives he obtained a transition from the quadrangle to the circle, the beautiful perfection of which he rendered peculiarly effective in the lofty drum. By sixteen double pilasters he gave a noble construction to this part of the building, and by an equal number of large windows he introduced an abundance of light;

[1] *Denkm. d. Kunst.* Pl. 87. Figs. 1–7.

thus rendering the mighty structure wonderfully bright. The vaults themselves, also distinctly constructed and covered with harmonious and effective mosaics, spring in a slender form, thus producing both externally and internally the effect of perfectly light and unlaboured suspension. Outside a projecting row of columns encircles the drum, above which rises the incomparable profile of the dome, which terminates with the slender lantern. In 1605, Carlo Maderna carried on the building; but he de-

Fig. 302. Section of St. Peter at Rome.

stroyed the effect of the dome on the front side by considerably lengthening the nave, by which the interior of the church was increased indeed to 600 feet in extent, but the harmony of the original idea was irrecoverably lost. In 1629, Bernini continued the building, to which he added the magnificent portico; and, in 1667, the whole design was finished by the gigantic double

colonnades, which surround the square. Apart from the lengthening of the front nave, the interior effect of the church is not a
little injured by the grotesque detail and the overloaded decoration. We can, besides, only regard the tunnel-vault with its
massive pillars as a retrograde movement. In spite of all this,
the mighty building, with its beautiful vast proportions and the
noble design of the principal parts, produces an effect which we
must call, it is true, not peculiarly ecclesiastical, but still in its
own way solemn and elevated. The façade, on the other hand,
is an insufferable and paltry, though gigantic decoration.

The example of St. Peter's Church became the standard for
church architecture. The system followed there, of a tunnel-
vaulted nave with massive pillars and a dome over the transept,
was adopted almost without exception. But in another respect,
also, Michael Angelo's work was still more fatal for the development of architecture, as by it for the first time the example was
given of a caprice which subsequently produced the bizarre
style. Nevertheless, some of the most distinguished of his
younger contemporaries were serious and independent enough,
not indeed to keep themselves free from his influence, but to
refrain from his errors. A noble and strict conception of the
antique is common to them, and their buildings have throughout
a stamp of worth and significance ; but there is a certain coldness
about them, which marks the character of the second half of this
epoch. In accordance with this, they were active also in forming a theory of their art, and their compendiums were for a long
time the canon for architects.

Among the earlier of these masters is Vignola, whose real
name was Giacomo Barozzio (1507–1573), and whose principal
works are the castle Caprarola at Viterbo and the church Del
Gesu in Rome. Next to him was Giorgio Vasari of Aretino,
known also as a painter (1512–1574), whose principal work is
the building of the Uffizi at Florence. In common with Vignola,
he built also the magnificent villa of Pope Julius III., outside
the Porta del Popolo in Rome. The third in the list is Andrea
Palladio of Vicenza (1518–1580), whose principal works are to

be found in Vicenza and Venice. In Vicenza he built, besides a number of palaces, the so-called Basilica (the town hall) and the Teatro Olimpico. In Venice, his works are the unfinished court of the monastery of Carità, the present Academy of Art, and the churches Del Redentore[1] and S. Giorgio Maggiore.

One of the greatest and most original masters of this epoch is Galeazzo Alessi of Perugia (1500–1572), whose works principally belong to Genoa. Here, in the course of the sixteenth century, favoured by a rich and pomp-loving aristocracy, a palatial style developed itself, which, by an independent culture of the elements hitherto less esteemed, again produced new and grand effects. Its æsthetic conditions resulted from the local circumstances of the situation. The narrowness of the Genoese streets made the form of the façade appear subordinate, and in this respect the Genoese masters dispensed with nobler forms and proportions. The limitation of the space, and the steeply rising ground, allowed them, for the most part, just as few important court designs ; and thus they hit upon the plan of seeking a more imposing effect in the splendid development of the vestibule and flight of steps. Both had been hitherto worthily but moderately designed, the latter usually rising simply in a corner of the court, to the right or left of the entrance. In Genoa they formed the vestibule into a broad and lofty hall, the vaults of which were frequently supported by independent columns. With this vestibule the ascent of the staircase was connected ; it was placed in the direct centre, and led up in two arms, right and left, resting on simple or coupled columns, and the imposing perspective of this hall was often finished with a decorated niche for a fountain. About 1550, the Palazzo Ducale was built by Rocco Pennone, the steps of which were among the earliest works of this kind. This style reached its highest perfection in Galeazzo's works, who exhibited perfect examples of grand space in the Palazzo Spinola, and still more in the now ruined Palazzo Sauli.[2]

---

[1] *Denkm. d. Kunst.* Pl. 71. Figs. 8-9.   [2] Ibid. Fig. 7.

(Fig. 303.) In church architecture, his splendid S. Maria da Carignano in Genoa deserves especial notice, inasmuch as it is a beautiful and consistently executed imitation of St. Peter's as Michael Angelo designed it.

Fig. 303. Court of Pal. Sauli in Genoa.

THIRD PERIOD : BIZARRE STYLE.

(1600–1800.)

If the sixteenth century had preserved the character of noble repose and well-proportioned beauty, the seventeenth century began by giving way to caprice and a violent exaggeration of forms; thus sufficiently proclaiming the passionate, unbridled, and degenerated taste of this period. All that the former epochs had produced now seemed no longer to satisfy. The desire arose for mightier masses, richer detail, effective construction, and picturesque effects. These were produced by colossal designs, surprising perspective contrivances, a multiplying of the members, and especially by an accumulation of rows of decorative columns and pilasters. Palatial architecture grasped those characteristics of a more imposing plan, which had been adopted by the Genoese school, and henceforth rather sought after perfection in gigantic vestibules and flights of steps than in noble and just execution. The courts were neglected, and the building

degenerated for the most part into a plain pillared structure, to
which greater effect was occasionally given by a colossal loggia.
An exception to these is formed by the splendid colonnades in
the Palazzo Borghese at Rome, which were built by Martino
Lunghi the elder, in the early part of the seventeenth century;
but here also ostentatious effect is sought after by the doubling
of the columns.

The most important master of this epoch is Lorenzo Bernini

Fig. 304. Pal. Pesaro, Venice.

(1589–1660), who was also engaged as a sculptor. We have
already spoken of his buildings connected with S. Peter's, especially the imposing colonnade. He exhibits all the error, all the
decorative frenzy, of the bizarre style in the colossal bronze
tabernacle of the high altar in S. Peter's. On the other hand,
the Scala Regia of the Vatican, and the winding staircase in the
Palazzo Barberini, evidence his talent for grand and effective
designs.

His rival, Francesco Borromini (1599–1667), endeavoured to surpass his adversary in violent flourishes and wild exaggeration. In his works the straight line almost entirely disappears, the ground-plans are composed of curves moving in and out, as, for instance, in the church of Sapienza and of S. Agnese, on the Piazza Navona in Rome; and even the gables, the window lintels, and the cornices are broken up, so that all severer composition ceases, and the whole seems to be in one vague confusion.

Where any trace of earlier models appears, many important and more worthy works were still executed, though the tendency to showy picturesque effect is never to be mistaken. Thus the Pal. Pesaro at Venice (Fig. 304) affords a splendid example of the after-influence of Sansovino's library; and the University palace at Genoa possesses hall and staircase in the utmost conceivable grandeur of design.

In the eighteenth century, there was a reaction from the exuberance of the earlier period, and it was endeavoured, by simpler execution and by the return to Palladio and Vignola, to lead the way to a new classic style. But although many an able work was produced, creative power was yet decidedly on the decline, and greater soberness and coldness confirmed the want of a fresh and living principle.

---

b. *Other Lands.*[1]

While in Italy the Renaissance had advanced with victorious power, and had arrived almost exclusively at sovereign sway, the other countries of Europe long clung to the traditions of the Gothic style; and far into the sixteenth century this last architectural form of the middle ages witnessed that late revival, the partially insipid or overloaded style of which we have already considered. Now, however, from the various relations with Italy, the Renaissance gradually advanced, and produced for a time a true chaos of forms, as the deeply rooted Gothic

[1] *Denkm. d. Kunst.* Pl. 87 A., 91, 91 A.

was not readily relinquished, and its details were strangely inter-mingled with the new mode of building. And even where architects began exclusively to use antique members, Gothic principles were often allowed to prevail in the whole conception and construction. Much that was attractive, but also much that was strange, arose from this fermenting process. It was not till the seventeenth century that the Italian style was universally employed; but no longer in the noble and severe manner of the golden period, but in the coldly correct or grotesquely over-loaded style of the later epoch. Under the sway of these prin-ciples, all independent national feeling vanished from the archi-tecture of the West; and even into the remote regions of the East and the extreme West, into the countries of the other hemisphere, the architectural rules of Vignola, Serlio, and Pal-ladio advanced with European civilisation; so that modern Roman architecture once more, and in a more extensive manner than had been the case in the early supremacy of Rome, made its triumphal progress through the whole civilised world.

The Renaissance was introduced into France by Italian artists, especially by Fra Giocondo, whom Louis XII. sum-moned to his court. Nevertheless, mediæval architecture re volted against the new style, which was often obliged to adapt its graceful details to a form of architecture completely Gothic in design, construction, and organisation. One of the most original examples of this blending of style is the church of St. Eustache in Paris, begun in 1532; and one of the richest and most tasteful is the choir of S. Pierre at Caen. But in castle architecture, also, the high roofs, the numerous projections and towers, the forest of lofty gables and fantastic chimneys, evi-dence the predilection for the picturesque and gay style of the middle ages, which now indeed degenerated into a deformity all the more monstrous as the obtruded details of classic architec-ture formed a striking contradiction to this style. The principal instance of this bizarre architecture is the château of Chambord,[1]

[1] *Denkm. d. Kunst.* Pl. 87 A. Fig. 1.

begun in 1523 by Pierre Nepveu, surnamed Trinqueau. In small buildings, as in the château of Chenonceaux, not far from Tours, and the château of Azay-le-rideau, this mixed style frequently exhibits an extremely graceful and picturesque effect. Somewhat more strict in composition, and at the same time elegantly finished in its details, is the château of Blois, built for Francis I.; the so-called ' Maison de François I.' is original and full of lively effect : it has recently been removed to Paris. The château of Fontainebleau also belongs to this period.[1]

Nevertheless, during the course of the century, a revolution took place in favour of a calmer plan and a more strict mode of composition ; for instance, in the château ' Madrid,' since destroyed in the Revolution, which Francis I. erected in the Bois de Boulogne in remembrance of his captivity. We here also find a French architect named Pierre Gadier. The west façade of the Louvre (Fig. 305), built by Pierre Lescot about 1541, is the most splendid specimen of perfect and nobly decorated French Renaissance.[2] The Hôtel de Ville also, begun in 1549, is a magnificent work in this style. Insipid, on the contrary, and exhibiting grotesque degeneracy, especially in its ugly rusticated columns, is the earlier part of the Tuileries, executed by Philibert Delorme about the year 1564. This style increased in the course of the following century still more decidedly ; and although a few stately works, such as the church of the Invalides and the Pantheon (Ste. Geneviève), were still produced, artistic feeling, on the whole, was feeble and exhausted. Only in the so-called rococo style, which at length appeared, and which produced many graceful works in rich interior decoration, did individual fancy rise, it is true, to the utmost extreme of caprice, but, at the same time, it was combined with undeniable skill and a certain piquant and fantastic humour.

Far more exuberant was the form which the new style assumed in Spain, where it likewise first appeared in a thoroughly decorative fashion towards the end of the fifteenth century ; but

[1] *Denkm. d. Kunst.* Pl. 87 A. Fig 3.   [2] Ibid. Fig. 2.

Fig. 305.   Façade of the Louvre.

it was combined here in the most lively manner with the rich
forms of detail belonging to all the earlier styles of the Peninsula, especially with those of the Moorish and the Gothic.

From these elements there arose here an early Renaissance, which, in spite of all caprices, reached a marvellous pitch of magic beauty, triumphantly fantastic power, and intensity of feeling. This style has therefore been justly styled the Plateresco, or goldsmith's style. The courts of the monasteries and palaces especially exhibit a degree of finish which approaches in richness the decoration of the courts of the Alhambra, though in delicacy and grace it is inferior to those Moorish works. The court of the palace Del Infantado at Guadalaxara displays an ostentatious mixture of the utmost conceivable splendour. The broad keel-shaped arches, with their indented edges, rest in the lower story on Doric columns, and in the upper on various spiral columns, with gaily decorated shafts crowned with dwarf Gothic finials. Towards the middle of this century, this style was moderated, retaining indeed the richness of decoration peculiar to it, but accommodating itself on the whole more to the forms of the Italian Renaissance. A splendid specimen of this nobler fantastic style is presented by the chapel of the New Kings in the cathedral of Toledo,[1] which was completed in 1546. (Fig. 306.) Not until the second half of the century, under Philip II., did the severer classic style become prevalent ; nevertheless, it here assumes a heavy grandezza and a gloomy massiveness. The monastery of the Escurial, built in 1563–84, may be mentioned as the principal work of this style.

The Netherlands exhibited at first a graceful style of decoration, in which Gothic forms were frequently mingled with classic, as in the church of St. Jacques at Liège, completed in 1538. Subsequently the stricter Renaissance penetrated here also, as is seen in the town hall at Antwerp, built in the year 1560, the later parts of the town hall at Ghent, built about 1595, the church of St. Charles at Antwerp, built by Rubens in the year 1614 ; and still more decidedly, though somewhat more insipidly, in the town hall of Amsterdam, built by Jacob van Campen about the middle of the seventeenth century.

---

[1] *Denkm. d. Kunst.* Pl. 87 A.

It was late before England yielded to the new style, and the forms of Gothic art continued here almost uninterruptedly. While in other lands the graceful early Renaissance was adopted, the Gothic style here witnessed that exuberantly rich revival which produced its finest and unsurpassable work in Henry the

Fig. 306. Chapel of the New Kings in the Cathedral of Toledo.

Seventh's Chapel at Westminster. Italian renaissance was, it is true, introduced by Pietro Torrigiano in 1518 in Henry the Seventh's Monument; but it was only imitated in similar smaller works. About the year 1544 another Italian architect, John of Padua, is mentioned; and shortly after Girolamo da Trevigi was occupied in architectural works. In the latter part of the century the heavy but ostentatious 'Elizabethan style' appeared, in which a number of spacious palaces were executed. John Thorpe stands conspicuous as the famous master of this epoch. About 1620, Inigo Jones brought the strict rules of Palladio into application in the palace of Whitehall and other buildings; and between the years 1675 and 1710, Christopher Wren produced a magnificent example of this style in the rebuilding of St. Paul's.

In Germany, where the Gothic style likewise held sway till far into the sixteenth century, an elegant early Renaissance advanced, at first in isolated instances, displaying simple and graceful forms in the noble hall of the Belvedere on the Hradschin at Prague, and in the attractive and cheerful arcades of the castle of Offenbach, displaying more ornamented and splendid forms in the Otto-Henry part of the castle at Heidelberg (Fig. 307), built between 1556 and 1559, to which is attached the heavier and broader style of the portion built by the Elector Frederic between 1601 and 1607.[1] One of the richest and most elegant works of the Renaissance in Germany is the castle of Brieg, begun in 1544, the magnificent portal of which was finished in 1553. Somewhat later, in the year 1571, the slender and finely arched hall of the town hall at Cologne was built.[2] One of the rare specimens of artistic brick building at this period is the royal palace at Wismar. The castle of Schwerin also preserves some remains of an older design in its modern restoration.

South Germany was the principal seat of this fantastic early Renaissance. The old castle at Stuttgart, with its picturesque arcades, built between 1553 and 1570, is one of the most attractive instances of the free adoption of Italian forms. The new pleasure house, which was destroyed in 1846, must have been unique in its character. It was built between 1580 and 1593, by George Beer, and contained in the lower story a vast hall, surrounded with arcades, and with a vaulted roof supported by pillars. This hall was furnished with a fountain and a great reservoir. The upper story, which was reached by a splendid

---

[1] *Denkm. d. Kunst.* Pl. 87 A. Figs. 7 and 8. [2] Ibid. Fig. 6.

Fig. 307. Portal of the Otto-Heinrichsbau at Heidelberg.

flight of steps, contained a single banquet hall, surrounded by an
open colonnade, which, like the whole building, displayed the
most magnificent plastic ornament.   An original specimen of

elegant wood building, with splendid coloured decoration, is afforded by the golden hall in the castle at Urach. In Bavaria the palace at Freising, with its arcades, begun in 1520, is one of the earliest works of German Renaissance. Somewhat later followed the palace at Landshut, and soon after the castle Trausnitz in the same place. It is ruder in form, but richly ornamented in the interior.

More strictly classic is the aspect of the Renaissance in the town hall at Nuremberg, which was built about the year 1616 by Eucharius Holzschuher. One of the noblest works of this style is the arsenal at Berlin, built by Nehring about 1685; and one of the grandest is the castle at Berlin, so far as it was rebuilt by Andreas Schlüter, from 1699 to 1706. In Vienna, at the same time, we find Fischer von Erlach, who executed buildings of imposing appearance in the palace of Prince Eugene and in the church of St. Charles Borromeus. These were followed by many palaces of importance in Prague.

The various lavish courts of Germany imitated, especially in the eighteenth century, the love of building exhibited by the French court, and there was scarcely one which did not believe it necessary to have a Versailles. All the palaces of that day with their environs swarm with splendid designs of this kind, of which we will only mention the richest and most distinguished in their way—namely, those of Dresden (Zwingerbau and Japanese palace), those of Munich (the châteaux of Schleissheim and Nymphenburg), and that at Würzburg (the magnificent royal castle). A more serious style was assumed by architecture in Berlin and Potsdam, under Frederic the Great, in buildings (the castle at Potsdam, and the palace at Sanssouci), which were for the most part erected by G. von Knobelsdorf, and exhibit great strictness of execution and grandeur of design.

CHAPTER III.

I. SCULPTURE.[1]

IF in the Gothic epoch, sculpture had obtained a freer footing in
Italy, it was now afforded both opportunity and means to
develope in a still more unfettered manner. Its principal
employment consisted in the adornment of tombs and altars,
which almost unfailingly were attached to the wall like triumphal arches, and various plastic ornaments were also required
for reliefs and insulated statues. Pulpits, fonts, holy water
vessels, the singers' galleries, and choir screens, were also
richly adorned with sculptures. An advance in technical power
corresponded with the abundance of works, but the kind of
subject was aided in its expression by the picturesque and
realistic taste of the period. In the portrait statues of the dead,
there was a decided effort after a perfectly true conception of
the outward appearance, and .in the numerous reliefs there was
an evident tendency to depict the varied scenes of life. If,
nevertheless, on the whole, even this age of energetic realism
preserved Italian artists from petty trifling execution, and from
straying into unessential and paltry details, this was not alone
due to the study of the antique, but still more to the grand
innate feeling of Italian art for all that was essential and
important, a feeling which had been already awakened in the
earlier epochs.

a. *The Schools of Tuscany.*

Tuscany, long the principal theatre of Italian art, is here
also to be placed at the head of our considerations. The first

---

[1] *Denkm. d. Kunst.* Pl. 65 and 66.

master of importance, who forms the transition from the earlier to the new mode of art, is Jacopo della Quercia, surnamed Della Fonte, and who lived between 1374 and 1438. His principal works are a monument in the sacristy of Lucca Cathedral, and an altar and two monuments in S. Frediano in the same city; also the plastic decorations of the main portal of S. Petronio at Bologna (about 1430), and sculptures on the fountain in the Piazza del Campo at Siena, executed considerably earlier, between 1412 and 1419, and from the excellence of which he received his surname. In these various works we see the artist, with a delicate feeling for lifelike action and distinct characterisation, working his way more and more from mediæval tradition to a new and independent style.

More important does the great Florentine master, Lorenzo Ghiberti, appear to us (1381–1455), as the founder of an epoch in the history of art, and at the same time one of the greatest sculptors of all ages. We find him also setting out with the laws prescribed by the older art; but the earliest work known by him—namely, a bronze relief of the Sacrifice of Isaac, executed in his twentieth year (1401), in the Uffizi at Florence, and which he made, in competition with other artists, for the bronze gates of the baptistry—displays in its noble and distinct arrangement a delicacy of form, especially of the naked form, which belongs to a new habit of thought. Between 1403 and 1424, he completed the bronze gate for the north portal of the baptistry at Florence, with twenty representations in relief from the scenes of the New Testament, and the figures of the Four Fathers of the Church and the Evangelists. The arrangement here follows that of Andrea Pisano on the south gate : it is still predominantly architectural, the relief is simply treated, though more richly grouped than the other, but with a few touches the master has diffused over the whole a fulness of life, and in some of the representations has produced unsurpassable works.[1] At the same period, Ghiberti executed three statues for the exterior niches of

[1] *Denkm. d. Kunst.* Pl. 65. Figs. 6-8.

Or San Micchele, in 1414—that of John the Baptist, which still evidences in its severity of form a considerable power of characteristic expression ; then, in 1422, that of the Apostle Matthias; and, lastly, that of St. Stephen, a youthful figure, of great beauty and perfection. To a somewhat later period (1427) belong two bronze reliefs on the baptismal font of S. Giovanni in Siena, representing the Baptism of Christ, and John before Herod— the latter especially exhibiting lively expression and excellent grouping.

Next follows his famous work, executed between 1424 and 1447—namely, the eastern gates of the baptistries at Florence, which, as is well known, inspired Michael Angelo's verdict that they were worthy to form the gates of Paradise.[1] The stories of the Old Testament are represented in ten large compartments. The Creation of the First Man begins the series; next, we see Adam and Eve, driven out of Paradise, labouring in hard toil; next, Noah's Thank-offering after the Deluge, the Promise of Abraham, and the Sacrifice on Moriah, Esau's Renunciation of his Birthright, Joseph and his Brethren, Moses in the Presence of the Lord on Mount Sinai, the Fall of the Walls of Jericho, the Battle with the Ammonites, and the Queen of Sheba before Solomon. In the treatment of the relief, the master has completely wandered into the picturesque. The crowded composition, the detailed delineation of landscape and architectural background, with its perspectively gradated groups of figures, is undoubtedly an error, as it passes beyond the limits of plastic art. In spite of this, the whole is filled with such lofty nobleness of characterisation, with such free elevation of the figures, with such truly classic perfection of form, and with such unsurpassable freedom and life in expression and action, that it will maintain its place of honour as one of the noblest and most glorious works of modern art. (Fig. 308.)

Lastly, Ghiberti was engaged, after 1439, upon the bronze sarcophagus of St. Zenobius in the cathedral of Florence, which

---

[1] *Denkm. d. Kunst.* Pl. 65. Figs. 1-5.

is adorned on three sides with reliefs from the life of the saint : it exhibits the same picturesque treatment, and is rich in beautiful figures and in various significant touches.

Side by side with Ghiberti, and undoubtedly under the influence of his works, a younger contemporary appeared, who in his own style adopted a similar path of scarcely less importance—we allude to Luca della Robbia (1400 to 1481). The chief works of this charming artist and of his able school consist of figures of burnt and glazed clay, for the most part executed in white on a light blue ground and with small additions of yellow, green, and violet. Many works in marble and bronze belong to

Fig. 308. From Ghiberti's Gate in the Baptistry. Florence.

his earlier life; and these may be reckoned among the most excellent of this period in purity and nobleness. The earliest of these, executed about 1445, is the beautiful marble frieze from the front of the organ in the cathedral, now placed in ten parts in the Uffizi. They represent boys and girls of different ages, dancing, singing, and making music; they are full of charming naïveté and childlike grace, rich in beautiful action and in happy expression of innocent and pure gladness : the figures occasionally stand completely separate from the background, especially in the representation of the dance. From 1446 to 1464, Luca della Robbia was engaged in the bronze gate of the sacristy of Florence Cathedral, containing in ten compartments the seated statues of the Madonna, John the Baptist, the Evangelists, and the Four Fathers of the Church surrounded by figures of Angels, all for the most part remarkably beautiful and noble in attitude, and in the pure arrangement of the drapery.

. The principal importance of this excellent master rests, however, on the numerous glazed terra-cotta works executed by him and his associates. They were made in great abundance by order, and form the most attractive ornament in almost all the churches, sacristies, and chapels of Florence and its neighbourhood. It may be imputed to the simple subjects and fine feeling of the master, that in these works the relief style appears with a distinctness and moderation strikingly different from the usually picturesque treatment prevalent at this epoch. The wise and moderate employment of colour is excellently suited to increase the agreeable effect of these unpretending works, and to enhance their value as architectural ornaments. Countlessly often is the representation repeated of the Madonna and Child (Fig. 309) surrounded by saints and angels ; but truly inexhaustible is the master—a Raphael in his kind—in new arrangements and modifications, ever varying with equal grace the same theme of charming and happy maternal love. These works are extremely abundant in the churches of Tuscany, and especially in those of Florence, occasionally appearing on lunettes of doors, as the Annunciation on the portal of the church of the Innocenti, the lunettes of the sacristy doors in the cathedral, which represent the Ascension and the Resurrection : these, however, are less happy than others. Lastly, the naïve and lovely medallions of infants on the portico of the building of the Innocenti, and the frieze on the Hospital of Pistoja, are some of the later, but still excellent works of this school.

The tendencies of the period are increased into extreme one-sidedness in a third Florentine artist, who by his true adherence to nature obtained a preponderating influence over contemporary and succeeding masters. Donatello, properly Donato di Betto Bardi (1386–1468), belonged, more than any other artist of his time, to a strict portrayal of nature; thus presenting a striking contrast both to the traditions of former epochs and to the nobleness of antique forms. It is true he was not wanting in studies after the antique, as his earlier works testify; but such traces soon disappeared, and gave way to the most regardless

Fig. 309. Madonna of Luca della Robbia.

striving after exact characterisation. He was at the same time indifferent to beauty, and rarely, and as it were only casually, allowed it to insinuate itself into his works. The great number of his productions still existing evidence his quick and energetic work. Among the most important of his earlier works are the marble reliefs which he executed for the front of the organ in the cathedral of Florence, and which are now in the Uffizi. Like the similar works of Luca della Robbia, they represent a band of dancing children, also evidencing freshness of conception,

but without exhibiting the happy proportions and delicate grace
of the other. His coarse adherence to nature reaches its height
in the larger single statues, many of which are to be found in
Florence. He is most successful in manly, strong, youthful
figures : the bronze David in the Uffizi is, indeed, not free from
exaggeration ; the marble John the Baptist is fearfully skeleton-
like ; and the bronze figure in the cathedral at Siena is somewhat better, though also very repulsive. On the other hand, the
two bronze statues of St. Mark and St. Peter, on the exterior of
Or San Micchele, are ably and worthily executed ; but, above all,
the figure of St. George, in another niche in the same building,
is distinguished by its bold and·youthfully elastic bearing. The
S. Magdalena in the baptistry is extremely clumsy and almost repulsive ; and the bronze Judith, represented as having conquered
Holofernes, in the Loggia de' Lanzi, is thoroughly grotesque.

How completely Donatello was called upon to strike out a
new path in his art is excellently shown in the bronze equestrian
statue of Francesco Gattamelata at Padua, the first equestrian
statue of importance in modern art, characteristic to excess, but
full of life and power.

In his relief compositions, Donatello exhibits a crowded
picturesque arrangement, after the model of antique sarcophagi,
and in harmony with the tendency of the age. In S. Antonio
at Padua, the high altar and the altar in the chapel of the Holy
Sacrament are adorned partly with singing angels of a childlike
naïveté and sweetness of expression,[1] and partly with miraculous
stories of the saint, executed in a picturesque but highly expressive style. (Fig. 310.) The bronze reliefs of the two pulpits
of S. Lorenzo at Florence, representing the history of the
Passion, are one of his latest works : they are conceived with
great life and confused action ; but they are thrilling and effective
in the delineation of the various feelings, especially in the pulpit
on the left side, the execution of which probably belongs entirely
to him. The bronze works are very excellent, with which he
adorned the old sacristy of the same church at an earlier period ;

----

[1] *Denkm. der Kunst.* Pl. 65. Figs. 9, 10.

works exhibiting a moderation and dignity of style generally rare with him, and harmonising well with Brunellesco's architecture.

Among the few older masters who counterbalanced Donatello's violent adherence to nature, we may place also Brunellesco himself, who took part with Ghiberti in the competition for the bronze gates of the baptistry, and executed a relief for them which is preserved by the side of Ghiberti's in the Uffizi. It exhibits a lively and distinct arrangement, and a thorough study

Fig. 310. Relief from S. Antonio at Padua, by Donatello.

of nature. A great wooden crucifix, of a noble and dignified style, placed on the altar in a side chapel of Sta. Maria Novella, was also executed by him.

Younger contemporaries followed predominantly Donatello's model. To these belong Antonio Pollajuolo, who carried the style to great hardness in his works, though he was skilful in bronze designs, as is evidenced by the monuments of Innocent VIII. and Sixtus IV. in St. Peter's at Rome; also Antonio Filarete, who executed the no less important bronze gates on the main portal of St. Peter; and Antonio Rosellini, whose distinguished marble monuments in S. Miniato in Florence, and in

the church of Monte Oliveto in Naples, still exist. Especially,
however, we must mention Andrea Verocchio (1432–1488), who
further developed Donatello's style by a conscientious and
thorough study of nature, and who obtained an important influence on the development of Italian art, as the teacher of
Lionardo. An able work executed by him is the bronze group
of Christ showing his Wounds to the doubting Thomas: it is in
a niche in Or San Micchele; and an especially important work,
full of energetic character and bold life, is the equestrian statue
of General Bartolommeo Colleoni, in front of the church of S.
Giovanni e Paolo in Venice, the execution of which was completed, after the master's death, by the Venetian Alessandro
Leopardo.

One of the most important and at the same time most amiable artists of this period is Benedetto da Majano (1442–1498).
The beautiful marble pulpit in Sta. Croce in Florence was furnished by him with representations in relief from the life of
St. Francis, which are among the freshest and most attractive
works of the century. (Fig. 311.) The arrangement, the distribution of the whole, and the ornament exhibit pure naïveté and
abundance of imagination. The small allegorical female figures,
in elegant niches, are full of grace and tenderness. Above them,
in the five compartments of the pulpit, are excellent scenes in
relief, distinctly arranged, and executed in a free, noble manner,
without crowding, and yet picturesquely grouped on landscape
and architectural backgrounds. Another work by the same
master is the noble monument of Filippo Strozzi in Sta. Maria
Novella in Florence. Matteo Civitali, also (1435–1501), is an
important master of this period, whose beautiful and nobly
finished works are chiefly to be found in the cathedral of his
native city Lucca. His last work (about 1492) was six Old
Testament marble statues in the chapel of St. John, in Genoa
Cathedral.

Truly inexhaustible is this artistic period in marble monuments, which are not merely to be met with in the churches of
Tuscany, but also in other parts of Italy. Rome is especially

rich in works of this kind. Almost every church there has some specimens to show of the rich and elegant, and often artistic, works of the Florentine school. Above all, S. Maria del Popolo is a perfect museum of such works. Mino da Fiesole, with his pupils and associates, seems to have had an important share in the execution of these monuments.

Fig. 311. Relief by Benedetto da Majano.

b. *The Schools of Upper and Lower Italy.*

Tuscan sculpture was at this epoch so rich in creative power and conspicuous talent, and it responded so perfectly to the taste of the period, that its artists were summoned everywhere throughout Italy, and a great part of the monumental works of this epoch was executed by them. Next to the Tuscan artists, we find many native masters engaged in Upper Italy, who, partly through Florentine influence, and frequently through their own independent striving to meet the general spirit of the age, had adopted the new style. The pomp-loving aristocracy of Venice especially afforded the sculptors an abundance of tasks, principally referring to monuments. The churches of Venice, above all, S. Giovanni e Paolo and S. Maria de' Frari, are almost overcrowded with these rich and noble marble works; and as such works required a number of different powers in their execution, they are rarely to be referred to one definite artist. Yet a series of names are mentioned by which whole families of sculptors were characterised, as bound together by the laws of a common atelier no less than by bonds of blood.

At the beginning of the new movement stands Bartolommeo Buono, who in his principal works gradually passes from the ideal style of the middle ages to the realistic style of the fifteenth century. In the portal lunettes of the church of Abbazia, there is a Madonna della Misericordia receiving the adoration of many small monkish figures, where the sweet grace and devotion of the earlier period still prevail. On the other hand, the portal lunette of the Scuola di S. Marco already indicates the revolution, which is completed in the year 1443, in the plastic ornament of the Porta della Carta of the Doge's Palace, and which appears to us full of life and beauty.

About the year 1450, the works of the before-mentioned ateliers followed the new movement, and their extensive and splendid productions furnish evidence of the power and abundance of creative gifts, with which here also the new style was adopted. It is not possible to attempt to mention the immense number of these works : but little can be stated with certainty with regard even to the productions of the different masters.[1] Yet these works possess a charming tenderness and grace, which often appear in this late period like an echo resounding from the middle ages. On the other hand, the execution of the

---

[1] O. Mothes, *Geschichte der Baukunst und Bildhauerei Venedigs.*

physical form is not equal to the Florentine works in sharpness and truth, nor is such richness and variety of action to be met with.

Antonio Rizzo, or Bregno, belongs to the first of those who advanced further in the path opened by Bartolommeo, as may be seen in the two Doge monuments in the choir of S. Maria de' Frari. The younger master, Lorenzo Bregno, appears, however, to have been the more important; he lived in the beginning of the sixteenth century, and several monuments may likewise be traced to him. Next comes the artist family of the Lombardi, ruling Venetian art both in architecture and sculpture. Pietro Lombardo, whom we have already met with as an architect, stands at the head of the family with his sons Tullio and Antonio. A great number of monuments are ascribed to these joint working artists, though the share of each separately has never been accurately ascertained. Their principal works are the tomb of the Doge Mocenigo, in S. Giovanni e Paolo, several reliefs on the façade of the Scuola di S. Marco; and to the more important Tullio a great altar relief is assigned in S. Giovanni Crisostomo, which represents the Coronation of the Virgin kneeling in an unusual manner before Christ, who, surrounded by apostles, is placing the crown upon her head. The expression is full of grace and fervour, the execution verges on the antique, especially in the well-folded drapery, while the heads and hair of the figures are somewhat stiff and hard.

Among the later and more certainly dated works of the two sons, we find several reliefs in the magnificent chapel of S. Antonio, in the church of the same name at Padua, which belong, it is true, to the following century, but which may be mentioned here on account of the connection. The ninth relief here is by Antonio : it represents the saint making a little child speak by a miracle, that it may bear witness to the innocence of its mother. Antonio here shows himself as the simplest and most distinct of the disciples of this school, both in arrangement and in the execution of the relief, more closely adhering to the antique than any other. The sixth relief, in which the saint is opening the corpse of a miser, and discovers a stone instead of a heart, is marked with the name of Tullio and the year 1525. To the same master also belongs the seventh relief, in which the saint is curing a young man's broken leg (Fig. 312): both works exhibit a certain rude, sharp, angular manner, especially the early ones, yet at the same time there is a lifelike and distinct arrangement.

This Venetian style is developed into pure and noble grace in the works of Alessandro Leopardo, who likewise, at the head of a great atelier, produced a number of important works. The most beautiful of the Venetian monuments, that of the Doge

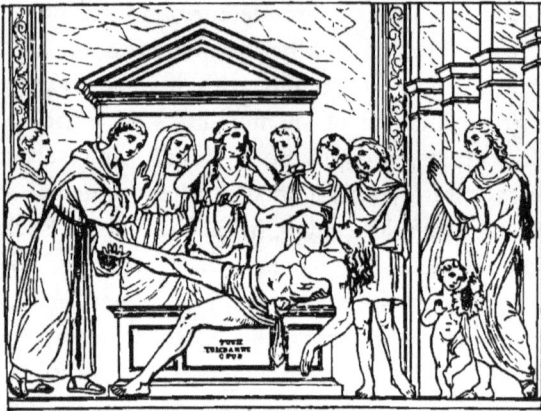

Fig. 312. Relief of Tullio Lombardo.

Andrea Vendramin, executed in the year 1479, in the choir of S. Giovanni e Paolo, is ascribed to him. The composition is extremely grand, and evidences an aim at general effect; there are a great number of figures in the simple antique style, only the graceful folds of the drapery exhibit the coldness peculiar to the Venetians, which is, however, counterbalanced by the charming sweetness of many of the heads. Leopardo was employed, with the Lombardi, in the splendid decoration of the chapel of Cardinal Zeno in San Marco, where the noble Madonna della Scarpa is especially referred to him. Lastly, he executed the three bronze standard-bearers in the square of San Marco, the sculptures on which evidence the same fine plastic feeling based on antique art.

In Lombardy, the façade of the Certosa at Pavia, with its rich sculptures, was a scene of action for many artists, whose works lasted far into the sixteenth century. It is still more difficult to distinguish here individual sculptors; in general, however, there prevails a sweet and charmingly tender expression. Similar works appear in the cathedral of Como, and in other churches of the country.

Besides all these works, which stand in direct relation to architecture, or require an architectural framework, another style now appeared in the works of the Modenese Guido Mazzoni, who completely freed sculpture from this connection, and aimed at a decided dramatic effect in insulated groups of painted clay figures. Gifted with undeniable power, this artist goes to such an extreme in passionate pathos and regardless adherence to nature, that while his works are thrilling in their effect, there is something in them absolutely distorted and repulsive. His principal work is the Madonna with the Body of Christ, who is lamented by His followers: it is in S. Giovanni Decollato at Modena. The same subject is treated by him in the funeral chapel of Monte Oliveto in Naples.

Lastly, we must mention the part which Lower Italy, especially Naples, took in the new movement. While here, as in Rome, it was chiefly Florentine artists who introduced renaissance into sculpture, yet native talents were not wholly wanting. Among them, in the early part of the fifteenth century, Andrea Ciccione in a charming manner marked the transition from the old to the new period. In S. Giovanni a Carbonara in Naples, the monument of King Ladislaus behind the high altar is his work. The composition is predominantly Gothic, but it is very effective as a whole, and is nobly executed. The figures, however, show the dawning of the realistic antique style: the figures of the Virtues, with their beautiful drapery and graceful expression; the sitting figures of the royal family; and at the head the equestrian statue of the deceased, noble and severe, though somewhat vacant in the effort after truthful portraiture. The sculptures which adorn the richly finished crypt of the cathedral belong to the end of the century. They were finished, according to their inscription, in 1504, and were executed by Tommaso Malvito of Como, thus by a Lombard artist. The Madonna, with angels and saints, is introduced in a peculiar manner in medallions on the ceiling, in a somewhat hard and unpleasing realistic style. The kneeling marble statue of the Cardinal Olivier Caraffa, executed at the same time, is able and lifelike, but coldly natural.

2. PAINTING.

How completely the taste of the new period was inclined to the picturesque we have already seen in the prevalence of this tendency in sculpture. All the more plainly did it manifest itself in painting, as that art which could far better satisfy the effort after the representation of truth and variety of life in its external and internal emotions. But that which procured a decided advantage to Italian painting in this epoch was the constant requirement for the execution of great frescoes; thus causing the lively development of a free monumental style, and by compositions on a large scale guarding the painters from the dangers of the northern art of this period—namely, a decline into details, non-essentials, and trifles. But that which also obtained for painting the advantage of a far freer position was the fact that it was affected less than sculpture by the imitation of antique art, and that the direct conception of the reality was its principal aim, the attainment of which was possible to various individual artists, ever according to their especial endowments. This explains the variety of painting at this epoch, which in this is far superior to sculpture.

a. *The Tuscan School.*[1]

As in the former period, the Tuscan school still appears foremost in the wealth and lasting power of its artistic works.

[1] *Denkm. d. Kunst.* Pl. 67, 67 A, and 68.

As Giotto and Orcagna, although with the more symbolic style of their age, had established the tendency of Florentine art to the delineation of lively action, so the masters of the present epoch again took up the same task in the spirit of their own time. But when they depict sacred story, the incident itself is no longer the main matter, but it serves them, as it were, with a pretext for the lifelike conception and representation·of reality. Hence they place the sacred figures in rich landscape scenes, and delight in magnificent architectural backgrounds, introducing their own contemporaries, in the costume of the day, as interested witnesses of the sacred events. Whilst thus the specific religious purport of their works is decidedly diminished, actual life is now for the first time completely made the object of art, and is so ennobled and elevated by the innate greatness of the Florentine school, that these figures, in spite of their temporal stamp, obtain an eternal value in art's world of beauty.

After some transition movements, which are exhibited in the works of Paolo Uccello (among them his frescoes in the cloisters of Sta. Maria Novella, and a bold battle piece in the National Gallery in London, one of his earliest representations from profane history), and still more decidedly by Masolino (in his wall paintings in the church and baptistry at Castiglione di Olona in Lombardy, about 1428), Masaccio, a pupil of Masolino, appeared as the decided pioneer of a newer style of art. A wavering between the earlier and later period is still expressed in the frescoes of a chapel in San Clemente in Rome, representing the history of St. Catharine and St. Clement. His principal works, however, are the frescoes which he executed in the chapel Brancacci in Sta. Maria del Carmine at Florence. Hitherto, the commencement of these works has been ascribed to Masolino, and the Preaching of Peter, the Curing of the Cripple, and the Recovery of Petronilla, have been assigned to him. But recent investigations[1] have proved that it was Masaccio who began the entire series, and executed them alone, with the excep-

---

[1] Cf. the acute remarks in Crowe and Cavalcaselle's works, to whose laborious investigations we owe these important results.

tion of parts subsequently finished by Filippino Lippi. On the
left pilaster, at the entrance into the chapel, he painted the Expulsion from Paradise, the earliest nude modelled figures of Italian
art; also Peter baptizing (Fig. 313) and in prison; Peter and John
healing the Cripple, and distributing alms. His two great principal paintings are, however, on the left wall. On the upper one

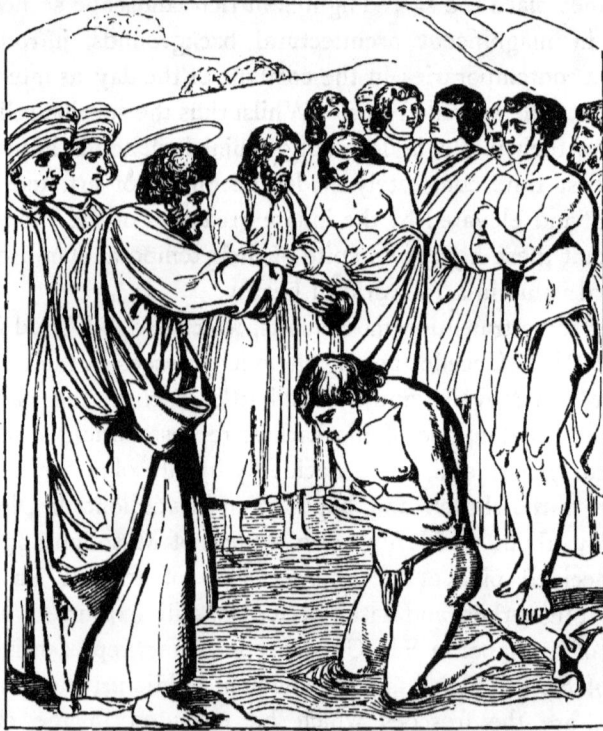

Fig. 313. From Masaccio's Frescoes in S. Maria del Carmine. Florence.

is Christ, ordering Peter to take the coin out of the fish's mouth,
a painting of commanding grandeur and power; below these is
Peter preaching, and the raising of the king's son to life, the
latter being partly finished by Filippino Lippi.[1] The figures are

[1] *Denkm. d. Kunst.* Pl. 67 A. Fig. 1.

throughout full of life ; they are distinctly modelled and grandly executed, the colouring is powerful and grave, the drapery free and bold in its arrangement, and the whole spirit of the representations is replete with historical interest. (The rest is by Filippino Lippi.)

The example of this bold and vigorous mode of representation excited all contemporaries to admiration and emulation. One of the first of these is Fra Filippo Lippi (about 1412 to 1469). Similar to the personal experiences of this passionate artist, who, carried away by unbridled feeling, burst asunder the fetters of monastic discipline, his artistic works also manifest similar boldness in their conception of life. He places sacred figures and events upon the level of every-day existence, but often dives so deeply into simple human feeling, that traits of the tenderest fervour appear in his works side by side with sensual and naïve reality. At the same time, he gives his colouring that glad cheerful brilliancy which pervades the whole life of his figures. Among his grand works, the wall paintings in the choir of the cathedral of Prato are the most important. (Fig. 314.) On the right wall there are the events in the life of John the Baptist ; on the left wall, those of St. Stephen, all depicted with much life and expression. The entertainment with the dancing Herodias is very beautiful. The heads are fine, intelligent, and somewhat melancholy ; the fine manly figures are grandly draped, and the whole is executed in warm and distinct colouring. On the other side, there is the Stoning of St. Stephen, depicted with affecting truth. The most splendid sorrowing figures are gathered round the dead saint, full of dignity and simple severity. The frescoes in the apsis of the choir of the cathedral of Spoleto belong to a much later period. They represent the Crowning of Mary, and three other scenes from her life, and are composed with much life and grace. His panel paintings are often executed with charming sweetness and feeling; the Madonnas are maternally solicitous, and the infant Christ appears for the first time the most gracious and yet thoroughly natural conception. The galleries of Florence, especially those of the academy, contain

numerous works of this kind; the Museum at Berlin possesses
likewise some admirable panel paintings; and there are two
pictures in our own National Gallery, originally painted for
Cosmo de' Medici, which are especially charming. The one
represents John the Baptist with six other saints, the other an
Annunciation of great sweetness.

Fig. 314. St. John bidding Farewell to his Parents. By Fra Filippo Lippi.

Among Fra Filippo's pupils, Sandro Botticelli (Alessandro
Filipepi, 1447–1515) is the most distinguished. He enlarged
the sphere of representation, by introducing occasionally antique
myths and allegories into his pictures. Thus, for instance, there
is a sweetly naïve painting of Venus, hovering over the sea on a
mussel shell, now in the gallery of the Uffizi in Florence.[1] Still

---

[1] *Denkm. d. Kunst.* Pl. 67 A. Fig. 5.

more remarkable is the allegorical painting of Calumny in the same collection, which displays Sandro's predilection for hasty movements and fluttering garments. In his religious panel paintings, which are in the Uffizi and many other galleries, a sweet and hearty feeling prevails, though by the constant repetition of the same type of countenance there is something monotonous. Lastly, Sandro took part in the frescoes with which Sixtus IV. adorned the chapel in the Vatican, designated Sistine after him. There are three great paintings by him, among which the Extermination of Korah and his Company is a composition full of dramatic life. Beautiful landscape, variety of action, and expressive figures distinguish these pictures.

The next master of importance was Filippino Lippi (1460–1505), the son of Fra Filippo, and the pupil of Sandro. Among his earlier works was the completion of the frescoes in the Cap. Brancacci in S. Maria del Carmine in Florence (Fig. 315), in which he painted the King's Son restored to Life, St. Peter and St. Paul before the Judge, and St. Peter's Sufferings and Release, all works of power and value, and full of dramatic life.[1] To his later period belong the frescoes in the Capella Strozzi in S. Maria Novella, executed in the year 1486, and containing scenes from the Acts of the Apostles. On the left is the Resuscitation of Drusiana by the Evangelist St. John, on the right the Expulsion of the Dragon from the Temple of Mars by St. Philip. The representations are full of life and expression, but somewhat restless in the drapery and attitudes, thus manifesting a certain fantastic inclination. Yet the whole stands out with great truth, and is almost surprising in its power; thus, in the Resuscitation of Drusiana, the astonishment expressed in the splendid group of women and children; and in the Expulsion of the Dragon, the expression of terror, fear, and horror—while the architecture appears rich and almost overloaded. On the vaulted roof there are the grand figures of Christ, the four Evangelists, and St. Antony.

Of a still later date are the frescoes in S. Maria sopra

[1] *Denkm. d. Kunst.* Pl. 67. Fig. 4.

Minerva, in Rome, where Filippino executed the wall paintings in the chapel of St. Thomas. The Triumph of St. Thomas over Averroes, i.e. of belief over heresy, is only interesting from the beautiful Florentine life exhibited in the spectators, who are expressing their sympathy. In the Ascension of the Virgin, the exaggerated vivacity of the angels, and the movements of the Madonna and the Apostles, who stand amazed round the empty coffin, are too much designed; but the beautiful warm colouring

Fig. 315. Peter and Paul before the Proconsul. By Filippino Lippi.

and the charming heads compensate for many defects. Among his panel paintings, which are repeatedly to be met with, a great altar painting in the church of the Badia at Florence is one of the best and most attractive works of his earlier period. The Madonna, accompanied by angels, is advancing to St. Bernard, who, in the midst of a rich rocky landscape, is giving himself up to pious contemplation. The Virgin, who, like the

angels, reminds us of Sandro, looks maternal and somewhat
suffering, the angels are full of feeling, with beautiful boy heads.
The tone of the whole is warm, mild, and distinct, only the
drapery of the angels has the gay colouring and restless folds,
which are so often to be remarked in the Florentine paintings of
the same period. An altar-piece, now in the National Gallery, and
originally executed for a chapel of the Ruccellai, bears much
affinity with this excellent work. It exhibits fine and deep
colouring, and represents the Madonna receiving the adoration
of Saint Hieronymus and Saint Dominicus. It is one of the
best works by this master.

Other painters of this period, carried away by the strong current of the time, passed from the school of Fiesole to the style of
Masaccio, but they retained at the same time a remnant of the
sweet softness and feeling of their first master. Among these
was Cosimo Rosselli, an early fresco by whom in S. Ambrogio
at Florence, executed in the year 1456, is rendered attractive
rather by separate beauties, such as an abundance of lovely
heads, than by excellence of arrangement. In his later life he
painted several pictures in the Sistine Chapel at Rome, among
which the Sermon on the Mount, and the Cure of the Leper,
contain a number of graceful and dignified figures, in a rich and
lovely landscape. He also executed panel paintings. A similar
course of development is seen in Benozzo Gozzoli (1424–1485),
who, in his principal work, the twenty-two great wall paintings
in the Campo Santo at Pisa, executed between 1469 and 1481,
evidences charming grace in the conception of actual life, and an
inexhaustible abundance of fresh, original, and deeply felt ideas.
They represent the stories of the Old Testament, beginning
with Noah and ending with Joseph, and their patriarchal simplicity and idyllic grace are depicted with incomparable naïveté.
(Fig. 316.) A number of lifelike figures stand in the background,
the richness of which, both as regards landscape and architecture,
is unrivalled even in this creative age, and surpasses all contemporaries in its joyous and cheerful expression. In the countless
groups of youthfully graceful and manly figures who crowd his

pictures, in the rich costume of the time, and engaged in every conceivable employment, the true purport, the biblical incident, passes into the background ; and the history of the patriarch Noah, with his vineyard and his drunkenness, only affords the merry artist occasion to depict the lively doings of the vintage. Other frescoes by him, in the church of Monte Falco at Foligno (about 1450), and in S. Agostino at S. Gimignano (1465), mark

Fig. 316. From the History of Noah. Benozzo Gozzoli.

the artist's gradual course of development. One of the most graceful of his panel pictures, an enthroned Madonna and Child, painted after 1461, and still recalling Fiesole to mind, although far more developed in the completion of the figures, is in the National Gallery in London. The Louvre possesses a Glorification of St. Thomas Aquinas.

One of the most important masters of this epoch is Domenico Ghirlandajo (1449 to about 1498), who, in grandeur of feeling and power of execution, surpassed most others, and may be regarded as the true inheritor of Masaccio's mental gifts. He invests not merely the ideal figures of his saints, but also the numerous band of contemporaries, who are grouped around as companions or spectators, with a true historical dignity, with a solemn sublimity and with a lifelike variety, enhanced by able execution and strong colouring. The wall painting in the Sistine Chapel, representing Peter and John called by Our Lord to the office of Apostles, belongs to his earlier works, and is full of dignity and freshness of life. More important and extensive are two cycles of fresco paintings, with which he adorned the Sassetti Chapel in S. Trinità in Florence, in the year 1485, and

Fig. 317. Zacharias writing the Name of John. By Domenico Ghirlandajo.

the choir of S. Maria Novella, in the same city, in 1490. The latter especially, representing the life of the Virgin and of John the Baptist, exhibit the mature and perfected art of the master.[1] The events themselves are depicted by few figures, with simple grand touches ; but the noble contemporaries of the painter appear throughout in great number as spectators—the maidens graceful and refined, the matrons bourgeois-like and pleasant, the youths slender and elegant, the men full of importance and character—splendid figures, betraying free manly dignity. (Fig. 317.) The Florentine life of that day is clearly reflected in

[1] *Denkm. d. Kunst.* Pl. 67. Figs. 5 and 6.

these attractive paintings. The events at the birth of Jesus and John, and the meeting of Mary and Elizabeth, are especially depicted with simple adherence to the actual life of the period. The scenes are generally placed upon noble architectural backgrounds or charming landscapes. In his panel pictures, Ghirlandajo does not work with the same freedom, although among them, also, there are works of great merit, such as the Adoration of the Shepherds, in the Academy at Florence, executed in the year 1485, in which the Madonna is represented as maidenlike, sweet, and lovely; the Child is one of the most charming of this epoch: the arrangement and execution are able, and the colouring full-bodied and enriched with a gold-brown tint.

Next to him, and likewise great and independent, Luca Signorelli of Cortona gleams forth as one of the mightiest minds of his time (about 1441 to 1524); he is bold and powerful, striving after the highest aims, and superior to his contemporaries in the passionate delineation of exciting scenes—at the same time, he is especially fond of representing the naked figure. Among his earlier works, are two of the frescoes in the Sistine Chapel, Moses' Journey to Egypt with his wife Zipporah, and his Death, in which the artist, after the usual Florentine manner, introduces a number of figures and ideas. The highest point to which his peculiar gifts attained is, however, marked by the frescoes, painted after the year 1499, with which he completed the decoration of the Madonna Chapel in the cathedral at Orvieto, which had been begun by Fra Angelico. Seldom have such contrasts been combined in the execution of the same work in so circumscribed a space. Beneath the pure and blessed figures of Fiesole, which looked down from the vaulted ceiling, the powerful creations of Signorelli cover the walls, like a race of mighty beings struggling against the universal annihilation. The demon-like and gloomy representation of Antichrist, the Resurrection of the Dead, Hell, and Paradise, are all the productions of his hand. In the Resurrection, he evidences his perfect knowledge of the human form in a number of naked figures, who appear in the most different attitudes in bold foreshortening.

The representation of the condemned is especially rich in powerful touches—the horror of those struck by the avenging lightning from heaven is well depicted. But the angels, too (Fig. 318), who are hovering down with lutes and lyres, bringing tokens of consolation to the fearful, are incomparably grand and beautiful. In the appalling ferryman, who transports the dead across, while various naked figures are wandering along the shore, we recognise the idea which subsequently the great follower of this master, Michael Angelo, again adopted in his Last Judgment. The frescoes in the monastery of Monte

Fig. 318. From the Last Judgment. By Signorelli.

Oliveto, near Siena, depicting the life of St. Benedict, belong to a later period. In his panel paintings, the same grand severe taste prevails, combined with a rude manly conception, strong dark shadows, and vigorous modelling. One of the most excellent is the Madonna enthroned among Saints, executed for the cathedral at Perugia in the year 1484 : it is nobly arranged, conceived with great freedom and naturalness, and is well executed. Many excellent works are to be found in his native city Cortona, and two valuable altar panels in the Museum in Berlin.

As plastic art had a lively influence upon painting, we find occasionally both arts even now united in the same master; thus, for example, in Andrea Verrocchio, and in a similar manner in Antonio Pollajuolo, whose panel paintings especially mark this combination of power by their unusually strong modelling. There is a remarkable representation of the martyrdom of S. Sebastian by the latter artist in the National Gallery, perhaps the most complete work of this master. Yet, while in these artists, form was the principal thing, to which the intellectual value of the work was subordinate, Lorenzo di Credi, on the other hand (1459–1537), a pupil of Verrocchio's, attained in his numerous panel pictures, with all his care of form, to a warmth and power of feeling which invest them with an especial power of attraction. Lastly, we have yet one remarkable master to mention, who, affected by Florentine and Paduan influences, forms a transition to the artists of Upper Italy; namely, Pier della Francesca, of Borgo S. Sepolcro (born about 1415, lived till 1494). The most delicate delineation of form and a rare study of perspective foreshortening is combined in his works with a tender and almost transparent clearness of colouring. Added to this, they possess a purity of feeling, and often a sense of beauty, such as is otherwise only found in the works of the Umbrian school. His principal works are the frescoes in the choir of S. Francesco at Arezzo, representing the history of the Passion. In the Uffizi at Florence, there are portraits of Federigo di Montefeltro and his wife, by his hand. There are other works in the sacristy of the cathedral at Urbino and in his native city Borgo S. Sepolcro. The excellent altar panel, representing the Baptism of Christ, now in the National Gallery in London, was executed there: it contains charming figures, bathed as it were in a flood of light, and surrounded by a gay but yet effectively dark landscape. Signorelli and Pietro Perugino are mentioned as pupils of Pietro.

b. *The Schools of Upper Italy.*[1]

The character of the painting of Upper Italy is based upon the expression of a certain tender sweetness and grace. In Padua, even at the end of the former epoch, an advance had been made by Aldighiero and Avanzo towards greater truth of delineation, but the conception had remained as before; and here also a new principle of life was wanting in order to produce a thorough revolution in painting. The first place in this effort is due to the scholarly Padua with its famous university. This was the city in which the study of the antique and the scientific practice of perspective were carried on with an energy elsewhere unequalled. In the Paduan paintings of this period we perceive just as clearly the soil from which they sprung, as in the Florentine pictures of the same period we trace the free and excited life of a grand and mighty commonwealth. This direct inclination to the portrayal of actual life is less perceptible in the Paduan paintings. On the contrary, they exhibit an antique mythological tendency; the study of the human body is pursued by means of antique plastic works, and where the naked figure itself is not delineated, the surrounding objects and the rich architectural designs are overloaded with representations in relief. While such was the prevailing tendency, the delicacy and grace which had formerly belonged to the painting of Upper Italy were for a long period checked, and gave place to a sharp and often harsh expression, and to an exaggerated distinctness of form. This tendency prevailed in the fifteenth century all the more absolutely, as the one Florentine artist of importance, Donatello, who at this time was executing numerous works for Padua, adhered to a similar style. Nevertheless, we can even here easily perceive that such a period of transition was necessary for painting, if it were not to sink into indistinctness and softness.

The first master of the Paduan school was Francesco Squar-

[1] *Denkm. d. Kunst.* Pl. 67 A and 69.

cione (1394–1474), famous rather for his instructions than for his own creative power, and who brought home from Greece a collection of antique sculptures which he made the basis of his teaching. His instruction alone, however, would not have aided the art to a new revival, had there not been one genius among his numerous pupils who stands out as one of the first in this brilliant and creative epoch.

Andrea Mantegna (1431–1506), assisted by the study of the antique, strove after an exact delineation of the physical form; so that we find in his figures a plastic rather than a picturesque character, which occasionally, especially in his earlier works, is not without a certain hardness and harshness. Yet at the same time he possesses such a lively dramatic feeling, that he is scarcely surpassed in the thrilling representation of events. His chief work in fresco is the wall painting in the church of the Eremitani in Padua, containing representations from the lives of St. James and St. Christopher. The walls of the chapels dedicated to these saints are each covered with six paintings. The division between them is made by pilasters and friezes, consisting of festoons beautifully painted on a dark ground: the upper part is finished by genii with garlands, and the whole work is full of grace and naïveté. On the right wall there is a more strictly architectural framework, with well-painted columns and entablature. In the compositions of the paintings, the master has limited himself to what is essential and necessary; but they are full of life and expression. The incidents in the life of St. James are the most remarkable, above all, the Cure of the Man sick of the Palsy. The manner in which he looks up at the apostle, who is blessing him, and in which the disciple, a noble figure, looks down on the poor man full of sympathy, while a powerfully delineated soldier clasps his hands in wonder, is as simple as it is touching. The colouring is distinct, bold, and smooth; the modelling is executed with much life; the drawing, as well as the rich architectural perspective, is managed with the utmost correctness and perfection. The upper ones, containing incidents from the life of St. Christopher, were exe cuted by some of his fellow pupils, and are more common and insignificant; the sufferings and death of the saint, on the other hand, though unfortunately much injured in the lower parts, are excellently delineated by the master's own hand. The decoration of the calottes of the vaulted roof, containing coloured arabesques, angels, and evangelists, in medallions formed by garlands, is devised and painted with much life and freshness.

The same charming spirit prevails exclusively in the frescoes with which Mantegna adorned the ducal palace at Mantua in 1474, now the Castello di Corte. The walls of one of the large apartments are covered with representations from the life of Lodovico Gonzaga. One picture brings before us the ducal family. While the conception is somewhat severe, there is wonderful distinctness of feeling depicted by the simplest means. The landscape which forms the background is a rich ideal representation of antique Rome. Another picture, much faded and destroyed, shows the duke with his consort Barbara sitting in the open air, surrounded by his children, courtiers, and friends. A third picture depicts a hunting scene in a poetically fantastic mountain landscape. The paintings of the ceilings are full of the utmost grace and cheerfulness. In the calottes there are representations of the deeds of Hercules, and other antique myths, painted in relief on a gold ground; in the lozenge-shaped compartments there are eight painted busts of Roman emperors in rich wreaths, each supported by a guardian angel, and all painted on a gold ground. Lastly, in the centre, the ceiling, which is entwined with green festoons, seems to open, and the eye falls upon a cylindrical and masterly painted aperture, through which may be seen the blue sky. On the upper edge there is a peacock strutting—beautiful female heads and lovely children are looking towards it; others are putting their heads roguishly through the opening of the balustrade, others are standing daringly on the lower socle;—one is seen from behind, another is obstinately squeezing himself in, and a third is looking roguishly at him : the whole is executed with delightful humour and masterly foreshortening, and is especially remarkable as the earliest example of such delusive ceiling painting.

Among his altar paintings, the grand and rich work in the high altar of S. Zeno at Verona occupies the foremost place. It represents the Madonna enthroned among many saints, among whom there is a wonderfully beautiful St. John: the figure is full of grace, and is surrounded by a rich architecture, and charming angels bearing garlands. A similar picture, belonging

Fig. 319. Christ mourned by Angels. By Mantegna.

to his later works, is the Madonna della Vittoria (executed in the year 1495), in the Museum of the Louvre, in which the Duke Gonzaga is introduced kneeling with his consort. Among the most splendid works of this kind, there is one in the National Gallery, representing an enthroned Virgin adored by John the Baptist and Mary Magdalene—the latter an exquisite figure, looking up full of heartfelt confidence. Another picture, now in the Museum at Berlin, depicting the body of Christ supported by two mourning angels (Fig. 319), is a work of thrilling expression and grand treatment of form. In many works Mantegna has treated antique subjects with especial delight, thus belonging to the first who opened this field of art to modern painting. The most important of these is the famous Triumphal March of Cæsar, originally painted for the hall of a palace in Mantua, and now one of the costly treasures in Hampton Court.[1] There are nine pictures executed in grey colour, and betraying, in an abundance of magnificent groups and lifelike ideas, a strict and thorough adherence to the spirit of the antique ; while the careful and conscientious treatment even in the smallest details evidences the gifted artist. In other representations of a similar kind, which are executed on a small scale, there is an almost miniature-like delicacy, which recalls the fact that Mantegna occupies an important place among the earliest Italian engravers. There is a charming representation of Parnassus in the Museum of the Louvre in this style.

Another artist who was under the influence of the Paduan school is Melozzo da Forli, thus named from the place of his birth. Only small remains of his works have come down to us : these, however, are of so much importance that he ranks both as an attractive and independent master. About the year 1472, he painted a large fresco picture of the Ascension in the choir of Santi Apostoli in Rome ; but the painting perished, in the beginning of the sixteenth century, on the rebuilding of the church : only small fragments were saved. In the palace of the Quirinal there is a figure of Christ rising, surrounded by angels ; and in the sacristy of S. Peter there are a number of angels making music. In these works, the art of Upper Italy again reached its utmost loveliness and tenderness of feeling ; but combined with this we find a masterliness of drawing, a rare delicacy and distinctness of colour, and a bold employment of those perspective rules which first meet us in Mantegna's Mantuan frescoes. The remarkable, though somewhat angular and gloomy, fresco in the Vatican Gallery, representing Sextus IV.

---

[1] *Denkm. d. Kunst.* Pl. 67. Figs. 2 and 3.

appointing Platina to be the superintendent of his library, is also Melozzo's work.

About this time in Lombardy the Milanese school especially distinguished itself, its early works also bearing great affinity with those of Padua. Besides many less important artists, among whom we may mention the architect Bramante, his pupil Bartolommeo Suardi, surnamed Bramantino, was the first to assume a more conspicuous position. Although his works extend far into the sixteenth century, he remained true to the earlier style ; and, although not free from peculiarities, he gave expression to a graceful tenderness of feeling, combined with which we perceive the Paduan predilection for bold and striking foreshortenings. A fresco painting of the Madonna with Angels, in the collection of the Brera in Milan, is remarkable for its conception. The works of Ambrogio Fossano, surnamed Borgognone, whom we have already mentioned as the architect engaged in the Certosa at Pavia, are of a similar style. Without great power or depth of thought, he is rendered attractive by a soft breath of charming feeling. Numerous works by him, especially frescoes, are to be found in the Certosa at Pavia. There is a noble crowning of the Virgin in S. Simpliciano at Milan (Fig. 320) ; and the Museum at Berlin possesses two excellent altar paintings of the Madonna and Saints, full of expressive feeling. Besides these artists, there were many other painters in Lombardy whom we must here pass over.

Works of greater importance were about this period produced by the Venetian school. At first it also stood under the influence of the Paduan, and Bartolommeo Vivarini, the first conspicuous artist of this new style, followed the masters of the Paduan school in exact treatment of form. His numerous works in the churches and museums of Venice, as well as in many foreign collections, are remarkable for their strictness of characterisation and elegance of execution. In a younger painter of the same family, Luigi Vivarini, we find the same style considerably softened, and already evidencing the influences of the great master, Giovanni Bellini, who stands as the founder of true

Venetian painting.[1] For now there begins a reaction to the
severity and hardness of the Paduan style, and the Venetians
find henceforth the true life of their representations in colour.
Even in the earlier epoch there had been here, far more than
elsewhere, a tender and richly blended colouring.   The splendidly

Fig. 320. Coronation of the Virgin. By Borgognone.

varied mirage, which arose from the wondrous position of the
City of the Lagunes, must indeed have early habituated the eye
of the painter to the effect and importance of colour.   The
festive cheerful spirit of the people, and the brilliant pomp of the
rich aristocracy, may have strengthened this taste for the full
colouring which gives a charm to earthly beauty; and it was just

---

[1] The same influence is not without its trace in Bartolommeo's works, as, for example,
in a Madonna with Saints, executed in the year 1482, in the right transept of Santa
Maria de' Frari, in Venice, where the colouring is deep and bright, and at the same
time warm and distinct as in Bellini's works.

now, about the middle of the century, that the oil painting cultivated by Van Eyck in Flanders was introduced into Italy.

Antonello da Messina was the medium of this important influence. His principal pictures are to be found in the Museum
at Berlin, and they plainly betray the transition to an independent conception of the subject. A male portrait, executed in the
year 1445, follows predominantly the Flemish style; a St.
Sebastian of the year 1478, and still more a Madonna and Child,
evidence even now that more free and noble beauty, and that
soft misty blending of colour which afterwards distinguished the
Venetian school. A Christ on the Cross, in the Academy at
Antwerp, executed in a masterly style on a small scale, and
belonging, it seems, to the year 1455, calls to mind the Netherland manner in its arrangement and miniature-like delicacy; but
in the more simple features of the landscape and in the character
of the heads, as well as in the bearing of the figures, there is a
decidedly Italian stamp. There is a half-length figure of Christ
in the English National Gallery, bearing Antonello's name and
the date 1465, which, with the exception of the somewhat
laboured hands, is remarkably freely and broadly painted, and
has a lustrous tint. A large Crowning of the Virgin, in the
Museum at Palermo, which is ascribed to Antonello, is of a
similar kind. It is a picture full of serious and severe beauty;
the heads of the angels are especially noble and graceful, Christ
and the Madonna are dignified and important, the colouring is
warm, and there is a transparent clearness in the shadows.
Besides these, the Academy at Venice possesses a reading
Madonna, designated by his name, which is powerfully modelled
and is interesting in expression. The gallery of the Belvedere
at Vienna has a Body of Christ mourned by Angels; and, lastly,
the collection of the Louvre contains a masterly male portrait,
which formerly belonged to the Galerie Pourtalès, and which is
designated with the name of the master and the year 1475.

Giovanni Bellini was the master who adopted these new
elements and means of representation with great judgment, and
during a life of ninety years (1426–1516) employed them with

rare power. Nevertheless, his authentic works all belong to the later period of his life, and form a series which furnish a noble testimony to the unwearied efforts and able mind of the master. Without deep thought, without especial poetic elevation, without richness and variety of composition, he knew how, by distinctness of character, to give his pictures the expression of a noble dignified life represented in solemn repose without passion and emotion. At the same time, colouring attains in his works to that splendour, that mild power and brilliancy, which henceforth remain the inalienable property of the Venetian school. His earliest known and dated work is a Madonna with the Child standing on a parapet before her, executed in the year 1487. It is in the Academy at Venice, and there is a similar one in the Museum at Berlin. It is free, grand, and noble, and at the same time exhibits great softness of colouring. That Bellini only reached this stage of art after long effort is evidenced by some of his apparently earlier works, such, for example, as a Madonna and Child, likewise designated by his name, in the Academy at Venice, which is painted hardly and clumsily. Next follows an altar-piece, of the year 1488, in the sacristy of Sta. Maria de' Frari at Venice, representing the enthroned Madonna, with angels and four saints on the side panels. Her expression is charming and humanly amiable; the angels, making music at the foot of the throne, are extremely lovely; the colouring is wonderfully soft and warm, with that delicate transparent grey shade which is peculiar to Bellini. There is a Circumcision of Christ in a choir-chapel in S. Zaccaria in Venice, which is soft in colour, and charmingly tender in expression. In his later pictures, even in those of his advanced age, far removed from weakness and declining power, his formerly more mild and sweet expression rises to grand dignity and importance, and the tender soft colouring acquires a splendour and glowing beauty which are truly Titian. This is the case in a picture, painted in his eighty-seventh year (1513), in a side chapel in S. Giovanni Crisostomo in Venice. In a splendid rocky landscape St. Hieronymus is sitting with a book; in the foreground on the right stands St.

Augustine; on the left St. Christopher, carrying the charmingly painted infant Jesus : there is a grandeur of character in them, and a free and masterly power, combined with brilliant colouring. Giovanni frequently painted the single figure of the Redeemer (Fig. 321), a representation in which, by grand nobleness of ex-

pression, solemn bearing, and the excellent arrangement of the drapery, he reached a dignity which has been rarely surpassed. His highest work of this kind is in a large altar-piece in S. Salvatore in Venice, which contains a representation of the Last Supper scene at Emmaus. The four disciples are serious and dignified figures; but Christ, portrayed in the noblest type of the divine Teacher and Master, is far superior to them in grandeur and solemnity. The colouring is bright and glowing, and the whole conception and treatment are those of a master striving after the utmost perfection.

Fig. 321.   Christ, by Giov. Bellini.

Next to Giovanni come the works of his elder brother, Gentile Bellini (1421–1501), who exhibited a similar style, but with less power and depth of characterisation. There are several large and interesting paintings by him, full of figures depicting events in Venetian history, in the Academy at Venice. It is true they are sacred events—a procession and a miracle—which he here represents, but in the constrained conception we here first perceive a genre-like character, unknown as yet to Italian art, and which, in Florentine art, with the exception perhaps of Benozzo Gozzoli, is counterbalanced by a certain grandness of historical feeling. The predilection for Oriental dress, which is observable in Gentile and other Venetians of the same period, is partly to be accounted for by the costumes which presented themselves to the eye in Venice at that time far more plentifully than now, and partly may have arisen from a journey to

Constantinople, whither the master was summoned by the sultan in the year 1479.

Giovanni's influence upon his younger contemporaries was of lasting importance, and decided the development of the Venetian school. Not merely the great masters of the following epoch, Titian and Giorgione, were his pupils, but many less important but able artists received their stamp from him. Among the most conspicuous of these is Vittore Carpaccio, a great number of whose historical paintings, full of fresh conception of life, are in the Academy at Venice; and the Museum at Stuttgart also possesses an important altar-piece executed by him in the year 1507, representing the Madonna with four Saints, and a kneeling figure of the giver of the picture. Cima da Conegliano also holds a conspicuous position; his devotional pictures are distinguished for power of characterisation and splendid colouring. Able works by him are to be found in Venice and in the Museum at Berlin.

c. *The Umbrian School.*[1]

In the midst of the preponderating realistic effort which pervaded almost all the schools of Italy in the fifteenth century, in Ancient Umbria, in the quiet wooded valleys of the Upper Tiber and its tributaries, an independence of feeling was preserved, such as belongs to remote mountainous regions, and which rests rather upon deep religious sentiments than upon a lively conception of outward life. This had early been the home of religious ecstasy; here had been the birthplace and the influential monastery of St. Francis of Assisi, with whom the fanciful tendency of the Umbrian school harmonises in the same manner as the tone of the Sienese works had before harmonised with St. Catharine of Siena. Notwithstanding, at this period the effort after powerful conception and detailed representation of reality was so deeply stamped in the general mind, that even in the secluded valleys of Umbria it was not to be altogether

---

[1] *Denkm. d. Kunst.* Pl. 70.

avoided. Thus, in the works of their painters, there arose a
blending of both elements, which added a new charm of tenderness of feeling and depth of expression to the rich productions of
Italian art.

Niccolo Alunno of Foligno appears as the true founder of
this style. He belongs to those masters who, without great
power of thought, are rendered charming by a simple agreeable
expression, purity of feeling, and grave dignity. One of his
finest works is the Annunciation in Sta. Maria Nuova at Perugia,
executed in the year 1466. The angel Gabriel is exquisitely
charming, and the Madonna, also, is full of loveliness, a picture
of maidenlike humility. Above are hovering graceful choirs of
angels, below are kneeling worshippers; among them are introduced the givers of the picture. The colouring of the picture is
brilliant, the expression is full of deep feeling—though it is kept
within bounds—the forms, especially the hands, are somewhat
empty and unfinished. An interesting Crucifixion of Christ,
executed in the year 1468, is in the Art Hall at Carlsruhe, and
a graceful Madonna seated on a throne, surrounded by angels
adoring and making music, executed in the year 1465, is in the
Brera at Milan.[1]

The work begun by Niccolo was taken up with great power
by Pietro Perugino (rightly Pietro Vanucci della Pieve), and was
brought to peculiar perfection during his long and active life
(1446–1524). Born in Città della Pieve, a small Umbrian town, he
gave himself up at first to the style prevailing in his own country,
though subsequently he endeavoured to perfect his art in Florence
under Andrea Verocchio and other influential masters, and to acquire a more significant and powerful conception of life. This tendency is shown in an Adoration of the Kings, in Sta. Maria Nuova
at Perugia, which in distinct characterisation and pure strong
colouring exhibits great affinity with the Florentine style. Still
more evident is this in the wall paintings, executed about 1480,
in the Sistine Chapel in Rome, only one of which—the Delivery

[1] *Denkm. d. Kunst.* Pl. 70. Fig. 2.

of the Keys to St. Peter—is preserved ; but in grandeur of character, in significant delineation of the incident, and in the
masterly perfection of the drapery and colouring, it is one of the
most remarkable of the whole series.

Soon after his fortieth year, he settled in Perugia, where he
henceforth formed the head of the Umbrian school, and drew
around him a great number of associates and pupils. He now
returned to his original tendency, which he endeavoured to
combine with the more perfect realism of the Florentine art.
A deep religious enthusiasm prevails throughout his works ; the
expression of devotion, resignation, supplication, and enthusiasm
has scarcely been depicted by any other master to the same
extent. There is a rare purity in his figures, and his female
and youthful heads especially, with their delicate oval, their
noble pure brow, tender dovelike eyes, slender nose and small
pretty mouth, are full of charming grace. He also succeeds
well with venerable old age, and only fails in the expression of
manly power, energetic will, and action. As, however, he had
limited himself to a narrow sphere, he soon fell into a stereotyped manner, not merely repeating the same heads and the
same expression, but also unweariedly the same positions and
movements. Thus his devout figures have constantly an
affected and even exaggerated air; and although the able hand
and care of the master cannot be mistaken in the finish, and
though the colouring is excellent with its warm and strong tints,
yet there is scarcely anything more unsatisfactory than the mechanical sentimentality which is observable in many of his pictures. Much of this may indeed be imputed to his associates,
whose assistance—owing to the increased demand for his productions—must have been very considerable.

The Madonna enthroned amid four Saints, originally in the
chapel attached to the town hall in Perugia, and now in the
Vatican Gallery, belongs to his best period. There is also
another able picture there, the execution of which is for the
most part ascribed to the young Raphael, and which represents
the Resurrection of Christ. Perhaps the most important of his

works is the Descent from the Cross, in the Pitti Gallery at
Florence. It was executed in the year 1495; the arrangement is
grand and distinct, the painting is excellent, and there is a
heartfelt expression of pain.[1] In Perugia, he adorned the walls
and ceiling of the Collegio del Cambio, in the year 1500, with
frescoes of superior colouring and beautiful detail, but of little
importance as regards general arrangement. Somewhat later,
he executed the beautiful altar-piece of the Madonna adoring
her Child, one of the most perfect works of this master, and full

Fig. 322. Madonna, by P. Perugino.

of brilliant colour. It was formerly in the Certosa of Pavia, and
now is in the English National Gallery; on the folding panels
there are the figures of the archangels Michael and Raphael,
the perfect beauty of which seems to intimate the co-operation
of the young Raphael. A more feeble repetition of the principal
picture is to be seen in the Pitti Gallery at Florence. (Fig. 322.)
He also painted at Perugia, in S. Francesco del Monte, a fresco
of the Adoration of the Kings: it is full of grace and dignity, and

[1] *Denkm. d. Kunst.* Pl. 70. Fig. 3.

is one of his finest works. Among the various smaller devotional pictures which are to be found in the different churches of Perugia, the Adoration of the Kings in S. Agostino, may be mentioned as one of the best. The painting of St. Sebastian in S. Fràncesco, executed in the year 1518, is, on the other hand, extremely feeble both in colour and drawing, and in expression also it is weak and powerless. Equally feeble is a fresco altarpiece in the cathedral at Spello, executed in the year 1521, representing Mary with the body of Jesus, although the head of the mother is not without depth of feeling.

Among the artists who followed Perugino's manner, we find less independent and individual conception than in other schools. Almost without exception they follow the model established by their master in type, expression, and style. One of the most gifted was Pinturicchio (whose real name was Bernardino di Betto, 1454–1513), who more than the other members of the school applied himself to historical representations, and was principally engaged in the execution of fresco painting. He executed most important works of this kind in Rome. In a side chapel of S. Maria in Araceli, he painted scenes from the life of St. Bernardino. They are somewhat in Perugino's style, and are rarely distinguished by greater nobleness or life, yet the colouring is bright and distinct. The frescoes in the Appartamento Borgia in the Vatican are by his hand. In the choir apsis of S. Croce in Gerusalemme he painted the events of the Crucifixion, which have been considerably retouched. There are also frescoes by him in S. Maria del Popolo and in S. Onofrio. The paintings which he executed in 1501 for a chapel in the cathedral at Spello are of a more attractive character. They contain the Annunciation, the Birth of Christ, and Christ at the Age of twelve Years in the Temple : there is also a half-length figure of the painter on a pilaster. The scale of the figures is often uncertain, and the perspective is not always managed correctly ; but the arrangement is distinct, the colouring is delicate and somewhat colder than with Perugino, and the feeling also, though hearty and fervent, is without the deeper ecstasy of the former master. The figures are truly excellent, the heads sometimes full of beauty and dignity; the Madonna especially is free and noble, and the details are finished with grace and delicacy. In the following year, 1502, he began to adorn the Libreria of the cathedral at Siena with frescoes, which, with those at Spello, may be regarded as his principal works. Here he depicted no religious incidents but the life of Pope Pius II., the famous Æneas Sylvius Piccolomini. Ten large wall paintings contain the various scenes, frequently of a very stirring character, judging from the designation given under each; but in the representation itself generally quiet, ceremonious, and with the utmost possible avoidance of all action. Yet the effect is attractive, partly on account of the skilful arrangement and happy proportions, able characterisation, free architectural or landscape background, and partly from the fresh glowing colouring, beautiful architectural framework, and the arabesques of the ceiling, all of which render the building one of the most cheerful and splendid of its kind. The fresco painting of the Last Supper, in S. Onofrio at Florence, which was formerly ascribed to Raphael, was probably also executed by Pinturicchio. His panel pictures are sometimes careless and unimportant. The academy at Perugia possesses one of the most beautiful, executed in the year 1495, and depicting the Annunciation, Death, and Crowning of the Virgin; another, which depicts the Adoration of the Kings in the attractive and cheerful style of this school, is to be found in the Pitti Gallery at Florence.[1]

Among Perugino's pupils, Giovanni lo Spagna (from Spain) was the most distinguished with the exception of Raphael, whom we shall consider presently. In the Palazzo Pubblico at Spoleto there is a fresco executed by him, representing the Madonna with the saints Thomas Aquinas, Hieronymus, Augustine, and Catharine: it is unfortunately somewhat injured, but it is charmingly beautiful and full of noble purity, such as the young

---

[1] *Denkm. d. Kunst.* Pl. 70. Fig. 7.

Raphael alone exhibits throughout the entire school. The frescoes, too, which he painted in the choir of the church of S. Giacomo at Foligno are very attractive. The principal picture, the Crowning of the Virgin, produced under the influence of Fra Filippo's frescoes in the cathedral of Spoleto, is, like Fra Filippo's, executed in a distinct architectural form; the figure of Christ is noble and mild, the Madonna humbly resigned; and to these are added glorious angels, and the apostles characteristically depicted.

Lastly, the Adoration of the Kings, in the Museum at Berlin, belonging to the Ancajani House, was also executed by him, though from its Raphael-like beauty it was regarded as one of the youthful works of that great master. Unfortunately the picture is partially effaced.

Besides Lo Spagna and various other pupils, two masters from the adjacent territory followed a similar style. The one was the father of the great Raphael, Giovanni Santi of Urbino (born previous to 1450, died 1494), whose works are for the most part to be found in his native country, the Marches of Ancona, and the most remarkable of which are the fresco paintings in the church of the Dominicans at Cagli. Without much depth, they are yet attractive from their earnest feeling, dignified expression, and careful execution.[1] The other more important master was Francesco Francia, whose real name was Raibolini (from about 1450–1517). Working in his early years as a goldsmith and medal-coiner, he only late in life
· devoted himself to painting, an art in which he obtained a position fully equal to Perugino's. Possibly he received many a stimulant through the works of the latter; yet his eye was open enough to accept also the influence of the Venetian and Lombard schools. His fundamental characteristic is also deep religious feeling, which, however, holds itself free from fanaticism and ecstasy, and yet finds expression in a tender and agreeable tone. He, moreover, bears great affinity with Perugino in his

[1] *Denkm. d. Kunst.* Pl. 70. Fig. 5.

predilection for the representation of calmness of mind, in avoiding much action, in the purity of his characters, in his delicate finish, and in his excellent and for the most part warm colouring. But his figures are more full of life, his forms are more vigorous, and he exhibits freer development than Perugino. His earliest known painting, which he executed in the year 1494, is an enthroned Madonna surrounded by six saints. It now belongs to the rare treasures of the Pinakothek at Bologna. One of his noblest and most perfect works is the altar-piece in the Bentivoglio Chapel in S. Giacomo Maggiore. It is also a Madonna seated on a throne with four saints—that is, a wonderfully beautiful St. Sebastian, an elevated St. John, and two charming angels, sitting on the foot of the throne making music. The colouring is full of depth and lustrous power. Besides other able works in the Pinakothek at Bologna, he painted with his pupils, in S. Cecilia, a series of frescoes depicting the life of the saint, which are among his most able works. Among the paintings to be found elsewhere, there is the Madonna adoring the infant Jesus lying before her, which is one of the most famous and attractive works in the Pinakothek at Munich. In the Brera at Milan, there is a noble Madonna and Child seated on a throne, surrounded by four saints.[1] Smaller paintings, for the most part depicting the Madonna or the Holy Family in half-length figures, are to be found in many galleries; one of the most graceful is at Dresden. (Fig. 323.) The Madonna has ever the same calm thoughtful expression, the same soft dark eyes, the same rounded oval countenance, yet the effect is always graceful and pleasing. Francia also belongs to those masters whose creative power remained in unbroken freshness into his advanced age. He died in 1517, shortly after Raphael's St. Cecilia had come to Bologna, overwhelmed, it is said, by the powerful effect of this work.

The ablest of Francia's pupils is Lorenzo Costa of Ferrara, who had formerly followed the influence of the Paduan school,

---

[1] *Denkm. d. Kunst.* Pl. 70. Fig. 1.

but subsequently worked at Bologna, and was impelled by Francia's example to attempt a similar style. There are some beautiful pictures by him, of warm and harmonious colouring, in the Pinakothek at Bologna, in S. Petronio in the same place, and in the Museum at Berlin. Giacomo and Giulio Francia, the son and the nephew of the older master, have less independence of style.

Fig. 323. Madonna, by Fr. Francia.

d. *The Neapolitan School.*

The direct influence of Flemish art penetrated into Naples more immediately than into the other parts of Italy, and under King René of Anjou, who was himself a pupil of Van Eyck, abundant cause was afforded for such a combination of styles. Although there is no lack of pictures which furnish significant examples of this connection, there is a great want of investigation regarding this point of art history. Even the records respecting Antonio Solario, the chief master of the Neapolitan school, called Lo Zingaro from his former smith's work, are vague, and do not agree with the pictures ascribed to him; for if Antonio really lived from 1382–1445, he cannot have painted the works imputed to him, as they all point to the latter end of the century. Tradition makes Antonio the Quintin Matsys of the South, for, according to it, he changed his smith's work for painting out of love to the daughter of Colantonio del Fiore. The panel pictures referred to him—a Madonna with Saints, in the Museum at Naples, exhibiting able conception of life, decided treatment of form, and warm harmonious colouring, and a Bearing of the Cross, in S. Domenico Maggiore—do not correspond with the frescoes in the court of S. Severino, which are likewise ascribed to him. These contain incidents from the life of St. Benedict divided into nineteen pictures, and are among the most charming works of the fifteenth century. Rather cold than warm, and thoroughly soft, mild, and harmonious in colour, with warm flesh-tints, they depict a series of scenes relating to monastic life. There is an air of calm quiet in the sweet religious peace portrayed, and without much action they are interesting from the groups of contemporaries; and still more from the landscape background, which displays a beauty, power, and depth of feeling unknown to the Italian art of the fifteenth century, and rare even in the following epoch. Grand and bold rocks, and soft idyllic spots with charming vistas, give a great value even to the less important scenes, and contribute to the delicious feeling of solitary peaceful repose, which corresponds with the character of the place, and is doubly agreeable in the midst of the noisy life of Naples.

CHAPTER IV.

ITALIAN ART IN THE SIXTEENTH CENTURY.

1. SCULPTURE.

ITALIAN plastic art had, in the course of the fifteenth century, acquired a new form of representation allied to the antique, and had attained to great importance in its restless striving after truth and life. In some cases it rose even to a height rarely attained subsequently. We have only to call to mind Ghiberti's gates, whose equal the following epoch never again produced. If, however, hitherto the expression of an exact and sometimes styleless realism had prevailed, the renewed study of antique works was now to produce a tendency to the ideal, the beautiful, and the sublime, which called forth a higher and freer style. In this change the delicious naïveté of the former period, the loving though often constrained devotion to natural appearances, gradually suffered and vanished, and for centuries was irrecoverably lost to plastic genius. On the other hand, plastic art acquired a free and grand conception, a broad and bold treatment of forms, and a simplification of style to all that was important and essential, which for a time could vie with the antique. Only, indeed, with the antique as it was understood in the best period of the Roman emperors, for it was works such as the Apollo Belvedere, the Torso, and the Laocoon, which were acknowledged and admired at this period as the highest productions of antique art. Important as these master-works are, they yet contain, compared with the true Greek works, the germ of theatrical effect in expression and of exaggeration in form. As, therefore, plastic art drew as little as the architecture of the period from the original source, but only secondhand, it could not long

remain pure from affectation, and at length fell into a mannerism,
to which truth and simplicity were compelled to give way.

Another cause that led still more to this erroneous path was
the course taken at this period in artistic subjects. It is true
religious matters were even now much represented; but these
subjects were treated in an idealistic antique conception, which
was too alien to the very nature of the religious subjects for
any true life to be produced in them. And when, in addition to
this, the figures and stories of antique mythology were lavishly
adopted, this revived antiquity soon stiffened into cold allegory,
since it was only intended for the cultivated minds of the educated, without regard to the opinions of the entire people. So
soon as art forsakes the basis of national ideas, so soon must it
become abstract, and go astray.

There was, it is true, a short period in which antiquity,
animated by modern taste, revived, and a series of noble creations
sprung from the union of Christian ideas and antique forms.
But it was only the rare power and purity of specially great
masters which could maintain this ideal height. Such a position
was impossible to the multitude of even able artists, for it required a more powerful intellectual counterpoise than the Christian ideas of this period afforded. Thus that mannered, hollow,
and exaggerated style was soon to take possession of plastic art,
and to expel first nature and then beauty from its territory. Yet
this transformation was not effected, until a short period, rich in
creative power and beauty, had passed away. And even in the
various styles of plastic art a various fate may be pointed out
within the general current. From the first, relief fared the
worst, as in the former epoch it had exhibited the utmost degree
of picturesque treatment; and even such masters as Ghiberti
followed the universal error. The same tendency, with few exceptions, marked the sixteenth century, so that even the idea of
the true relief style was lost until recent times.

It was otherwise with the insulated statues and groups,
which for a long period retained the nobleness and grandeur of
a truly ideal style. But here also the too great freedom allowed

to modern art proved fatal, and the complete dissolution of the old bond which had combined plastic art with architecture was at length as pernicious to the one as it was good for the other. In the fifteenth century a light and decorative framework had as signed to plastic art its position and its limits. In the noblest works of this new epoch this law is still to be found. But soon sculpture emancipated itself so completely that it spread beyond the framework of architecture, and so completely disregarded the relation that architecture was obliged to conform to its caprices. Thus at length architecture as well as plastic art must have been ruined. Freed from its close union with nature by an excessive and one-sided imitation of the antique, and now also completely released from the rule of architecture, it rushed unbridled into caprice and degeneracy.

As may be seen from these remarks, the period under consideration comprises several epochs, the progress of which we shall gather from separate investigations. We shall trace the short period of the perfection of art, which truly ceased soon after Raphael's death, the beautiful remnants of which, however, animate Italian sculpture until about the year 1540. Then begins that process of decline which unceasingly advances, and irresistibly carries with it even the most distinguished masters.

a. *Florentine Artists.*[1]

Among the sculptors of this epoch, Lionardo da Vinci, the pupil of Verocchio, would, without doubt, hold a most distinguished place, were it not that his admired work, the colossal equestrian statue of Francesco Sforza, perished without a trace being left, with the exception of a few studies and sketches for it which are preserved in engravings. The execution of the cast had been hindered; and when, in the year 1499, the French took possession of Milan, their archers chose Lionardo's clay model for their mark, by which means it was wantonly destroyed. The noble mind of the master, however, early exer-

[1] *Denkm. d. Kunst.* Pl. 72.

cised decided influence over many other artists of his time, especially his fellow pupil Giov. Franc. Rustici, whose bronze group of John preaching between a Pharisee and Levite is admired as one of the noblest and ripest works of this period : it still stands over the north portal of the baptistry at Florence. Other. works by this highly gifted artist are no longer known.

We possess, on the other hand, more extensive knowledge of the works of another Florentine sculptor, whose progress was likewise not uninfluenced by Lionardo—namely, the noble Andrea Contucci, surnamed Sansovino, who lived from 1460– 1529. In purity of taste, perfection of form, harmonious beauty of feeling, and graceful mode of treatment, he may be called the Raphael of plastic art, although in depth and range of subject he must give place to the prince of painters. The sculptures of the altar in S. Spirito at Florence belong to his earlier period— at least, the reliefs exhibit a hand still fettered by the customary style ; while the noble statues of the two Apostles, the Angel with the Candelabrum, and the Infant Christ, were undoubtedly subsequently added by him. One of his most perfect works, and indeed one of the freest and most beautiful creations of modern plastic art (Fig. 324), is the bronze group of the Baptism of Christ, executed about the year 1500, and placed over the east portal of the baptistry. The figure of the angel was added by another hand. The figure of John the Baptist is grand in expression and full of strong feeling, though remaining perfectly free from artificial pathos; the form of Christ is nobly and freely executed, expressing in gesture and position the gravity and seriousness of the solemn moment. The cathedral of Genoa possesses statues of the Madonna and of John the Baptist, executed by him (1503). There are also in Rome many of his most excellent works—among them the two most splendid marble monuments in Italy, in the choir of S. Maria del Popolo, belonging to the years 1505 and 1507. The arrangement is still essentially that of the former century. A niche deeply hollowed, formed like a triumphal arch, and enclosed by columns, contains the sarcophagus, on which the figure of the deceased lies outstretched with the soft expression of slumber. Insulated statues, angels, and allegorical figures of the Virtues are introduced as ornaments for the smaller niches : the whole is finished above by the figure of the Saviour, with two angels holding torches, and full of lively action. While all the decorative part is treated with graceful elegance, the style reaches its purest perfection in the insulated plastic works. In the allegorical figures, the artist has shown an attempt at freedom, by the peculiar bending forward of one shoulder, although the means for attaining this freedom are

Fig. 324. The Baptism of Christ. By Andrea Sansovino.

almost monotonous in effect. In the older monument, the drapery somewhat bulges, but in the later one there is such a distinct harmonious flow, and such simple rhythm, that the figures stand out purely and nobly as in antique works. Unsurpassably beautiful, in the figures of the deceased, is the expression of life depicted under the tender veil of a soft slumber: in the earlier work, the recumbent figure is supporting his head on his hand ; in the later one, the arm is lightly drawn up to the head—in

both there is perfect repose and mildness of expression, and
harmonious beauty in the action and features. Another Roman
work is the group, in S. Agostino, of the Madonna and Child,
and St. Anna, executed in the year 1512; a work of noble
arrangement, heartfelt expression, and perfectly finished forms,
only unfortunately placed in an unfavourable manner, and therefore scarcely to be enjoyed. Lastly, Andrea conducted, in the
year 1513, the rich marble adornment at San Loreto, only a part
of which, however, was executed by himself. He produced the
great relief of the Annunciation about the year 1523; the Birth
of Christ, with adoring shepherds and angels, he completed in
1528. The rest were executed by his pupils and associates.

We must here also briefly mention Raphael, who made the
sketches for many of his plastic works, and perhaps executed
one of them with his own hands—at least, the marble sitting
figure of Jonas, in the Capella Chigi, in S. Maria del Popolo,
corresponds with the idea which one entertains of Raphael's
genius, both in its splendid expression and finished beauty;
while the Elijah, in the same place, betrays another and an inferior hand, at least in the execution.

More powerful was the influence of Raphael's great rival,
Michael Angelo Buonarrotti of Florence (1475–1564), in the whole
sphere of plastic art; indeed, so decided was the effect of his
artist nature upon his younger contemporaries, that on his death
he only left behind him imitators of his style and weaknesses.
Although Michael Angelo created great works in architecture
(cf. vol. ii. p. 128), and still more in painting, he considered himself to be truly a sculptor, and designated sculpture as the art in
which he felt himself especially at home. If we compare his plastic
works with all previous ones—even with those of a Rustici and a
Sansovino—we at once see that with him art reached one of those
turning points which form the entrance to a new period of power
never before anticipated. His deep passionate mind was neither
satisfied with the ingenious realism of the fifteenth century, with
its truth to nature, nor with the harmonious and calm beauty
which had been produced by earlier masters. Each of his works

existed only for its own sake, and in this there lies an affinity with the antique; but each was also the product of the stormy inward struggle of a mind incessantly striving after a high ideal, and unweariedly wrestling for a new expression of its ideas, to whom that which was once won afforded such small satisfaction that it was often left as incomplete—and in this there lies the strongest contrast to antique art. Almost all his plastic works are, in some part, unfinished; many he must have allowed to lie so, because, in the strong impulse to free from the marble the soul slumbering within it, he spoiled the block, or chiselled it faultily.

While Michael Angelo thus deeply examined the master-works of antiquity, and created from them an independent ideal style, which proclaims itself the offspring of the antique in the bold conception of the forms, in the free grand treatment of the surfaces, and in the almost abstract and typical form of countenance, he is, on the other side, the first who disregarded tradition, and, in the subjects represented by him, only sought an opportunity for expressing a totally different purport, belonging to himself alone. Thus first begins modern art and the rule of subjectivity. Indeed, so absolutely does this new principle appear in him that, delighting in the most touching expression of an idea, he trifles recklessly with the laws of natural organisation —which no one had more deeply studied than Michael Angelo —makes them yield to his purpose, violating truth and beauty, while he seeks out constrained and even impossible positions, exaggerates certain physical forms into colossal size, and, in the proud endeavour to set aside all alluring grace, not unfrequently falls into the reverse. Hence a true estimation and a genuine enjoyment of his works are extremely difficult; hence it is generally false when any one, not deeply acquainted with art, breaks forth into ecstasy over these mighty creations, just as the enthusiasm expressed for the later Titanic works of Beethoven is frequently only empty talk. The sincere critic will allow that an unprejudiced eye is at first repelled by these works of Michael Angelo, but that a mysterious elementary power draws the thoughtful and intelligent spectator back again to the great solitary master; that then a deep examination and serious study begin, in which gradually the key to their understanding is found. Then alone can an estimation of these sublime creations begin; but at the same time there is a consciousness that the enjoyment they afford has a tragic tinge, for he makes us participators of the sufferings and struggles amid which a great mind has here revealed its innermost feelings.

Even his earliest works betray the lofty genius, and show how he was striving to rise from the prevailing adherence to nature to a higher style and an ideal conception. This is the case in the shallow relief of a Madonna in the Buonarrotti palace at Florence; and in a high relief there, executed when he was but seventeen years of age, representing Hercules in battle with the Centaurs, a work full of bold and vigorous life, though somewhat overloaded in the style of antique Roman sculptures. There is an angel holding a candelabrum, full of charming grace and true ideal beauty, which he also executed in his early youth (1494) on the monument of S. Dominicus in the church of the Dominicans at Bologna.[1] With what restlessness the youthful master now sought to express his artistic ideas in the most different subjects, is evidenced by the marble statue of Bacchus in the Uffizi at Florence, likewise belonging to this period, and not merely betraying considerable study of nature, but also depicting with great truth the expression of drunkenness. The last of the works of this youthful epoch was the Pietas, executed in the year 1499 in S. Peter's at Rome, representing the Madonna mourning over the corpse of her Son: it is a splendidly constructed marble group, full of deep feeling and noble perfection, and there is a touching expression in the heads.[2] The grandly beautiful marble Madonna in the Liebfrauenkirche at Bruges belongs to about the same time.

Hitherto the creative power of the master was still pure and naïve. Now, however, that epoch of his life begins in which the violent struggles of his nature burst all bounds, thrust aside

[1] Photographie in H. Grimm's *Ueber Künstler und Kunstwerke.* May Number, 1865. [2] *Denkm. d. Kunst.* Pl. 72. Fig. 4.

tradition, and followed the wild paths of fancy. About 1501, appeared the colossal marble statue of David, in front of the Palazzo Vecchio at Florence, executed out of one single hewn block.[1] The constraint which this circumstance imposed upon him renders the excellent execution of the work doubly admirable ; yet the effect is not entirely perfect, as the colossal size is in contradiction to the supposed boyish age. The epoch of his highest power begins with the year 1503, in which Michael Angelo was summoned to Rome by Pope Julius II. The design of a monument for this high-minded and art-loving Pope seemed to afford the master opportunity for venturing on the boldest flights of imagination. In 1504, he designed a mighty insulated building, an idea of the arrangement of which is given in a sketch in the Uffizi. Chained figures are introduced upon the pilasters in expressive allegory, personifying the provinces conquered by the Pope, and the arts which at his death would be interrupted in their progress. Other figures were placed in niches and on pedestals, such as Moses and Paul, as representatives of active and contemplative life, all in arbitrary symbolism, but even in the hasty sketches full of grand expression and bold action. It is readily perceived that sculpture here, no longer as in former times, and even in Sansovino's works, is subordinate to architecture, but that the latter is only created on account of the plastic figures. Unfortunately the work, which would have been an incomparable gigantic monument of modern sculpture, was never executed—a fact which long proved a source of bitterness to the master. After many alterations, and after a second smaller design had been made in vain, forty years afterwards (1545), that insignificant and inconsistent monument was erected which stands in S. Pietro in Vincoli. Most of it is the work of pupils, as is also the figure of the Pope, who, with his sarcophagus, is squeezed in between two plain pilasters. The figures of Rachel and Leah are the work of the master himself, and are likewise intended to symbolise contemplative and active life : the famous colossal sitting figure of Moses is also his.[2] In

---

[1] *Denkm. d. Kunst.* Pl. 72. Fig. 2.   [2] Ibid. Fig. 5.

this figure the artist has allowed himself to be carried away from his symbolic intention, and has endeavoured to give the idea of mighty energy. (Fig. 325.)　It is not the circumspect chief, the

Fig. 325.　Moses.　By Michael Angelo.

wise lawgiver, whom we see, but the stormy zealot dashing asunder the tables of the law in furious anger at the idolatry of his people. He seems to have just witnessed the worship of the golden calf; his head, with his flashing eye, is turned threat-eningly to the left; his beard, disturbed by internal emotion, flows down over his breast; his right hand is resting on the tables of the law, and with his left he is pressing his beard to him, as if he would repress the violent outburst—but the ad-vance of the right foot and the re-ceding of the left betray to us that in the next moment the mighty figure will arise, and pour forth his unbridled, annihilating anger on the recreants. This mighty Titanic ex-pression, the agitating character of the moment chosen, combined with a masterly perfection of technical execution, do not nevertheless con-ceal the fact that the form of the head is in no wise noble, and that it expresses rather physical power and passion than intellectual greatness. Besides this figure, there are in the Louvre two unfinished statues of slaves, which seem likewise to have been executed for this monument, and are in parts of great beauty. (Fig. 326.)

Fig. 326. Slave. By Michael Angelo.

Several works belonging to the middle period of his life, and exe-cuted earlier than those we have just considered, still stand within the limits of a noble well-regulated beauty. Thus, for instance, the marble statue of the naked figure of a risen Christ with the cross, in Sta. Maria sopra Minerva in Rome, which was produced about the year 1521. The attitude is very noble, the intellectual expression of the head somewhat common, and the beauty of the elegant naked body (to which modern precaution has added a bronze apron and a shoe of the

same metal, against the injurious fervour of the kisses of the
faithful) is rather antique than Christian.   In the Uffizi of Florence there is also the splendid unfinished youthful figure of an
Apollo, whose free and light action is extremely beautifully conceived and indicated.   There is also there a medallion relief of
the Madonna, with the infant Jesus resting against a book, and
the little St. John by the side : this work is likewise unfinished,
but it is arranged in the space with unsurpassable beauty, and
is full of noble feeling.

Fig. 327.   Tomb of Giuliano's de' Medici.   By Michael Angelo.

Next follow the two monuments of Giuliano and Lorenzo's
de' Medici in S. Lorenzo in Florence ; an order of Pope Leo X.,
but not begun till about 1529.   The architecture of this monument is full of paltry decoration ; but it is well calculated to give
more effect to the plastic work.   The sitting statues of the two
princes are placed in niches in the wall ; and below these, on the
rounded lid of Giuliano's sarcophagus, rest the figures of Day
and Night ; and on Lorenzo's, Dawn and Evening.   There is no

idea here of a definite thought and characterisation. They are heroic figures, whose forms are, it is true, grand and powerful, but neither nobly nor beautifully treated. In the rhythmical display of grand action this effect is increasingly produced by violent straining of the limbs. Nevertheless, in these figures, executed as they are with regardless boldness, there is touching feeling. The figure of Night especially is conceived with wonderful grandeur, in all the repose of sleep, the weary head bent forward over the right arm, which rests artistically on the left thigh. The lower parts are executed with power and energy ; but the upper are thoroughly repulsive, as if the master, in bitter defiance, had wished to check all easy enjoyment and labourless intrusion into his thoughts. The Day is naturally conceived, with his (unfinished) head turned over his shoulder, and lying outstretched with a noble rhythm in the arrangement of the limbs (not without constraint, it is true) ; at the same time the forms are wonderfully and powerfully executed. The statue of Giuliano, in military equipment, with his small and somewhat malicious head, has great simplicity and dignity of bearing.

This figure is far surpassed by that of Lorenzo, who is resting his contemplative head on his hand, and seems like thought turned into marble. Hence he has received the designation of ' Il Pensiero.' The two reposing figures on his monument are easy and free in their grand outline, and in their simple natural arrangement. The figure of Twilight is noble and less repulsive in its forms ; but it is also not so grand in expression as that of Night. The lines of the whole work exhibit the utmost harmony and true architectural rhythm.

In the same chapel there is an unfinished sitting statue of the Madonna and Child,[1] another grand and nobly conceived composition. The head of the Madonna has an almost tragic expression ; the arrangement, especially in the too restless action of the Child, is not free from exaggeration, yet the whole has a touching pathos. Similar excellences and similar deficiencies are

---

[1] *Denkm. d. Kunst.* Pl. 72. Fig. 3.

to be found in the outstretched dying Adonis in the Uffizi—a figure likewise grandly conceived, though the head is mannered and masklike. The statue of an apostle, unfinished, like so many of his works, and still partly in the rude marble block, is to be found in the court of the Academy at Florence. The group of the Descent from the Cross, in the cathedral of Florence, is a laboured and unsuccessful work. On the other hand, the likewise unfinished bust of Brutus, in the Uffizi, exhibits a powerful energy of characterisation. A portrait of the master, a bronze bust in the Conservatore Palace in Rome, belongs to the most able works of this kind, but can scarcely proceed from his own hand.

The bold caprice to which this great master more and more abandoned himself was fatal to art. As in architecture, so also in sculpture, he gave the signal for the introduction of an unbridled subjectiveness, which became all the more dangerous the less inward greatness lay in his imitators, and the more this deficiency was concealed by exaggerated Michael Angelo mannerism. Yet there were at first some artists who knew how to maintain, with tolerable freedom, a more moderate style. Among these we may mention Tribolo, or more rightly Niccolo Pericoli (1485–1550), who was employed under Andrea Sansovino in the Casa Santa at Loreto, and who adopted the noble graceful style of that master. He evidenced this independently in the reliefs of the two side portals of the façade of S. Petronio in Bologna, where he depicted in an attractive manner incidents from the lives of Moses and Joseph. In the interior of the same church there is a relief of the Ascension of the Virgin, likewise an able work. We must also here mention Benvenuto Cellini (1500–1572), interesting from his decorative works as well as from his autobiography. Summoned to France by Francis I., he was there entrusted with extensive works; but nothing is preserved of the life-size silver statues nor of the colossal figure of Mars, which possibly did not rise above a common decorative level. On the other hand, in the Museum of the Louvre, there is the delicate and elegantly finished bronze relief of the Nymph of Fontainebleau; in the Ambraser Collection at Vienna there is a richly adorned salt cellar, worked in gold; and in Windsor Castle there is an extremely splendid shield. Florence possesses his principal work of a later period, under the Loggia de' Lanzi, in the bronze statue of Perseus, with the head of Medusa. In its careful execution it is not without some constraint; but the expression is powerful and the outline happy.

b. *Masters of Upper Italy.*[1]

Owing to the preponderating influence of the Tuscan-Roman school, the hard natural style of the schools of Upper Italy received a softer breath of grace and beauty, especially through the medium of Andrea Sansovino. One of the most able of these masters is Alfonso Lombardo (1488–1537), who worked in Bologna at the same time as Tribolo, and through him acquired a more ideal style. The clay figures of the apostles in the cathedral of Ferrara belong to his earlier and more realistic period. His most important works are in Bologna. There is a Descent from the Cross, likewise in clay, in the church of S. Pietro in that city. There are also many able works in S. Petronio; above all, in the arched compartment of the left side portal, the Resurrection is distinctly and nobly executed. In S. Domenico there are the miniature-like and graceful reliefs on the supporter of the Arca di S. Domenico; and in the oratory of S. Maria della Vita there is a life-size clay group of the Death of Mary, exhibiting freedom of action and excellent composition.

Modena also at this period possessed a fertile and talented artist, Antonio Begarelli (until 1565), who took his own course; though within the general current. His principal works consist of large groups in burnt clay. His style bears much affinity with Correggio's paintings; his figures are full of sweet beauty, but in the composition he follows predominantly the laws of painting. The more important churches in his native city possess his greatest works. Thus in S. Maria Pomposa there is a group of

---

[1] *Denkm. d. Kunst.* Pl. 73.

mourners over the body of Our Lord ; in S. Francesco there is a Descent from the Cross, full of passionate action, entirely producing the effect of a large painting ; more noble and simple is the dead figure of Christ surrounded by mourners, in S. Pietro ; in S. Domenico there is a group of Christ between Martha and Mary; and, lastly, in the Museum at Berlin there is an altar, with a crucifix and four angels, executed with simple grace.

To this series of artists belongs also Andrea Riccio, surnamed Il Briosco (1480-1532), whose works principally belong to his native city Padua. A peculiar delicate feeling for lifelike arrangement and able execution was combined in him with an ingenious freshness of creative power. Yet the richness of his imagination was so great that it guarded him just as little as most of his contemporaries from a certain overloading in his reliefs. His two bronze reliefs, David dancing before the Ark of the Covenant, and Judith and Holofernes, in front of the choir of S. Antonio, are free and lifelike. Similar in character is the famous bronze candelabrum, erected in the same place in the year 1507; it is true it is overloaded, in the taste of the time, throughout its entire height of eleven feet, with a lavish show of ornament, and especially with all the conceivable fantastic creations of ancient mythology, but in its excellent execution and in the reliefs at its base it is full of life and spirit. We have given an illustration of its lower parts in Fig. 328, as an evidence of the decorative style of this epoch. A number of reliefs, belonging to the tomb of the Torriani at Verona, now in Paris in the Museum of the Louvre, were also executed by him.

The most celebrated master of Upper Italian sculpture is, however, the Florentine Jacopo Tatti, usually called Jacopo Sansovino, after his great teacher Andrea Sansovino, and who, in his long life (1479-1570), governed the architecture and sculpture of Venice for half a century. In his earlier epoch, he followed successfully, and not without independent feeling, the pure and noble style of his master, as is evidenced by the great marble statue of a seated Madonna and Child, in S. Agostino in Rome. To this period also belongs the statue of the Apostle James in the cathedral of Florence; and, in evidence of his lifelike and original conception of antique subjects, there is a marble statue of a Bacchus in the Uffizi, a work excellently executed and designed with much freshness. In the year 1527, after the taking and plundering of Rome by the French, Jacopo repaired to Venice, where henceforth he

Fig. 328.   Riccio's Candelabrum in S. Antonio.   Padua.

assumed his splendid position in matters of art, and, assisted by a great number of pupils and associates, created many important works.   The value of these is not always equal, and is affected by his greater or lesser participation in their execution.   Occasionally the hard adherence to nature belonging to this school prevails, and overloading and exaggeration are also apparent; on the whole, however, Jacopo maintained his art—at a period when almost all artists had fallen into the mannerism produced by Michael Angelo—at a height similar to that of the Venetian painters of the time, and exhibited, like them, an attractive warmth of life and able conception of nature. Among his numerous works in Venice, we must mention, above all, the Bronze Gate of the Sacristy of S. Marco, the arrangement of which calls to mind the famous Ghiberti gate at Florence. An elegant frame, adorned with statuettes of the prophets, and single strongly projecting heads, encloses two larger reliefs, the Entombment of Christ (Fig. 329) and His Resurrection, which are composed

Fig. 329. Relief rom the Bronze Gate in S. Marco. By Jacopo Sansovino.

with great excellence and cleverness. No less lifelike in conception, though somewhat exaggerated and deficient in moderation, are the six bronze reliefs, which represent the miracles of St. Mark, and are introduced on the choir screen of S. Marco. On the other hand, the small sitting bronze figures of the four evangelists on the balustrade of the high altar betray the preponderating influence of Michael Angelo. About the year 1540, he adorned the Loggia at the foot of the bell tower with allegorical and mythological reliefs and statues, the former of which especially exhibit much grace. Also the colossal marble statues of Mars and Neptune, at the foot of the giant staircase of the Doge's palace, are full of power and life, and are ably executed. Extremely delicate and charming, and among his finest works of this kind, are the statues of the Virtues, especially that of Hope, on the tomb of the Doge Venier, in S. Salvatore, executed about the year 1556. Lastly, Jacopo proves himself to have been a distinguished portrait painter by the sitting statue of Thomas of Ravenna, above the portal of S. Giuliano. In S. Antonio, in Padua, the rich ornament of the chapel dedicated to the saint belongs to him and his pupils, with the exception of the before-mentioned reliefs of the Lombardi. But the relief ascribed to Jacopo, the Revival of a Suicide, is one of his most meagre works; it is true, not without his usual spirit and life, but exaggerated in effect, the figures sharp and angular to ugliness, and the drapery straggling. On the other hand, one of the noblest and most feeling compositions, the Bringing to Life of a dead Youth, is the work of the most talented and able of his pupils, the Veronese Girolamo · Campagna.

c. *Imitators of Michael Angelo.*[1]

Through Michael Angelo, sculpture had obtained a new grand ideal style, but at the same time that fatal inclination to violent effect, which allowed the great master himself occasionally to fall into mannerism. That which with him, however, was ever the expression of an inward conviction, and the result of a powerful creative process, sank in his imitators into external form and hollow mannerism. Even artists of great talent could not escape this mighty influence, which, like a tragic destiny,

---

[1] *Denkm. d. Kunst.* Pl. 72.

exposed modern art to decline after a short period of extreme perfection. Among the associates of Michael Angelo, Montorsoli worked for the most part in Genoa, whither he was summoned by Andrea Doria; Guglielmo della Porta, who also first worked in Genoa, executed the splendid monument of Pope Paul III. in St. Peter's in Rome; and Bartolommeo Ammanati executed the clumsy and unpretending fountain in the Piazza del Granduca at Florence.

Giovanni da Bologna, a Netherland artist, whose main activity was concentrated in Florence (1524–1608), enjoys greater importance. He knew how to impart to his figures, in spite of their general expression, an air of vigorous reality and harmonious beauty, and to give his architectural works abundance of effect. The great fountain at Bologna, executed in the year 1564, is splendid and effective; the famous marble group of the Rape of the Sabine Women, under the Loggia de' Lanzi at Florence, is a masterly work, though disagreeably mannered in form and expression; the bronze equestrian statue of Cosmo I., on the Piazza del Granduca, is ably executed; and, lastly, his cleverest work, and one at the same time distinguished for delicate treatment of form, is in the Uffizi—namely, the famous Mercury, who, certainly whimsically enough, is supported by a bronze zephyr; but the figure is full of lightness and grace, as though he were about to shoot upwards with the speed of an arrow.

We must here, lastly, mention an older master, who in an unworthy and envious manner strove to declare himself a rival of Michael Angelo, and who through the irony of fate belongs, against his will, to the most mannered imitators of the great master— namely, Baccio Bandinelli (1487–1559). His most able work is a relief on the marble screen of the choir in Florence Cathedral, representing the prophets, the apostles, the Virtues, and other personifications.[1] They are cleverly composed within the space, and possess great interest as shallow reliefs; the ideas for the most part are beautifully conceived, and the arrangement is

[1] *Denkm. d. Kunst.* Pl. 72. Fig. 9.

varied ; the drapery is frequently grand, though occasionally somewhat hard. The marble group of Hercules and Cacus, in front of the Palazzo Vecchio at Florence, is, on the other hand, disagreeably exaggerated and affected, and is an imitation of the colossal form and grand style of Michael Angelo.[1]

2. PAINTING.

What the age of Pericles was for sculpture, the sixteenth century was for painting. We have already unfolded to view, why it was that the modern world was compelled to express its highest feelings in this art. The fifteenth century had in various manners opened the way for this ; it had penetrated with energy the whole range of ideas, and had depicted life with characteristic truth. Thus painting had acquired absolute authority over the world of form, and could now with the utmost freedom turn to the representation of the profoundest ideas and the most sublime beauty. The noble style which distinguishes the works of this golden age from all earlier and later works, was the necessary natural result of the noble artistic feeling, which had been gradually developed more and more in the Italian people. The affinity with antique art was no longer the result of study or imitation, it was the expression of an inward harmony.

Had this utmost perfection of art been only concentrated in a single master, this would have been sufficient to impress the classic stamp for ever upon the Italian painting of that period. But all the more wonderful seems the creative power of this incomparable epoch, when a whole series of masters of the first rank appear side by side, who each in his own original style, took the same final step to the summit of ideal beauty and classic perfection. So deep were the ideas of this epoch, so grandly were the antique and Christian views conceived and raised to a height at which each exclusive limitation ceased, and the human mind appeared wholly filled with eternal truth and beauty, that even artists of a second rank were carried away by

[1] *Denkm. d. Kunst.* Pl. 72. Fig. 10.

the mighty stream, were upheld on the height of its powerful waves, and created works, imperishably pervaded by the beauty, nobleness, and perfection of the great masters. The strict limits within which the masters of the former century had each pursued his own course, yielded to the lively interchange into which the masters of the different schools now entered. Only thus could the versatile and grand artistic characters of the masters rise above the one-sided tendency of the schools, and the freedom of art be accomplished. It is true, this epoch also of purest and noblest painting lasted but for a short period; it is true that here also the ideal style soon became shallow and superficial, and the covering was preserved after the spirit had fled; but this short period comprises such an abundance of noble and beautiful works, that in its wonderful radiance all past productions stand forth only as an intimation and a promise, and the master-works, which contain the brilliant realisation, send forth into the remotest ages a gleam of beauty and magnificence which sheds its undying light on subsequent generations.

a. *Leonardo da Vinci and his School.*

The founder of this new and highest epoch of painting is Leonardo da Vinci;[1] born in 1452, in the Castle Vinci, in the neighbourhood of Florence, and died in France in 1519. He was one of those rare phenomena, in whom nature loves to combine all conceivable human perfections; his beauty was as graceful as it was dignified, his physical strength was scarcely conceivable, and his mental gifts were of a character more versatile than is scarcely ever combined in the same person. For not merely in sculpture and painting did he appear among the first artists of his time, not merely did he establish the theory of his art by acute scientific investigations in anatomy and perspective, the results of which he has given in his treatise upon painting, but in all

---

[1] C. Amoretti, *Memorie storiche sulla Vita, gli Studj e le Opere di Leonardo da Vinci.* Milano, 1804. Leonardo da Vinci, by Count H. v. Gallenberg. Leipzig, 1834. *Léonard de Vinci et son École,* by Rio. Paris, 1855. *Vies et Œuvres des Peintres les plus célèbres, &c.,* by Landon. Paris. Cf. *Denkm. d. Kunst.* Pl. 74.

other branches of practical and mechanical science he was far in advance of the knowledge of his age. He studied the laws of geometry, physic, and chemistry; he was active as an engineer and an architect; he built canals, sewers, and fortresses; he invented machines and mechanical works of all kinds, and was besides a zealous cultivator of music and a skilful poet and improvisatore. The yearning for knowledge led him, throughout his restless life, unremittingly to new studies and inventions; and although he only devoted a small portion of his time and power to painting, the art owes to him especially its perfection and freedom.

Like the other artists of the fifteenth century, he started at first with the natural characteristic conception of life, and carried the art to perfect mastery over form; at the same time, he knew how to combine with this the highest expression of beauty, the deepest power of thought, and the manifestation of the divine. In the artistic carrying out of his ideas, he satisfied himself, however, so little, that after long unwearied labour he left many of his works unfinished, or employed new technical means for their perfect representation, which unfortunately hastened the destruction of his most important works. An unsurpassable care in the most delicate execution, a purity of form, combined with a tender blending of colour and a delicious softness of outline, the result of his thorough study of aerial perspective, are peculiar to Leonardo's works. In expression he unites dignity and grandeur with a charm which passes into the sweetest grace, especially in the female heads. The type of his female heads, with their large dark eyes, the somewhat long straight nose, the smiling mouth, and the small tapering chin, has become the common property of all his pupils and imitators; yet in his original works there is a sad dreamy expression mingled with this sweet smile, evidencing the deep and feeling character of his conception.

As Leonardo early showed decided talent for painting, he was entrusted to Verrocchio, whom he soon so far surpassed that the latter is said to have renounced painting. There is a picture

by this master, the Baptism of Christ, still in the academy at
Florence; it exhibits an unpleasing adherence to nature, and an
almost skeleton-like drawing of the figures. By far the most
beautiful figure of the whole is that of an angel, which, according
to Vasari's testimony, was executed by Leonardo. Other works
belonging to this youthful period have either perished or disappeared : not a trace is left of his two cartoons of Neptune and
the Fall of Man, nor of a fantastic monster which he painted on
a shield; and the Medusa Head in the Uffizi at Florence is
erroneously named as one of Leonardo's works. The finely
executed portrait of Ginevra Benci, and the no less excellent
painting of a goldsmith (by Lorenzo di Credi), in the Pitti
Gallery, are equally little to be regarded as genuine works of
Leonardo. On the other hand, the fresco of the Madonna with
a kneeling figure of the donator, in the monastery of S. Onofrio
in Rome, is assuredly by Leonardo, and must indeed belong to
this period, as in its characterisation and simply cold colouring
it shows the influence of the Florentine school. We find the
master, on the other hand, freer and more independent in style
in the Adoration of the Kings; a large picture in the Uffizi, still
in its brown first colour, and in which the touching sweetness of
the Madonna, the fervour of the adoring kings, and the poetry
of the arrangement evidence advanced masterly power.

Towards the year 1482, Leonardo was summoned to Milan,
to the court of Ludovico Sforza, at first in his capacity of
musician and improvisatore. But there is still a letter by the
artist, drawn up as a memorial, in which he offers his services
to the Milanese ruler as an engineer, military architect, architect,
sculptor, and painter. Besides the theoretical treatises on his
art, which he wrote there, there were two great artistic undertakings to which he devoted his powers until about 1499. The
one was the equestrian statue before mentioned, and the loss of
which is ever to be lamented ; the other (1496–1498) was the
famous Last Supper, in the refectory of S. Maria delle Grazie,[1]

---

[1] Bossi, *Del Cenacolo di Leonardo da Vinci.* Milano, 1819. Cf. Goethe's beautiful treatise.—*Denkm. d. Kunst.* Pl. 74. Fig. 2.

a work whose disgraceful destruction is yet still more to be deplored. Much injury and ruin, arising from the inundation of the hall, from the thoughtless barbarousness which introduced a door at the lower centre of the picture, and certainly also from the original faulty condition of the wall, have contributed to the destruction of the work. More than all these circumstances, however, its ruin has been aided by the fatal idea of the master to paint his work on the wall in oil colours; and, lastly, in order to finish the fate of this misused picture, two miserable bunglers in the last century, Bellotti and Mazza, committed the outrage of completely painting over Leonardo's greatest creation. Only recently has this addition been carefully removed; and after all this havoc, the gleam of its former beauty is still so indestructible, that the effect of the original surpasses that produced by Raphael Morghen's excellent engraving. It is true, the previous accurate study of this important engraving is indispensable. The original cartoons of the heads, which are still in preservation—that of Christ in the Brera Gallery, and the Apostles in the Grand Ducal collection at Weimar—also afford the most important assistance.

√ After the comprehensive remarks which we owe to Goethe, it would be superfluous and presumptuous to give a detailed description of the work. Besides, who does not know it from the engraving? Who has not admired, again and again, the incomparable majesty of the Divine Master and Teacher—a majesty which no artist has conceived and represented with the same depth—the grand characterisation of the figures of the disciples round Him—and who has not been touched by the thrilling effect of this deeply tragic incident? For Leonardo has not contented himself with the quiet representation of the Last Supper, as it had previously been so often depicted; equally little was he satisfied with the task of awakening new interest, in the simple delineation of the sacred scene, by the deep conception and completion of the separate characters. All this was done in a perfect manner; but while Leonardo chose to depict the moment in which Christ sorrowfully and seriously

utters the words, 'One of you shall betray me,' he broke with
all past tradition, cast a spark of fire into the assembly, and
boldly ventures to change the quiet familiar celebration of
Christ's Last Supper into a scene of passionate dramatic action.
And yet only such a master could maintain that noble moderation
in the midst of this ferment of feeling, in which sadness, pain,
uncertainty, anger, indignation, and even horror are combined;
only such as he could, with his profound knowledge of the

Fig. 330.   Group from Leonardo da Vinci's Last Supper.

human mind, develope each various expression as the result of
each various character, and, amid the struggle of contending
feelings, place the Divine Master in the midst in calm resignation and wonderful majesty, only slightly dimmed by the expression of sadness.   The composition itself—two groups of
three disciples being placed on each side, thus making the figure
of Christ more effectively conspicuous—is one of the greatest

master-pieces of art. Added to this arrangement, the fine contrasts of character are inexhaustible, and are evidenced in the expression of the heads, in the action, the drapery, and, above all, in the hands. As an example of this, we have given one of these groups, that placed at the right hand of Christ, comprising the loved disciple, sunk in sorrow, the ardent and angrily excited Peter, and the alarmed and skrinking traitor.

Many other pictures, especially portraits, belong to the same period of his Milanese residence. Thus, in the Ambrosian Library at Milan, there are several beautiful portraits in crayon, also the portrait of Gio. Galeazzo Sforza, executed in a free, broad, and bold style; while the profile likeness of his wife, Isabella of Aragon, exhibits the detailed work of the earlier epoch. To this period also belongs the portrait of Lucrezia Crivelli, a loved one of Ludovico; it is similar in style, and is poetically attractive : it is in the Louvre, and is designated there as the ' Belle Ferronière.' There is also there a half-length figure of John the Baptist in the Wilderness, which, however, from its chiaro oscuro, and the enthusiastic expression of the head, marks the transition to the later epoch. On the other hand, a nude female portrait, according to Waagen now in the Hermitage at St. Petersburg, seems to belong to this early period.

When the French entered Milan in the year 1499, Leonardo repaired to his native city Florence, and was for many years engaged there in artistic works. At this period he produced the cartoon of a large painting, the Battle at Anghiari,[1] which he executed, between 1503 and 1504, for the hall of the Palazzo Vecchio. Michael Angelo also was soon after invited to execute a similar work, and entered the lists with his great countryman. The two cartoons, designed by the first masters of that day, were, as it were, the public manifesto, with which art designated the moment when she was prepared to rise to the highest point of perfection. The younger artists, among them Raphael and

---

[1] *Denkm. d. Kunst.* Pl. 74. Fig. 3.

many others, assembled to admire and study these works, which founded truly the new era of painting. This cartoon of Leonardo, and that of his rival also, have perished. Only a group of four horsemen, fighting passionately for a standard, has come down to us through a drawing of Rubens, which has been engraved by Edelingk, and is sufficient to furnish evidence of the boldness and power of the composition. Shortly before, Leonardo had drawn a cartoon of the Holy Family, which also excited the greatest admiration, and is now in the National

Fig. 331. The Holy Family, after Leonardo da Vinci.

Gallery in London. The Virgin is nursing the Child, who is turning caressingly to the little St. John, while St. Anna is sitting beside full of happiness. Another composition of the Holy Family exists in several copies by his pupils, the best of which, partly by the hand of the master himself, is in the Louvre. (Fig. 331.) The Madonna is here sitting on the lap of St. Anna, and is looking smilingly on the Child, who is getting up on a small lamb. The freedom with which this genre-like idea is adopted,

and yet at the same time the true womanly majesty and grace
preserved, point with certainty to the great master. There is
also the splendid portrait of Mona Lisa, the wife of his Florentine friend Giocondo, at which he worked for four years continuously, and yet at the end pronounced it unfinished. The
original in the Louvre at Paris, although in parts severely
criticised, attracts, from the grace of the conception, as well as
from the sweet charm of the almost seductive smile.

In the year 1513 Leonardo repaired to Rome; but in 1516
he obeyed the summons of Francis I. to the royal court of
France, where he died three years after, deeply lamented by the
art-loving King, but not, as tradition reports, in his arms. All
that is to be found under his name in the different galleries are
works of his pupils, often indeed of great perfection, and of high
value from the intellectual merit of the composition being trace-
able to him. For he himself worked but slowly, never did
enough, and constantly allowed works begun to remain unfinished; but he possessed sufficient glorious ideas to furnish
material for the work of a whole school. Among the most
famous of these works there are many Holy Families, especially
that in the Louvre, and one in the possession of Lord Suffolk,
known under the name of ' La Vierge aux Rochers.'[1] The
Madonna, with the infant Christ and the little St. John, accompanied by an angel, are sitting in a rocky cleft by a flower-
wreathed fountain, one of the most charming idylls of Christian
art. Another Holy Family, known as ' Vierge au Bas-relief'
(Fig. 332), appears frequently repeated. There is also an important composition, which, without doubt, owes its first idea to
Leonardo, representing Christ as a youth between four Pharisees,
the best copy of which, one of Luini's most perfect panel pictures,
and only perhaps a little too laboriously modelled in the hands,
is in the English National Gallery; a feebler copy is in the Pal.
Spada in Rome. The beautiful picture of Vanity and Modesty
in the Pal. Sciarra, probably executed by Bernardino Luini, may

---

[1] *Denkm. d. Kunst.* Pl. 74. Fig. 6.

lay claim to the same origin, and is charming from its deep poetry and tender blending of colour. There is also a small figure in the Pal. Borghese of Christ blessing. It is especially

Fig. 332. Leonardo's Vierge au Bas-relief.

finely executed, and full of mysterious charm, and may be traced to a sketch of Leonardo.

√ A great number of pupils and imitators followed Leonardo,[1]

---

[1] *Denkm. d. Kunst.* Pl. 74. Fumagalli, *Scuola di Leonardo da Vinci in Lombardia.* Milano, 1811. J. D. Passavant, *Beiträge zur Geschichte der alten Malerschulen in der Lombardei.* Kunstblatt of the year 1838.

among them some of distinguished gifts. So powerful, however, was Leonardo's intellectual superiority, that not merely his types, but also his ideas, form the true value of this able school, and many of his compositions, as we have said, only live in the pictures of his pupils. The common characteristic of these Lombard painters is a calm grace and loveliness, which are especially agreeable in religious subjects, avoiding the expression of deeper passionate excitement as well as of energetic action. In drawing and outline of form inferior to their master, who stands unsurpassed in thorough anatomical knowledge, Leonardo's pupils have, on the other hand, cultivated his tendency to tender blending of colour and a fine chiaro-oscuro—this, indeed, not seldom to excess. In the same manner, the sweet charm of his female heads, especially of the Madonna, occasionally degenerates into a stereotyped mannered expression, in which a soulless smile prevails.

The first place among Leonardo's pupils is due to Bernardino Luini, who was especially distinguished by the grace and feeling, by the agreeable and often enchanting beauty, of his figures, and by the clear warm tint of his colouring. He displayed considerable activity as a fresco painter. The Brera Gallery at Milan contains a number of these works, belonging to his earlier and somewhat constrained period, which have been gathered from the churches of the surrounding neighbourhood, and in some of the heads of which traces of Raphael's influence are perceptible. In the library of the Ambrosiana in the same city, there is a fresco of the Scoffing of Christ, which betrays a certain limit of the artist in the representation of strong and malicious characters. He also adorned the church of the Monastero Maggiore (S. Maurizio) at Milan with an abundance of the most beautiful frescoes, representing figures of saints, the Passion of Christ, and incidents from legends. He shows himself at the height of his power in the frescoes, executed about the year 1529, in the Franciscan Church at Lugano, where a large painting of the Crucifixion, full of splendid figures of touching expression, and a lunette picture of the Madonna, with the Child and the little

St. John, exhibit all the charm of the master; also the equally excellent fresco, executed about 1530, in the church at Saronno, which depicts the life of the Madonna. His numerous easel paintings are often regarded as works of Leonardo, from their feeling, beauty, and perfection. A painting, bearing the date 1515, and representing the Madonna, with saints and several kneeling donators, in the Brera Gallery, has a somewhat colder red for its first colour; but it is nevertheless inferior to his frescoes in warmth of feeling.

Leonardo's other pupils exhibit less independent power; among them is the graceful and tender Andrea Salaino, whose pictures are distinguished for a soft reddish grounding in the flesh tints; also Beltraffio, who is not without constraint both in expression and drawing; Marco d'Oggione, conspicuous for a somewhat colder colouring; Francesco Melzi, who approaches Leonardo in depth of feeling and grace of expression; and, lastly, Cesare da Sesto, who at first with considerable talent emulated the master, but subsequently, to the disadvantage of his art, adopted the external manner of the Raphael school.

Under the influence of Leonardo, which was blended, however, with that of the Umbrian school and of Raphael's art into a peculiarly modified style, stands also the talented and fertile Piedmontese painter, Gaudenzio Ferrari (1484–1549).[1] Springing from the older Lombard school, he adhered to a certain inclination to a lively and even exaggerated expression belonging to those masters. His chief work was the execution of several extensive frescoes, some of which are in the Brera Gallery. Another very able picture, full of dramatic life, is in a chapel in S. Maria delle Grazie. It is a representation of the Crucifixion, and is rich in figures. More important are the wall paintings, executed about 1510, in the Minorite Church at Varallo in Piedmont, representing the history of Christ; and also those in the Capella del sagro Monte, representing the Crucifixion of Christ, the principal figures of which are sculptured and painted

---

[1] *Denkm. d. Kunst.* Pl. 79 A. Cf. the Illustrated work, *Le Opere del Pittore G. Ferrari, dis. e inc. da Silv. Pianazzi, dir. da Berdiga.* Milano, 1835.

like nature, while on the walls and vaults around he painted
spectators and lamenting angels.   He executed a Last Supper
in the refectory of S. Paolo at Vercelli; and in S. Cristoforo, in
the same place, he painted, between 1532 and 1535, a series of
large frescoes from the Birth of the Virgin to her Ascension.
Lastly, in 1535, he painted beautiful bands of angels in the dome
of the church at Saronno, near Milan.   One of the earliest and
most important of his panel pictures is a lament over the dead

Fig. 333.   The Ecstasy of St. Catharine.

body of Christ, in the Turin Gallery. The Martyrdom of
S. Catharine, in the Brera Gallery, is a work of strong and somewhat coarse expression.   The scene of torture is well executed,
though the colouring is somewhat glaring; the saint is noble
and gentle, and the executioners full of effective action.

Another excellent Lombard master is Andrea Solario of

Milan, surnamed Del Gobbo, whose earlier pictures—for example, a Holy Family of 1495, in the Milan Gallery—evidence the influence of Giov. Bellini, and occasionally that of Mantegna, as in the Crucifixion, in the Louvre (1503). Subsequently he followed Leonardo's manner, exhibiting, however, independent feeling and a delicate sense of beauty. This is evident in the touching figure of the Madonna nursing the Child, in the Louvre, and in the Ascension of the Virgin, in the Certosa at Pavia.

Gianantonio Bazzi, surnamed Il Soddoma (1474–1549), was also produced by the Lombard school. Born in Vercelli, he was at first, without doubt, under Leonardo's influence, but subsequently, during a stirring life, he received lasting impressions from acquaintance with Florentine art, and also during his sojourn in Rome from the works of Raphael. The importance of this artist lies less in grandeur of conception or distinctness of composition, than in an extraordinary sense of beauty, and in the expression of deep enthusiastic feeling, which he clothed in the noblest forms and with the softest blending of colour. The frescoes, representing incidents from the life of St. Benedict, which he executed about the year 1505 by the side of Signorelli's works in the court of Monte Oliveto, not far from Siena, are full of able characterisation. Shortly after he was summoned to Rome by Pope Julius II., in order to carry out the wall paintings in the apartments of the Vatican, only few of which, however, are still in existence. On the other hand, there are two beautiful frescoes in the Villa Farnesina, which he painted for Agostino Chigi—Alexander's Marriage with Roxana, and the Wife of Darius imploring Mercy of the victorious Alexander. The first especially is full of beauty, and is admirably painted, with warm colouring and unsurpassable softness. Even by the side of Raphael the charming sweetness of Roxana's head (Fig. 334) is striking.[1] The numerous Cupids who appear below and in the air are charmingly naïve, and the foremost figure of Alexander's suite is full of the utmost youthful magnificence. Yet we miss

[1] The Illustration is taken from an engraving by Louis Jacoby.

in the drapery the noble style to which Raphael and Michael Angelo accustom us; and in the second picture especially there is a want of any higher law of composition, although there is sufficient to occupy the eye in the extremely beautiful female figures.

The master subsequently returned to Siena, where he created

Fig. 334. Head of Roxana. By Soddoma.

his most perfect works, and infused new life into the decayed Sienese school. Among his most beautiful works are the frescoes, which he executed in the Oratorium of S. Bernardino, together with Beccafumi and Girolamo del Pacchia, hitherto erroneously confused with the unimportant Pacchiarotto. The Ascension of the Virgin, the Visitation, Mary in the Temple,

and her Crowning, are by his hand, and are rich in beauty and
deep feeling : the latter picture alone is ill arranged, and is not
equal to the others in characterisation. There are also some
figures of saints in the corners, which are magnificent in expression. No less excellent are the figures of saints, especially S.
Sebastian and S. Hieronymus, in a chapel of S. Spirito. In the
oratory of S. Caterina he painted several wall pictures of the life
of the saint, which are difficult to estimate on account of the
darkness of their position. He painted the same legends in a
chapel of S. Domenico (Fig. 333), where he represented the saint
in a swoon, with the deepest feeling and the noblest expression
of pain. There are also several frescoes by him in the Pal.
Pubblico, single figures of S. Victor and S. Ansanius, which are
full of nobleness and grace. Among his somewhat rare panel
paintings there is an Adoration of the Kings, in S. Agostino,
and a large Descent from the Cross, in S. Francesco, which are
worthy of mention ; but, above all, S. Sebastian, in the Uffizi
Gallery at Florence, is one of the noblest creations of the time,
with its wonderful depth of mental pain and its enchanting
beauty. Soddoma's influence, blended with the more important
influence of Raphael, may be perceived in the paintings of the
able architect Baldassare Peruzzi, who, it is true, was not always
free from mannerism, but who in the beautiful fresco of the Madonna in S. Maria della Pace, in Rome, produced a thoroughly
noble and ably executed work.   .

Lastly, we must here add a Veronese artist, Gianfrancesco
Carotto, who belonged to Mantegna's school; his beautifully
composed pictures, with their tender feeling, exhibit an independent reception of Leonardo's influence. One of his principal works, of the year 1528, is the altar-piece, in S. Fermo at
Verona, of the Madonna and S. Anna, hovering on clouds and
surrounded by beautiful angels : below these are four saints depicted with lively action.

b. *Michael Angelo and his Followers.*

Michael Angelo Buonarroti,[1] of Florence (1475–1564), with whom we have already become acquainted as an architect and sculptor, has a position in painting also by the side of Leonardo, as a fellow founder of the new period, and at the same time as one of the first and highest masters of this art; indeed, it may be said that in sublimity, power, depth of thought, bold action, and grand outline, he has never been equalled by any other artist. Although he himself gave preference to sculpture, yet it was from the abundance and richness of his ideas that he produced his most perfect works in painting, which could alone afford him sufficient scope for his designs. The same Titanic mind, which filled his sculptures, also lives in the great paintings which he executed. Easel pictures were not his forte: whatever had to be compressed into such a space he preferred to express in marble, or he gave it to others to execute. On the other hand, he created alone, without assistance, the two largest frescoes which had until now been completed, and he did this independent of all artistic as well as ecclesiastical tradition. In these wonderful works he exhibited a power before which even the greatest of his successors have bent in reverence.

Michael Angelo received his first instruction from Domenico Ghirlandajo, whom he astonished by the rapid development of his talent. At the same time, he copied, of his own accord, Masaccio's splendid frescoes in S. Maria del Carmine, and gave the most careful study to the remains of the antique. How boldly and independently he worked, even at an early period, is shown in a panel painting of the Holy Family, still in the Tribuna of the Uffizi, as well as in his early plastic works. The Madonna is sitting on the ground with her feet crossed; she has just closed the prayer book that is lying on her lap, and is stretching out her hand to the Child, held to her by Joseph, who

[1] *Denkm. d. Kunst.* Pl. 77. Cf. Vasari, *Vita del gran Michelangelo Buonarroti.* Quatremère de Quincy, *Histoire de Michelangelo Buonarroti.* Paris, 1835. J, Harford, *The Life of M. A. Buonarroti.* London, 1858. 2 vols. H. Grimm, *Leben Michelangelo's.* Hanover, 1863. 2 vols.

is sitting behind her. The background is filled with naked figures, who are leaning against a parapet, and who owe their origin, it is true, to no other reason than the need of the artist to satisfy himself in drawing the human form. The group itself is extremely far-fetched in idea, and therefore, in spite of its able drawing, it is less attractive. All external charm of the senses was even here so completely disdained by the painter, that he executed his work in a cold colour in tempera.

More according to his taste undoubtedly was a commission of the Florentine civil authorities, to sketch a battle piece for the great hall of the Palazzo Vecchio, in which Leonardo had already painted. He chose a moment before the battle, in which the soldiers had heedlessly given themselves up to bathing in the Arno, and were suddenly called to battle by the sound of the trumpets. (Fig. 335.) When he had finished his cartoon (1505), it so much excited the admiration of his contemporaries, that it even eclipsed Leonardo's work. With perfect knowledge of the human body, to the study of which he had devoted twelve years of his life, he here exhibited in bold groups the most various movements—the sudden surprise, the manifold attempts to put on their clothes, to seize their weapons, and to hasten to the combat. The cartoon was set up, and was studied with eagerness by all younger artists, among them Raphael; unfortunately, however, it was destroyed, though not, as Vasari alleges, by Bandinelli's malice, so that it has only come down to us in old copies and engravings.

By this painting and several plastic works, Michael Angelo's fame speedily rose so high, that he received a summons to Rome, as we have before mentioned, from Julius II., in order to prepare a design for the monument of this pope; and when this undertaking came to a standstill, to paint the ceiling of the Sistine Chapel. Unwillingly and with reluctance he went to the work; and only the iron will of a pope like Julius II. could have brought the passionate mind of the master to the accomplishment of this mighty work, after he had even precipitously quitted Rome in anger at an imagined offence, and was only persuaded to return at the personal request of the pope. Solitary and thrown upon his own resources, secluded from all the world, Michael Angelo began the work towards the year 1508, and

Fig. 335. Michael Angelo's Cartoon of the Bathing Soldiers.

accomplished it in a few years; yet, reckoning the interruptions that occurred in its progress, he is said to have required for it, on the whole, only the incredibly short period of twenty months.

This ceiling is one of the most perfect of the master's works, and the mightiest monument of painting throughout all ages. In the arrangement of the whole, Michael Angelo not merely adhered to the form of the vault, which is that of a vault with an even surface in the middle, but he added a rich architectural construction, which appears in itself not devoid of caprice, but was well adapted to his object. The long central surface contained scenes from Genesis, from the Creation to the Deluge, in eight

Fig. 336. The Persian Sibyl.   Fig. 337. The Prophet Isaiah.
By Michael Angelo.

alternate broader and narrower paintings. On the large triangular compartments of the vault he painted the sitting figures of the Prophets and Sibyls, prophetically pointing to the Messiah; in the four corresponding corners, he depicted the fourfold deliverance of the people of Israel, the Brazen Serpent, Goliath, Judith, and Esther. In the pendentives and window arches, there are groups of the ancestors of Mary, waiting in quiet expectation for the Redeemer. To these thoughtful and profound scenes and figures, he added a world of magnificent figures, executed in grey and bronze, and placed on painted pedestals, or other subordinate places; figures which possess no other importance than 'that they invest the architectural framework with an inexhaustibly rich life, without confusing the eye or destroying the repose of the whole.

The immeasurable depth and inexhaustible value of this work can only be remotely intimated. We can only, therefore, slightly point out the most important parts. The stories of Genesis, in the first place, are here treated with a grandeur such as art can never again produce. The figure of God the Father

Fig. 338. Creation of Light. By Michael Angelo.

exhibits the utmost majesty; accompanied by spirits, He hovers as if upborne by the tempest, to separate the light from the darkness, to give their course to the heavenly bodies, and to create the first man. In the Creation of Adam, an electric spark of life seems to pass through the limbs of the slumberer by the contact of the Creator, and to awaken the body into being. The first human beings are represented as a primitive race full of beauty and unbroken power; and over the figure of Eve, who stands forth shy and childlike at the command of God, the master has diffused a charming grace which is generally foreign to his works. Throughout he combines in a few touches the deepest and the highest feelings. Thus the Prophets and Sibyls belong to the most wonderful creations of his art. Sublime above all human measure, and at the same time exhibiting the deepest expression of reflection and reverie, of investigation and looking forward, they seem to represent, in their solemn seclusion, the longing, the desire, and the painful waiting of whole nations and ages for the promised redemption. Grand and simple in design are the four representations of the Deliverance of the People of Israel, which, like all the other paintings, refer to the Messiah and His work of redemption. In

Fig. 339.　Group of the Ancestors of Mary.　By Michael Angelo.

the thirty-six groups of the ancestors of Mary (Fig. 339) there is the same tone of painfully contemplative and longing waiting, exhibited in an abundance of touching scenes, and at the same time an overwhelming wealth of invention is displayed in the positions, grouping, and gestures. Lastly, the numerous naked figures which, on pedestals, cornices, and tympanons, fill all the vacant spaces with their intellectual beauty, are among the most splendid things of the kind produced by modern art. They testify most astonishingly to the masterly sense of form, and to the boldness and power of imagination, with which Michael

Angelo employed his art. Added to this, although the plastic character predominates, they possess a power and warmth of colouring, which still gleams forth victoriously from the coating of incense smoke, which unfortunately increases from year to year. They afford us a most remarkable evidence of the all-conquering energy of the master, when we reflect that they were his first attempt to meet the technical difficulties of fresco painting.

About thirty years later, in his old age, Michael Angelo, by commission of Pope Paul III., executed his Last Judgment on the altar wall of the same chapel (1534–1544). More boldly than ever before, he here renounced all traditionary forms of Christian art. He who would seek to find here the beautifully arranged ranks of the elect and the blessed, and the bands of angels, which form a halo of heavenly glory round the Redeemer, enthroned in etherial light, would be sadly disappointed. Michael Angelo intended to express the storm of passions by the most violent action of the human body; he could choose but one moment for this, namely, that afforded him in the world-annihilating ' Depart from me, ye cursed.' Fear, despair, powerless fury, struggle between fear and hope, fill the immense painting. But they are not the feelings of sinful, unsaved Christians, waking to the terrible tidings that heaven is lost to them for ever; but one might imagine them the antique race of Titans and Giants, dashed into the abyss by the Thunderer Jupiter. Thus, in harmony with them, the angels are rushing through the air with instruments of torture, and crying for vengeance; thus the advance of the blessed becomes an equally absolute call for justice, the struggle of the condemned against the demons of darkness becomes an athletic contest of life and death, and even the gloomy and fearful ferryman in the boat below, driving back suppliants with strokes of his oar—an idea already employed by Signorelli and taken from Dante's ' Purgatorio'—harmonises with the general merciless tone of the whole. And, in order to show that all hope of mercy had vanished, Mary, the mother of Christ, is hiding herself fearfully by the side of her Son, and turns tremblingly away her usually gracious countenance.

Placing ourselves upon this high point of the master's works, we must confess that he has expressed his ideas with a depth and power unequalled in the whole realm of art, exhibiting to us his wonderful mind, contrary to all the rules of nature, rising to its utmost might instead of declining with extreme old age. Who has ever, as he has here, almost in his seventieth year, with such absolute power over the realm of form and with never-failing hand, compelled into life every conceivable grouping and foreshortening, every possible movement of the human form —hovering, falling, rising, and wildly confused? Although subsequent prudery (at the order of Pope Paul IV.) materially altered the original condition of the picture by painting over many of the naked forms; although the smoke of incense has dimmed the once clear and distinct colouring; yet even now it is easy to perceive with what masterly power the artist knew how to produce an unsurpassable distinctness and harmony in this picture of 60 feet in height, in spite of its immeasurable abundance of figures. While he thus here also must ever stand forth as one of the greatest artists, we must, nevertheless, not conceal the fact, that the inner majesty, the consecrated feeling, the calm beauty of his ceiling paintings, is not existing here; and that in his Last Judgment he fully let loose that mighty and exaggerated power, which speedily carried art to its decline.

Two other frescoes, in the Capella Paolina in the Vatican, belong to the same late period—namely, the Conversion of Saul and the Crucifixion of St. Peter—both of which were for a long time blackened, but have been now cleaned, and likewise, especially the former, show a striking power of dramatic life.

Easel pictures by Michael Angelo seem not to exist, except that earlier Holy Family and an unfinished Madonna with Angels, in Mr. Labouchère's possession in London. As we have said, he did not care for panel painting, and only rarely occupied himself with it. An old copy is still existing, in the royal castle at Berlin, of the painting of the Leda, which he executed in tempera. Others were painted by his pupils and imitators, after his sketches. He especially employed Fra Sebastiano del

Piombo for this purpose (1485–1547), who, in the Venetian school, under the influence of Bellini and Giorgione, had attained to masterly power of colouring, and well knew how to adapt this to the grand ideas and forms of Michael Angelo.   There is a painting in the National Gallery which is probably his work,

Fig. 340.   Raising of Lazarus to Life.   By Sebastian del Piombo.

representing the ' Dream,' a poetical and allegorical composition by the great master, copies of which are to be found elsewhere. The principal work of this able artist, in the same collection— the Raising of Lazarus to Life (Fig. 340) — probably also originated from a sketch of Michael Angelo.   It was executed in 1519, in competition with Raphael's famous picture of the Transfiguration on Mount Tabor. At the same period (1520) appeared the grand and beautiful painting of the Sufferings of S. Apollonia, in the Pitti Gallery in Florence. A Crucifixion full of deep expression and nobleness, by Sebastiano's hand, is in the Museum at Berlin; and in the same place there is also a dead figure of Christ mourned over by Mary Magdalene and Joseph of Arimathea, in colossal half-figures, strikingly tragical and grand in form. That Sebastiano had even before risen to great independent importance, as Giorgione's pupil, is evidenced by the principal picture of his earlier period, in S. Giovanni Crisostomo, in Venice, representing S. Chrysostom engaged in lively conversation with several saints — a painting of great beauty and grave deep colouring. As a portrait painter, also, this artist was highly important, as is evidenced by his grand and freely conceived painting of Andrea Doria in the Pal. Doria in Rome; by the splendid female portrait of the erroneously called Fornarina, of the year 1512, in the Tribuna der Uffizi, a portrait hitherto ascribed to Raphael; and by another excellent female portrait in the Städel Museum at Frankfort.

Several of Michael Angelo's compositions were likewise executed by Pontormo (rightly Jacopo Carucci), a pupil of Andrea del Sarto. Thus, for instance, there is a painting, full of exuberant life, in Kensington Palace; and also in the Museum at Berlin, representing Venus caressed by Cupid. Marcello Venusti also frequently imitated Michael Angelo's compositions. The most excellent of these is a small copy of the Last Judgment in the Museum at Naples, especially important because it was painted previous to the violent attempt to render the picture more suitable to the general view.

Of all these imitators of Michael Angelo, Daniele da Volterra (rightly Ricciarelli), who belonged to Soddoma's and Peruzzi's school, showed most original mental power and importance. His principal work is the famous Descent from the Cross, in the church of Trinità de' Monti at Rome, which is full of bold action and deep pathos. Less agreeable, on the other hand, is the crowded representation of the Murder of the Innocents, in the Uffizi at Florence.

The later painting of the sixteenth century in Rome and Florence[1] followed almost entirely the one-sided imitation of Michael Angelo, round whose grand forms and bold ideas the whole age feebly revolved, to the complete loss of all original creative power. They displayed the exaggerated muscular development of his figures, without his knowledge of anatomy; they aped their attitudes, their positions, and actions, without being able to breathe into them the animating soul; they delighted in colossal productions, in gigantic paintings, and unex-. ampled rapidity of painting, without thinking of true life, solid execution, and faithful characterisation. The high ideal style became repulsive mannerism, in which conscientious drawing yielded to superficial handicraft, and colouring completely lost all truth, warmth, and harmony. It was only when simple tasks of portrait painting were to be produced, that able works still appeared. The principal representative of this style in Florence was Giorgio Vasari of Arezzo (1512–1574), one of Michael Angelo's truest admirers, and of great merit, from his attractive history of the Italian painters, the invaluable basis of modern art history. Francesco Salviati (rightly de' Rossi) and Angiolo Bronzino were also of great importance, the latter from his portraits. In Rome, the brothers Taddeo and Federigo Zuccaro are the foremost representatives of this mannered and degenerated tendency in art. In almost all artists we find able original talent ruined by the false taste of the whole epoch.

c. *The other Masters of Florence.*[2]

So rich in artistic powers was Florence that, besides the two great masters, Leonardo and Michael Angelo, other able artists rose to independent importance, and to a free and nobly developed style. The first of these is Fra Bartolommeo or, by

---

[1] *Denkm. d. Kunst.* Pl. 88.   [2] Ibid. Pl. 76.

his secular name, Baccio della Porta (1469–1517). He received his first instruction from Cosimo Rosselli; but he soon felt the influence of the mighty mind of Leonardo, whose depth of characterisation and tender colouring he strove to imitate. There are two small paintings in the Uffizi belonging to this earlier period, representing the Birth and Circumcision of Christ, which are executed with miniature-like delicacy. Baccio had already reached great fame in his art, when the condemnation and burning of his friend Savonarola (1498) shattered him so deeply that he entered the Dominican order, and renounced his art for four years. Only at the urgent exhortation of his friends and the brethren of his order did he apply himself again to his forsaken art; and when Raphael came to Florence in 1504, he attached himself to the excellent frate, learned from him his treatment of colour, and gave him instruction in perspective in return. Fra Bartolommeo's true sphere is devotional painting, and in this branch of art he is equal to the greatest and noblest masters. His figures are full of deep feeling, and at the same time exhibit freedom of action and ripe beauty. That which, however, gives his paintings an especially solemn effect is their magnificent arrangement, and, with all their freedom, the strict architectural construction of the whole. In colouring he has that soft blending peculiar to Leonardo, and by means of which he introduced and still further developed aerial perspective, combining in his best works a rare power and depth, with freshness of colour. He executed but little in fresco, and of that little few works are preserved. The remains of a Last Judgment in the monastery of Sta. Maria Nuova in Florence are, however, of great importance. They exhibit two rows of magnificent figures of the Apostles and Saints, enthroned on clouds, with Christ in the centre, full of nobleness and heavenly repose. A number of the most beautiful of his numerous altar-pieces are still to be seen in Florence. In the collection of the Academy there is a Madonna appearing to St. Bernard, belonging to his youthful period. In the expression of the Virgin and the Angel it is not quite successful, and the colouring is still as untoned and as

inharmonious as most of the earlier Florentine works ; but the
figure of the Saint is full of dignity. Most of his other works
belong, on the contrary, to his second epoch. Thus, for instance,
there is a Madonna with Saints in S. Marco, which is extremely
important and powerful, and deep and warm in colour. There
is also the Risen Christ with four Saints, in the Pitti Gallery, a
painting full of solemn dignity and beauty. In the same place
there is the Descent from the Cross, one of the master's most
splendid works (Fig. 341), full of deep agony of mind, and presenting a striking gradation in the mourning John, the Mother

Fig. 341. The Descent from the Cross. By Fra Bartolommeo.

bent with sorrow, and Mary Magdalene completely sunk in tears
and woe. There is a famous painting in the same gallery representing the colossal figure of S. Mark, a work which the master
expressly executed, in order to meet the objection that he could
not create any grand figures. The drapery is extremely beautiful and significant ; but the action is somewhat formal, the head
is somewhat empty in expression, and the unfavourable influence
of Michael Angelo's ceiling paintings in the Sistine Chapel is not
to be mistaken. One of the master's most beautiful compositions
is an unfinished picture in the Uffizi, only painted in the brown

grounding, and representing the sitting Madonna and Child, with
the little St. John and St. Anna, surrounded by several saints.
It is full of the utmost grace and beauty, well and symmetrically
grouped, and powerful and solemn in effect.   The churches of
Lucca possess other important paintings of the master.   In the
cathedral S. Martino, there is an altar-piece of the enthroned
Madonna, with Saints and Angels making music, belonging to
the year 1509, which is full of noble expression and bright harmonious colouring.   To about the same period belongs a painting in S. Romano, representing God the Father, surrounded by
Angels, and below Mary Magdalene and St. Catharine of Siena,
one of his most perfect creations, and only to be compared with
Raphael in beauty, grace, and dignity.   The Madonna della
Misericordia, on the other hand, in the same church, and belonging to the master's later period, with all its great beauties in
parts, is not free from designed arrangement and formal attitudes,
and hence produces a chilling effect.   Works of this artist are
rarely to be found out of Italy.   The collection of the Belvedere
at Vienna possesses a Presentation in the Temple; two important altar-pieces of the Madonna enthroned with Saints are
in the Museum of the Louvre, and a similar painting is in the
cathedral at Besançon.

   An able colleague of Fra Bartolommeo was Mariotto Albertinelli, who followed the style of his friend, and completed many
of his works.   This was the case with a fresco painting in
Sta. Maria Nuova, and an altar-piece of the Ascension of the
Virgin, in the Berlin Museum.   His finest work, full of grace
and depth of feeling, and at the same time distinguished by the
flow of the drapery and its noble rhythm, is the representation of
the Visitation, in the gallery of the Uffizi.   The hearty meeting
of Mary and Elizabeth is here conceived in a similar manner to
that in which Andrea Pisano had treated it on the bronze gate
of the baptistry, only the painter has increased the expression of
feeling, and has developed still further the picturesque contrasts.

   More independently and freely did the power of a younger

artist, Andrea del Sarto (1488–1530), develope itself.[1] Formed
in the school of Pier di Cosimo, he experienced, like so many of
his contemporaries, the greatest stimulant by the study of the
two famous cartoons of Leonardo and Michael Angelo ; but, in
his further development, the gifted Andrea differed from all
former styles of Florentine art, and formed himself into a
colourist such as Italy hitherto had never possessed, except in
the Venetians and in Correggio, and has never since possessed.
The beautiful heritage, however, of Florentine art which de-
volved upon Andrea, not without the special influence of Fra
Bartolommeo, almost twenty years his senior, was the important
style of composition, the delicate feeling for architectural arrangement, raised to greater freedom by the rich and varied life of the
separate figures, and, lastly, a dignified fall of the drapery. The
main excellence, however, in which Andrea stands unique among
his art contemporaries rests in the incomparable blending of
colour, in the soft flesh tints, in the exquisite chiaro oscuro,
in the transparent clearness even of his deepest shadows, and in
his entirely new manner of perfect modelling. Andrea was
astonishingly fruitful in works during a life of no great length,
and, moreover, saddened by a fatal passion ; he executed extensive frescoes, and brought this technical power in them to a
hitherto unexampled perfection of colouring. The number also
of his panel paintings is extremely great ; and although there are
among them some less finished, and even some exhibiting motley
or faded tints, yet the greater number of his genuine works are
of extreme beauty. His sphere, like Fra Bartolommeo's, was
limited to devotional paintings ; yet he does not undertake his
task like the other, impelled by deep religious feeling and grand
views, but rather in the spirit of worldly grace and loveliness.
Occasionally the warmer sympathy of the master is thus missed,
and there is a certain indifference apparent in the constant repetition of the same type of countenance. Sometimes, however,

---

[1] *Denkm. d. Kunst.* Pl. 76 and 79 A. *Andrea del Sarto,* by A. v. Reumont.
Leipzig, 1835.

there is a noble expression of true feeling, and almost always there is a touch of heartiness which attracts the spectator.

Among his frescoes,[1] the three first in the porch of the Compagnia dello Scalzo, at Florence, are the earliest. Executed in grey tint, they depict the Life of John the Baptist, and especially the scene in which John is baptizing the people is full of life and character. In his later life he completed this cycle by adding six pictures, some of them of great value. Between 1511 and 1514, he painted the frescoes in the porch of S. Annunziata, five scenes from the life of St. Philip Benizzi, the Adoration of

Fig. 342. Madonna. By Andrea del Sarto.

the Kings, and the Birth of Mary, not indeed exhibiting high dramatic power, but excellently arranged, full of fresh life, and in finished high colouring. His style and his beauty of colour are exhibited to the utmost in the famous Madonna del Sacco, a fresco in the transept of the same church, of a much later date.[2] The Last Supper, which he executed in the refectory of the monastery of S. Salvi, exhibits equal perfection with the Madonna del Sacco; it is indeed not to be compared with Leonardo's in depth and power, but it is well grouped and is full of lively action.

Of the numerous panel paintings of the master, it is sufficient to mention some of the most important. The Pitti Gallery contains several Madonnas and Holy Families, which exhibit the same simple subject with manifold variety. A Madonna enthroned on clouds, with four saints below, is not one of his most

[1] See the *Pitture a Fresco d'Andrea del Sarto nella compagnia dello Scalzo.* Firenze, 1830.   [2] *Denkm. d. Kunst.* Pl. 79 A. Fig. 1.

expressive paintings, but it is delicate in its tints, and is executed in warm chiaro oscuro. There is an Annunciation, which is painted with more freshness and energy, but it is at the same time harder, and the drapery is too variegated ; another, a smaller Annunciation, where the angel is represented kneeling and the Madonna sitting, is without sufficient expression, though 'light and glowing in colour. One of the most important paintings in the same gallery represents four saints disputing over the Trinity : in the free grand action of the noble figures, in power and softness of execution, and in splendid grouping, this is one of the most perfect of his works. The Tribuna degli Uffizi possesses the famous Madonna di S. Francesco of the year 1517, one of Andrea's principal works. Mary is standing, as a figure of grand freedom, on a pedestal, holding in her arms the Child, who is twining its little arms lovingly round her neck; on the right is S. Francis, on the left is S. John : the expression is noble and full of feeling, and the colouring exhibits wonderful depth and clearness.

Soon after the completion of this painting, in 1518, Andrea received a summons to the court of Francis I. of France, who welcomed him with great honours. Unfortunately the master, so important as an artist, but as a man so weak and character- less, allowed himself soon after to be again allured to Florence, abused the king's confidence in an unjustifiable manner, and was now obliged to spend the rest of his life in his native city, with- out obtaining a larger sphere of activity, depressed by the cir- cumstances he had brought upon himself. That, in spite of these, he could produce so many excellent works (among them the later frescoes before mentioned) tends to increase the fame of his better genius. Of the paintings executed in France, there is a beautiful picture in the Louvre of a Caritas holding a child in her arms, and bending down lovingly to two other children—a work of delightful naïveté and excellent colouring. During the latter years of the artist, in the year 1528, he produced a grand representation of the Madonna enthroned with Saints—a work in which splendid arrangement, figures of lifelike character, and brilliant clearness of colouring, combine to produce a beautiful effect. It is now in the Museum at Berlin.[1] Still later, in 1529, he executed a no less famous picture, in the Dresden Gallery, the Sacrifice of Abraham.

As a colleague and imitator of Andrea, we must mention Marcantonio Franciabigio, who, in competition with him, executed, al fresco, two paintings from the Life of St. John, in the vestibule Dello Scalzo, and the Sposalizio of Mary, in the porch of S. Annunziata, approaching in the latter work the manner of his far more important friend. Among Andrea's pupils, Pontormo appears not unworthy of his master as an able portrait painter, while in his historical paintings he yielded to the influence of Michael Angelo. Other pupils, such as Domenico Puligo and Rosso de' Rossi (1541), who was much engaged in France, fell into a diluted mannerism, and allowed Andrea's beautiful colouring to degenerate into unnatural softness and external effect.

Lastly, we must here also mention Ridolfo Ghirlandajo, the son of Domenico, and the pupil of Fra Bartolommeo, who, in his earlier works (two scenes from the life of St. Zenobius, in the gallery of the Uffizi), exhibited much able effort, but subsequently fell into lifeless mannerism and the old inharmonious want of tone of the earlier Florentine artists.

d. *Raphael and his School.*

If the masters of painting we have hitherto considered emanated from the Florentine school, we have now to turn to another great master of the art, who, in his early development, sprung from the Umbrian school. We allude to Raphael Santi (erroneously Sanzio) d'Urbino, born 1483, died in Rome 1520.[2] The most wonderful thing conspicuous in him is a harmony of all intellectual talents, only rarely found even in the greatest artists, and never seen in similar perfection but in one kindred

---

[1] *Denkm. d. Kunst.* Pl. 76. Fig. 6.
[2] Ibid. Pl. 78 and 79. J. D. Passavant, *Rafael von Urbino.* Leipzig, 1839.

master of another art—namely, Mozart. While in other masters, even the first, one tendency predominates, whether that to energetic characterisation or to the highest expression of the sublime, we find in him every trait of intellectual life combined with incomparable harmony, and the highest expression of this harmony is perfect beauty. But this beauty consists not merely in sensual charms and in fascinating grace, but it is filled with depth of thought, animated by powerful characterisation, and in its creations every feeling of the mind rises nobly and vigorously from loving tenderness to solemn sublimity. It is a noble mind which invests it with its own nobleness.

This moral power is perceived, above all, in Raphael's course of development. As a tender boy he grew up amid artistic work, his father, Giovanni Santi, being himself an estimable painter in Perugino's style. After the early death of his father in 1494, the little Raphael was sent to Perugia, to receive the instruction of the chief master of the Umbrian school. It was of great value for the youthful pupil, that his first bias was given by a school which created works full of heart-sprung feeling, and imparted to them a breath of tender contemplativeness. But that which gradually in Perugino and most others had degenerated into stereotyped and external mannerism, received in the young Raphael a new and genuine life, conceived as it was by his fresh and devout mind. When he had grown up to be an intelligent and vigorous youth, and the school had nothing more to offer him, yearning for higher development, he sought further stimulant at Florence; whither he repaired for a short period in the autumn of 1504, and for a longer residence in 1508. · The cartoons of Leonardo and Michael Angelo, the wonder of the time, attracted him also to enthusiastic study; but at the same time the splendid works of the earlier Florentine art of Masaccio, and above all the artist himself, opened his eye to the whole fulness, variety, and depth of actual life. None the less did he indulge in lively intercourse with contemporaneous artists; and above all it was the noble Fra Bartolommeo, from whom he not only learned a fresher treatment of colour, but also the secret of architectural and yet free grouping. But with all this soft, almost womanly susceptibility of nature, Raphael's greatness lay in a manly power of mind, with which he knew how to blend together these various influences, and, far from all eclecticism, to develope a style peculiar to himself by his innate and lofty gifts.

At this stage he received the summons to Rome, in the year 1508, from the art-loving Pope Julius II., who wished to entrust him with the execution of the most important tasks. Now began the epoch of Raphael's most masterly power, which was evidenced in the most sublime and extensive subjects, and in an almost immeasurable series of splendid works. But even now the master did not remain standing at the point to which he had attained. In the presence of the works of Michael Angelo, in the presence of the remains of antique art, which he studied deeply, the manly ripeness of his mind urged him to new and higher advance, so that each following work became the result of advanced knowledge. No acquisition of the art of the period was disregarded by him; everywhere he knew how to adopt freely essential merits, and even in colour many of his creations vie with those of the Venetians in clearness, depth, and glow. He knew no limits in the whole range of subjects at that time open to art; he is just as important in solemn symbolic representations as in bold historical compositions; just as perfect in the dignified treatment of Christian subjects as in the graceful animation of antique mythology; just as great in portraiture as he is inexhaustibly rich and feeling in true religious painting, above all, in the Madonnas and Holy Families; and in all this extensive creative power, he knows but of one self-imposed limit, and that is beauty. Thus, in a short space of time, he produced imperishable works, remaining in his restless advance ever true, beautiful, and pure, freer than any other master from superficial mannerism, and creating a world of works, edifying to every generation and age, and before the immortal beauty of which all parties are united in common adoration.

Among the works of his early epoch, there are several Madonnas, two of which are in the Museum at Berlin. The earlier is somewhat constrained in form and action, and is somewhat hard in colouring; the later one, however, representing the Madonna

Fig. 343. Raphael's Sposalizio.

between S. Franciscus and S. Hieronymus, is full of graceful feeling, noble action, and has a clear brilliant colouring.[1] Still more delicately finished, but with the same warmth of feeling, is a small circular picture of the Madonna in the Palazzo Conne-

[1] *Denkm. d. Kunst.* Pl. 78. Fig. 2.

stabile at Perugia. There is also a Crowning of the Virgin in the Vatican Collection, still likewise in Perugio's style, but one of the most charming and purest remnants of the Umbrian school.

At the close of this early youthful epoch we may place the famous 'Sposalizio' in the Brera at Milan (Fig. 343), the Marriage of Mary, executed in the year 1504. Combined with perfect clearness and warmth of colouring, there is here a freedom in the arrangement, a lifelike beauty in the figures, a lightness and grace of movement, which far surpass the power of the whole Umbrian school, and speak to us like a voice from Florence. A noble domed building gives a solemn finish to the background.

About this time, Raphael quitted Perugino's school, and the following four years of his residence in Florence mark the epoch of his greatest artistic crisis, in which his Umbrian feeling and beauty were counterbalanced by the Florentine taste for stronger life and characterisation. Under these new ideas, his style rose to nobler freedom and more cheerful freshness. His Madonnas, hitherto almost childlike in their girlishness, became charming virgins, and expressed a vigorous independence in drawing, form, and colour. Among the earliest works which exhibit this change, we may mention the simple and yet touchingly beautiful Madonna del Granduca in the Palazzo Pitti at Florence. Many more extensive works were executed soon after his first shorter residence in Florence. One of these is the excellent painting, still breathing forth the spirit of Fra Bartolommeo, which he painted in Padua for the nuns of S. Antonius, of Padua, and which is now in the royal palace at Naples. It represents the Madonna enthroned with St. Peter, St. Catharine, St. Paul, and St. Rosalia; at the foot of the throne the little St. John is approaching, full of eagerness to testify his adoration of the infant Christ. The latter raises His little hand as if in blessing, and the mother is drawing the Child lovingly to her. A splendid enthroned Madonna of the year 1505, with the grand figures of John the Baptist and St. Nicolas of Bari, is now at Blenheim, and was originally painted for the church of the Servi at Perugia. In the year 1505, Raphael executed his first independent fresco, also at Perugia, in the church of S. Severo. It represents Christ in Glory, enthroned between two hovering angels; over Him is the dove of the Holy Spirit and God the Father in clouds; below Him, on both sides, there are three splendid figures of saints, likewise sitting on clouds. The spirit of Florentine art is here also combined with Umbrian beauty and sweetness, and the grand structure of the whole may be regarded as an imitation of Fra Bartolommeo's fresco in S. Maria Nuova.[1]

The second longer residence in Florence induced Raphael more definitely to follow the style of Florentine art, and the works of this period exhibit a gradually increasing abandonment of his former manner. In the early part of this epoch, he produced the Madonna of the Tempi family, now in the Pinakothek at Munich.[2] She is represented standing, and pressing the Child to her heart with tender warmth. Next followed three representations of the Madonna, all of a similar character, depicting her as sitting in a bright landscape, watching the graceful play of her Child with the little St. John. The idea is exhibited with some constraint in the Madonna with the Bird, in the Tribuna degli Uffizi; it is more free and unconstrained in the 'Madonna im Grünen,' in the Belvedere at Vienna; and with perfect grace is the same idea depicted in the 'Belle Jardinière,' in the Museum of the Louvre. Still further did Raphael carry out this idea in a picture of the Holy Family, in the Pinakothek at Munich, in which Elizabeth and Mary, kneeling together, are delighting in the naïve doings of the children; and Joseph completes the group, which is strictly pyramidal in its arrangement, though full of noble freedom. To the same period also belongs the St. Catharine, now in the National Gallery in London; it is one of his most charming figures, similar in treatment and expression to the 'Belle Jardinière' in the Louvre, but

---

[1] Well engraved by J. Keller.   [2] *Denkm. d. Kunst.* Pl. 78. Fig. 2.

in colouring somewhat warmer and more atmospheric.   At the end of this epoch he painted the ' Madonna del Baldacchino,' in the Pitti Gallery at Florence, which remained unfinished; and in the year 1507 the famous Entombment, now in the Palazzo Borghese in Rome.   This picture, which is the first work in which Raphael attempted to depict a dramatic incident, shows the wonderfully rapidly developed power of the artist of twenty-four years of age, though both in expression and action there is still a want of perfect freedom.

About the middle of the year 1508, Raphael received that honourable summons to the court of Julius II., in order to undertake there one of the grandest tasks which could have been assigned to the art of that day.   This task was to adorn the splendid apartments of the Vatican with paintings in which the spiritual power of the Papacy was to be glorified.   Under Raphael's hand these paintings became the highest expression of the whole knowledge and of the profoundest ideas of the period ; and at the same time they were the fulfilment, as it were, of that which monumental painting in Italy had striven after, and had pursued in uninterrupted advance since the time of Giotto.   Three apartments (stanze) of the Vatican and a great hall were covered with these works on their walls and vaulted ceilings, and consequently they bear the name of the ' Raphael Stanze.'

The paintings begin in the Camera della Segnatura with the representations of Theology, Poetry, Philosophy, and Jurisprudence, forming the sum of the ideas of intellectual power at that day.   Theology is depicted in the so-called Disputa.[1]   We see above the glory of the triumphant Church, Christ in the centre, enthroned on clouds, and with an expression of divine mildness and mercy ; by His side are the humbly interceding Madonna and John the Baptist, who is pointing to Him as the Redeemer of the world ; below is the dove of the Holy Spirit ; and above all is God the Father in a glory of angels.   On both sides, seated on clouds, are splendid figures of the glorified, ex-

---

[1] Recently engraved in a masterly manner by Joseph Keller.

hibiting perfect beauty and freedom.   The whole upper part is
the highest development of the work already executed in S.
Severo at Perugia.   Below, on the ground, there are a number
of Fathers of the Church, bishops, and teachers, grouped on
both sides of an altar containing the monstrance with the consecrated host.   Here, with incomparable power and depth of characterisation, we find lively action, enthusiastic belief, and profound investigation, fervent devotion, dispute, and doubt.   The
picture stands at the head of all religious symbolic painting, and
yet at the same time it is full of true life and enchanting beauty.
The execution exhibits careful finish even in the smallest details ;
the colouring is charming, clear, and fresh.

No less splendidly, on the opposite wall, does the school of
Athens embody the grandeur of antique intellectual life.[1]   Plato
and Aristotle—figures of the most delicate characterisation—
form, in the centre of a lofty hall, the most splendid contrasts as
regards idea and painting.   The other philosophers of antiquity
are gathered round them in free and animated groups—by
lively interest, eager dispute, proof, doubting or believing attention, a marvellous world of distinguished men exhibit various
degrees of character, age, and temperament.   Here, also, the
execution exhibits the utmost finish, although general effect
seems more aimed at.

The third painting, the Parnassus, presents the cheerful
picture of a highly poetic existence, and depicts Apollo playing
the lyre with charming naïveté, enthroned in youthful grace
between the noble figures of the Muses and the famous poets of
ancient and modern times.   The insertion of the window in the
picture is here admirably taken advantage of for the composition, so that a new beauty is obtained from the apparent inter-
ference.

On the opposite wall Jurisprudence is represented in two
pictures, which are likewise rich in beauties.   The allegorical
and smaller historical scenes of the vaults also contain many
excellences.

[1] *Denkm. d. Kunst.* Pl. 79. Fig. 1.

In the year 1511 these works were finished, and in the fol
lowing year Raphael began the paintings in the Stanza d' Elio-
doro. Here he depicted the Divine protection and assistance
which accompany the Church, with various references to existing events. The mode of representation therefore abandoned
the calm tone of the symbolical compositions: it exhibited
vigorous action, breathed the utmost dramatic life, and at the
same time showed greater energy and boldness in the forms and
colouring. Probably Michael Angelo's ceiling paintings in the
Sistine Chapel exercised considerable influence over these works.
The first painting was Heliodorus expelled by avenging Angels
from the Temple which he intended to plunder. The terror of
the sacrilegious plunderer, the grand anger of the gold-glittering
horseman, and the fear of the spectators, are depicted with such
power of expression that the work stands as one of the highest
productions of dramatic historic art. And with what majesty
and repose is this stormy scene counterbalanced by the group of
the advancing Pope! We scarcely consider the anachronism; it
seems cancelled by the simple grandeur and truth of the representation. Still more distinctly and admirably is this blending
of different periods effected in the Mass of Bolsena, which is
executed on the wall of the window, and which, like the other
painting, is rich in portraits of importance, and at the same time
affords a new proof of the playful ease with which Raphael knew
how to overcome the difficulties of space.

In these works, which were completed by 1512, the hand of
Raphael's pupils is already perceptible in their execution. When
Julius II. now died, and Leo X. succeeded him in the Pontificate,
so many tasks were heaped upon the master that he was compelled to allow his pupils to take greater part in his future
frescoes, and at length only superintended their execution after
his own cartoons. Thus, for instance, in the same room, the
Deliverance of Peter was executed on the wall of the second
window, also one of the most perfect historical compositions, and
admirable, moreover, from its excellent chiaro oscuro, which imparts an especially characteristic tone to the incident. This was

followed by the painting of Attila, deterred from an Attack on Rome by the Appearance of the Apostles St. Peter and St. Paul; likewise a scene of passionate excitement, contrasted in a masterly manner with the sublime repose of the heavenly figures, and the calm dignity of the Pope and his suite. Yet we must bear in mind that this somewhat indifferent bearing (equally so as in Heliodorus), although artistically legitimate and used with wisdom, is perhaps a remnant, not yet wholly overcome, of the manner of the fifteenth century. The ceiling paintings contain scenes from the Old Testament, and exhibit much dignity of composition.

The Stanza dell' Incendio, begun about 1515, contains in the first place the representation of a Fire in the Borgo, which was extinguished through the intercession of the Pope. This scene is placed in the background, where the Pope appears on the balcony of the old church of St. Peter. But his relation to the scene is beautifully explained by the women imploring assistance; and the foreground is filled with groups of people seeking safety and flight. In these for the most part naked figures, which are represented full of effort and terror, we can undoubtedly trace the influence of Michael Angelo. In the execution they are not free from hardness.

The three other wall paintings in the same room are of a less important kind : the Victory over the Saracens at Ostia, the Oath of Leo III., and the Coronation of Charlemagne. On the other hand, the Sala di Costantino contains one of Raphael's finest compositions—a work, indeed, which was only executed after his death by Giulio Romano—namely, the Battle of Constantine, in which Maxentius was conquered at the Flaminian Bridge, near Rome. The scene is extremely rich, and full of magnificent figures and various incidents belonging to the battle; yet the great master understood how to give conspicuous prominence to the principal figures, and thus to create the most perfect battle-piece of modern art.

A second extensive work were the ten cartoons for tapestries, which Raphael designed, between 1513 and 1514, by order of

Leo X. The tapestries were woven at Arras in Flanders after his drawings, and were intended for the walls of the Sistine Chapel. Seven of these cartoons are still to be seen at Hampton Court. The tapestries themselves are in the Vatican Gallery. They depict the most important points in the history of the Apostles, with such grandeur and majesty of conception that they are among the most perfect of the master's creations, and exhibit him to us once more at the height of historical dramatic

Fig. 344. The Punishment of Elymas the Sorcerer. From Raphael's Cartoons.

representation. Peter's Miraculous Draught of Fishes begins the series, and is full of cheerful life and action. The Consigning of the Keys is noble and expressive; the Curing of the Lame Man is rich in ingenuity and arrangement; the Death of Ananias is a picture full of thrilling tragic power;[1] and the Stoning of Stephen is full of beautiful expressiveness. In the Conversion of St. Paul, the miraculous nature of the event is splendidly depicted; in the Punishment of the sorcerer Elymas (Fig. 344), who is struck with blindness, a fearful and sudden

[1] *Denkm. d. Kunst.* Pl. 79. Fig. 3.

terror is depicted in the same thrilling manner as in the Death
of Ananias. The Preaching of St. Paul at Athens and at Lystra
are works of great beauty, and the series is concluded by Paul
a Prisoner at Philippi. (There are copies of these tapestries in
the Museums of Berlin and Dresden.)

A second series of tapestries, twelve in number, and likewise
to be found in the Vatican, seem, like the others, to have been
partially executed from Raphael's designs, and contain some
beautiful compositions.

At the same time, by order of Leo X., Raphael conducted
the decoration of the Loggie, in the court of the Vatican, which
had been begun by Bramante. In the compartments of the
vaulting he made his pupils execute that series of scenes from
the Old, and occasionally from the New Testament, which are
known under the name of 'Raphael's Bible.' Although somewhat hard and variegated in colouring, in the style of Giulio
Romano and his other pupils, they exhibit the genuine beauty of
Raphael, in that simple patriarchal dignity and grace which
speak to us from the stories of the Old Testament. In the
scenes of the Creation we perceive the somewhat softened influence of Michael Angelo. On the walls and pilasters (Fig. 345),
the master introduced the most charming ornaments, executed
after his own designs by Giovanni da Udine, who was especially
skilful in these delineations, and in their charming variety and
cheerful colouring the utmost splendour of antique art was
revived with increased richness. Even in the present sad state
of destruction, these halls are among the most attractive works
that modern art has produced.

While Raphael required the assistance of his pupils in these
extensive works, he himself painted the colossal figure of the
Prophet Isaiah, in the year 1512, in the church of S. Agostino,
a work in which he paid his tribute to Michael Angelo's powerful style, to the disadvantage of his own. On the other hand,
two years later, in 1514, he produced, entirely in his own style,
in the little church of S. Maria della Pace, a wall painting representing four Sibyls with Angels; a work full of enchanting

beauty, splendidly arranged within the space, and displaying a
colouring, power, and distinctness unsurpassed in fresco painting.   The designs for the dome paintings of the Capella Chigi
in S. Maria del Popolo were also prepared by Raphael about
this period.

In the frescoes of the Farnesina, in which he painted the
Triumph of Galatea,[1] in the year 1514, the inexhaustible master

Fig. 345.　Raphael's Decorations.　From the Loggie of the Vatican.

entered the mythological world of the ancients.   Drawn by dol-
phins, the goddess hovers over the flood in her sea-shell, surrounded by Nereids and Tritons, while charming Cupids hover
in the air, shooting down their arrows.   Laughing, exulting
happiness and bright beautiful life pervade the figures, fill the
sea and the air, and speak to us in the warm and tender colouring, and in the delicate and graceful delineation.   In 1518,
Raphael executed, with his pupils, on the ceiling of a hall in the

[1] *Denkm. d. Kunst.*　Pl. 78.　Fig. 8.

same villa, the History of Psyche.[1] On the even surface of the vault he painted two scenes rich in figures—the one representing the Judgment of the Gods, and the other the Marriage of Cupid and Psyche.   In the calottes, Cupid appears again in unsurpassably wanton grace and variety, with the attributes of the different gods. The pendentives contain separate scenes of the same story, incomparably composed within the space, and full of beautiful action and lively expression. (Fig. 346.)   Although some-

Fig. 346. Soaring Psyche. By Raphael.

what coarse in execution, these charming paintings still testify of the purity, freedom, and beauty of soul which pervade all that Raphael has created.

With all these important and vast monumental works, the activity of this wonderful mind was by no means exhausted. Besides all these, besides his architectural productions, besides the building of St. Peter's and his researches in antique Rome, he still found time to execute a number of easel paintings, Madonnas, Holy

[1] Etched by F. Schubert. Munich. Fol.

Families, larger altar paintings, and even portraits, about forty of which may be enumerated as belonging to this epoch of the master's life. We will limit ourselves to the most important.

Above all, we must mention the Madonnas and Holy Families, in which Raphael has infused his full soul, and has raised the originally mere ecclesiastical theme to the highest human perfection and freedom. Although Raphael was never married, yet no master has ever glorified with such devotion as he has done the happiness of family life. About fifty Madonnas may be pointed out as his production, since from his earliest youth to the last day of his life he ever anew treated this favourite subject; but he ever knew how to vary this simplest and purely human theme of maternal love, so that these works alone plainly enough reflect his course of development. His Madonnas advance from childlike constraint to graceful maidenliness, and pass from thence, in his maturer works, to the expression of grandly free and true motherly dignity, which is consecrated by a mysterious charm of innocence and purity. Thus these pictures are the most attractive human delineations of simple hearty family life, and yet, without halo or golden ground, they are more divine than all former Madonnas. Among the most splendid works of this kind belonging to his early years in Rome, there is a ' Madonna of Duke Alba,' now in the Hermitage at St. Petersburg, a circular picture, representing the Virgin sitting in a cheerful landscape, looking at the play of the two children. There is also the ' Vierge au Diadême ' (likewise called Vierge au Linge), in the Museum at Paris. Full of sweetness, Mary is depicted as raising the veil from the sleeping infant Jesus, in order to show Him the little St. John. Another circular picture, exhibiting exquisite beauty of composition, is the famous Madonna della Sedia, in the Pitti Gallery at Florence, which was executed about the year 1516, and in clearness and warmth of colouring, and in the ripe though tender beauty of the Madonna, shows great affinity with the Sibyls in S. Maria della Pace. More simple, but similar in action, is the Madonna della Tenda, in the Pinakothek at Munich. Extreme grace also marks the circular painting of the Vierge aux Candelabres, now in England, and the Madonna del Passeggio, in the Bridgewater Gallery : both of these, however, belong to the master's later period, and were only partially executed by himself.

This range of thought is extended in the Holy Families, and is more richly executed in them. Here, too, Raphael is inexhaustible in new and splendid ideas, and shows himself the first master of all ages in nobleness of conception, in beauty of lines,

Fig. 347. Madonna della Sedia. By Raphael.

and in perfect rhythm of composition. The Madonna dell' Impannata, in the Pitti Palace at Florence, is among his noblest works as regards design, though the execution betrays less evidence of his hand. Another grandly finished composition is the so-called ' Perle,' in the Museum at Madrid, where there is also another and a still richer Holy Family, under the name of the ' Madonna della Lucertola' (with the lizard), or the ' Madonna under the Oak.' Of a similar character, but still more magnificent, free, and full of life, is the Madonna of Francis I. in the Louvre, which Raphael painted for the King of France in 1518.[1]

[1] *Denkm. d. Kunst.* Pl. 78. Fig. 6.

The 'Rest after the Flight to Egypt,' in the Belvedere at Vienna, is a picture full of cheerful and happy peace. In all these larger compositions of his later period, Raphael placed the execution for the most part in the hand of his pupils, even in the case of the Madonna of Francis I.

Lastly, belonging to this epoch of the master's works, there are three great Madonna pictures, which, as altar-pieces or devotional pieces, had a special place to fill, and required a more solemn conception. Here, also, Raphael reached a point unattained both before and after him. The Madonna enthroned as the Queen of Heaven is surrounded by hovering angels; some figures of distinguished saints are also added. Raphael has repressed all superfluous richness, and has transformed the choirs of angels into an aureole of lovely heads; but in the few principal figures he has reached a dignity and sublimity which are combined, notwithstanding, with the freest action and the most graceful characteristics. The earliest of these works, executed about 1511, is the Madonna di Fuligno, now in the Vatican Gallery. Floating on clouds is the magnificent figure of the Madonna, who, full of hearty maternal love, is devoting her attention to the holy Child. Below, there are St. Franciscus, John the Baptist, and S. Hieronymus, who is bringing forward the kneeling donator of the picture. Between is a graceful angel with an inscription tablet. Higher in composition and in the harmony of its internal relations is the Madonna del Pesce, in the Museum at Madrid, painted, about 1513, for the church of S. Domenico at Naples. Here the enthroned mother of God is depicted turning graciously to the young Tobias, who is kneeling shyly at her feet offering a fish, and who is introduced by a beautiful angel; while on the other side the venerable Hieronymus is reading from a book. The painting was originally intended for a chapel in which prayers were offered for the curing of eye diseases: hence the figure of Tobias was justifiable, and the gracious expression of the Madonna received especial significance. The most glorious delineation was, however, reached by Raphael in the world-famed Sistine Madonna,[1] which was painted, about the year 1518, for the church of S. Sisto in Piacenza, and is now the celebrated masterpiece of the Dresden Gallery. Who does not know this wondrous figure, which, veiled by magnificent drapery, floats on the clouds like a heavenly apparition, surrounded by a glory of lovely angel-heads? A veil flows down from her head, which seems as if lost in thought, reflecting on the divine Mystery which her arms embrace with maternal fervour; for enthroned in her arms in calm majesty is a Boy, in whose childlike features is stamped the sublimity of His mission, and whose eyes with their power and depth allow us to forebode His vocation as Redeemer of the world. Pope Sixtus is looking up with reverence, forming by his grand dignified appearance a splendid contrast to St. Barbara, who, opposite to him, bows her graceful head with humble gesture, and casts her eye downwards at the majesty before her. Lastly, the groundwork is finished by two enchanting boy angels resting on the lower breastwork. It is as if Raphael had wished to combine in this incomparable creation his deepest thoughts, his most sublime ideas, and his most perfect beauty, that it might be and might remain the highest production of all religious art. His Madonnas, and the Sistine Madonna especially, are not created for any definite epoch or for any special religious views; they live for all times and for all nations, because they reveal an eternal truth in a form eternally acceptable.

Other important paintings of a religious purport must yet be added. In the first place there was the small miniature-like and clever representation of the Vision of Ezekiel, in the Pitti Gallery at Florence, which, in its grand and bold conception, betrayed Michael Angelo's influence. There was the St. Cecilia, in the Pinakothek at Bologna, which was completed in 1516, and which made so overwhelming an impression on the old Francesco Francia; there was the painting of St. Michael, now in the Louvre, which was executed in the following year, and is

---

[1] *Denkm. d. Kunst.* Pl. 78. Fig. 7.

full of expression and bold action ; there was the painting of
S. Margaretha as Vanquisher of the Dragon, in the same place ;
and the same subject, conceived more boldly, in the Belvedere
Gallery at Vienna. There was also the youthful and spirited
figure of St. John in the Desert, in the Tribuna degli Uffizi,
many good old copies of which exist elsewhere. Lastly, the
highest importance belongs to two great altar-pieces, in which a
dramatic incident is depicted instead of the calm condition delineated in most of the other works. The one is the Bearing
of the Cross, known under the name of Lo Spasimo di Sicilia,
because it was painted for the monastery Dello Spasmo at
Palermo : it is now in the Museum at Madrid. Belonging to
the master's maturest period (between 1516 and 1518), this work
exhibits a composition full of thought, combined with perfect
power in the expression of passionately excited feelings. The
height of dramatic greatness and powerful composition was,
however, reached by Raphael's last work, which remained unfinished at his death—namely, the Transfiguration of Christ on
Mount Tabor, now the most costly jewel of the Vatican Collection. (Fig. 348.) With wonderful profoundness, the master in
this painting combines two wholly separate incidents, representing above a gleam of the blessedness of Paradise in the
majestic soaring figures of Christ, Moses, and Elias ; and depicting at the same time below, in striking contrast, in the passionately excited groups gathered around the possessed boy, the
sorrow and distress of earthly life. But while he opens heaven
to us, and reveals to us the everlasting majesty of Christ, he
casts a divine ray of consolation on the night of struggling
earthly existence, and resolves its doubts into blessed trustful
certainty.

In conclusion, we have yet to mention that Raphael also
belonged to the greatest portrait painters of all ages, and that his
portraits combine a truly historical conception of important points
with the most delicate shades of characterisation, and a clearness
and warmth of colouring, often reminding of the Venetian school.
The Pitti Gallery at Florence is especially rich in such works.

The portraits of Angelo Doni and his wife, painted about 1505, previous to his Roman period, still bear traces of constraint; the portrait, on the other hand, of Pope Julius II. exhibits maturity of finish and cleverness of conception. There is also in the same place the portrait of Pope Leo X., with the cardinals

Fig. 348. Transfiguration of Christ. By Raphael.

Giulio de' Medici and De' Rossi, that of Cardinal Bibbiena, his friend and patron, and of Fedra Inghirami. There are also many excellent works in Rome—for instance, the youthful and charming violin player of the year 1518, in the Pal. Sciarra;

an excellent double portrait of two men in the Pal. Doria; and the so-called Fornarina in the Pal. Barberini, often repeated, but to our taste the only Raphael work which shows no nobleness of conception. The Museum at Paris contains the extolled but somewhat cold Johanna of Aragon, also the distinguished portrait of Count Castiglione. Lastly, in the Pinakothek at Munich, there is a charming youthful half-length portrait of Bindo Altoviti, which was formerly regarded as Raphael's own likeness.

Thus Raphael in his short life of thirty-seven years, full of creative power and energy, traversed and exhausted the whole mental range of his time, and revealed, in an almost countless number of splendid works, that highest idea of the beautiful, which, as he himself said, ever floated before him. At the same time, more than any other artist he remained true to his genius, unweariedly endeavouring to rise still higher in the grandest tasks, but also to invest the seemingly insignificant and accidental elements of his work with the enduring stamp of beauty and inward nobleness. When he died, Rome seemed desolate to his contemporaries, and painting bereft of its parent. Round his catafalco, where his last and yet unfinished work, the Transfiguration, was placed as his noblest monument, all classes, ages, and generations were gathered together, to pay by their common sorrow the last tribute of respect to the famous artist as well as to the great man.

Raphael's style soon became the common property of the Roman artists; and as the master, from the multitude of his orders, had needed assistance in his frescoes, as well as in many of his panel pictures, most of the painters at that time in Rome, both native and foreign, were connected with him.[1] So long as he himself was living, his mind inspired them in their works, and his just ideas of beauty were diffused over them like a precious

---

[1] *Denkm. d. Kunst.* Pl. 79 A.

remnant of his own creations; after his death, however, the more important and able of these artists soon fell into a certain want of moderation, while the less gifted degraded his style into a lifeless unpleasing mannerism, and even in colouring could no longer attain to his softness, repose, and harmony. To the first of these two classes belongs Giulio Romano, whose real name was Pippi, one of the few artists whom Rome herself has produced (1492–1546). As Raphael's most talented pupil, he had the greatest share in the execution of the larger works of his master; as, for instance, in the Battle of Constantine, which was very ably painted by him, although somewhat hard and coarse. Among his independent works at this epoch are the mythological frescoes in Villa Lante and Villa Madama; also some

Fig. 349. Amphitrite, from the Villa Lante. By Giulio Romano.

excellent altar-pieces, such as the painting of the enthroned Madonna in S. Maria dell' Anima, a smaller Madonna in the sacristy of St. Peter at Rome, a Madonna on the point of washing the infant Christ, now in the Gallery at Dresden, and the Sufferings of St. Stephen in S. Stefano at Genoa. Four years after Raphael's death, Giulio was summoned to Mantua by Francesco Gonzaga, and important works were entrusted to him; but in these he increasingly yielded to a coarser taste, which led him in his delineations to violent action, exaggerated forms, and a rude and even common conception. In the frescoes in the Ducal Palace, representing the story of Diana and scenes from the Trojan war, he still exhibits a more moderate style ; but, on the other hand, in the extensive frescoes of the Palazzo del Te, especially in the Overthrow of the Giants, and the story of Psyche, he oversteps more and more all nobler moderation. Though not without power and richness of invention, he contributed more than any other, by this unbridled style, to the desecration of art. The coloured sketches for these works, which may be seen in the Villa Albani at Rome, belong, on the contrary, to the most perfect and splendid things of their kind. Francesco Primaticcio, who directed the decoration of the palace of Fontainebleau for Francis I., may be mentioned as a follower of his style.

Among the less important artists, we must mention Francesco Penni, surnamed Il Fattore, who took great part in the execution of Raphael's works, but has himself produced scarcely anything worthy of mention ; Andrea Sabbatini of Salerno, an attractive artist, many works by whom are to be found in the churches and the Museum at Naples ; Polidoro da Caravaggio, rightly Caldara, who painted many able frescoes in grey on the outer walls of many Roman palaces ; and Perino del Vaga, whose real name was Buonaccorsi of Florence, who transplanted Raphael's style to Genoa, where he adorned the palace of Andrea Doria with frescoes. His influence may be traced upon Luca Cambiaso, who was painting in Genoa, an artist of great truth and sound feeling in the midst of a period wholly sunk into mannerism.

From other schools also many artists adopted Raphael's style. This was the case, for instance, with a gifted pupil of Francia, Bartolommeo Ramenghi, surnamed Bagnacavallo, who executed a grand altar-piece of the Virgin enthroned on Clouds and surrounded with Saints, now in the Dresden Museum ; also the graceful Timoteo della Vite, who had belonged to the same school. There were also some Ferrarese, among them the fertile Benvenuto Garofalo, whose real name was Tisio, many paintings by whom are in the galleries of Italy and other countries; and the gifted Dosso Dossi, who is distinguished by the splendid colouring and the poetic charm of his works.

e. *Correggio and his School.*

In decided contrast to all former artists, and yet one of the most distinguished, and indeed a bold conqueror in the field of art, appears Antonio Allegri da Correggio (1494–1534).[1] Formed in the schools of Upper Italy, he was probably trained by a Lombard artist, Francesco Bianchi Ferrari, and by the influence of Mantegna's school, and subsequently received considerable stimulant from Leonardo's works. The sweet grace that appeared in that great master, though with him fettered by strict limits, and which formed its expression in a tender blending of colour, acquired in Correggio its consistent though regardless development. Even as a youthful painter he must have possessed an unusual susceptibility of feeling, for he is one of the most precocious artists that the history of art can produce. Gifted with an intense capacity of feeling, and with nervous excitability, he aimed in his works at manifesting this side of the inner life; he bathes his figures in a sea of joy and rapture, fills them with intoxicating mirth and delight, and gives even to the feelings of pain a partly sweet and partly sorrowful expression. He scarcely knows what is grandeur, seriousness, and nobleness of form, just architectural rhythm, and delicate balance of lines. He only desires to represent his figures in the lively expression of passion, full of inward excitement and in restless outward action; and, in order to do this, he bursts asunder all traditionary rules, and overleaps both the laws of religious conception and artistic custom. When we see his figures, we readily perceive that they have another home than that of other great masters. His Madonnas and his Magdalenes exhibit the same genre-like

---

[1] *Denkm. d. Kunst.* Pl. 75.

form of countenance, the same moist swimming, tenderly longing glance, the small nose, and the pretty and everlastingly smiling mouth as his Danaë, Leda, or Io. He delights in depicting the joy of passionate devotion, but the expression is the same whether he is painting heavenly or earthly love. How enchantingly he knows how to depict the charm of the latter, how he makes the soft undulating limbs vibrate with intoxicating rapture, how, with rare exceptions, his feeling ever remains pure and true! and for this reason he does not in his own mind degrade even his sacred figures, when he stamps them as partakers of the same feelings. He transports all into the state of paradisiacal innocence, and–in this lies the justice of his representations.

His true mode of expression is, however, light, as, in soft blending with twilight, it is interwoven with delicate reflections and transparent shadows, as it plays around the figures, and, like an electric fluid, pervades the atmosphere, as it were, with the breath of sweet feeling. In the execution of this chiaro oscuro, with its lightest gradations and shades, Correggio is one of the first masters of painting. He discovered and brought to wonderful perfection this new medium, by which his figures, half-veiled and half revealed, appear all the more charming and captivating. To him it is the true means by which he renders his art effective. To it he sacrifices higher style, nobler drawing, worthier arrangement; from delight in it, he loses himself in faulty outline, in general characterisation degenerating even into coquetry, and into a mode of composition, in which the effect of colour is everything, in which every ideal qualification is completely repressed, and unlimited use is made of all conceivable foreshortenings.

His earliest work, belonging to the twentieth year of the artist's life (1514), is the great altar-piece of the enthroned Madonna with St. Francis and St. Anthony, John the Baptist and St. Catharine, in the Dresden Gallery. There is still some constraint apparent, but in expression and characterisation it reminds of Leonardo, and the colouring is soft and well blended.

The attractive picture of the Rest after the Flight into Egypt, in the Tribuna degli Uffizi, belongs likewise to his earlier period, and is a graceful idyll, beautifully finished as regards colouring, and still free from all his subsequent mannerism of expression. The Madonna, in the same place, represented as adoring the Child lying before her, is also among his most graceful and most purely conceived works, exhibiting splendid tints in chiaro oscuro : the Madonna indeed is deficient in ideal conception, but full of sweet maternal love.

With the year 1518, a turning point occurred in Correggio's life, which was destined to lead him to perfection in his art. He was summoned to Parma, in order to execute a number of highly important and extensive frescoes. At first he was engaged in decorating a hall in the convent of S. Paolo.[1] The subject of these representations affords a striking evidence of the thoroughly worldly and brilliant life in the ecclesiastical institutions of that day. They are scenes of antique mythology, stories of Diana, and other smaller paintings, which he here executed, and in which he displayed the brightest charm and the sweetest grace of his style. Peculiarly gracefully is the vault painted as a vine arbour, and through the oval openings of which roguish genii are looking in, full of charming naïveté. Two years afterwards, Correggio received the far more important commission to paint the dome vault of S. Giovanni, as well as the altar apsis.[2] Very little is preserved of the frescoes of the former, as it was subsequently pulled down : the paintings of the dome still exist uninjured. In the centre is Christ hovering above in glory ; below Him are the figures of the Apostles seated on clouds, looking up to Him adoringly ; and still further below, in the triangular spaces, are the four Evangelists, and the four Fathers of the Church, likewise on clouds. The figures are full of grand power ; but the artist has set aside every remembrance of an architectural background, and allowed us to gaze into apparently boundless ether. At the same time, he subjects his

[1] *Denkm. d. Kunst.* Pl. 75. Figs. 8-10. [2] Ibid. Fig. 4.

figures to all the consequences arising from a background, foreshortens them therefore for a definite point of view, by which all nobler development of the body and all higher expression is completely lost. Mantegna had already in Mantua applied perspective rules in a similar manner, but only in a small space and in subjects of a roguish and cheerful style. Melozzo da Forli was the first who had introduced this principle in serious religious representations, in his paintings in SS. Apostoli in Rome. Correggio, however, knew no limits to it; and while he thus adapted it to a lofty dome, a foreshortening of the figures was necessary, which sacrificed the upper nobler parts at the expense of the lower. Without moderation he yielded to this delight in a thoroughly new mode of representation in the dome frescoes

Fig. 350. Madonna della Scodella. Correggio.

of the cathedral at Parma, executed between 1526 and 1530, and depicting the Ascension of the Virgin.[1] Here also the triangular spaces were filled with large figures of saints, the patron saints of the city, accompanied by angels and genii. Above them, between the windows of the dome, stand the Apostles, looking upwards with rapture towards the Madonna, who is being borne above by a band of rejoicing angels. Soaring in heavenly glory, Christ appears advancing to receive her. The boundless undulation of figures, in all conceivable foreshorten-

[1] *Denkm. d. Kunst.* Pl. 75. Fig. 5.

ings, is like a sea of joy and blessedness. Scarcely anything is to be seen of the figures but the legs and lower parts; the upper part of the body and the countenance are so strongly foreshortened, that even at that day the sharp wit was current that Correggio had painted a ragoût of frogs. Notwithstanding, the success of his innovation was immense among his admiring contemporaries; and henceforth through two centuries this mode of representation prevailed, unworthy as it was of both place and subject.

Besides these works, various excellent easel pictures were produced in this epoch of masterly power. There are many works of this kind in the Museum at Parma, among others the ' Madonna della Scodella,' a further development of that earlier picture of the Rest during the Flight into Egypt. (Fig. 350.) The painting of S. Hieronymus,[1] or rather of the enthroned Madonna with S. Hieronymus, a beautiful Angel, and Mary Magdalene, is so filled with magic light that it is also frequently designated as 'the Day.' The Descent from the Cross exhibits a touching expression of pain; while, on the other hand, the equally well-painted picture of the Sufferings of S. Placidus and S. Flavia produces a repulsive effect, as one of the earliest torture pictures of modern times. We have yet to mention the fresco painting of a Madonna and Child, which forms one of the noblest and grandest of Correggio's conceptions. He frequently represented with naïve grace the Marriage of Christ with St. Catharine, conceiving the subject thoroughly as a charming child's play. The most excellent of these representations is in the Louvre; one somewhat altered is in the Museum at Naples, where there is also a Rest on the Flight to Egypt, designated as the ' Zingarella.'[2] The Madonna, full of hearty maternal feeling, wears a turban-like headdress, and charming angels are hovering in the air.

Many very important works by him are in the Dresden Gallery. Thus, there is a small and extremely tenderly executed

---

[1] *Denkm. d. Kunst.* Pl. 75. Fig. 2.   [2] Ibid. Fig. 3.

picture of S. Magdalena (Fig. 351), in which, indeed, there is nothing of the expression of a repentant sinner, but only a very beautiful woman, who, while the dreamy twilight of the wood is playing round her, is lying on the luxuriant turf absorbed in a book. There are also some larger altar-pieces, which represent the enthroned Madonna surrounded by Saints, and which betray all the perfection, but also the weaknesses of the master; for the expression of Mary here verges on the wilful and the amorous, and the saints look towards her with a fervour which scarcely belongs to a religious painting. The same style is ex-

Fig. 351. Magdalene. By Correggio.

hibited in the 'S. Sebastian,' and still more in the 'S. George,' in which these saints profane the effect still more by a somewhat tender physical beauty, coquettishly displayed. One of the most famous pictures in the same gallery is 'the Holy Night,' the birth of the infant Christ, who is worshipped by the assembled shepherds, and by beautiful angels in the air above. The light streams out from the Child, and with a wonderful charm encircles the happy mother, who is bending over the new-born Babe, and dazzles the shepherds and shepherdesses, whose features betray naïve astonishment. As a work of the same kind, we must also mention a grand Ecce Homo, executed at a somewhat earlier and stricter period, and now in the National Gallery in London, where there is also a charming small picture of the Holy Family.

Lastly, there is a series of pictures existing in which Correggio treated scenes from ancient mythology. In these works his style is more in harmony with the subjects depicted than in his religious paintings. All that in them diverted from the sanctity of the incident, and mingled with it a doubtful element— the joyous expression of the heads, the captivating prominence of physical charms—here accords perfectly with the subject, and allows the master to display with exquisite grace some of his happiest inspirations. To these belongs the charming picture of the Training of Cupid by Venus and Mercury, in the London National Gallery; also Ganymede carried away by the Eagle, in the Belvedere at Vienna; above all, however, several pictures in which Correggio has ventured to depict the utmost rapture of love without becoming low or ignoble. The two most famous of these works are in the Berlin Museum, and in the Belvedere at Vienna. Leda with the Swan (Berlin), in a charming wooded landscape, accompanied by her bathing companions, is undoubtedly the most fascinating and innocent of these pictures.[1] But the highest expression of loving desire is reached in the painting of Jupiter in a Cloud embracing Io, a work of mighty power and wonderful perfection. The finest copy is in the Belvedere at Vienna: there is a lesser one at Berlin. On the other hand, the picture in the Louvre of Jupiter and Antiope borders on voluptuousness; and the Danaë in the Borghese Palace in Rome, exquisitely as it is painted, exhibits in expression and attitude a touch of commonness; while Cupid catching the Golden Rain is extremely graceful, and two little genii engaged in whetting a golden arrow are full of fascinating naïveté. Lastly, the Dresden Gallery possesses a masterly male portrait, said to represent the painter's physician.

---

[1] *Denkm. d. Kunst.* Pl. 75. Fig. 6.

Correggio's pupils, without exception, fell into the grossest mannerism, and sought in effects of light, sweet coquettish gestures, and affected forms to surpass him, or, in a no less superficial manner, attempted an imitation of Raphael's style. Even the most gifted among them, Francesco Mazzuola, surnamed Il Parmigianino (1503–1540), is not to be enjoyed in his religious frescoes and paintings, and is only admirable as a portrait painter, when he had to adhere to nature. Somewhat later (1528–1612), Federigo Baroccio of Urbino adopted Correggio's style, and generalised it into a mannered type, which subsequently was regarded as the true expression of what was called 'grazie.' Occasionally, however, in the works of this artist there is a touch of that charming naïveté, which too speedily vanished from painting with its golden age.

f. *The Venetian School.*[1]

Less affected by the common interchange of style which prevailed in other schools, and favoured by the peculiar local circumstances of the city, the masters of the Venetian school now carried to perfection those principles of representation which had been newly established among them in the former epoch. We have already seen Giovanni Bellini introducing *colour* as this new element, and in a long and active life bringing it, by unwearied study, to an almost unsurpassable power, warmth, and distinctness. On this basis, Venetian painting advanced. Unaffected by other styles, it sought the beautiful in its own manner, and found it in the glorification of simple reality, in the brightness and joy of life, which at that time had reached its highest festive splendour in the proud, rich City of the Lagunes, the queen of the Adriatic. This glittering splendour is reflected in the master-works of painting, but they have raised it to lasting beauty and ideal majesty; not by any peculiar and strictly finished forms, not by deep and thoughtful purport, not even by the violent emotions of the inner life, but simply by the power

[1] *Denkm. d. Kunst.* Pl. 80.

of a state of being filled with beauty, and lifted above all trouble and restraint, and exulting in its peaceful condition with the happiness of Olympic gods. There is a noble, but still more worldly grandeur in all these splendid figures, even when they appear as Madonnas and Christian saints. They no longer stand in lifelike relation with the spectator, as in Correggio's works ; they rather repose in calm grace, like the antique gods. The struggles and sorrows of the world, strong action, and passionate feeling are utterly remote from them, for they are only created for luxurious enjoyment.

Hence, pictures representing a state of life form the true power of the Venetian school, and the simplest incidents are sufficient to render it attractive. Above all, however, there is a beauty of colouring diffused through their works, which entirely remains their own. They discovered the secrets of colour effect, the bloom of flesh tints, the charm of gradation and contrasts, in a manner nowhere else so thoroughly fathomed. At the same time, however, this warm, glowing colouring is not, as in Correggio, the expression of a nervously excited feeling, but the emanation of an inward harmony, of a natural healthfulness of mind and body, manifested as perfect sensual beauty full of nobleness and purity.

The first step towards the complete freedom of Venetian art was made by Giorgione, whose real name was Giorgio Barbarelli, of Castelfranco (1477–1511), who was only prevented by the shortness of his life from proving himself an equal rival of his great fellow pupil Titian. From his master, Giovanni Bellini, he acquired a deep bright glow of colour and power of characterisation, though he increased both to an almost coarse intensity. He is the first master in whose works landscape is conceived in a poetic manner. This remains henceforth a great excellence in the Venetian school, which, perhaps from the very want of it, was attracted to the beauties of landscape scenery. Among his earlier works, there is an altar-piece in the parish church of his native city, Castelfranco, representing the enthroned Madonna, honoured by St. Liberale and St. Francis ; there is also in the

Monte di Pietà at Treviso a dead Christ supported on the
Brink of the Grave by mourning Angels, which is full of thrilling
power of expression.   A grand originally sketched, but unfinished, Judgment of Solomon is at Kingston Lacy, near Wim-
borne, in England.   The same poetic mind is evidenced by
Giorgione in the conception of many historical scenes, which
acquire under his hand the character of highly romantic tales,
and are often peculiarly fascinating from the mysterious character
of the representation.   Thus, in the Dresden Gallery there is a

Fig. 352. The Concert. By Giorgione. Pitti Gallery.

Meeting of Jacob and Rachel, in which a touch of patriarchal
feeling is given by the peculiarly rural character of the scene.
The Sea Storm, in the Academy at Venice, which has been
sadly retouched and destroyed, exhibits the master at the height
of his mysterious and fantastic style.   Even in his portraits,
which are distinguished by noble conception and warmth of
colouring, he delights in yielding to this poetic inclination, and
thus raises the simple portrait into a genre painting, full of
character and attraction.   This is the case in the splendid
picture in the Pitti Gallery at Florence, which bears the name of

the 'Concert.' (Fig. 352.) It represents a priest at the piano; by his side is another with the violoncello, and on the other side is a youth with a stately plumed hat. The conception of the figures is so full of historical life, that a repetition of the painting in the Pal. Doria at Rome is naïvely enough designated as the portraits of Luther, Melanchthon, and Catharine von Bora.

As we have before mentioned Giorgione's single pupil of importance, Sebastian del Piombo, we will here pass to an artist who carried on Giorgione's style in an independent manner— namely, Jacopo Palma Vecchio, that is, the elder, although he likewise at first followed Giovanni Bellini.[1] Without Giorgione's coarse power, Jacopo gives his pictures a mild, thoughtful, and attractive tone, which is expressed by a corresponding soft and warm colouring. His most splendid work is an altar-piece of seven parts, in S. Maria Formosa, at Venice. In the centre is St. Barbara, grand and almost heroic in action, and glowing in colour; by the side there are other saints, and above is Mary with the corpse of Christ. Noble life is expressed in an excellently finished painting in the Dresden Museum, representing three young maidens, alleged to be the daughters of the master, and splendid types of voluptuous but noble and golden-haired Venetian beauty. A number of excellent pictures in the Belvedere at Vienna have been partly destroyed by unsparing 're-storation.' On the other hand, one of the master's most enchanting works, the 'Bella di Tiziano,' erroneously ascribed to Titian, is in the Sciarra Gallery in Rome.

The chief master of the Venetian school, the splendid Tiziano Vecellio, also emanated from Giovanni Bellini's school. He was born at Cadore, in the Friulian Alps, in 1477, and, after a life of almost a hundred years, was carried off by the plague at Venice in 1576. Starting with the strict and still antique style of his master, he received various new impulses from his gifted fellow pupil Giorgione, and concentrated the whole ability of the

---

[1] *Denkm. d. Kunst.* Pl. 80. Figs. 8 and 9.

Venetian school into incomparable power and depth, raising it to perfect freedom. His works, above all, breathe that majesty and life and that pure beauty which are only to be attained by a truly great conception of reality. At the same time his genius is all-embracing, and although the delineation of calmly beautiful existence harmonises most deeply with his own nature, yet there is no sphere of representation in which he has not produced masterly

Fig. 353. The Daughters of Palma Vecchio. Dresden Gallery.

works. In his long life, he adhered with indestructible energy and unerring fidelity to the principle which guides him from the beginning; and by this splendid example he showed pupils and contemporaries the path by which with persistent step they brought to light ever new treasures, while all the other schools of Italy had long forfeited their life, and had fallen into joyless mannerism.

One of this master's earliest works is the famous Tribute Money, at Dresden.[1] The treatment still appears tender and neat, and the rich beard and hair show the detail of a loving

[1] *Denkm. d. Kunst.* Pl. 80. Fig. 2.

hand; but the colouring exhibits the utmost warmth and power, and at the same time the expression of Christ is full of wondrous depth and calmness, as with His searching glance He rejects the Pharisee, with his crafty effrontery. In his later works, Titian paints with a broad bold brush, with grand free forms and distinct colours, which are blended into unsurpassable harmony by the wondrous brilliancy of his light tints. There are some frescoes which he executed with his pupils in Padua, and which excite interest as the only works of the kind of the Venetian school, besides the wall paintings of the Doge's Palace, which were destroyed by fire. In the Scuola del Santo there are three Miracles of St. Antony, by his hand, not indeed important as historical compositions, but highly attractive as grandly conceived figures in a poetic landscape, and for their glowing and perfect colouring. Similar importance belongs to the picture of Joachim and Anna in the Scuola del Carmine.

We can only mention the most important of the numerous oil paintings of this master. Among his representations of a religious character, the Entombment of Christ, in the Louvre (there is a copy in the Pal. Manfrin at Venice), stands foremost.[1] Although inferior to Raphael's Entombment in grandness of structure and purity of outline, this work attains to true and feeling beauty in its deep and solemn colouring, and in its noble moderation, the thrilling expression of suffering being beautifully subordinate to the physical action of supporting. Another masterly work belonging to his most vigorous period is the Ascension of Mary, in the Academy at Venice.[2] Surrounded by a charming group of jubilant angels, the grand figure of the Madonna solemnly rises upwards. A wondrous ray of glory bursts from her divine countenance, which beams with the glory of heaven, for above her appears God the Father, with extended arms, on a glory of angels; below, full of passionate longing, are the Apostles, whom she has left behind on earth, and who feel themselves impelled to follow the glorified one. All this is

[1] *Denkm. d. Kunst.* Pl. 80. Fig. 4.   [2] Ibid. Fig. 5.

portrayed freely and boldly in grand touches, and in splendid colouring, and only the somewhat confused and too stormy group of the Apostles exhibits a trace of violent delineation. The master, however, reaches the utmost moderation of passionate excitement in the grand representation of the Murder of Peter Martyr,

Fig. 354. Peter Martyr. By Titian.

in S. Giovanni e Paolo. (Fig. 354.) The saint has been already hurled to the ground, and is lying helpless with his arm stretched out to the murderer, who is on the point of taking a fatal thrust. The fearfully tragic nature of the picture is, however, concentrated in his companion, who, full of terror, is turning to fly. The representation has here scarcely anything in common with the religious conception, yet in the light-encircled angel genii, rushing down among the lofty trees, swinging palm branches, the master has given the fearful scene an atoning finish. The splendid landscape in this painting is of the highest importance. There is another painting, now almost entirely destroyed, in the Jesuitenkirche, representing the sufferings of S. Laurentius, in which the fearful character of the incident is softened by the gloom of night, and the most wonderful ghastly reflection is produced by the gleams of the moon breaking in, and by the light of two torches. We must also mention the grand Crowning of Thorns, in the Louvre, formerly in S. Maria delle Grazie at Milan, a work of dramatic pathos, yet with all its greatness it is not free from violence. Lastly, in the Belvedere in Vienna, there is a grand ' Ecce Homo ' of the year 1543, a picture of great power and boldness, though not devoid of jarring detail.

By preference Titian adhered to calmer devotional pictures, of which he painted a great number. The Madonna appears here as a true maternal woman full of majesty and graciousness, in mature and womanly beauty, and no longer in the shy constrained expression of the Virgin. The other saints display grandly conceived characters; the portraits of the donators of the paintings, which are usually added, appear as dignified figures, full of nobleness and grace. One of the most important works of this kind is the great altar-piece of the enthroned Madonna surrounded by Saints, and by the Pesaro family, in S. Maria de' Frari. Many others of smaller dimensions exhibit charming feeling, and acquire a peculiarly human and touching character from the freer arrangement, especially the omission of the throne. Thus there is a beautiful picture in the Dresden Gallery, in which the Madonna is turning graciously with her Child to a young woman humbly approaching her, who is presented to her by St. Peter. (Fig. 355.) St. John is kindly helping to hold the Child, who is eagerly reaching towards the shy petitioner; and St. Hieronymus, on the other side, completes the group, which is distinguished by the noble characterisation of the heads, and rich picturesque contrasts. One of his latest devotional pictures is the Annunciation in S. Salvatore in Venice; yet here also the expression is full of feeling, and it is only the somewhat gloomy and heavy tone of colouring, and the less distinct delineation of the forms, that betray the master's extreme age. This is the case also with his last picture, the Descent from the Cross, which he left unfinished, and which is now in the collection of the Academy.

Fig. 355. Madonna with Saints. By Titian. Dresden Gallery.

The same freedom with which Titian developed an abundance of truly human ideas from the range of religious subjects, and represented them in perfect works, led him also in the conception of scenes of antique mythology. The greatest master of nobly glorified and sensual beauty must indeed with especial delight have had recourse to the bright fable world of the Greek Olympus, as here more than elsewhere the opportunity was afforded of depicting the full charm of human beauty. Titian proceeded at the same time more innocently and less designedly than Correggio, for while the figures of this master of ardent

desire address themselves to the spectator, the noble and
majestic women of Titian are only there for their own sake, and
it is only pure delight in beauty to which they owe their existence. Only rarely do we meet with exceptional instances, in
which beauty is exhibited with a certain passionate design.
Among the representations of this kind, three splendid paintings,
executed in the year 1514 for the Duke of Ferrara, are the
earliest. One of these, Bacchus and Ariadne, still exhibiting a
strict and formal beauty, is in the possession of the National
Gallery in London; the two others are in the Museum at
Madrid, where there is also a Bacchanal full of enchantingly free
life, and justly estimated as one of his most excellent works.
We may here also class a grand representation of the discovery
of Callisto's devious Course, which has been repeatedly copied.
The copy painted for Phillip II. is still in the Museum at
Madrid.[1] Surrounded by nymphs, Diana is enthroned by a
clear spring in a bright landscape. On the other side of the
spring, some of her companions are engaged in discovering
Callisto's misfortune. There are other copies in the Belvedere at
Vienna, and in the London Bridgewater Gallery. We may also
here add a picture of mysterious power, more passionately conceived than the other works of the kind—namely, Venus, on the
Point of Revealing to a young Girl the Mysteries of the Service
of Bacchus, in the Pinakothek at Munich. Lastly, we must here
number several highly poetical pictures of an allegorical purport.
One of these, in the Borghese Gallery in Rome, peculiarly noble
in its feeling, bears the designation of 'Heavenly and Earthly
Love.' On the edge of a marble sarcophagus which serves as a
fountain, two female figures are sitting—the one naked, with a
noble, finely developed form, seems turning, as if persuasively, to
the other, who is sitting opposite to her, wholly attired, and with
an expression of resolve. A splendid landscape encloses this
beautiful group. The other picture, in the Bridgewater Gallery,
and designated as 'the Three Ages of Man,' breathes the idyllic

[1] *Denkm. d. Kunst.* Pl. 80. Fig. 3.

cheerfulness of an innocent paradisiacal existence. There is a copy by Sassoferato in the Pal. Borghese in Rome.

A great number of other works of this kind belong here, · pictures for the most part of smaller size and few figures. It is constantly Venus, who is conceived in various graceful attitudes. Sometimes the master satisfied himself with representing a single female figure, usually entirely or in a great measure unclothed, which he frequently characterised as Venus. In these pictures, Titian gives the ideal of womanly beauty, not as a noble and glorified creation of the senses, but for the most part with a grandeur of conception, and an absence of design, such as only have been known in the best epoch of antiquity among the Hellenists. His colouring here reaches its highest triumph, for almost without shade, and often in the brightest light, he is able to give such a roundness to his forms that they seem as though animated by glowing life. Although exhibiting full maturity and magnificent splendour of form, these female figures are yet so noble that they happily avoid the excess of too great voluptuousness. One of the most beautiful of these paintings is in the Fitzwilliam Museum at Cambridge (a copy is in the Dresden Gallery), representing a Venus outstretched nobly and easily on a couch, and crowned by Cupid, while a young man beside her is playing the lute. (Fig. 356.) A similar scene is depicted in one of the two pictures in the Tribuna degli Uffizi at Florence, and the landscape also is highly poetical; the other picture, on the contrary, a masterpiece of painting, is not so purely and undesignedly treated as the former, as the naked body stands out in full light from the white linen of the couch. We find the same subject with different variations twice again in the Museum at Madrid.

That Titian, lastly, must occupy one of the first places among the portrait painters of all ages, may be inferred from the character and tendency of his art; indeed, few equal him in grand conception and in the power of giving prominence to all that is beautiful and important in individual appearance. The calm feeling of a free and noble existence pervades all his numerous portraits, evidenced in the unconstrained dignity of bearing, in the lifelike glow of the colouring, and in the delicacy of feeling with which they are placed within the space allotted. We can here, also, only mention a small number of the most important. Although the master is equally happy in the representation of youth and age, the female and male sex, yet some incomparable female portraits are among the most splendid productions of his art. They are conceived with so much love,

Fig. 356. Venus. By Titian.

and, although thoroughly individual, they are of such perfect beauty, that for a long period they have been designated as 'Titian's beloved Ones.' One of the most beautiful is the 'Maîtresse de Titien,' in the Louvre; in a free, idealised costume, the same type returns as 'Flora,' in the Gallery of the Uffizi; and full of fresh youthful grace, in rich Venetian costume, with pearls, chains of gold, velvet, and silk, we find it again in the charming portrait in the Pitti Gallery in Florence. One of the noblest figures is the youthful female portrait in the Berlin Museum, designated 'Titian's Daughter,' to which a pleasing genre style is added in the upheld vessel of fruits. In a repetition of this painting at Madrid, the young woman is receiving in return a dish with the head of John the Baptist, and is therefore transformed into the daughter of Herodias. His numerous male portraits represent the most important men of his time, kings and princes, poets, scholars, warriors, and noble patricians, all grandly conceived, with free and bold touches, an aristocracy in the full meaning of the word.

None of his contemporaries in Venice and in the territories belonging could escape the overwhelming influence of the great master; yet, however, as his art ever pointed to nature as its true source, even insignificant painters remained free from his manner, maintained their vigour and freshness, and adhered to the faithful conception of life and to beautiful and warm colouring as the best heritage of the school. Bonifazio, with his good and solidly executed pictures; the Paduan Domenico Campagnola, who successfully emulated the master in the Paduan frescoes; the able Geronimo Savoldo of Brescia; Girolamo Rumanino, who strove after deeper pathos in his works; the feeling and excitable Lorenzo Lotto of Trevisa, whose paintings we find in Bergamo (in the cathedral, S. Bartolommeo, S. Bernardino, and S. Spirito); and the gifted Calisto Piazza of Lodi, trained in the Lombard school, all belong to this list of artists, but are, however, all surpassed by one master, in whom a thoroughly noble mind and a true religious feeling alien to the Venetians were combined with great beauty of colouring—namely, Alessandro Bonvicino, known under the name of Moretto of Brescia (1500–1547). Upon him, also, Titian exercised a decided influence; yet the glowing Venetian colouring assumed in his works a softer atmospheric tint, which appears like the natural emanation of his own tender feeling. He delighted most in painting devotional pictures, which from their excellent arrangement suggest the influence of Raphael's school. A number of his finest works are still in his native city Brescia. In the old cathedral there is an Ascension of the Virgin by him, a beautiful work full of deep feeling, the colouring tempered, though of great power and depth. Titian's Ascension has exercised evident influence upon the composition. There is also a large altar-piece in S. Clemente of the Madonna enthroned on Clouds, with several saints below: it is especially sweet and charming, and at the same time exhibits splendid colouring and

Fig. 357. Holy Family. By Moretto. Berlin.

tender harmony. In SS. Nazaro e Celso there is a Crowning of the Virgin, one of his most excellent works, nobly arranged and bathed as it were in silver light. The Städel Museum at Frankfort-on-the-Maine possesses a Madonna on a Throne, surrounded by the grand figures of the four Fathers of the Church, and also another beautiful enthroned Madonna with S. Sebastian and S. Antony; the gallery of the Belvedere at Vienna has the majestic S. Justina with the kneeling figure of the donator of the picture; and, lastly, the Museum at Berlin possesses an Adoration of the Shepherds, in parts extremely excellent, and one of his most poetic devotional paintings; a glorified Madonna hovering in the air with her Child, St. Anna, and the little St. John, surrounded by lovely angels. Below two expressive and grandly conceived priestly figures are kneeling, filled with the deepest devotion: a splendid landscape forms the background. (Fig. 357.)

Many other important artists were produced by the Venetian school at about the same time. Above all, we may mention Giov. Antonio Licinio Regillo, surnamed Pordenone, from the place of his birth (1484–1539), who is in nowise inferior to Titian in the glow and softness of his colouring, especially in in his flesh-tints; and he also rivals the great master in his lifelike characterisation and grandeur of conception;[1] also the talented Paris Bordone (1500–1570), a master distinguished for his lifelike conception, who combined a soft tenderness with the glowing Venetian colouring, and produced excellent works, both in historical pictures and portraits. Moretto's pupil, also, Giov. Battista Moroni, must be named as a distinguished portrait painter.

While the other schools of Italy, in the latter part of the sixteenth century, speedily fell into mannerism and affectation, Venetian painting exhibits at this period an important revival, inferior, indeed, in purity and majesty to the works of the earlier masters, but scarcely yielding to them in creative power, and even carrying on the principles of the Venetian school to new and splendid results. The reason for this phenomenon lies partly in the uninterrupted prosperity which Venice now enjoyed both as regards her power and her well-being; principally, however, in the sound basis which characterised Venetian painting.

[1] *Denkm. d. Kunst.* Pl. 80. Fig. 10.

The ideal types which the great minds of Raphael and Michael Angelo had given to Roman Florentine art were only living so long as the deep thoughts of those masters pervaded them; so soon as this essential was lacking, the forms appeared lifeless and repulsively cold. It was otherwise with the Venetians, who followed nature directly; and though they thus never attained to the richness of thought and ideal majesty of those two heroes, they all the more surely maintained themselves with healthful creative power on the basis of lifelike reality.

In two great masters of considerable genius the vigorous activity and the fertile productive power of this later epoch culminated.[1] One of these is the Venetian Jacopo Robusti, known as Tintoretto (1512–1594). He at first frequented the school of Titian; but he soon withdrew, and studied henceforth with the express intention of combining Michael Angelo's outline with Titian's colouring. He certainly thus acquired more exact and more plastic forms by means of deeper shadows and more forcible modelling; but the irreconcilability of these contrasts made him, for the most part, lose the clearness, delicacy, and harmony of the colouring of the Venetian school, without affording an essential compensation for the loss. He belongs, indeed, to the boldest and most unfailing painters known in the history of art; his pictures are immense in number and extent—a circumstance especially produced by the fact that the Venetians were never fond of frescoes, and preferred adorning the walls and ceilings of their large and splendid halls with gigantic oil paintings. Tintoretto produced marvellous things in the execution of these works; and not the least admirable part in them is that for a long time he guarded himself from the danger of falling into coarse decoration painting. It is true, it could not be otherwise but that his style no longer reached the height of the Titian period, that he aimed only at great effects of light and shade, and at length he also fell into gross mechanical painting.

[1] *Denkm. d. Kunst.* Pl. 88.

Some noble altar-pieces belonging to his earlier period are in the churches of Venice, and elsewhere in galleries. There are also some ably treated mythological paintings. Among the numerous pictures with which he adorned the Doge's Palace (Fig. 358), there are many excellent ones, happily conceived and beautifully painted. In the great Council Hall, he executed a gigantic oil painting of Paradise, 30 feet high by 74 feet broad— a tolerably wild medley, it is true. The Marriage at Cana, in the sacristy of S. Maria della Salute, and the Miracles of St. Mark, in the Academy, are important compositions. In the

Fig. 358. Allegorical Picture. By Tintoretto.

Scuola di San Rocco there are more than fifty large oil paintings, among them a Crucifixion. He appears more pleasing on other occasions than in these colossal works; in his numerous portraits, for instance, which, from their able conception and excellent colouring, occupy a high rank.

The second of these two later masters—nobler and greater than Tintoretto—is Paul Veronese, as he is called from his native city; but his real name was P. Caliari (about 1528–1588). He entered, indeed, upon Titian's heritage, and by his grand creative power and noble beauty upheld the banner of Venetian art until the end of the century. In him, also, the conception is no longer so noble and simple as in the earlier masters—he likewise paid his tribute to the age—but it is yet nobler, freer, and more beautiful than in any other of his contemporaries. He portrays the old splendid Venetian life yet once more in all its glory and intoxicating mirth; a rejoicing, festive feeling is expressed in his large pictures, a strong expiring tone, in which the golden age of Italian life dies away for ever. In the refectories of the rich monasteries and fraternities, they delighted at that time in painting some biblical feast, especially the Marriage at Cana. In these pictures the painter could unscrupulously introduce his joyous age, with its rich and splendid costumes, into their marble-columned halls; and Paul Veronese did this with a gladsomeness and taste for the beautiful, which make us even now regard with pleasure these mere scenes of earthly pageantry. But in more serious subjects, also, he knew how to produce a thrilling effect by deep feeling and lively expression. At the same time he endeavoured to enrich the composition, to pass beyond the simplicity of Titian's works, to obtain in colouring a more varied gradation, to blend the colours and to form certain transition tints, giving stronger emphasis to splendid drapery, ornament, architecture, and other externals. But the clearness, warmth, and harmony which he, nevertheless, imparted to his paintings are all the more worthy of admiration.

A series of Paul's most splendid paintings, executed at the period of his prime (between 1560–1565), are in the church of S. Sebastiano, in Venice, where the master lies buried. The first place in merit belongs to S. Sebastian going to the Place of Execution. The incident is forcibly depicted in its full importance, with its multitude of eager spectators, and it is at the same time full of truly grand dramatic life. The other paintings, also, on the walls and ceiling of this church are among his most excellent historical compositions. Other religious votive pictures are calmer in their treatment; but yet a thrill of inward emotion passes through the worshipper as it does through the divine

figures. An extremely beautiful painting of this kind is the
Adoration of the Kings, in the Dresden Museum. (Fig. 359.)
The Holy Family is here arranged on one side as an independent group, while on the other side all the pomp and power of
the world bow adoringly, represented as it is in the kings with
their purple garments of sparkling gold brocade. A wonderful
abundance of powerful colours is blended into perfect harmony;
and the dignity of the figures, the splendour of the colouring,
the grand arrangement within the space, and the noble life

Fig. 359. From the Adoration of the Kings. By Paul Veronese. Dresden Gallery.

which pervades the whole representation, raise the work to one
of the most masterly creations. Paul's other styles are also
worthily represented in the same collection. In the Good Sa-
maritan, the predominant feature is the simple grand landscape,
with its splendid and glowing colouring; in a small Christ on
the Cross mourned by his Followers, a deep pathos of feeling is
expressed; in the Finding of Moses, an Old Testament subject
is transformed into a graceful legend by the costume of the time

and the poetical landscape around ; and, lastly, the Marriage at Cana is a beautiful specimen of those great banquet paintings in which Paul's art shone. The principal picture of this kind is, however, the representation of the same scene in the Louvre. On a canvas of six hundred square feet, the master displayed the cheerful splendour, the festive life of his own day ; the chief personages —Christ and His mother—are entirely thrown into the background, and appear almost like unbidden guests at this lavish banquet. The painting of the Entertainment of Levi, in the Academy at Venice, is not much smaller, and by its light colouring and the charming broad colonnades, it produces a pleasant feeling of free cheerful life. A series of the same works are to be found in various galleries, creating astonishment at the indestructible vigour of the master, who ever knew how to infuse into them new and attractive ideas from actual life.

He also painted a great number of mythological and allegorical pictures, in his later life, for the walls and ceilings of the Doge's Palace at Venice ; and although these representations are not always purely and nobly conceived, they possess at least great splendour of colouring, and a strong breath of life which makes us forget the coldness of allegory.

While we thus see this highly gifted master in one entire class of his pictures—and certainly in those most preferred in his own day—using sacred history only as a pretext for the splendid portrayal of life, another able artist of the same school descended a step further into lower life, and thus became the founder of true genre painting. We allude to Jacopo da Ponte, surnamed Bassano, after his native city (1510–1592), whose art was first formed in Venice by Titian's works, but who subsequently created a mode of representation peculiar to himself, and never before seen. He sought out lower life—peasants' cottages with their rude inhabitants, with their cattle, poultry, farming implements, and other accompaniments — represented them with splendid colouring and bold brush ; introducing occasionally a sacred or profane incident as accessories, but omitting these additions with equal readiness, and delighting in the delineation of lower life, and even in the representation of lifeless objects. While he produced these works with true pleasure, with cheerful assiduity, and with ever-skilful colouring, he disregarded, it is true, all former excellence of painting; but he opened the way to a new era, which subsequently availed itself of his example as far as lay in its power. As associates in these works he employed his four sons; and these five able men inundated the galleries with a flood of pictures which, without especial wealth of invention, exhibit a strong family likeness, and in their style and fresh colouring are able representations of a low sphere of life.

CHAPTER V.

I. SCULPTURE.

WITH the beginning of the fifteenth century that realistic taste was awakened in the North, which was to supplant the art of the middle ages, and was to procure the victory to that modern style, which was based on the study of nature. It seems that it was the numerous portraits on grave monuments which first induced the necessity for the utmost faithfulness in the delineation of individual character, and resulted in a fuller and more exact portrayal of the form. Even in the course of the fourteenth century this tendency produced remarkable results, as is evidenced by the before-mentioned (vol. ii. p. 65) sculpture schools of Tournay and Dijon. With increased exercise, the desire now soon arose to give a similar perfection to the physical form of the ideal figures of sacred history. Painting soon emulated sculpture, and reacted so decidedly on the latter that at that time both arts were most closely connected. Although northern plastic art, on the whole, does not reach the height of the Italian, this may be imputed partly to the want of antique ideas, and to the absence of the marble so necessary for its higher perfection; and partly, and still more, to the striving too much after detail, and to a strong inclination to the fantastic, by which the grand, calm, and harmonious conception of the whole could but rarely assert itself in its essential features.

Numerous as are the plastic works of this period, the investigation of them has hitherto been unsatisfactory, and has at all events been impeded by the fact that a countless number of local schools appeared side by side, and only rarely did masters of greater importance rise like luminous central points from the uniform mass. We are most informed respecting German plastic art; but scantily, on the contrary, with regard to that of other lands, whose course of development seems notwithstanding tolerably analogous with the German. The universal system of idealistic Gothic art, which had become somewhat empty and conventional, was forsaken almost without exception, and in its stead appeared the tendency to natural individual representation, with a one-sidedness verging on the extreme. The exact and fixed expression of the physiognomy, the attention to all the small peculiarities of figure, bearing, and even costume, the delight in representing the various materials according to their especial texture and quality, all these were the immediate results of this tendency. While the ideas, compositions, and the whole arrangement were still mediæval, they yet were all expressed in a manner which had no longer any connection with tradition, and indeed not seldom exhibited a contrast with the ideal purport. When the subjects of sacred history were treated, a passionate and even violent element pervaded the representation, and in the striving after effect nothing was so gladly and constantly treated as the Passion of Christ and the Martyrdom of the Saints. All this produced in the reliefs an overloaded style, inclining to the picturesque; and this style, wholly devoid of antique influence, harmonised with the intellectual disposition of the age, and produced an effect all the more glaring, as antique plastic art did not, as in Italy, afford a more noble and harmonious law for the individual forms.

With the sixteenth century, the influence of modern Italian plastic art began to be generally diffused. It was especially the splendid works, tombs, and other monuments which, both in construction, decoration, and in the execution of the figures, first adopted the antique Italian style. So long as adherence to nature and the characteristic individual representation of the northern art were combined with this modern ideal style, the interchange produced many lifelike and attractive works; when, however, about 1550, the natural warmth and naïveté of the northern taste declined, and yielded to a conventional and formal classic style, true freedom vanished for the most part from the plastic works, and gave way to theatrical effect and cold allegory.

a. *Germany.*[1]

WOOD CARVING.

The carved wooden altars are most immediately connected with mediæval tradition both in technical workmanship and in subject, while in the mode of expression they evidence the realistic tendency and dramatic picturesque style of the period. The construction, on the whole, remains the same as before, only much more freely developed, so that these works, in their extensive arrangement, massive plastic ornament, and lustre of gold and brilliant colours, appear as the most lively expression of the artistic effort of their time. The predilection for this peculiar combination of the plastic art with that of painting increased from the beginning of the fifteenth century in an incredible manner, and lasted uninterruptedly until the middle of the sixteenth.

The strong realistic character of the representations required above all a deep cutting in relief of the altar, in the divisions of which the separate scenes were represented. Each compartment thus appeared as a small theatre, with a varied landscape background, on which, in rich perspective gradation, the events were amply delineated. The figures, at the same time, were small in proportion; the foremost not unfrequently were completely insulated like statuettes, and the rest were executed in high relief. When, in some instances, larger statues, such as the Madonna or other saints, were placed in the chief niches, they exhibited a completely developed plastic style, which nevertheless was likewise affected by painting and gilding. A picturesque effort is apparent, moreover, when in all these figures

---

[1] *Denkm. d. Kunst.* Pl. 85. Cf. Lübke's *Geschichte der Plastik*, pp. 516-617.

the drapery is broken restlessly in many sharp folds, often even degenerating into creases.   This was partly caused by the gay attire worn at that period, which, not heavy and bulging enough with its own magnificent material, with its silk and velvet, demeaned itself in this way ; but partly also it was caused by the technical part of wood carving, and the desire to increase the splendour of the gold and colours by many broken folds led to this style, which was for a long time adhered to in all branches of plastic art.   The more gorgeous, however, the display in the figures, the freer became the architectural framework which enclosed these works.   Hence the fantastically curved decorations of the late Gothic style appeared as the framework and termination of the separate divisions, until even here the impulse to natural delineation fully burst forth, and an intricate flourish of leaves and branches exclusively prevailed.

From the countless abundance of such works, scattered through most old churches in all parts of Germany, we will only mention some of the most important.   Swabia is especially rich in early altars of the kind.   Among them, and one of the earliest, is the altar of Lucas Moser at Tiefenbronn, belonging to the year 1431, and representing a St. Magdalene borne upwards by angels.   One of the most excellent of the works there is the high altar in the Jacobskirche at Rothenburg on the Tauber, belonging to the year 1466, which likewise contains only single figures of Christ, an Ecce Homo and several saints ; but these are executed in a considerably advanced and genuine plastic style.   There is a splendid Marien altar in the Pilgrims' Church at Creglingen, belonging to the year 1487 ; and there is an altar executed in a masterly manner in the Kilianskirche at Heilbronn, belonging to the year 1498.   There is another skilfully executed altar in the Kreuzkirche at Gmünd.   We may also mention as excellent works the high altar in the monastery church at Blaubeuren, belonging to the year 1496 ; that in the cathedral at Ulm, belonging to the year 1521 ; and the delicately and nobly executed altar in the cathedral at Breisach, representing a Crowning of the Virgin, and belonging to the later date of

1526. The cathedral of Chur in Switzerland also possesses in its high altar, executed in 1491 by Jacob Rösch, one of the choicest and most complete works of this kind, comprising in an ingenious manner the whole cycle of sacred incidents from the Passion to the Crowning of the Virgin.

In the Austrian lands, also, there are a great number of such works, many of which, such as the splendid altar of St. Wolfgang [1] in Upper Austria, belonging to the year 1481, and that of Weissenbach in the Tyrol, may be traced. to the skilful hand of the sculptor Michael Pacher. The altar of the church at Clausen on the Rhine,[2] with its lifelike representation of the Passion, is famous as one of the most able productions of the late period of the sixteenth century. The two altars in the church at Calcar are, however, of great importance; also an altar in the collegiate church at Xanten, all of them likewise valuable works belonging to the latter part of the same century, and all without coloured decoration. The carved works in Westphalia are also numerous and skilful; among them an altar at Kirchlinde is distinguished for its especially noble and just style. The later mode of representation, for the most part confused and overloaded, may be seen in the colossal altars of the church of S. Peter at Dortmund, and in the church at Schwerte, the latter belonging to the year 1523. On the other hand, the high altar of the parish church at Vreden is distinguished as one of the richest and most excellent of these works, and is, moreover, of great interest from its well-preserved polychromatic ornament. Further in the north, we must mention, as one of the principal works of this latest period, the large and splendid altar in the cathedral at Schleswig,[3] executed between 1515 and 1521 by Hans Brüggemann, and containing the scenes of the Passion, represented in a strong and lifelike manner, but without colour. Pomerania also

[1] See Heider's and Eitelberger's *Mittelalterl. Kunstdenkm. des österr. Kaiserstaates.* Vol. I. Pl. 19.

[2] E. aus'm Weerth, *Kunstdenkmäler des christlichen Mittelalters in den Rheinlanden.* Vols. I. and II. Leipzig, 1857.

[3] Cf. the Illustrations by Böhndel, *Der Altarschrein in der Schleswiger Domkirche.* See Lübke's *Gesch. der Plastik.* Leipzig, 1863.

possesses a number of these carved altars, of which we must mention one in the Marienkirche at Greifswald, containing a representation of the Entombment of Christ. Lastly, in the frontier lands, in Silesia, and especially in Breslau and Cracow, and as far as Hungary, many similar works may be pointed cut.

The Franconian works of this kind also possess great importance, and were for the most part executed under the direction of Michael Wohlgemuth, also known as a painter. Thus there is the high altar of the Marienkirche at Zwickau, belonging to the year 1479, the carvings of which represent Mary with other saints; also the altar in the Ulrichskirche at Halle, executed in the year 1488, likewise containing Christ and the Virgin with various saints.

Towards the end of this period, there flourished in Nuremberg an excellent master in the art of wood carving, Veit Stoss of Cracow [1] (1438–1533), who devoted his earlier activity to his native city. The principal work of his early epoch was the high altar in the Frauenkirche at Cracow (1472–1484), representing a Crowning of the Virgin with other smaller biblical scenes. In Nuremberg, where he settled in the year 1496, there are many of his works existing, which are distinguished by tender feeling and grace, softness of form, and by a relief style, exhibiting distinctness of arrangement, though full of life. Although he could not escape the influence of his time in the petty creased style of his folds, his drapery is at the same time conceived in grand masses, and there is freedom in its arrangement. His principal work is the Rosenkranz in the church of S. Laurence, executed in the year 1518, an ingenious and attractive work.[2] In the centre there are the insulated figures of the Madonna and of the Angel of the Annunciation, surrounded by a chain of medallions carved in the same manner, containing in each medallion the seven joys of the Virgin—the Annunciation, the Visitation, the Birth of Christ, the Adoration of the Wise Men, the Resurrection of Christ, the Outpouring of the Holy Spirit,

[1] *Denkm. d. Kunst.* Pl. 85. Figs. 1 and 2.
[2] Cf. R. von Rettberg, *Nürnbergs Kunstleben, &c.* P. 145.

and the Crowning of the Virgin. These reliefs are especially distinct in their arrangement, they are beautifully composed within the space, and are full of naïve and charming feeling. Under the cross, the serpent with the apple betokens original sin; graceful angels are hovering round the whole, which is terminated by the enthroned figure of God the Father. Among the other authentic works of this master, there are also the former high altar panels in the upper parish church at Bamberg, with representations from the life of Christ and His mother; also a large Christ on the Cross, together with the figures of the Virgin and St. John, in the church of St. Sebald at Nuremberg, executed in the year 1526.

Lastly, we must here mention another able master of the Swabian school, Jörg Syrlin, the elder, whose principal works

Birth of Christ.   Adoration of the Wise Men.   Crowning of Mary.
Fig. 360. From the Rosenkranz.

were the splendid choir stalls in the cathedral of his native city Ulm (1469–1474); works of the highest decorative luxury, in which, however, besides the rich development of architectural ornament, a great number of half-length portraits of heathen sages, Old Testament prophets and patriarchs, as well as Christian saints and apostles, and, lastly, those of the honest master himself and his wife (Fig. 361), are introduced in a powerful though graceful realistic style. In 1482, he executed in stone the fountain in the market-place at Ulm, the so-called ' Fischkasten,' a simple Gothic pyramid with three stately figures of knights. Jörg Syrlin, the younger, was no less skilful than his father in executing a number of excellent works in carved wood; among them the splendid choir stalls in the monastery church at Blaubeuren, in the year 1496, and the sounding-board for the pulpit of Ulm Cathedral, executed with much rich decoration in the year 1510.

Fig. 361. Jörg Syrlin's Portrait. Ulm.

STONE SCULPTURE.

Stone sculpture was at this time also carried on with great eagerness, and found constant application in portals, buttresses, lectoriums, and choir pillars. Some able works of this kind here also point to the especial activity and power of the Swabian school.[1] Among the earlier works, in which the new tendency is exhibited with nobleness and moderation, there is a statue of Count Ulric, the 'much beloved,' which was executed about 1440, and formerly stood in the market-place at Stuttgart. The

[1] Heideloff's *Schwäbische Denkmale.*

restoration of the Collegiate Church there, during the entire course of the fifteenth century, and especially towards the end of it, afforded manifold opportunity for works of sculpture. Both the lectorium and the splendid pulpit in this church, as well as the originally designed and richly adorned Gate of the Apostles, are furnished with reliefs and statues, in which vigorous realistic execution is attractively combined with dignity of conception. In the beginning of the following century (1501), the excellent 'Mount of Olives,' in the Leonhardskirche, was executed, representing a figure of Christ on the Cross as large as life, lamented by Mary, St. John, and Mary Magdalene—a work in which a rare depth of feeling is evidenced with powerful conception of form. No less lifelike and varied is the display of plastic art, during the later part of the fifteenth century, in the portals and pillars of the elegant Frauenkirche at Esslingen (cf. Fig. 280 in vol. ii. p. 64), as well as on the portals of Ulm Cathedral. Among the most splendid works of the Swabian school, we must also mention the 'Sacramentsgehäuse'[1] in Ulm Cathedral, executed in the year 1469, the fountain in the market-place, and the baptismal font in the church at Urach—the latter executed in 1518 by Meister Cristoph—and the font and tomb in the Marienkirche at Reutlichen.

Among the most excellent works of this kind, which belong partly to architecture and partly to sculpture, we may number the pulpit of the cathedral of Freiburg in the Ore mountains, produced about the year 1470, and just as original in its design as it is masterly in its execution; also the beautiful pulpit in Strasburg Cathedral, belonging to the year 1486; also the pulpit in St. Stephen's in Vienna, which was finished about 1512, by Meister Pilgram, and is adorned with excellent half-length figures of the fathers of the Church; besides many rich tabernacles and lectoriums, which are to be found in good preservation throughout Germany. A number of good monuments in the Rhine lands afford a distinct view of the development of the style. Among the earlier of these belongs the monument of Ruprecht of

---

[1] Receptacle for the sacred elements of the Communion.

the Palatinate († 1410), in the Holy Ghost Church at Heidelberg. Many others of the same kind are in the cathedral at Mayence.[1] The monument of Archbishop Conrad III., in the year 1434, still wavers between the usual style and a freer individual conception. In the monument of Diether von Isenburg (1482), the latter gains the ascendancy, and henceforth ever appears in all subsequent monuments. Many others are to be seen in other churches.

The monument of King Louis of Bavaria, placed in the

From the Portal of the Apostles.　　　　　　From the Lectorium.

Fig. 362. Statues from the Collegiate Church at Stuttgart.

Frauenkirche at Munich soon after 1468, is also of great value, and with all its realistic accuracy exhibits great nobleness and freedom of delineation. The Maximilian Museum at Augsburg possesses some stone reliefs belonging to this epoch, which evidence a pure taste for the beautiful.

[1] See Emden, *Der Dom zu Mainz und seine Denkmäler, &c.*

The Franconian school produced in Adam Krafft one of the most important masters of this period. He lived till 1507,[1] and was chiefly engaged in Nuremberg. Powerful conception of life, exact delineation of form, and a tinge of hearty feeling often rising to a touching expression, characterise his works. The somewhat crowded arrangement, and the restless folds of the drapery,, are a tribute which all the masters of the period paid more or less to the extravagant taste of those around them. Added to this, there is in Krafft's works a certain coarse stoutness in the figures. His earliest known works are the Seven Stages on the way to the Johannis Cemetery, in which he has depicted in strong

Fig. 363. Krafft's Third Stage.

relief, with great life and thrilling force of expression, the seven times that Christ fainted under the burden of the cross. (Fig. 363.) His style reaches an agitating depth of feeling in the reliefs representing the History of the Passion, which he executed, in 1492, on the exterior of S. Sebald: the Entombment of Christ is especially full of heartfelt inspiration. Joseph of Arimathea and Nicodemus have reverentially taken up the

[1] R. v. Rettberg, *Nürnbergs Kunstleben*, p. 50. *Denkm. d. Kunst.* Pl. 85. Figs. 4–6.

body of the Lord, and are on the point of consigning it to the sarcophagus; the grief of the bereaved followers breaks forth uncontrollably—most passionately in Mary Magdalene, who, wringing her hands, sinks down at the foot of the tomb; and most deeply in the mother, who is pressing her lips yet once more on the deathly pale features of her beloved Son. One of the most artistic works of this master is the stone sacraments-gehäuse, 62 feet high, in the church of S. Laurence, which he executed between 1496 and 1500. The lower structure rests on three strong kneeling figures, which represent the master himself and two of his associates. From here there rises a slender boldly soaring Gothic pyramid, adorned with statuettes and relief scenes from the History of the Passion, terminating at the top in a curved form.

With what fresh and lifelike simplicity Krafft knew how to grasp the events of ordinary life is evidenced in the beautiful relief of the Public Scales, executed in the year 1497. The weigher at the town hall is standing in the middle, and conscientiously observing the wavering of the beam, beneath which the motto, 'To thyself as to others,' guarantees strict justice; while the man on the left is on the point of adding another weight, the merchant opposite, whose bales of goods are to be taxed, is putting his hand slowly into his money bag. It would not be possible to depict this incident more significantly, more strikingly, or more distinctly. (Fig. 364.)

About the same time there lived in Würzburg an equally able master, Tilman Riemenschneider[1] (about 1460–1531), whose style never indeed reached the power of the Nuremberg school, but who exhibited instead a touching depth and softness of feeling, though fettered by the realistic spirit of the time. His statues of Adam and Eve and the Apostles, executed for the Frauenkirche at Würzburg, are able works. His Madonnas, in the Neumünster Church in the same place, and in the Pilgrims' Chapel at Volkach, are full of charming tenderness, combined

---

[1] C. Becker, *Leben und Werke des Bildhauers Tilmann Riemenschneider.* Leipzig, 1849.

with a certain exuberance of form.   Elegiac tones of pain are brought out by the master in the representations of the Mourn-ing over the dead Christ, one of which he executed for the church at Heidingsfeld, and another still richer one for the church at Maidbrunn (1525).   From 1499 to 1513, he worked at the marble monuments of the Emperor Henry II. and his wife

Fig. 364. Relief on the Nuremberg Public Scales. By A. Krafft.

Kunigunde, for the cathedral of Bamberg.   Both figures are represented as resting on the lid of the sarcophagus; the sides of the latter are adorned with relief scenes from their life, and are executed in a fresh vigorous realistic style.   At a somewhat later period, about 1495, he produced the equally excellent marble monument of Bishop Rudolph of Scherenberg, in the cathedral at Würzburg, the ably characterised figure of the bishop, in somewhat heavy and hard drapery, being placed under a Gothic baldachin. On the other hand, in the marble monument, in the same place, of Bishop Lorenzo of Bibra, executed in 1519, the master reaches a grand dignity and skilfulness of execution, such as belong to the modern adoption of the antique.

But the stateliest monument of this whole epoch is the marble memorial to the Emperor Frederic III., in St. Stephen's Cathedral at Vienna, which was begun, in 1467, by Meister Niclas Lerch of Leyden, and was continued after his death by Meister Michael Dichter, who completed it in 1513. The whole design appears as originally as it is grandly conceived : on a broad projecting base, adorned with statuettes and reliefs, rises the equally richly sculptured sarcophagus, on which rests the dignified figure of the emperor in full robes, with his sceptre and imperial orb. Although occasionally Gothic details have been employed, the composition has, on the whole, a distinctness and repose, which call to mind the Renaissance style.

Other German monuments belonging to the sixteenth century decidedly exhibit the Renaissance forms in the arrangement of the whole, still combining with them in the representation of figures the individual freshness and variety of the former style. This is the case with the beautiful monument of Johann Eltz and his wife in the Carmelite Church at Boppart, belonging to the year 1548 ; also with the monuments of two archbishops in the cathedral at Treves, belonging to a somewhat earlier period; also the monument of Archbishop Albrecht, in Mainz Cathedral, executed in the year 1546, several monuments in the church at Wertheim, and many others. In the latter part of the century a decorative style, in the manner of the Italian Renaissance, gained ground in these works, thus giving them a place in the following epoch.

BRONZE WORKS.

In the German bronze work of this epoch, no school stands forth so prominently as the Nuremberg school; this old imperial city occupying, in the variety of its artistic productions, almost the same position as Florence did to Italy. Here, also, in a similar manner, it was the striving after a thoroughly complete and characteristic form of expression, which belonged as a common basis to the different productions of the Nuremberg masters. Nowhere, however, did this tendency reach such perfection, such nobleness of conception, and such delicacy of execution, as in the bronze works. Established tradition placed the basis for this development in the artist family of Vischer, and the special gifts of one particularly important master carried the efforts of the school to a point never otherwise reached in the same manner by the works of northern art. The earliest known work of this school is the bronze font of the church at Wittenberg, executed in 1457 by Hermann Vischer.[1] The form is Gothic, finished with various graceful ornaments; but the figures of the Apostles, which surround it, are especially important, because we trace in them a happy remnant of the simple lines of Gothic works, and we also perceive a conscious and independent adoption of the antique style of drapery.

The principal master of the Nuremberg school, and one of the greatest of German art generally, is, however, the son of this Hermann, the famous Peter Vischer, of whom we know that he became a master in the art in 1489, and died in 1529.[2] Among all the gifted masters of that period, not even excepting Albert Dürer, he has the freest perception; a gift which enabled him to rise above the narrow barriers of the taste of the age, and by a restless striving after purity to reach a dignity and nobleness of style which stands unique in the northern lands throughout the whole of this long period. The earliest authentic work by his hand is the monument of the Archbishop Ernst, in the cathedral of Magdeburg, completed in the year 1495: it is a sarco-

---

[1] Illustrations in Schadow's *Denkmälern Wittenbergs.*
[2] *Denkm. d. Kunst.* Pl. 85. Figs. 7–11.

phagus, adorned with figures of the Apostles and other sculptures, and upon it rests the figure of the archbishop. The master here, more than in any other work, aims at the coarse characterisation and exact mode of treatment peculiar to Nuremberg art at that period; but in the figures of the Apostles, he already betrays his own grand sense of the beautiful. At about the same time (1496), he executed the gravestone of Bishop Johann, in the cathedral of Breslau, which inclines in its conception to the same tendency. Other monuments of this earlier epoch, which, however, cannot with certainty be traced back to this master, evidence, on the other hand, a free advance towards the more simple and pure style of his father. Many things, designed by others, were only moulded in Vischer's atelier : this was the case, for instance, with the monument of Bishop George II., in the cathedral at Bamberg, completed in 1506, and which in its conception belongs to his earlier manner.

The famous masterpiece of the master, the tomb of St. Sebald, in the church of that Saint at Nuremberg,[1] which he executed with his five sons between 1508 and 1519, marks a decided change in his artistic style. As early as the year 1488, a design was sketched for it—it appears probably by his own hand—though it has, without foundation, been ascribed to Veit Stoss. According to this, the monument was to be a slender building, rising with three pyramidal points, and constructed in the conventional Gothic style. If, as has been supposed, utterly without foundation, mere economical considerations prevented the execution of this plan, and favoured that now existing, we may extol this as a most fortunate circumstance; for to it, combined with his own more matured artistic feeling, we owe a work which stands unique of its kind, while the former would have been similar to many others. The whole conception of the work shows the master to have reached perfect freedom and independence.[2] The sarcophagus, which belongs to an earlier period,

---

[1] Engraved by Reindel. Cf. *Denkm. d. Kunst.* Pl. 85. Figs. 7–10.

[2] Rettberg's remarks on this evince singular narrowmindedness. See Nürnberg's *Kunstleben*, p. 150.

rests on a support, the surfaces of which are adorned with reliefs representing incidents from the life of the Saint. This essential part of the monument was enclosed within a light shrine rising on eight slender pillars, and the whole was crowned by three rich baldachins. While the latter are a free imitation of the finish repeatedly to be seen in monuments of the thirteenth century,

Fig. 365. Tomb of S. Sebald. By P. Vischer.

the structure of the whole exhibits the slender light arrangements of the Gothic style, and the details point to the most elegant Renaissance. These various elements are, however, blended together so ingeniously and so freely, that the work is admirable even in this respect. Still more versatile, however, does the genius of the master appear in the extremely rich plastic ornament, with which he covered the monument from the socle to its uppermost point.

The reliefs on the surface of the support (cf. Fig. 367) exhibit a grace and naïveté, and at the same time a simplicity of treatment, and a just conception of the relief style, scarcely equalled in the North or even in Italy. The shrine rests—an ingenious idea of the artist—upon twelve gigantic snails, which support it on the back of their strong shells; and on its richly decorated base it exhibits an abundance of excellent little figures, recumbent lions, and all sorts of mythological beings—nymphs and genii, antique and Old Testament heroes, and the allegorical figures of the cardinal virtues. The cornice, triangular compartments, and other places, are peopled with various small creations. At the four corners there are light-bearers in the form of fabulous mermaids, which, like the rest, exhibit perfect grace and lightness in design and execution. (Fig. 366.) In small niches in the beautifully constructed pillars there are the figures of the Apostles, in which the master has reached the utmost nobleness, and the most perfect freedom and grandeur. In the noble flow of the drapery the idealism of the fourteenth century lingers purified and glorified, combined with classic simplicity and delicacy of feeling, with perfect knowledge of the natural organisation, giving the whole character a grand beauty, such as is only found, in a similar manner, in Lorenzo Ghiberti. (Cf. Fig. 368.) On one of the narrow sides of the support, the master has introduced the simple dignified figure of S. Sebald, and on the other a corresponding figure of himself with a cap and leathern apron. The columns do not terminate in finials as in the Gothic style, but are crowned with twelve statues of the prophets; but above the central baldachin, the highest point of the whole, stands the infant Christ with the orb. Thus the master has not only blended the profound cycles and the idealism of the middle ages with the striving of his age after lifelike characterisation, but with the grace of antique forms and ideas, thus producing a work full of enchanting harmony.

Still more decidedly does Vischer in his subsequent works adopt the antique style, such as we find it at that time disseminated far beyond Italy by innumerable artistic influences; but even now he belongs to those rare masters, who relinquish therefore nothing of their own, nothing of the naïveté and life-like freshness of their native art. It was just in him a touch of

Fig. 366. Mermaids from the Tomb of S. Sebald.

inner affinity with this art, which had restrained him from the very beginning of his work from the eccentricity, fancy, and frequent peculiarities of his German contemporaries. One of his most perfect works is the splendid relief in the cathedral at

Fig. 367. Relief from the Tomb of S. Sebald. Sebald curing a blind Man.

Ratisbon,[1] in the year 1521, representing Christ soothing the sorrowing sisters of Lazarus : it is touching in its plain truth, and is full of deep expression and beautiful clear arrangement : the

[1] *Denkm. d. Kunst.* Pl. 65. Fig. 1.

style of the relief is as simple as Ghiberti's, and is equally noble
and free in every part.   No less full of noble feeling and ideal
beauty is a relief of the Crowning of the Virgin, belonging to the
same year: the original is in Erfurt Cathedral, and there is a
copy in the Castle Church at Wittenberg.   We must also mention
two monuments belonging to the master's later period—that of
Cardinal Albrecht of Brandenburg, in the Collegiate Church at
Aschaffenburg, executed, in 1525, during the prince's lifetime;

Thaddæus.   Paul.
Fig. 368.   From the Tomb of S. Sebald.

and the masterly monument of the Elector Frederic the Wise, in
the Castle Church at Wittenberg, in the year 1527.   That Peter
Vischer, lastly, occasionally also handled antique subjects, is
evidenced by a statuette of Apollo in the Art School at Nuremberg, full of life and freshness, though the forms are somewhat
hard; and a relief of Orpheus and Eurydice, in the cabinet of
curiosities in the Museum at Berlin.

Besides these numerous and important works, we have yet to mention some which indeed also emanated from the master's atelier, but which do not evidence so distinctly his own hand, and betray a certain dissimilarity in the treatment. We may reckon among these the monuments of the Henneberg counts in the church at Römhild near Meiningen[1]—that of Count Otto IV., executed previous to the year 1500, and especially that of Hermann VIII. and his wife Elizabeth, completed after 1507, in which the characterisation of the principal figures appears extremely excellent, and must certainly be traced back to Peter Vischer himself. There is also a double monument to the Elector John Cicero, in Berlin Cathedral, bearing the date of 1530, and the name of Johann Vischer, the earlier part of which must, however, be denied as the work of the great master. Lastly, the partially beautiful slab with the Burial of Christ, in the Ægidienkirche at Nuremberg, of the year 1522, points to the master himself, both in its design and in the execution of the finely foreshortened body of Christ in shallow relief. The above-named Johann Vischer executed, in 1530, the old bronze relief of the Virgin Mary, preserved in the Collegiate Church at Aschaffenburg. To another son, Hermann Vischer, the younger, the beautiful monument of the Elector Johann, in the Collegiate Church at Wittenberg, is ascribed, which was executed in the year 1534, though, indeed, it is no longer wholly free from mannerism in the treatment of the drapery. Of Hermann we also know that he was in Italy, and brought from thence a number of drawings; so that a direct connection with the art of the South is thus authenticated. Lastly, the monument of the Count Eitel Frederic of Zollern, in the church at Hechingen, executed about 1510, seems to belong to Peter Vischer: it shows great affinity to one of the Römhild monuments, but is superior to it in beauty and freedom of treatment. Whether the monument of Cardinal Frederic, in the cathedral at Cracow, likewise emanated from Vischer's atelier must for a time remain uncertain.

[1] Döbner, *Die ehernen Denkmale in der Stiftskirche zu Römhild, &c.* Munich, 1840.

There is, on the other hand, no doubt that the two colossal bronze statues of King Arthur and Theodoric on the monument of the Emperor Maximilian, in the Collegiate Church at Innsbruck, owe their origin to Peter Vischer's hand.[1] This monument, one of the most extensive and most splendidly sculptured memorial in the world, was begun about 1508, according to an idea of the art-loving emperor, under the direction of his court painter, Gilg Sesslschreiber of Augsburg. The twenty-eight bronze colossal figures of the ancestors of the imperial house, and of half legendary hero kings in the early middle ages, were first undertaken, and these surround the real monument in solemn rows. The noblest of them are the figures of Arthur and Theodoric, bearing the date of 1513, and their elegant bearing, delicate proportions, and perfect execution (the latter especially the case in Arthur) prove them to be works of Peter Vischer. The greater number of the female figures, moreover, are distinguished for their graceful bearing, richly damasked and softly flowing drapery. Most of these, as well as the statues of the knights, generally less successfully executed, and occasionally coarse to heaviness, or insipid and fantastic, and astonishingly rich in costume, were designed by Meister Gilg. Steffen and Melchior Godl and Gregor Löffler are chiefly named as casters. The latter cast in 1549 the statue of Chlodwig, designed by Christoph Amberger. The work advanced but slowly, owing to its extent, and the whole was not completed until the second half of the century. For there were, besides, twenty-three bronze statues of saints of the Austrian House, about two feet high, which were originally intended to be connected with the monument, but they are now placed separately in the Silver Chapel of this same church. These also are able and lifelike works, though without particular delicacy of conception. At last the splendid marble cenotaph was executed, on which is placed the noble and feeling bronze statue of the emperor kneeling in prayer. The latter, as well as the fine statues of the four cardinal virtues, treated in an

[1] Cf. Lübke's *Gesch. der Plastik*, pp. 605 and 611 et seq. *Denkm. d. Kunst.* Pl. 86. Fig. 2.

antique style, which surround the emperor, were designed by Alexander Colin of Mecheln, and were cast by Hans Lenden-strauch of Munich in 1572 ; the emperor's statue being 'recast' in 1582 by the Italian Lodovico Scalza, surnamed Del Duca. Colin also executed twenty of the marble reliefs which cover the monument, the first four of which were the work of Gregor and Peter Abel of Cologne. These works, containing the heroic deeds and brilliant events in the life of the emperor, are certainly composed in pure picturesque effect, with crowded arrangement, according to the taste of the time ; but they are pleasing from their neat miniature-like execution, as well as from many fresh lifelike characteristics, and great skill in the handling of the chisel. Thus the whole monument stands unique in its kind.

The monuments of the Saxon princes in the choir of Frei-burg Cathedral are another grand memorial of the plastic art of this period. They begin with Henry the Pious († 1541), and con-tain in the rich marble architecture of the Renaissance six gilded bronze statues of princes and princesses, as well as the figures of Caritas and Justitia—able works, occasionally exhibiting the most lively power of conception, though inclining to the general ideal style. Thus in the bronze work also, at the close of the century, that revolution took place, which we have already desig-nated as a turning point in the history of German plastic art, and the monuments of which we must reserve for the following chapter.

b. *France, Spain, and England.*

The plastic art of the other non-Italian lands still require much study and investigation before we can obtain a connected glance at its development. We will for a time follow the separate notices which we possess respecting it.

In France[1] the influence of the realistic style is evidenced in the before-mentioned works at Dijon, at the end of the fourteenth century. In the course of the following epoch, this effort rises to

---

[1] *Denkm. d. Kunst.* Pl. 86. Cf. Lübke's *Geschichte der Plastik*, p. 617 et seq., 680 et seq.

peculiar power and importance; but it is frequently combined with an attractive softness and mildness of expression. In the beginning of the sixteenth century the Italian Renaissance style prevails, and is especially employed with richness and dignity in monuments. In carved work there are many richly executed choir seats preserved, such as those in Amiens Cathedral, executed by Jean Trupin, in the year 1508, and in many other churches. Stone sculpture displays great luxuriance and splendour occasionally in the reliefs for the decoration of the choir screen, which frequently exhibit a restless crowded arrangement, as in the cathedral at Chartres, and still more in that of Amiens (about 1531); but it is especially in some extremely rich monuments that the realistic style is often exhibited with nobleness and moderation. Among the earlier of these works, we may mention the monument of Duke John Sanspeur and his wife, begun in 1444, and not finished in 1461, and which was removed from the Chartreuse at Dijon to the Museum in the same city. At about 1504, the splendid royal tombs in the church at Brou were executed, which are as charming from the perfect tenderness of their execution as they are from their agreeable conception. No less costly and ingenious is the double monument of the two cardinals of Amboise, in Rouen Cathedral, which was executed in 1510 by Roullant de Roux, with a peculiar blending of the mediæval and antique styles; also the monument of Louis XII. in St. Denis, a work executed by the distinguished Jean Juste of Tours, at a somewhat later period (about 1530). The arrangement employed in Italy for such monuments here appears in great splendour. The monument consists of an open arcade building, on the upper platform of which kneel the two expressive and noble marble statues of the deceased. Through the arcades, however, the eye falls on the figures of both lying outstretched in the fearful reality of death, executed with striking design, as though the casts had been taken from the corpse. Northern realism here appears in its most unpleasing exactness. The lower structure is adorned with statues of the Apostles and other sculptured work by an inferior hand. The same master previously produced the tender charming monumental figures, in Tours Cathedral, of two young princes of the royal house, who had died early. Lastly, the unsurpassably noble figures of the minister, Louis de Poncher, and his wife, Roberte Legendre, in the Louvre, must be ascribed to him.

The antique tendency which is here perceived, and the adoption of which was brought about by the influence of various Italian artists, made its way more and more exclusively towards the middle of the sixteenth century. Increasingly few are those works which exhibit an affinity with the middle ages in form and idea; such, for instance, as a group representing the Burial of Christ, in the crypt of Bourges Cathedral, executed in the year 1545; or such as the works of a humble artist, named G. Richier, who executed a Mount Calvary, in the church of Hatton-le-Châtel (1523), and the monument of Duke René of Chalons, in S. Etienne at Bar-le-Duc, at a later period (1544). The greater number of artists were employed by the court, and hence followed the Renaissance style, so much in favour there. Thus there was the famous Pierre Bontemps, who executed the monument of Francis I. in S. Denis in 1552; a work which, fashioned after the tomb of Louis XII., surpasses its model in splendour. But it was especially the splendid works for the decoration of the palace of Fontainebleau which engaged a number of able artists, known under the name of the 'School of Fontainebleau.' The principal master was Jean Goujon (–1572), whose plastic works are full of grace from their softness and elegance of form. He produced the tender and nobly executed reliefs on the fountain 'Des Innocens,' in the Museum of the* Louvre; also the somewhat affected representation of Diana of Poitiers, the mistress of Henry II., who is depicted as Diana resting by the side of a splendid stag, according to the conception of the period; originally in the Château Anet, and now likewise in the Louvre. There are also many other works there by his hand. Germain Pilon's works exhibit a similar style; he was engaged in the execution of Francis the First's monument, and also took part in the monument of Henry II., from 1564 to 1583. Some-

what earlier (about 1560), he executed the three charming
Graces, now in the Louvre, which formerly bore the heart of
Henry II. in an urn, in the church of the Celestines. These and
other works by the same versatile artist evidence great ease and
technical power, but at the same time they show that the simple
period of French art was for ever vanished, and was supplanted
by an affected, studied, and even mannered style. In Henry the
Second's monument, the Italian Ponzio also took part, who as
' Maître Ponce ' occupies no unimportant position in the French
school of that day; and Frémin Roussel, who also worked at
Fontainebleau. We have yet to mention Jean Cousin and Barthélemy Prieur, many portraits by whom are in the Louvre, and
furnish proof that this branch of plastic art preserved its nobleness and simplicity of style for a longer period.

In the Netherlands, the brilliant advance of painting seems
to have been an impediment to plastic work; yet there are some
monuments which afford a favourable idea of the skill of the
artists. The monument of Mary of Burgundy, in the Liebfrauenkirche at Bruges, executed in 1495 by Jan de Baker, and
full of noble truth, and the monument of Charles the Bold, added
subsequently (1558) by a far feebler hand, are important bronze
works. A finely conceived and delicately executed marble
monument, of the year 1544, is to be seen in a side chapel in
St. Jacques at Bruges; and the chimney of the Hall of Justice,
in the same city, executed in the year 1529, is a splendid specimen of carving.

Spain[1] is rich in the plastic works of this epoch, in which
mediæval composition is often combined with antique influences,
thus producing a fantastic and magnificent effect. This is the
case especially in the lofty carved altars, the details of which, it
is true, correspond more with the Renaissance, although the
style, on the whole, may be called Gothic. Numerous statues
in niches, as well as picturesquely treated reliefs, adorn these
rich works. Among the most costly works of this kind, we must

---

[1] *Denkm. d. Kunst.* Pl. 86.

mention the high altar of the cathedral of Toledo, which was executed in 1500, and is resplendent with gold and coloured ornament. No less magnificent are the monuments of this period : sarcophagi covered with decorations and reliefs, and crowned with insulated figures, which surround the recumbent figure of the deceased. Thus in the Carthusian House of Miraflores, there are some monuments which Gil de Siloê executed, about 1490, for King Juan II., his consort, and the Infant Don Alonso. The style subsequently attained to greater simplicity through the influence of Raphael and Michael Angelo, while in the decorative parts there is still an agreeable remnant left of imaginative freshness. The works of Alonso Berruguete (1480– 1562), famous as architect, sculptor, and painter, are especially of this kind : there is a splendid monument by him, erected to the great inquisitor and archbishop, Don Juan Tavera, in the church of S. Johann Baptista, at Toledo. The reliefs here are especially praised for their simple and noble style.

In England,[1] we find some instances of the advance of realistic conceptions, especially in monuments, which here, in harmony with mediæval tendencies, are still formed as bronze slabs engraved with the figures of the deceased. The tomb of Richard Beauchamps, in Warwick Church, is executed with more power and greater costliness, and surpasses all English monuments of the period. It is true, William Austen's statue of the knight is tolerably stiff, but the head exhibits lifelike adherence to nature. The monumental slab was the work of Thomas Stevyns, the marble sarcophagus that of John Bourd, and the chiseling and gilding was superintended by Barthol. Lambespring. There are also many wood carvings, and several reliefs, handled with much character and exactness, in the church at Barnak, which may be mentioned as works of the same style. With the sixteenth century, however, here also Italian artists appear, who transplant the style of their own country to England. First among these is Pietro Torrigiano, who, with a number of English asso-

---

[1] *Denkm. d. Kunst.* Pl. 86.

ciates, completed in 1519 the splendid monument of Henry VII.,
in the chapel of this king at Westminster. The somewhat earlier
monument of the mother of this king, in the same church, seems
also from his hand. About 1530, we have authentic proof of the
activity of many other Italian artists in England, especially of
Benedetto da Rovezzano. English plastic art, however, did not
even now rise to lasting independent importance.

2. PAINTING.

In the North, as in Italy, painting was the favourite art of
this epoch, and it acquired there, especially in the Netherlands
and Germany, preponderating importance ; but, although in it
the same tendency of the age is expressed, it is manifested in a
wholly different manner, and leads to essentially different results.
The beginning of modern painting in the North by Hubert van
Eyck is more splendid, grand, and free than it was in Italy by
Masaccio or Mantegna. Not merely by the improvement of
the old invention of oil painting, and its perfect and masterly
adaptation and cultivation, but also by the sublimity of style,
which blended the old ideal grandeur with the youthful freshness of a developed taste for nature, the founder of the modern
painting of the North occupies a position which renders him
equal to any other great pioneering genius. He goes indeed
a step beyond the Italian artists. Without damaging in any way
the sacredness of the subject, he adheres rather faithfully to the
profound ideas of the earlier art ; he transports his figures into
the midst of smiling life, releases them from the strict ban of the
gold ground, and spreads around them the glory of nature in
the splendid light of spring. All this he conceives with a depth
and power, such as the Italian art of that day has nowhere
attempted with equal success ; and yet at the same time, amid
the boundless variety which opens to his eye, he adheres strictly
to essentials without losing himself in paltriness.

If, after such beginnings, northern painting in its further
development never reached the height of Italian art, if it forfeited the great mind of a Hubert van Eyck, and in many

respects rather went backwards than forwards, the reasons for this are very various.   In the first place, it had great influence upon the art that painting in the North had long lost those wall surfaces on which the larger cycles of events had been displayed, and on which connected historical compositions could be carried out.   It is, above all, the preponderating development of Gothic art, which cut off from northern painting all possibility of extensive display, and bound up the very veins of life.   Thus the artists saw themselves limited to miniature and panel painting, and more and more lost the opportunity of depicting their figures as large as life and in all the fulness of existence. Indeed, the preponderating delight in wood carving for altars, which we have just considered, limited the activity of painting to this narrow sphere, and allotted to it for the most part only the decoration of the wings, or even merely of the outer sides. Thus it was, therefore, that in such altar-pieces the carved works possessed usually higher artistic value than the paintings.

Upon the small panels the art could indeed advance in grace and delicacy; it could devote itself lovingly to the inexhaustible charms of natural life; it could refresh itself with the old Germanic taste for trees and plants, weeds, flowers, and grass blades; and, even in the representation of the human figure, it could lay the main stress upon depth of expression, and upon feeling and tenderness.   In all these respects northern painting had its indubitable advantages.   But it lessened them by the fact that it lost the taste for all that is grand and essential, that in the delineation of the most casual details it wandered into excessive adherence to nature, and constantly degenerated into artificial ornament and extravagance.   The figures lack the feeling of life, and while the heads, in their exquisite perfection, have an expression of mind produced by the most exact delineation of the individual character, the imperfectly formed heads with their singular movements cannot follow the movements of the mind.   Added to this, there is a magnificence which appears outwardly heavy from the predilection for stiff material, for velvet and silk, brocade and satin, which gives rise to those hard angular creased folds, which are increased to the utmost by the commonplace tastelessness and fantastic inclination to intricacy and overloading, permitting neither repose nor beauty.

Public life in the North in general had not that free and noble appearance, which it acquired in the powerful cities of Italy from a cultivated aristocracy, and under a grand modern princely power. In the commercial cities of the North, wealth had led to almost barbarous pomp, which found its corresponding and unpleasing expression in the strange, motley, and overloaded attire. The perfect grace and refined customs of outward deportment, innate to the Italian from of old, and disseminated through all classes, was at that time as now rare among the northern nations; and, lastly, still more than now, the southern races were superior to the northern in natural beauty. All these circumstances are reflected most immediately in the works of plastic art. Moreover, in the North there was an utter lack of that grand perception which recognised in art the highest ornament of life. The magistrates and princes could only rarely rise to that height which in Italy produced those extensive monumental works which rendered art so great there. Added to this, the artist was never granted that free position, in which he delighted in Italy. Albert Dürer gives us the most positive evidence of this, when he writes from Venice to his friend Pirkheimer, 'Oh, how I shall freeze for the sun! Here I am lord, at home I am a parasite.' The guilds and corporations, with all their narrowmindedness, held the artist fettered, and made freer advance almost impossible even to the boldest minds.

It was from these reasons that northern painting adhered to the one-sided views of the fifteenth century, sank into formal ossification, and in this manner placed almost insurmountable obstacles in the way of even the great masters who were produced by northern art towards the beginning of the following century—among them even an Albert Dürer; and in the struggle with these obstacles they lost their best powers and time, without being able wholly to extricate themselves from the fetters of a one-sided age. Added to this, there was that great reformatory movement of Luther's, which took possession of all more serious and deep minds, and put an end to all quiet artistic work. In struggling for the highest blessing of freedom of conscience, the North had for a long period to renounce the choicest gifts of art.

While by these various internal and external circumstances, northern painting was kept behind Italian art in its highest value, yet it also had its peculiar excellences, which promised its independent importance, in spite of all formal constraint and all inclination to unessential and paltry details. These excellences are, in the first place, a depth and warmth of feeling, which burst forth through the defective form—simple truth and naïveté, combined with a thorough sincerity and purity, qualities which all together cannot compensate indeed for the want cf beauty, but by virtue of their strong moral power have a refreshing effect and can make amends for much; above all, however, the truly inexhaustible abundance of individual life, which speaks to us in the works of the northern masters with a power and variety, such as is known by no other artistic epoch or school. Added to this, also, is the popular style to which northern art adhered, and which resulted in the splendid perfection cf the arts for multiplying works, such as engraving and woodcut. In this manner the masters spoke intelligibly to all nations, disseminated their ideas afar, so that everyone could comprehend them and make them his own, and by this lively interchange they were strengthened in the rude popular mode of expression which was natural to them. Thus we may say that art in the North bore a democratic stamp, while in Italy it appears more aristocratic, and, we shall readily here perceive, analogous with other spheres of intellectual life. Lastly, German thought at this period trod more independently than ever the fantastic world, and in many productions, especially in the famous ‘Dance of Death,’ and similar designs, it reached a height of grand and touching humour, unattained in this manner by any other people, and certainly not by the Italian.

a. *The Netherland Schools.*[1]

Commercial Flanders was to be the birthplace of modern painting in the North.[2] In the rich old cities of the country, trade and industry of every kind had flourished for some time, and all foreign seafaring nations found emporiums for the exchange of their goods. Added to this, she possessed a court, which just at this period was one of the first in splendour and consideration, and was conducive to the advance of the newly awakened art. It is not improbable that that old miniature school, famous in former times, which had its seat on the banks of the Maas, was of great importance in the development of Flemish art; although, on the other side, the sculptures of the monuments of Tournay had already powerfully excited the taste for natural lifelike conception and perfection of form. If, however, the eye of the artist had once been opened to conscious perception of the surrounding reality, such a splendid rich and varied life as had at that time reached its height in the Flemish cities operated powerfully on the development of such a tendency. Not in vain did the painter see the most different commercial nations—Germans and Italians, Sclavonians and Prussians, Spanish and Portuguese, bustling actively in the marketplaces of Bruges and Ghent. The endless variety in physiognomy, gesture, costume, and manners, called forth observation, and rendered the eye more acute.

From these favourable circumstances, a new and grand rise took place in painting in the person of a master who obtained an influence over his time such as few others have had, and who carried on the painting of his century to new and astonishing advance. Hubert van Eyck was, it appears, probably born in the little market town of Maaseyck, about the year 1366. He

---

[1] *Denkm. d. Kunst.* Pl. 81.
[2] Cf. Hotho, *Die Malerschule Huberts van Eyck.* Vol. II. Berlin, 1858. Schnaase, *Niederländische Briefe.* Stuttgart, 1834. Cavalcaselle, *The Early Flemish Painters.* Waagen, *Ueber Hubert und Johann van Eyck.* Breslau, 1822. Michiels, *Histoire de la Peinture flamande.* Bruxelles, 1846. E. Förster, *Gesch. der deutschen Kunst.* Vol. II. Leipzig, 1853.

seems to have been of an old painter family, as not merely a brother, but also a sister was devoted to the same art. Nevertheless, little is known of the nearer home circumstances of the great master ; and only so much is certain, that in the latter years of his life he was occupied in Ghent in the execution of his famous work, while he probably passed the middle years of his life at Bruges. His merits as the founder of an entirely new mode of painting are, on the contrary, established indubitably. In his subjects he followed most sincerely the thoughtful symbolic art of the middle ages, and by his own intellectual power he was able to give it depth and breadth. But at the same time he boldly depicted actual life, placed his sacred incidents in the midst of verdant nature, and stamped the true and exact impress of his own time and country in the physiognomy and dress of his sacred figures, and in his architectural backgrounds and furniture. For these new requirements he devised new advantages in the preparation and use of colours, and made wonderful progress in the application of oil as a cement, by means of which he produced a power and depth never previously known, and an incomparably fine blending of colour. To this was added an excellent varnish, which gave the colours a freshness and brilliancy, so that the paintings, from their perfect appearance of reality, surprised all contemporaries to the highest degree. Thus, as ever, the advance of technical skill grew out of the increased intellectual requirements.

The importance of the master is expressed in a painting in the Gallery at Madrid, which only recently has been attributed to him, although, according to experienced judgment, the composition alone, and not the manner of execution, can be traced to him.[1] A fine and richly constructed Gothic building, with arches and small slender towers, forms, like the mediæval altarpieces, the framework of the whole. Above, under a light graceful baldachin, God the Father is enthroned in mild sublimity, surrounded by rich and splendid drapery. On the steps of the

---

[1] Passavant, *Die christliche Kunst in Spanien.* Leipzig, 1853. O. Mündler, on the other hand, has expressed doubts as to Hubert's authorship.

throne lies the Lamb; on the right sits Mary, humbly reading in a prayer book; on the left is the youthful evangelist St. John, on the point of writing his Revelation. Further below, on a terrace, there are charming angels making music; while others, looking forth from the open courts of the side architecture, mingle their voices joyfully with the sound of the instruments. From the central slender baldachin the water of life is gushing forth clearly into a spring, towards which, on one side, the band of the faithful, with the Pope at their head, are approaching reverently; whilst the synagogue opposite, represented by the High Priest and his train, is turning away with a broken banner, and full of terror and despair. The grand architectural structure of the whole, within which the most lively action is exhibited, seems certainly, as far, at least, as regards the composition, to justify the assumption of such a master as Hubert.

His principal work, however, is the famous Adoration of the Lamb, which he painted by order of the patrician Judocus Vyts and his wife Lisbetta, for their funeral chapel in S. Bavo, in Ghent. The principal panels of this large altar picture are still in their original place, but six of the most beautiful side wings are in the Berlin Museum. Here, also, the subject is profoundly symbolic, and occupies a number of large panels. The work is divided into an upper and lower piece, each furnished with the wings necessary, which, according to mediæval custom, are painted both inside and out. Above, on opening the wings, God the Father appears enthroned, bearing the triple Papal crown, sceptre, and orb, with a splendid red mantle falling in magnificent folds, and forming one of the most solemn figures known in Christian art. At one side, in humble adoration, is the seated figure of the Madonna, and on the other, John the Baptist; and next to these, on the folding wings, are angels singing and making music; and on the outermost compartments are the figures of Adam and Eve, the representatives of mankind, imploring help and redemption. (These have been recently placed in the Museum at Brussels.) The lower row displays in the centre, on a vast flowery meadow, the Fountain of Life with the

Lamb, who is approached adoringly on both sides by groups of saints and angels, patriarchs, prophets, apostles, and martyrs. These groups are continued on the side wings by bands of hermits and pilgrims (Fig. 369), the champions of Christ and the just judges, who are advancing likewise to the Fountain of Salvation. On the outside the Annunciation is depicted (Fig. 370), and the kneeling figures of the donator and his wife, which are masterly in execution, and the patron saints of the church at Ghent, which are painted as statues.

This grand work was begun in 1420, and stands just as much at the head of the modern advance in painting, as the dome of the cathedral at Florence, begun at about the same time, introduces a revolution in architecture. Hubert is confirmed as an inventor by contemporary records. To no other was such a depth of thought imputed combined with such abundance of ideas, and with such grand power of characterisation. After the master's death, however (1426), his younger brother John was appointed to finish his work, which he completed in the year 1432. There has been much dispute with regard to John's share in it, and united opinion has at length

Fig. 369. The Anchorites. From the Ghent Painting of Hubert van Eyck.

ascribed to him about half of the panels.[1] We may certainly
presume that Hubert's hand alone executed the principal figures,
for there is a solemnity of expression, a majestic and yet soft
flow of drapery, a handling so broad and free with all its tenderness, and at the same time a warmth in the dusky flesh tints,
such as John never exhibits in the works certified by their
inscription to be his own.

Hubert's principal pupil was this same brother John, who

Fig. 370. The Annunciation. By Hubert van Eyck.

.was about twenty years younger; he was born in 1390, and
lived till 1440. All the fame of his brother seems to have been
transferred to him, so that for a time Hubert was almost forgotten. John was appointed in 1425 court painter to Duke
John of Bavaria; he then gained the favour of Philip the Good
of Burgundy, and was sent by him to Portugal in 1428, to paint
the Infanta Isabella, the Duke's betrothed. John gave his

---

[1] In disputing which Hotho limits John's share to a disproportionate minimum.

brother's style more fineness of detail, and went a step further in nicety of execution, renouncing in general all larger dimensions, and preferring a miniature-like style. With all his feeling and tenderness, which especially qualified him for representations of the enthroned Madonna, he lacked his brother's grand serious-ness and thoughtful depth; and while he devoted himself to the delineation of reality even in its most subtile details, he pointed out the way to the following school, by which a wonderful delicacy of detail was obtained. But freedom of physical form and grandeur of mind were for a long time lost.

The earliest of his authentic works is the Consecration of Thomas à Becket as Archbishop of Canterbury, executed in the year 1421, and now in the gallery of the Duke of Devonshire at Chatsworth. The scene is depicted in the interior of a church built in the circular arch style; an arrangement to which John adheres in his subsequent devotional pictures, and which was followed by other masters of his school. Whether the Madonna is represented in familiar simplicity, as in the painting in the Städel Museum at Frankfort; or in a garden amid orange trees, cypresses, and palm trees, as in a picture in the possession of Herr Suermondt at Aix-la-Chapelle; or in a pleasing landscape, as in a picture in the Belvedere in Vienna, erroneously imputed to Hugo van der Goes; or whether, as is generally the case, she is enthroned in a splendid church, as in the picture in the academy at Bruges, completed in 1436 (there is an excellent old copy in the academy at Antwerp), and in the costly gem in the Dresden Gallery; or in an open court, as in the magnificent picture in the Louvre, there is ever a tender idyllic trait, a thoroughly lyric feeling, which is expressed in his works. In many of his portraits, the master has exhibited great delicacy and exactness of characterisation—thus, for instance, in the splendid double portrait of a married couple, Jean Arnolfini and Jeanne Chenany, painted in the year 1434, and now in the English National Gallery; also in the portrait of Judocus Vyts, and in that of the Dean Jan van Löwen, painted in the year 1436, in the gallery of the Belvedere at Vienna; and, lastly, in the half-length picture of his own wife, painted in the year 1439, in the academy at Bruges. On the other hand, the Head of Christ, in the Berlin Museum, painted in 1438, and that in the academy at Bruges, painted in 1440, exhibit a certain want of expression, seeming to intimate to us the limits of John's genius.

The stamp of Eyck's style is, lastly, to be traced in the excellent miniatures of the prayer book, executed in 1424 for the Duke of Bedford, Regent of France, and which is now in the Library in Paris. As three hands are to be discerned in it, one is inclined to impute a share in it to Margaretha v. Eyck, the sister of the two masters, likewise certified to have been a painter. More doubtful is the participation of a third brother, Lambert, who is likewise known, though in a vague and uncertain manner.

The style established by the Eycks exercised irresistible influence upon all contemporaries, and was followed in Flanders by a great number of artists, of whom, however, there is too little known, but that the multitude of nameless pictures scattered in various galleries may be traced positively to separate masters. From this flood of wavering statements and hypotheses, we will therefore only bring forward a few points that have been established with some degree of certainty.[1] Thus the Städel Museum at Frankfort possesses a Madonna by Pieter Christus (Peter Christophsen), bearing the date 1447, hitherto erroneously read 1417; and the Museum at Berlin has two panels by the same painter, bearing the date of 1452, and representing in splendid colouring the Annunciation, the Adoration, and the Last Judgment. Like this artist, Gerhard van der Meere, by whom there is an altar-piece of the Crucifixion in St. Bavo in Ghent, seems also to have been a pupil of Hubert. In the same list, we may also mention Justus van Gent, whose principal work is a Last Supper in S. Agata in Urbino; and the equally highly esteemed Hugo van der Goes, who executed a Birth of

---

[1] James Weale has recently afforded important historical information respecting the masters of this school, in his catalogue of the Collection of the Academy at Bruges, as well as in the Journal edited by him, *Le Beffroi.* Bruges, 1863.

Christ in S. Maria Nuova in Florence, a double portrait in the Uffizi, and a St. John, bearing the date of 1472, in the Pinakothek at Munich.

More independent than these, Rogier van der Weyden, the elder, also called Rogier van Brügge (1400-1464), appears one of the most famous of Van Eyck's pupils. He was appointed painter of the city of Brussels in 1436, and at a subsequent period he was for some time in Italy. He surpassed John in his realistic fidelity and accuracy of representation, and in the detailed character of his delineations; he carried his exactness of form into coldness and hardness, but he considerably extended the range of his art, by introducing the most varied scenes of sacred history, and at the same time touching new chords of deep and thrilling feeling. His figures are for the most part somewhat hard, angular, and thin; but his heads possess great power and depth of physiognomy, and the colouring is softer and lighter than with the other masters.

One of his most famous paintings was the erroneously called Travelling Altar of Charles V., recently (in a careful old copy?) in the possession of the Museum at Berlin. In the centre there is the dead body of Christ on the lap of His sorrowing mother, on the folding wings the Birth of Christ and His Resurrection are depicted, all three scenes being enclosed in richly decorated architectural framework. A similar work in the same gallery, but thoroughly bearing the stamp of originality, contains representations from the history of John the Baptist. Here also there are the three chief incidents—his Birth, the Baptism of Christ, and his Beheading—enclosed in rich architectural frames, in which other scenes referring to it are painted as plastic groups; while in these works, the principal pictures show all the sharpness of the realistic style, the plastic representations adhere almost unchanged to the ideal softer style of the earlier period. The large folding picture of the Last Judgment, at Beaune in Burgundy, seems likewise to belong to this master's early epoch; while another folding altar, in the Museum at Berlin, is one of the most perfect works of his later life. The Birth of Christ is here depicted in a charming manner, and the folding panels contain the representation of the New Light of the World arising to the heathen; for, on the one side, the three kings are bringing their gifts of homage; and on the other, the Emperor Augustus, who, according to an old legend, has his attention drawn to the wonderful event by the Cumæan Sibyl, is raising the censer in worship. There is a similar work bearing much affinity with this, representing the Adoration of the Kings, in the Pinakothek at Munich. In the Städel Museum at Frankfort, there is an excellent Madonna with St. Peter, John the Baptist, Cosmas, and Damianus, which exhibits splendid colouring and careful execution.

Fig. 371. Sibyl and Augustus. Rogier v. d. Weyden.

A follower of Rogier, probably his pupil, is the much-praised Hans Memling, formerly erroneously called Hemling (about 1495), one of the most gifted and attractive masters of his time. Little is known of the circumstances of his life; his German origin seems certified by the name Hans. That he came to Bruges after the battle of Nancy, in 1477, as a wounded soldier, and was nursed in the Johannis Hospital, is a legend without foundation. Extensive travels through Germany, Italy, France, and Spain made him everywhere known and sought after. He aimed more than all at a neat miniature-like style; and, while adhering to this, he acquired a still higher degree of life and realistic perfection. At the same time, however, a breath of sweet feeling pervades his pictures, and manifests itself in an abundance of poetical ideas. Subjects such as the Life of Mary were rendered still more rich by him, and displayed an enchanting truth and grace. He frequently extended the landscape of his pictures, and embraced, at the same time, a number of scenes together, which were for the most part conceived in succession as regards time. It is as if those old carved wooden altars, with their many divisions, were transformed in harmony with the realistic requirements of the age.

Of the works which are ascribed to this attractive master in the present day, most are attributed to him merely on account of their similarity of style, and are without name or other designation. The earliest of these appears to be the Last Judgment, in the Marienkirche at Dantzic, painted in 1467, and purchased in 1473 from the Dutch, together with a richly freighted galley, by a Dantzic sea captain. It is also executed with folding panels, and contains one of the most detailed and thoughtful representations which northern art has produced of the Last Judgment, Paradise, and Hell. The Johannis Hospital at Bruges possesses some of the most important works of his middle life, among them the only work marked with his name. This is the Johannis-altar of the year 1479, the central picture of which represents the enthroned Virgin and Child, who, according to an old legend, is putting the betrothal ring on St. Catharine; on the folding panels the Martyrdoms of the two St. Johns are depicted. We must also mention, though it belongs to a somewhat later period, the famous Chest of S. Ursula, one of the most graceful legends of the saints, executed in neat and light miniature style, and full of fine and tender feeling. The six compartments contain the Arrival of S. Ursula and her Maidens at Cologne (Fig. 372), their Arrival at Basle, and then at Rome; their Journey Home; their Return to Cologne; and their Martyrdom.

Two panels, depicting the Seven Joys and the Seven Sufferings of the Virgin, also belong to this master—the former in the Pinakothek at Munich, the latter in the gallery at Turin. Both

portray with great distinctness, on a rich landscape, a number of
scenes full of figures, in which true feeling and an agreeable
depth of expression is vividly expressed. Lastly, in the year
1491, a most important work was produced, which is likewise
ascribed to this master—namely, the large panel painting in the
cathedral at Lübeck, containing a copious representation of the

Fig. 372. From the Church of S. Ursula. By Hans Memling.

history of the Passion up to the Crucifixion, and the Annunciation, and some saints upon the folding panels. In all these
pictures, Memling exhibits the height to which the Flemish
school could attain in its own way, and at the same time the
barriers against which it must at length be wrecked. As the
rich fancy of the most gifted artists ever found itself limited to

moderate panels, this school could never more rise to that complete understanding of the human figure in its free power of life, which is given in such grand touches in the works of Hubert van Eyck. Miniature-like execution prevailed more and more ; and with all its warmth and delicacy of feeling, with its keenness of observation, and with its charming depth of characterisation, this art remained formal and constrained, and could not in its own strength acquire that noble freedom and completion which raised Italian painting to classic perfection.

Towards the end of the century, the Flemish artists began, however, to feel this deficiency, pointed out as it was to them for the most part by their acquaintance with Italian works. They now endeavoured to study the human figure more thoroughly, to conceive the forms on a larger scale, and to exhibit them in lifelike proportions. This is seen in the gifted master, Gerhard David of Oudewater, who has only recently been known,[1] and who settled at Bruges about the year 1487, and died there in 1523. The academy at Bruges possesses two of his pictures, bearing the date of 1498, and which were painted for the Hall of Justice. They represent in figures of three-quarter life-size the Judgment of Cambyses and its Execution. Powerfully painted with warm colouring, with expressive heads, and careful neatness of detail, their only fault is a somewhat too confused arrangement, and the subject of the latter is too glaringly horrible. The younger Rogier van der Weyden, probably the son of the elder, displayed similar energy ; and his most important work, a Descent from the Cross, executed in the year 1488, and now in the Museum at Berlin, exhibits grand and even excessive passionate expression, and bold treatment of form. Noble and more idealistic appears the able Quintin Messys (Matsys), who, tradition tells us, out of love for the daughter of the painter Franz Floris, left the smith's workshop for painting, and who lived till 1531. He, too, produced a Descent from the Cross as his principal picture, a work full of

[1] Cf. Weale's *Beffroi*, 1863, p. 223 et seq.

power and dramatic life, now in the academy at Antwerp. There is a soft and graceful picture by him in the Berlin Gallery, representing a Madonna kissing her Child ; and, lastly, there are some genre paintings by him, which exhibit great acuteness of characterisation—for instance, the Two Misers, the original of which is in Windsor Castle. (Fig. 373.)

Johann Mabuse (–1532) also at first followed a similar style, till he subsequently went to Italy, and fell into the mannerism of the Roman school. This was the case likewise with Bernardin van Orley, who afterwards became a pupil of Raphael; also with Jan van Schoreel, the pupil of Mabuse (1495–1562), Michael Coxcie, and many other masters. These all endeavoured at first to develope themselves independently on the basis of their native tradition; but the Flemish school, in its further course, had become so one-sidedly realistic, that it had completely lost those fundamental principles of a great style which had belonged to it in the time of Hubert van Eyck. It was, therefore, natural that it linked itself where it found a formed ideal style—namely, with the masters of the Roman school. The fruit, however, that had slowly ripened there, as the result of a century of national art prosperity, was not to be transplanted to foreign soil without betraying the character of a borrowed and, as it were, exotic civilisation.

The artists belonging to the succeeding period of development, though for the most part unpleasing, and standing under

Fig. 373. The Two Misers. By Q. Messys.

the ban which burdens all such transition epochs, were, however, of importance, and opened the way by which Netherland art was subsequently again to reach a great independent position. As the principal representative of this transition period we may mention Lambert Lombard (rightly L. Suterman), who produced works until 1560; Franz Floris, rightly De Vriendt, one of the most renowned of his time, whose fame, however, did not survive his century (1520-1570) ; also Otto Venius, or Octavius van Veen, who lived till 1634, and, as Rubens' master, connects the old expiring period with the new revival of art. Others, such as Antonis Moro and Franz Pourbus, preserved even now in their portraits a simple ability and freshness of conception.

In Holland, soon after the middle of the fifteenth century, the decided influence of the Van Eyck school, as formed by Johann van Eyck, became perceptible. We know no certain picture by Albert van Ouwater, who lived at Harlem, and who is regarded as the founder of the school there. On the other hand, his early deceased pupil, Gerhard van Harlem, also called Geertgen van St. Jans, in his two altar panels, now in the Belvedere at Vienna, and representing the Mourning of Christ and the History of the Remains of St. John, shows himself an energetic follower of the Eycks' style, the realism of which, however, often led him to depict unpleasing heads and angular movements, and many fantastic and caricatured features. He devoted especial care to his landscape backgrounds. Among Hubert's immediate followers, we must mention another Harlem artist, Dierick Bouts, or Stuerbout (1391–1478), who subsequently settled at Löwen. The deep glow and brilliancy of his colouring are almost unrivalled even in this school, and his delicacy of characterisation and tenderness of execution are only thrown into the shade by the stiffness of bearing in most of the almost too tall figures. Among his principal authentic works is the altar panel of the Sufferings of S. Erasmus, in S. Peter's, at Löwen, executed about 1463, a painting of incomparable delicacy of execution, though awkward in action ; but the expression of the head is excellent, and the colouring is velvet-like in its softness. There is also an altar panel in the same church, completed in the year 1467, containing a representation of the Last Supper, which, from the greater size of the figures, appears less powerful in the colouring, but equally careful in the execution. There are two of the folding panels of this altar in the Pinakothek at Munich, representing the Gathering of the Manna, and Abraham meeting Melchizedek; the other two, containing

Fig. 374. Christ and the Tempter. After Lucas v. Leyden.

the Feast of the Passover,[1] and Elijah fed by Angels, are in the Museum at Berlin. Less excellent are the two paintings from the Legend of the Emperor Otto III., completed in 1472, which are in the possession of the King of the Netherlands, and are in the Museum at Brussels.

[1] See *Denkm. d. Kunst* (Pl. 81. Fig. 4), under the designation Memling.

We must also here mention Cornelius Engelbrechtsen, of Leyden (1468–1533), who, nevertheless, is more renowned from his pupil Lucas van Leyden [1] (1494–1533) than from his own importance. Lucas, one of the most precocious geniuses in the history of art, made himself noticed even in his ninth year as an engraver, and soon also as a wood carver and painter. Possessed of versatile gifts and restless activity, and astonishingly skilful in the technical work of painting, he yet is devoid of a deeper and nobler conception, and falls generally into that low and genre-like character, which suited his countrymen, or into a bizarre and fantastic extravagance. (Fig. 374.) Among his paintings, we may mention an extensive Last Judgment, in the Town Hall at Leyden, a Madonna of the year 1522, in the Pinakothek at Munich, which is one of his best productions, and a portrait of the Emperor Maximilian, in the gallery of the Belvedere at Vienna.

While thus, in some Dutch artists, the fantastic bias of the age led to the monstrosities depicted by Hieronymus Bosch (there is a work of this kind in the Berlin Gallery), in other painters the inclination to the simple portrayal of reality produced new tendencies, which were subsequently to have a grand future. It was Joachim Patenier (1490–1550), who for the first time made the backgrounds, which had been already an object of especial care with the Netherlanders, the principal matter, treated the sacred stories as unimportant accessories, and thus became the creator of modern northern landscape painting. In his pictures, however, there is a preponderating predilection for varied, rich, and gay colours, which he sometimes counterbalanced by a rather monotonous blue-green tint. His innovations were carried out still more decidedly by his contemporary, Herri de Bles, and the way was prepared for further developments. Thus Dutch painting, when left to its own course, unavoidably falls into an exaggerated adherence to nature, either rude or fantastic.

[1] *Denkm. d. Kunst.* Pl. 84 A.

b. *The German Schools.*[1]

The great effect of the mode of representation introduced by
the Van Eycks appeared first of all in the adjacent districts of
the Lower Rhine. The typical idealism of the Cologne school,
which had arrived at such perfection in the works of Meister
Stephan, declined and vanished, without leaving a trace, before
the brilliant Flemish realism. This was first evidenced in these
lands in a master, formerly erroneously called ' Israel von Mekenem,' but now designated, after his principal work, ' the Master
of the Lyversberg Passion.' This picture depicts, in eight panels,
the history of Christ's Passion, thoroughly in the style of the
older Rogier, with similar exactness of form and characterisation,
and with great power and glow of colour; yet the ideas are not
striking, and occasionally incline strongly to caricature and exaggeration. How long this tendency remained exclusively predominant in Cologne is evidenced, among many other artists, by
Bartholomäus de Bruyn, who in 1536 painted the high altar of
the Collegiate Church at Xanten. Another master of the earlier
period, who lived at Calcar, appears as one of the ablest independent emulators of Flemish art,[2] as is shown in his principal
work, the high altar in the church there, containing a representation of the Life of Christ in a series of pictures. On the other
hand, at the same time, in Westphalia, the ideal majesty of the
earlier school was preserved; and in the ' Meister von Liesborn,'
a rare combination was produced of that solemn style, with its
harmonious beauty, and the characteristic and more lifelike
reality of the later style. This is evidenced in the high altar
of the year 1465 in the Liesborn Monastery, which contains the
Life and Sufferings of Christ, and the remains of which have
been recently purchased by the English National Gallery.

With far more independence and freedom, the Flemish influence was received by the schools of Upper and Central Germany. They do not so fully abandon the beautiful soft feeling

---

[1] *Denkm. d. Kunst.* Pl. 82, 83, 83 A, 84. E. Förster, *Gesch. d. deutschen Kunst.*
Vol. II.   [2] E. aus'm Weerth, *Kunst denkmäler in den Rheinlanden.*

and ideal spirit of the former period, nor do they adopt the same exactness of execution, but by a more middle course they arrive at a thoroughly peculiar style, in which occasionally we find a happy blending of the two fundamental elements.   It may have partially contributed to this, that in Swabia, more than elsewhere in the North, extensive wall paintings were executed, many traces of which are to be found in the numerous late Gothic churches of the country.

In the Swabian school we must first mention the pleasing painter Lucas Moser, by whom there is an altar-piece in the church at Tie-fenbronn, executed in the year 1431.   In the latter part of the century, Frie-drich Herlen appears as a zealous follower of the Van Eyck style, without, how-ever, obtaining greater im-portance, or any thorough influence.   On the other hand, Martin Schongauer (also called M. Schön) is reckoned as one of the most distinguished artists of his time.[1]   He was, it seems, born at Colmar, about 1420, studied at

Fig. 375.   Christ on the Cross.   By Martin Schongauer.

Bruges under the elder Rogier, and subsequently settled in his native city, where he died in 1499.   Besides the few paintings at Colmar, his artistic worth is attested by the grandly conceived, though not perhaps beautiful, Madonna in St. Martin's Church there, and by two altar panels in the Museum, the figures of which exhibit a more ideal and fuller type, and also by the numerous

[1] *Denkm. d. Kunst.*   Pl. 82.   Figs. 1-3.

engravings executed by him. In these works Martin appears sometimes in tolerably close affinity with Flemish art, and sometimes in
a style of his own, the outward characteristics of which are a certain restlessness in the folds of the drapery, a sharp angular outline, and a strong admixture of the costumes of Upper Germany.
His excellences, on the other hand, consist in a noble, and often
even grand style of composition, in a depth of expression, and in
the refined beauty of his ideal heads. We have given a specimen of this in a Christ on the Cross, with Mary and John, from
one of his own engravings. Besides these religious subjects, he
often in his engravings handled scenes of low life with much
fresh and even coarse humour, and thus stands forth as one of
the earliest masters of genre painting.

One of the most important artists of the Swabian school was
Bartholomäus Zeitblom of Ulm, who was born about 1450, and
is mentioned until 1517. In him, more than in any other of his
contemporaries, there lived that high ideal spirit of earlier art.
His figures have a freer action, a grander physical form, a more
simple drapery than those of most of the artists of his time.
The modelling is soft, the colour light and tender, almost recalling fresco painting to mind ; the heads have a gentle expression,
but in form are somewhat blunt, and he never falls into sharpness of detail. His most important pictures are in the public
collection at Stuttgart. Among them, we must especially mention the folding panels of an altar executed in the year 1496,
containing the Annunciation, the two St. Johns, and two Angels
with the sacred cloth of Veronica—the latter panel is in the
Berlin Gallery (Fig. 376), and is a work of simple grandeur
and touching depth of expression. The splendid high altar at
Blaubeuren exhibits, in the representations on the inner side, the
influence and partly even the hand of the master.

Lastly, belonging to the Ulm school, there was the attractive
and feeling artist Martin Schaffner, whose works are mentioned
from 1508 to 1535. Still more than Zeitblom, he adhered to an
ideal view, and in his later years even yielded to the influence of
Italian art, to the greater purification of his style. The four

panels, painted in the year 1524, now in the Pinakothek at
Munich, and representing the Annunciation, the Scene in the
Temple, the Outpouring of the Holy Spirit, and the Death of
Mary, are among his most excellent works. Noble arrangement,
delicacy of feeling, and great sense of beauty, here almost com-

Fig. 376. The Angels with the Cloth of Veronica. By Zeitblom.

pletely triumph over the constrained conception peculiar to the
whole German art of this period.

Next to Ulm, the rich and ancient Augsburg was the second
central point of Swabian art. We here find in successive generations the painter family Holbein. About the middle of the
century, the family begins with a Hans Holbein, the grandfather
of the famous later master. The gallery at Augsburg possesses
pictures by him, in which he exhibits a simple and preponderating idealistic mode of conception, but combined with an
execution strictly adhering to nature. His son, Hans Holbein,
the elder, who was born about 1460, worked at first in his
native city, and subsequently at Basle, whither he was summoned
in 1504, and where he died in 1523. In the Augsburg Gallery,
in the Städel Museum at Frankfort, and in the Pinakothek at
Munich, there are pictures by him, which harmonise with the
Flemish style, without renouncing the art traditions of his native
country.

A similar style is exhibited by Hans Burgkmair, who was
born at Augsburg in 1472, and lived till 1559; an able skilful
master, who produced a great number of designs for woodcuts;

among others the 'Triumphal March of the Emperor Maximilian,' and the 'Weisskunig,' a poetical glorification of the same prince.

Far more important than all these is, however, the son of the elder Holbein, Hans Holbein, the younger, one of the greatest and noblest masters of German art.[1] He was born at Augsburg in 1495,[2] worked at Lucerne in 1517, settled at Basle two years subsequently, and was summoned to England in 1526, where, through the influence of Sir Thomas More, he entered the service of King Henry VIII. In the year 1529, he went again to Basle, and spent several years there, engaged, by order of the Council, in the execution of larger works.[3] He then returned to England, where, as has been recently proved, he died in London in 1543. While he is one of the most precocious geniuses of art history—appearing as an able painter at the age of fourteen—he is also among the few masters of the North who evidenced the decided influence of Italian art, and used it with perfect independence. Among the northern painters of that time, he is the only one, Dürer not even excepted, who reached a perfectly free and grand style, freed himself from the petty tastelessness of those around him, and conceived the human figure in its perfect truth and beauty. In many respects he is here equal to the great Peter Vischer, who likewise rose above the narrow barriers of the art of his native country, yet without losing the power, the feeling, and the freshness of the true German master. Holbein found, besides, in the art of his native city, especially in the works of his grandfather, a more ideal tone and a greater nobleness of form aimed at; and as is often the case with grandchildren that they resemble their grandparents, so the young Holbein inherited the mental peculiarity of his grandfather. In the same manner we saw Peter Vischer

---

[1] Ulrich Hegner, *Hans Holbein der Jüngere.* Berlin, 1827. A. Woltmann, *Holbein und seine Zeit.* 2 vols. Leipzig, 1866. Wornum, *Some Account of the Life and Works of Hans Holbein.* Lond. 1867. Ch. de Mechel, *Œuvres de J. Holbein.* Fol. Basle, 1780. *Denkm. d. Kunst.* Pl. 84. Figs. 1–6.

[2] Cf. A. Woltmann, in the Viennese, *Recensionen f. bild. Kunst,* 1863, July number. On the other hand, Grimm, *Ueber Holbeins Geburtsjahr.*

[3] From the recent archival researches of Hrn. His-Heusler at Basle.

employing the idealised types of a former age as a basis for new development. Holbein must, moreover, have been himself in Italy in his early years, and have studied the Lombard and Roman masters, for this alone can explain many of the excellences of his works.

The first authentic work by his hand are the four altar panels in the gallery at Augsburg, bearing the date of 1512, and thus produced in his seventeenth year. It exhibits, among other scenes, the Virgin and St. Anna, sitting together on a bench, upon which the infant Christ is trying to walk. The original and naïve character of this conception betrays at once with what decision the youthful Holbein was on his side making his first essay in the career of art. Three other pictures in the same collection prove how vigorously he strove to pursue the path of a healthful observance of nature. He next executed an altar-piece of the year 1516, depicting the sufferings of S. Sebastian, in which he displays noble grandeur in his treatment of form, perfect delicacy of outline, and beautiful and distinct colouring; part of this work is in the Augsburg Gallery, and part in the Pinakothek at Munich. He here already attains a height unrivalled by any of his northern art contemporaries.

Next come the works in the gallery at Basle, among which there are several portraits and an Ecce Homo of the year 1521, which exhibit his masterly power, both in the conception and reproduction of nature. At the same period he painted two excellent panel pictures in the minster at Freiburg, containing the Birth of Christ and the Adoration of the Kings. More important than all, however, are the eight pictures of the Passion in the collection at Basle, which were produced between 1520 and 1525, and proclaim him to be one of the first masters of religious historical painting. The series begins with the Prayer on the Mount of Olives; then follow the Capture, Christ before the High Priest, His Mocking and Scourging, His Bearing the Cross, His Crucifixion and Burial. In these highly dramatic, bold, and stirring compositions, the whole power and depth of German art is breathed forth, though purified by the influence

of Raphael and of other great Italians. The simple clearness of
the arrangement, which exhausts the subject in a few thrilling
touches, the broad free drawing, the strong modelling of the
figures, and the powerful colouring, all this invests these pictures
with an imperishable value. Still more important, however, is a
series of ten paintings of the Passion in the same place, executed
in a masterly manner in indian ink, and exhibiting Holbein's dramatic power and talent for composition still more thoroughly. (Fig. 377.)

Fig. 377. The Deriding of Christ. By Holbein.

While here the master has unsurpassably depicted the energy of passionately excited action, he appears also in simple devotional painting as one of the first artists, in another famous work, the Madonna of the Burgomaster Meier of Basle, which is in the possession of the Princess Elizabeth of Hesse at Darmstadt, and a copy of which, by his own hand, is in the Dresden Gallery.[1] (Fig. 378.) It is not the enchanting power of lofty beauty, nor the intellectual nobleness of significant character, but alone the warm feeling and true-hearted sentiment, which ever fascinate all hearts to this work as one of the most touching delineations of genuine German life. Scarcely less important, and equally

[1] The Darmstadt copy decidedly bears the stamp of greater freshness, originality, and power, and seems to me not only more beautiful and animated in the heads, but the execution also appears more fine and detailed than that of the justly praised Dresden painting.

attractive from its soft beauty, power of characterisation, and clear harmonious colouring, is a devotional picture lately discovered in private possession at Solothurn, bearing the master's monogram and the date 1522. (Fig. 379.)

Fig. 378. The Madonna of the Burgomaster Meier. By Holbein. Dresden.

It exhibits the enthroned Madonna, one of Holbein's most exquisite creations, with the Child on her lap; on either side are the saints Ursus and Martinus—the one a grave military figure in glittering armour; the other in the rich robes of a

bishop, looking down beneficently on a beggar who is asking
alms.[1]

How Holbein treated monumental subjects, we can perceive
from the large wall paintings, with which he decorated the hall
of the town hall at Basle in 1521.   Early injured by the damp-
ness of the locality, they are only to be recognised by small

Fig. 379.   Enthroned Madonna and Child.   By Holbein.

remains and by sketches and copies in the Basle Museum.
They contained, after the custom of the time, representations
from ancient history and from the Old Testament, as types of

[1] The illustration is taken from a photograph by Julius Schnor, for which I am
indebted to Herr Eigner, the excellent restorer of the original.

Fig. 380.   The Meeting of Saul and Samuel.   By Holbein.

republican severity and justice : the sacrificial death of Charondas ; Zaleucus, who suffers his own eye and that of his son to be put out on account of a crime committed by the latter ; Curius Dentatus, who rejects the embassy of the Samnites ; King Sapor, who humbles the captive emperor Valerian ;—among them, as single figures, Christ, King David, Justice, Wisdom, and Moderation. Besides these, there are the two important pictures executed during his subsequent sojourn there — Rehoboam, scornfully rejecting the messengers of his people, and the meeting of Saul and Samuel. (Fig. 380.) In dramatic value, great historical feeling, and perfect freedom of action, these creations of profane historical painting appear all the more remarkable, as the subsequent works of the kind degenerate into conventional forms.[1]

After his settlement in England, where he executed a number of splendid orders, both for Henry VIII. and for the nobles of the kingdom, Holbein devoted himself almost exclusively to portrait painting. His numerous likenesses are among the most excellent works in this branch of art, owing to their delicacy of conception, incomparably simple and unsurpassably true portrayal of life, their noble simplicity of feeling and loving finish, which are combined with a great freedom of treatment. Among his excellent works in England, are his drawings in Windsor Castle, the portrait of Thomas More in the possession of Mr. Huth, of the year 1527, Archbishop Warham, in Lambeth Palace, London, and the charming portrait of the Duchess Christina of Milan, as large as life, in Arundel Castle. Also we must not forget the elaborate portrait of the goldsmith Morett in the Dresden Gallery; that of the merchant Gyzen, of the year 1532, in the Berlin Museum, which is well executed in cold clear tints; that of Anne of Cleves; and the fine miniature-like one of Erasmus in the Louvre. The museum at Basle possesses some excellent portraits belonging to his earlier life; that of the burgomaster Meier and his wife, executed in the year 1515; the freshly conceived and warmly and tenderly

[1] Woltmann gives an excellent description of this ; we borrow our illustration from his work.

finished portrait of Bonifacius Amorbach in 1519; the wonderful family portrait of his wife with the children, in which a subject scarcely pleasing is ennobled by the highest art; and, lastly, the two charming female portraits (1526) of a young lady at Offenburg. Many of his most excellent portraits are to be found in the Belvedere at Vienna. There is a masterly portrait in brown tint of a young man, bearing the date of 1541, and resembling the Berlin portrait, with beautifully painted hands, apparently erroneously marked 1541, as it shows the warm colouring of his earlier works; that of Geryck Tybis, of the year 1533, painted in cold tints with grey shadows; and about the same year, the splendid portrait of the aged John Chambers, physician to Henry VIII; lastly, two charming female portraits —a young lady with gold embroidered cap and a gold ornament on her breast, and resembling in delicacy and tenderness the Basle portraits of the Offenburg Lady; and a wonderfully perfect picture of Jane Seymour, the king's third consort, with velvet-like hair, exquisite hands, and delicate form, wearing a costly necklace of pearls, and executed probably in 1536. The other pictures in the Belvedere imputed to the master erroneously bear his name. As miniature painter, also, Holbein produced some excellent works, as is testified by several miniatures in Windsor Castle, and in the Ambraser Collection at Vienna.

While the great master shows himself in these portraits to be an able portrayer of life, he knows also how to depict actual existence with deeper feeling and wider significance. This is evidenced in the most gifted manner in his famous Dance of Death, probably belonging to his early period at Basle, and which first appeared at Lyons in 1538. He here employed wood-engraving, and a forcible popular representation, to give suitable expression to his genuinely national conception, filled as it was with profound poetry and grand humour. The striking contrasts of a social condition of many gradations, such as appeared at that period of universal ferment, and found fearful expression in the insurrectionary movements of the peasant war, were here transformed by the artist's mind into a series of pic-

tures, in which the nothingness of all earthly things is depicted
with cutting irony. As the same idea of the almighty power
of death, before which all the power and pomp of the world
must bow, had in earlier times.inspired a thoughtful artist in
Italy to produce that sublime picture of the Triumph of Death ;
so here we likewise meet with a Triumphal March of Death, but
broken into separate representations, each of which has its own
significance. No class is too rich and powerful, no age too
tender and beautiful, no lot too high or too low—they all find
their common inexorable conqueror. But to each he appears
differently, to each he comes either unobserved or with force.
He places his crown on the emperor's head, and unrecognised
holds out the fatal cup tơ the king. He allures the empress
from the midst of her brilliant train to the open grave ; he seizes
on the queen by force, and deridingly with one kick casts the
helping physician away. He surprises the pope on his golden
throne, and merrily dances away with the bishop ; he pierces the

Fig. 381. From Holbein's Dance of Death.

warrior in spite of his armour, and
steals into the presence of the
priest as a willing sacristan. He
snatches the joyous child from its
mother ; he adorns the bride with
horrible dead men's bones. He
carries the gamester away from the
very claws of the devil ; he seizes
the robber in the very act ; he joins
the blind man as a treacherous
guide (Fig. 381) ; and he only forgets the poor leper Lazarus, the
only one to whom he appears as
a friend, and who supplicates him
imploringly for deliverance.

A similar cycle of ideas is depicted by Holbein, though in
another manner, in an allegorical antique style, in the paintings
which he executed in the house of Hansa in London, which,
however, have only come down to us in some engravings. The

subject here was the Triumph of Fortune and Poverty ; a work of great beauty and perfection, well worthy of a Raphael, a new proof of the wonderful versatility of this rare master.

Cristoph Amberger, born in Nuremberg in 1490, and subsequently engaged at Augsburg, followed Holbein's style, and from his excellent and simple portraits was a valuable master. Holbein also exercised decided influence on a Swiss artist, Niklas Manuel of Berne, surnamed Deutsch (1484–1530), who, as a zealous partisan of the Reformation, sketched many satirical representations full of striking humour, and appears to have been an artist of great skill and richness of idea, though strongly inclined to mannerism in his forms. There are many able pictures by him in the gallery at Basle ; but the Dance of Death, executed by him in fresco on the cemetery wall of the Dominican Monastery at Berne, has perished, and only exists in copies.

Deviating from the tendency of this Upper German school, Bavaria seems, so far as the deficient state of investigation will allow us to form a judgment, to have adhered more strictly to Flemish art ; and Austria also, in all that we have hitherto known of her paintings, shows a similar tendency. Here, among other subordinate productions, Michael Pacher completed, in the year 1481, the splendid altar in S. Wolfgang (cf. vol. ii. p. 299), in which he appears as an able and attractive artist in the Van Eyck style.

More important productions are afforded, at the same time, by the Franconian school, the principal seat of which, Nuremberg, we have already found active in the production of every kind of sculptured work. The plastic spirit here, now as ever, controls the development of painting, though we must not forget that the plastic art of this entire period has a preponderating picturesque character. A striking sharpness of form and vigorous modelling, combined with an effort after characterisation which becomes one-sided and ugly, are the distinguishing marks of the Nuremberg school. In no master is this so unpleasingly expressed as in Michael Wohlgemuth, who lived from 1434–1519, and at the head of a numerous band of painters produced with alarming mechanical skill a number of altar-pieces, in which wood carving is combined with panel painting. His principal piece is the altar in the Marienkirche at Zwickau,[1] in the year 1479, containing an extensive represen· tation of the life and sufferings of Christ, in which the realistic tendency results almost entirely in ugly and mean forms, though at the same time the able workmanship of a well-guided atelier is not to be mistaken. In his better works the master is often charming, from the almost ideal beauty of his heads and his powerful harmonious colouring.

It was a fatal destiny for the development of German art that from this very school, and from this very teacher, that artist was to proceed, who in depth of genius, in creative richness of fancy, in extensive power of thought, and in moral energy and earnest striving, must be called the first of all German masters. Albert Dürer,[2] as regards artistic gifts, need fear no comparison with any master in the world, not even with Raphael and Michael Angelo. Notwithstanding, in all that concerns the true means of expressing art, the clothing of the idea in the garment of the exquisite form, he lies so deeply fettered within the bonds of his own limited world, that he rarely rises to the same height of thought and expression. Dürer is justly the love and the pride of the German people; but we must not forget that, while he is the highest expression of their excellences and virtues, he is also the representative of their weaknesses and failings. Blind idolising is never becoming, least of all when the object of it is such a true, severe master. We must not hurry over the coarse harsh externals of his style either with indiffer- ence or false enthusiasm. It is difficult to estimate him justly; but if we earnestly seek to understand him, we shall best learn to love him.

[1] J. G. Quandt, *Die Gemälde des Michael Wohlgemuth in der Frauenkirche zu Zwickau.* Fol.
[2] J. Heller, *Das Leben und die Werke Albrecht Dürer's.* Leipzig, 1831. *Reli- quien von Albrecht Dürer.* Nürnb. 1828. *Leben und Wirken Albrecht Dürer's,* von A. v. Eye. Nördl. 1860. *Denkm. d. Kunst.* Pl. 83, 83 A.

Dürer has thoroughly fathomed reality in all its indications, and he has done this in a manner such as few other masters have done. His knowledge of the human organisation, and his observation of natural life, are just as surprisingly certain as his ideas seem inexhaustible, and the power of his imagination unbounded. But he rarely attains to perfect beauty of form. He is so filled with the effort after striking, fascinating reality that he cannot adopt a higher style, even in his ideal themes. Just as he followed the world-agitating reformation struggles of his time with enthusiastic conviction, just as, with clear keen understanding, the usual symbolic conception of the divine was resolved into the human, so throughout his representations he gives evidence of this revolution. His sacred figures are only the Nuremberg citizens of his time, and indeed most of them are taken from the sphere of common life with all the tokens of casual existence. He obtained even the subject from surrounding things, not seeking after models full of dignity and beauty, but especially after strongly marked characteristic heads, which constantly verge rather on the coarse than on the noble and graceful. And even this motley band, with their coarse individuality, he represented for the most part in a style of form, which, in the drawing of the head and hands, and also of other parts, necessitated an arbitrary mannerism, and broke up the drapery with its beautiful grand masses into creased and restless folds. Hence his sense of form knew no distinction; whether he was representing the sacred personages of belief, the rude figures of common life, or the wonderful creations of his fancy, they were all taken from the same sphere, and never appeared otherwise than what they were.

That Dürer was surrounded with a motley fantastic life, by the commonplace personages of his native home, and not by a fine noble cultivated southern race, is not sufficient to explain this strange tendency. Just as little can we trace it to the fact that in those creased and restless folds he yielded to the influence of the wood carving of the time. His countryman, Peter Vischer, had gradually in his creations overcome both influences, and had reached a style full of purity and beauty. In Dürer, there evidently lay an inner affinity with those characteristic touches of life. It is the fantastic tendency of his age which reaches its highest expression in him, and necessitates all those extravagances of form as well as the inexhaustible fulness and depth of his creations. Both are inseparable from him, and both must be accepted alike. But coarse and repulsive as much appears at first sight, we cannot but admire the power with which truth, depth, and fervour of feeling is expressed; and if even Italian masters like Raphael cannot be restrained from offering their homage to the greatness of the German artist, the understanding of his art, genuinely national as it is even in its imperfections, will not be unattainable by his fellow countrymen. We shall find that scarcely any other master has given forth with such a lavish hand all that the heart possesses of deep, affecting, and touching feelings, all that the mind possesses of mighty and sublime thoughts, and the imagination of poetic riches; that in none other is the depth and power of the German mind revealed so grandly as in him.

Dürer was born in Nuremberg in 1471, and was at first brought up to his father's trade, who was a goldsmith; but in 1486, as his inclination turned to painting, he was sent to Wohlgemuth for instruction. He remained for three years in his atelier; and in 1490 set forth on his travels, from which he returned in 1494, and settled as a painter in his native city. He here worked for ten years, not merely as a painter, but also engaged in extensive works in engraving and woodcuts; until, in 1505, he made a journey to Italy, in which, however, he only became acquainted with Venice, Padua, and Bologna. Towards the end of the following year, he returned to Nuremberg, where, with fresh and restless activity, he executed a countless number of important works, not merely paintings, drawings, engravings, and woodcuts, but even produced excellent carved works in boxwood and steatite. In 1520 he made a second journey, this time to the Netherlands, from whence he returned in the following year. From this period he lived and worked uninterruptedly in his native city until his death in 1528. (He died, like Raphael, on a Good Friday.) In these latter years, besides his artistic works, he produced many scientific works—instructions on geometry, the art of fortification, and the proportions of the human body, thus evidencing his extensive and thorough information.

All this astonishing fertility of mind unfolded in him wholly from personal inclination without outward stimulus, and indeed under the pressure of sad domestic circumstances and unfavourable relations of life. Germany had no Julius II. or Leo X., no Medici or Gonzaga, no art-loving aristocracy, no noble-minded governments. Venice offered our master a salary of 200 ducats a year, if he would remain there. In Antwerp they sought to attract him by similar proposals; but the true German returned to his own country, although 'within thirty years the commissions she gave him only amounted to 500 guilders;' and as his sole recompense he begged the council of the mighty imperial city to grant him the favour of paying him five per cent. interest upon a capital of 1,000 guilders obtained with 'labour and toil!' The Emperor Maximilian, much as he was inclined towards the excellent master, employed him on nothing greater than the decoration of the pommel of a sword and a prayer book, and in the execution of that colossal woodcut of Maximilian's Triumphal Arch, a somewhat insipid allegorical glorification of the monarch, which Dürer indeed executed with all the charm of his imagination. It is true the emperor granted him an annual stipend, but the arrangements necessary lasted for years, and the payment only reached him shortly before his death. Equally little was he benefited by exemption from civil taxes, a favour which the emperor himself endeavoured to procure for him; for the fathers of the city contrived to persuade the good-hearted artist to forego the exemption. Thus 'lamentable and shameful,' as Dürer once expressed himself with just indignation, were his circumstances. All the higher stands the sacred moral earnestness with which he unremittingly pursued his art.

In considering the most important works of this versatile

master, we will begin with his religious representations. In these Dürer burst asunder the fetters of ecclesiastical views, and depicted the sacred incidents with wondrous power, with all the non-essentials, it is true, belonging to the time, but also with perfectly pure human feeling. The sublimity of a fancy often roving into extravagance and formlessness is exhibited in the woodcut of the Revelation of St. John, which appeared in 1498. Among the sixteen (or rightly fifteen) sheets, some exhibit a demon-like power scarcely ever surpassed; as, for example, the Angels killing the third Part of Men, or the Dispute of the Archangel Michael and his Adherents with the Dragon. Other sheets, with all their grandeur, fall into formlessness and want of moderation; such, for instance, as that depicting the enthroned Judge of the World, from whose eyes glance flames of fire, and from whose mouth a sword issues, while in His outstretched right hand He holds the stars.

The Tribuna degli Uffizi at Florence possesses a splendid picture of the Adoration of the Kings, executed in the year 1504, one of the most feeling and attractive works of this master, full of poetic touches, with a beautiful landscape, and executed with warm and harmonious colouring. In 1506 followed the picture of the Feast of Roses, now in the Monastery Strahof, in Prague, a highly poetical composition, conceived with freedom and life, and which met with much acknowledgment from the Venetian masters. Less pleasing, and full of coarse and terrible truth, is the martyr scene of the Ten Thousand Saints, painted in 1508, and now in the gallery of the Belvedere at Vienna. The picture of the Ascension and Crowning of the Virgin, executed in the year 1509, by order of the merchant Jacob Heller, in Frankfort-on-the-Maine, has unfortunately perished; but there is a large and solemn representation of heavenly majesty in the painting of the Trinity, executed in the year 1511, and now in the gallery at Vienna. Surrounded by choirs of angels and saints, and by bands of adoring believers, God the Father is enthroned above; over Him is the dove of the Holy Spirit; and in His arms He holds the body of His Son, extended on the cross;

certainly one of the most profound conceptions of this theme. The colour, as in the master's other pictures, is clear, light, and fresh, though not free from a want of harmony, owing to the play of varied colour in the drapery.

Fig. 382. The Crowning of the Virgin. By Dürer.

In this and the following years (1511–1515) we see the master astonishingly active in religious tasks; and in quick suc-

cession he produced the extensive large woodcuts of the Passion
of Christ, in twelve sheets, the smaller series in thirty-six sheets,
the Life of the Virgin, in nineteen sheets, and the engraving of
the Passion, in sixteen sheets. It is impossible here even to
glance at them separately; it is enough that in them the master's
whole depth, feeling, and power are exhibited in inexhaustible
richness. Highly poetical are his introductions of natural
scenery, true German landscape, with mountain and valley,
rivers and woods, with their delightful variety of fortresses,
villages, and towns; and, in his Madonnas especially, he delights the heart by a world of charming, naïve, and pleasing
touches.

How far Dürer entered occasionally into the representation
of perfect reality, is evidenced by the remarkable painting,
executed in 1518, now in England, depicting the Death of the
Virgin, in which he gave the Virgin the features of Mary of Burgundy, the lately deceased wife of the Emperor Maximilian; and
in harmony with this he travestied the other sacred figures into
living personages. On the other hand, in one of Dürer's last
works—the Four Pillars of the Church—which he presented to
his native city, and which the latter gave to the Pinakothek at
Munich, he made the profoundest acknowledgment of his faith;
and declared, in the accompanying writing, that he considered
these the fundamental pillars of the original Christian doctrines
in their purity. On two panels, depicted with strong characteristic marks, St. John and St. Peter, St. Paul and St. Mark,
are represented as striking contrasts, so distinctly individualised
that they have been also designated ' the Four Temperaments.'
Dürer has here, shortly before his death, attained to a grandness
and simplicity of style, a depth and harmony of colour, and a
perfect freedom of form, and has overcome all paltry mannerisms
even in his wonderfully grand drapery.

Dürer's portraits are distinguished by a true and simple conception of life, and by careful execution combined with unsurpassably fine drawing and able modelling. The half-length
portrait of his father, now in the Pinakothek at Munich, was

executed in the year 1491 ; and his own portrait, now in the same gallery, bears the date of the year 1500. There is a peculiarly beautiful male portrait, dated 1507, on the back of which is depicted the fearful allegory of Avarice : this is in the Belvedere at Vienna. There is also in the same place the portrait of the Emperor Maximilian, executed in 1519. There is a splendid male likeness in the Museum of Madrid of the year 1521 ; and a masterly finished portrait of Hieronymus Holzschuher, executed in 1526, in the possession of the family at Nuremberg, the exact image of a thorough worthy German—true, solid, and firm.

Lastly, there are still many free compositions, both drawings and engravings, worthy of mention, in which the master has often given vent to his rich imagination with charming poetic power, and wonderful depth of feeling. Thus, for instance, there are the Four Witches of the year 1497, the St. Hieronymus and St. Eustachius, pleasant representations of solitude and idyllic forest life ; but, above all, the highly poetical 'Melancholy,' of the year 1514, one of the most perfect productions of the graving tool ; and the no less important sheet of the year 1513, which represents an armed knight, pursuing his way calmly and undismayed through the thick forest in the midst of threatening and horrible forms. (Fig. 383.) Lastly, the border drawings on the prayer book of the Emperor Maximilian must here be mentioned : they were executed in the year 1515, and are now in the Royal Library at Munich.[1] Humour and fancy are combined in them with ingenious playfulness. Natural and human life, the fairy world, and the vast realm of poetic invention are fashioned into bright arabesques, which in this sense must be regarded as a thoroughly original creation of the great master's, displaying his magnificent mind from a fresh aspect.

Many pupils and imitators followed Dürer, among whom we can only mention the able portrait painter George Pencz, Hans von Kulmbach, especially known by his engravings, Bartholo-

---

[1] Published in fac-simile by N. Strixner. New edit by F. Stöger. Munich, 1850.

mäus, and Hans Sebald Beham, who pursued the same branch
of art, the talented Matthias Grünewald and Albrecht Altdorfer,
conspicuous above all for mind and imagination.

More important than all these imitators is one master, who

Fig. 383. Knight: Death and Devil. By Albert Dürer.

carried the influence of the Franconian school to Saxony, and
during a long and active life stood at the head of an extremely
skilful school there. We allude to Lucas Cranach,[1] rightly

---

[1] Chr. Schuchardt, *Lucas Cranach des Aelteren Leben und Werke.* Leipzig, 1851.
Denkm. d. Kunst. Pl. 84. Figs. 7-11.

Lucas Sunder, who was born in a small place in Franconia, and lived from 1472 to 1553. In 1504 he became court painter to the Elector Frederic the Wise of Saxony, and remained in the same capacity with his successors, John the Constant, and John Frederic the Magnanimous. He followed the latter as a faithful servant and friend even to prison. He afterwards returned with his prince to Weimar, where he died in 1553. Cranach was a zealous adherent of the Reformation, and stood on terms of friendship with the Reformers. In many of his altar-pieces he endeavoured to express the relation of the new doctrines to the traditionary religious notions. He was distinguished more for his productiveness than for his depth of thought. He lacks Dürer's sublime ideas and mighty gifts of composition; on the other hand, his pictures have a peculiarly agreeable and harmless character, which has procured his works a sort of national popularity. Many of his graceful Madonnas have the thoughtful kindly air of German housewives. His round fair-haired female heads, with wise clear eyes, smiling lips, and rosy blooming complexions, are easy to recognise. The countless pictures which are dispersed everywhere under his name are, however, very various in execution, as he prepared his vast orders by the help of his unwearied associates; and although holding offices of importance as electoral court painter and burgomaster of Wittenberg, he accepted without scruple not merely commissions for pictures, but for the painting of arms, escutcheons, and horse-cloths, and even for room decorations.

The most important of his altar-pieces is the great work in the church at Schneeberg, containing the Crucifixion, the Last Supper, the Resurrection of the Dead, and the Last Judgment; also the altar-piece in the cathedral at Meissen, likewise containing the Crucifixion, with other scenes relating to it; also the altar-piece in the parish church of Wittenberg, representing the Last Supper, with the Reformers preaching, baptizing, and hearing confession below; and, lastly, the most important work of this kind in the parish church at Weimar, which was completed by his son after his death. Christ is here represented on the cross, and at the same time by the side as the Conqueror of Hell; on the other side stand Luther and Cranach, the latter of whom is touched by the blood that is gushing forth from the side of Christ.

Besides these religious pictures, Cranach produced a great number of representations, in which he sought to make use of his study of the naked figure, especially the female, combined with fresh, tender, and warm flesh tints. In biblical history, Adam and Eve furnished the subject; but he chiefly resorted to antique material, which he handled with coarse humour and travesty. Dignity and noble form are generally lacking, but a charmingly naïve character, often full of roguishness and grace, renders some of the best of these representations extremely attractive. (Fig. 384.)

After Cranach, the Saxon school soon relapses into obscurity, and only his son, of the same name, inherits somewhat of his father's fame and art.

Fig. 384. Group from a Painting of Cranach's in the possession of Schuchardt.

c. *French and Spanish Painters.*[1]

In France, in this epoch also, painting did not attain to great independent importance, although many traces may be seen of a lively reception of the influence exercised by the art of the Eycks.   It was again especially miniature painting, which was eagerly pursued, as may be perceived by many works to be found in the library at Paris.   The most excellent among them, by Jean Fouquet, court painter to Louis XI., about 1488, are distinguished by their noble style, as well as by their splendour and ability.   Herr Brentano at Frankfort possesses a number of excellent miniatures by this master, executed in a manuscript belonging to an officer of the State under Charles VII.   There is a great deficiency, on the other hand, in panel pictures ; and there are only a few works of this kind in the cathedral at Aix, and in the hospital at Villeneuve, near Avignon, ascribed, in consequence of an utterly groundless tradition, to King René of Anjou, who is regarded as a pupil of Johann van Eyck.   A similar style was embraced in the sixteenth century by François Clouet, also called Janet, who about 1550 distinguished himself as a portrait painter by his true, simple, and yet delicate conception of life (there is a small miniature-like likeness of Charles IX. in the Belvedere in Vienna belonging to the year 1563) ; while about this time most of his countrymen had yielded to the style introduced by the Italian artists, and had already begun to transform it into superficial and exaggerated grace.   French painting subsequently fell completely into this mannered style.

Spain, standing as she did in much closer connection with the Netherlands, possessed in the fifteenth century no independent painting of her own, but constantly drew Flemish artists into the country, in order to satisfy the requirement for religious pictures by their art-practised hand.   How far this constant contact may have influenced the development of a national school cannot be decided in the present unsatisfactory state of investigation on the

[1] *Denkm. d. Kunst.*   Pl. 84 A.

subject. Yet Louis Morales, surnamed ' El Divino' (the divine), who lived till 1586, is famous as a master who maintained a severe antique style of art against the inroads of the Italian views. Still even he was not free from these influences, while at the same time the deep ecstatic glow in his paintings evidences itself as a decidedly national element. Other painters gave themselves up implicitly to the study of the great Italian masters. Thus many artists at the beginning of the sixteenth century gained their renown as imitators of Leonardo.

This revolution in art was, however, decided in Alonso Berruguete (1480–1562), known also as an architect and sculptor, who followed Michael Angelo's manner in his paintings. Another master, born in Flanders, Pedro Campana (1503–1580), took a similar path, but with greater independence, and a happy adherence to the more antique style. His principal work, the Descent from the Cross, in the cathedral of Seville, is famous as a touching dramatic composition. Luis de Vargas (1502–1568), who worked in Seville, where there are a number of his altar-pieces still existing, is regarded as an artist of importance, more in Raphael's style. A similar tendency appears also in Vicente Joanez of Valencia (1523–1579), who is conspicuous for feeling and grace, and whom the Spaniards like to call their Raphael. Other artists gave themselves up more to the study of the Venetian masters, and distinguished themselves as important colourists ; thus, for instance, the two court painters of Philip II., Alonso Sanchez Coello—many able portraits by whom are in the gallery at Madrid—and Juan Fernandez Navarrete, surnamed El Mudo (1526–1579), and who is designated the Spanish Titian.

CHAPTER VI.

PLASTIC ART IN THE SEVENTEENTH AND EIGHTEENTH CENTURIES.

I. SCULPTURE.[1]

AFTER the decline into which sculpture had fallen during the latter period of the sixteenth century in Italy and elsewhere, the art was revived towards the beginning of the following century in a new style, which emanated from Italy, and which, with slight deviations, prevailed universally for nearly two hundred years. But the spirit of art generally was wholly changed. As we have already seen in the architecture of this bizarre period, everything now aimed at the utmost possible expression and the most dazzling effect. If the strict laws of architecture had been compelled to yield to this tendency, how much more easily must the plastic arts have been affected by it! Painting from its innermost nature was most inclined to realise this desire; indeed, a new and truly important revival for that art arose out of it. Plastic art, however, could only approach towards a similar effect by renouncing her peculiarly fundamental principle and becoming picturesque. The Relief style had already led the way to this; insulated sculpture now followed in the same track, cast aside all the fetters of the art, and resigned itself regardlessly to the inclination for effect.

Henceforth all plastic work was under every circumstance to be animated and full of passionate action; the expression of inward emotion was to be rendered powerfully effective by ges-

---

[1] *Denkm. d. Kunst.* Pl. 92 and 93.

ture, bearing, and attitude. The tendency of the modern age to strict adherence to nature required the utmost possible truth of form, which, however, lapsed immediately again into mannerism in the male figures, from exaggerated muscular development ; and in the female figures from an offensively luxurious, smooth, and occasionally too finical style. The same treatment was observed in the drapery, which was also arranged after the laws of painting, almost concealing the figure in its immense masses, or letting it appear in glimpses by all sorts of refined artifices, but at all events impeding the noble and distinct revelation of the natural form. Moreover, the drapery, by various effective arrangement — swelling, fluttering, and overloaded — was intended to aid the expression of the emotion, which was the principal matter aimed at. Thus all the dignity, simplicity, and truth of sculpture, and all plastic style, were lost, and outward effect and mere decoration became the objects of composition. A great number of highly talented artists, an immeasurable amount of creative power and resources, were swallowed up by this effort, and the world was deluged by an incalculable multitude of magnificent but inwardly empty works. While this fatally devious course prevailed, we can only wonder that some few artists still remained simple and natural, and that portraiture especially produced many able works. In the North especially, a more healthy style so far predominated that the old heritage of Germanic art—the taste for individual and characteristic representation—may be traced in numerous able works, combined with this degenerated tendency.

There is a youthful work by the sculptor Stefano Maderno, the marble statue of St. Cecilia, in the church of the same name in Rome, which is not without nobleness and simplicity. Yet it is characteristic here, that the saint is represented lying on the ground, as if she were just stretched out dead, and thus the effective and passing incident completely swallows up the deeper religious purport. The master, on the other hand, who obtained most decided influence on the sculpture of his day is Lorenzo Bernini, also active as an architect (1598–1680). Possessed of great gifts and astonishing facility of production, he carried the tendency to effective dramatic action to the utmost point, especially in plastic art. Scenes such as the Rape of Proserpine, or Daphne flying before Apollo (Fig. 385), both of which are

in the Villa Borghese in Rome, were his favourite subjects. But in the portrayal also of religious ecstasy he rivalled the painters of his time, in such works as St. Therese, in S. Maria della Vittoria in Rome, in which indeed the expression of powerless rapture verges upon a refined sensual representation. In monumental works, such as the marble equestrian statue of Constantine, on the Scala Regia in the Vatican, there is also an empty pathos, and in his monuments of Pope Urban VIII. and Pope Alexander VII., in St. Peter's, the allegorical apparatus and the coquettish arrangement of the various draperies are significant.

Fig. 385. Apollo and Daphne. By Bernini.

Among the countless Italian artists who followed Bernini's style, Alessandro Algardi (1598–1654) is among the best known and the most important. His colossal relief of Attila, in St. Peter's in Rome, exhibits, with all its masterly technical execution, the strange extravagances into which the relief style of this period erred, long accustomed as it had been to be entirely picturesque.

The French, already familiar with Italian influence during the former epoch, followed Bernini's style, carrying it to a degree of over-elegance and external theatrical effect. Among the most famous masters are Pierre Puget (1622–1694), who worked much at Genoa, and executed in S. Maria da Carignano, in that city, an exaggerated representation of the martyrdom of

S. Sebastian; and François Girardon (1630–1715), who was distinguished especially for his over-graceful female figures. Legros, also, was active in Rome; and in the church Del Gesù there is a statue by him of S. Ignatius, and a mannered allegory of Belief, dashed to pieces by heresy. In the eighteenth century, this plastic style was continued by artists such as J. Bapt. Pigalle (1714–1785), who executed the monument of Marshal Saxe in the St. Thomas' Church at Strasburg, a theatrical and effective work. Another French artist of this period, Houdon, executed the marble statue of St. Bruno, for S. Maria degli Angeli in Rome: it is simple and noble, and expresses much humble piety.

In the Netherlands, there are some sculptors of note, who follow the same tendency in essentials, owing as they do their artistic culture to Italy, but who arrive at happy results from their noble and more moderate style. Among these is François Duquesnoy, surnamed 'Il Fiammingo,' from his native country (1594–1644), who, in com-

Fig. 386. Statue of Count Eberhard the Mild, in the Collegiate Church at Stuttgart.

petition with Bernini, produced many works, especially in Rome. One of the most beautiful statues of the whole epoch is his S. Susanna in S. Maria di Loreto, which is simple and feeling in its conception, such as few are at that time. His naïve and fresh figures of children are also justly famed. His pupil Arthur Quellinus executed with great talent, and in a lifelike and powerful style, numerous plastic works, which adorn the town hall at Amsterdam, especially the extensive groups on the two pediments, which contain allegorical glorifications of the commercial city. In Berlin, also, traces are to be found of the works of this able master.

Germany, in the last few years of the sixteenth century, possessed a great number of monuments in her churches and cathedrals, witnesses of a lively artistic feeling, which often produced works of able and natural conception, and for the most part of great decorative value. The cathedrals of Cologne, Mayence, and Würzburg are rich in valuable works of this kind, and the eleven statues of Würtemburg princes, which were placed, about 1574, in the choir of the Collegiate Church at Stuttgart, are among the ablest productions of the epoch ; while among its most splendid, are the numerous monuments in the choir of the Collegiate Church at Tübingen. A magnificent work, likewise executed at the end of the sixteenth century, is the marble monument of the Elector Maurice of Saxony in Freiberg Cathedral. The kneeling marble figure of the prince is placed on the lid of the sarcophagus, which is supported by eight bronze griffins. The works of Netherland artists in Germany, which constantly appeared at this time, are also worthy of mention. Thus, the Hercules Fountain at Augsburg was executed in the year 1599 by Adrian de Vries ; the graceful fountain in a small court of the royal palace at Munich was the work of Peter de Witte, who was also much employed as a painter at the electoral court there, and who Italianised his name into Candido ; while, somewhat earlier (1589), a German artist, named Benedict Wurzelbauer, executed the rich and gracefully decorated fountain near the Church of St. Laurence in Nuremberg.

Flemish influence is also to be traced in Berlin, where Andreas Schlüter (about 1662 to 1714), both as architect and sculptor, appears as one of the greatest artists of this long epoch. His high importance in sculpture is evidenced in the numerous decorative reliefs, which he executed in the royal palace, as well as in the affecting heads of dying warriors, which

Fig. 387. Equestrian Statue of the great Elector. By A. Schlüter.

he introduced above the windows in the court of the arsenal ; but, above all, in the colossal bronze equestrian statue on the bridge of the great Elector, a magnificent work, and grand in form and attitude. Somewhat later, Rafael Donner produced many works in Vienna, likewise conspicuous for their noble and natural conception ; in 1739, he adorned the fountain on the new market-place with the leaden statues of Providence and the four Rivers of Austria. These last-named masters stand forth as rare and unique phenomena in an age wholly enervated and sunk into mannerism.

2. PAINTING.

The same tendency which led sculpture into error and degeneracy brought about for painting, in the course of the seventeenth century, a wonderful rise, and indeed a new and peculiar revival. The painting of this epoch is one of the most remarkable and splendid phenomena in the history of civilisation. While the public condition of Europe was not cheering, while modern absolutism was spreading over the lands, and all fresh national life was stifled, painting experienced a more varied and a more extensive culture than she had ever previously enjoyed. It is as though the modern mind had found in painting the most suitable medium for the expression of its manifold nature, and had revealed this nature most clearly in it. For, in the first place, this favourite art of the period spread over a much larger geographical territory than ever before, and was not merely cultivated with eagerness and success in Italy, Brabant, and Holland, but also in Spain, France, and England ; while alone in Germany, lacerated as she was by the thirty years' war, did the desire for artistic production become extinct. In the next place, however, the circle of ideas from which painting drew her works became as varied and diverse as the different countries which afforded them ; for while in Catholic countries, art obtained new suggestions from the almost inexhaustible source of ecclesiastical material, on the other side, the sway of the modern Protestant mind sundered the old ban of tradition, and turned the eye upon the boundless variety of actual life, even to its most insignificant daily incidents, upon the eternal beauty of landscape nature, upon the characteristic significance of the animal world and even of lifelike things, which only obtain an expressive physiognomy from the pervading mind of man. In all these spheres of art, painting displayed incomparable versatility, and drew from them points for artistic representation. Now, historical painting stood distinct ; and beside it, as independent styles, appeared genre painting, landscapes, animal pieces, and still life. The freedom of the individual from the usual range of subjects was therefore now complete, and each separate artist felt himself again confronted with the whole universe, as though he were only now created, and were placed in the enjoyment and aspect of God's rich and magnificent world. Wholly new forms and modes of representation thus resulted, new productions for technical skill, and, above all, for advance in colouring, were thus obtained ; and hence, also, great works were called forth which were to form a fresh era in the history of painting.

Diverse, however, as all these branches of painting are in intellectual tendencies, subjects, conception, and technical execution, their common characteristic feature is a strict adherence to nature, a perfect breach in every respect with tradition, and an effort to depict all subjects, whether sacred or profane, whether treated in a grand historical style or in the graceful manner of cabinet painting, with the utmost possible imitation of reality. That in different lands and styles of painting this produced very diverse results, will be evidenced in our considerations. In them, however, we can only briefly touch upon essential points, as the immeasurable abundance of the works of this period render any special detail impossible, and, besides, sufficient connecting links for the modern investigator are given in the generally intelligible principle of adherence to nature. We have only yet to observe that in the eighteenth century a general decay in artistic power befell painting also, which in this was at last compelled to share the ultimate lot of the sister arts.

a. *Italian Historical Painting.*[1]

In Italy, it is again the Church which claims to a great extent the service of the arts, especially of painting. But the style is a thoroughly new one. The Reformation had shaken the world, and had robbed even the Catholic hierarchy of the former feeling of quiet security and firmly established existence.

[1] *Denkm. d. Kunst.* Pl. 94.

They had perceived the necessity of arming themselves with all their strength against the dangerous foe. Hence arose a new and mighty revival of Catholicism, a bold and dexterous wrestling after the recovery of the old power, after the repression and extermination of the adversaries ; and the order of the Jesuits appeared as the most formidable representative of the movement. If the clergy, however, were to regain their old dominion over the minds of men, they must not avoid the league with the new powers which ruled the world ; and thus we now suddenly see the Church making a compact with the new style of art. As by splendid new houses of worship she sought to gain over the excited multitude, so in all the works of art which she required, she endeavoured, by passionate effect and the enchanting brilliancy of reality, to interest the faithful anew in the sacred figures and events. Painting could in this best meet her demands, because painting experienced the same impulse of the period after thrilling pathos and forcible adherence to nature.

After almost all the Italian schools had fallen, during the course of the sixteenth century, into an empty mannerism, two independent styles arose side by side, which sought a new starting-point for a freer development corresponding with the impulse of the period. The one style found it in a return to the great masters of the prime of art, and in a one-sided study of their admired qualities : these were the Eclectics. The other style returned to a still more original source, casting themselves regardlessly into the arms of nature, and striving after its forcible reproduction : these were therefore called Naturalists. We must consider both separately.

Even at the end of the sixteenth century, a similar effort to bring back painting from its errors of mannerism into a more healthy principle of life had appeared in some of the schools of Upper Italy, and had led to noticeable results. The artist families of Campi at Cremona, and of Procaccini at Milan, may be named as the main vehicles of this tendency. More successful and important appears the Bolognese school, the founder of which was Lodovico Caracci (1555–1619). He founded an academy in Bologna, and introduced the most extensive study of the greatest masters of the art as á basis for the remodelling of painting. While at the same time he referred to the antique for design, for grandeur to Michael Angelo, for composition to Raphael, for colouring to the Venetians, and for grace to Correggio, he never intended the literal execution of a programme so conflicting; but the serious and varied study of nature led his pupils of itself to a style in which much certainly remains of the highest qualities of these masters, but based upon a thoroughly independent and new feeling of life. It is this which in a remarkable manner, in the productions of the great artists of this period, counterbalances by far the previous coldness and academical regularity of the style.

Lodovico, who was principally active as a teacher, produced many paintings in the Pinakothek at Bologna, which exhibit him as an emulator of Correggio; the frescoes also in S. Micchele in Bosco there, depicting scenes from the life of S. Benedict and S. Cecilia, he executed with his pupils. Among these, his two nephews, Agostino Caracci (1558–1601) and Annibale Caracci (1560–1609), must be first mentioned; Agostino also being more remarkable for his teaching and engraving, while Annibale was distinguished as a painter. He was the first to realise the principles of the schools with great independent power, and in many of his paintings there is a considerable remembrance of the great masters whom he reverenced as his models. A Madonna with Saints, in the Pinakothek at Bologna, an excellent representation of S. Rochus, distributing alms, in the Dresden Gallery, a noble and touching Virgin with the Body of Christ, in the Palazzo Borghese in Rome, are among his most able works. This last subject he has frequently repeated, and in it he has done homage to that tendency to effect which impels the religious painting of this epoch to choose similar subjects of sorrow, pain, or ecstasy. The frescoes of a mythological character, which he executed in the gallery of the Farnese Palace in Rome, are Annibale's principal work. In arrangement and style, we can here trace the influence of Michael Angelo's

ceiling of the Sistine Chapel, at the same time there is a beauty
and clearness of colour, such as is only rarely obtained in fresco ;
and although the subjects are not represented with the freshness
and lifelike power of the Raphael period, they have yet distinguishing excellences in arrangement, drawing, and modelling.
(Fig. 388.) Annibale also painted genre pictures of low life
with fresh and often coarse humour, and he likewise belongs to
the first who ventured upon independent landscapes.

One of the most important pupils of the Caracci is Domenichino, rightly Domenico Zampieri (1591–1641), who was superior

Fig. 388. Venus and Mars. By Annibale Caracci.

to most of his contemporaries, not by great power of imagination,
but by a free and happy feeling for nature, extreme technical
skill and command of all artistic resources, and by an attractive
naïveté. Many partly important frescoes are by his hand ;
among others, the grand figures of the Evangelists on the
pendentives of the dome of S. Andrea della Valle, in Rome ;
the life of S. Cecilia, in S. Luigi de' Francesi ; and the history of
S. Nilus, in the church at Grotta Ferrata. In these works he
endeavoured for the most part to give a new charm to sacred
incidents by lifelike and characteristic national figures ; and this

charm is enhanced by the delicacy and truth of the delineation, furnishing evidence that even among the so-called eclectics, adherence to nature was the true moving principle in representation.

Among his panel pictures the Communion of S. Hieronymus, in the Vatican Gallery, is one of the most important, full of excellent touches taken from life, effective in arrangement, and

Fig. 389. S. Cecilia. By Domenichino.

painted in a masterly style. We must also mention the Evangelist St. John, looking upwards with enthusiasm—a work repeatedly copied; and the naïve picture of S. Cecilia, in the Louvre at Paris (Fig. 389)—the latter in a fantastic headdress, with turban and rich drapery, which was generally adopted by the painters of this school. There is an attractive mythological picture in the Borghese Gallery in Rome, representing Diana and her Nymphs; some of whom are bathing, and others are engaged with bows and arrows. The landscape here is especially noticeable, and it is even independently treated in many of this master's pictures. In other representatives of the school, such as Francesco Albani (1578-1660), the inclination to landscape, and especially to idyllic representations with mythological accessories, prevails almost exclusively.

One of the most brilliant masters of this period is, next, Guido Reni (1575-1642), an extremely fertile artist, who at first adhered rather to a strict imitation of nature. This effort rises into terrible one-sidedness in the Crucifixion of Peter, in the Vatican Collection, one of the many favourite executioner scenes of this period, which betray a repulsive barbarousness of feeling. To this early epoch also belong several pictures in the Pinakothek at Bologna; for instance, the grand painting of Christ on the Cross, with Mary and St. John, also the effective and dramatically composed Murder of the Innocents, and an excellent picture of the holy hermits Antony and Paul, in the Berlin Museum, figures of powerful characterisation and grand form.

In his middle life, Guido more inclined to the effort after delicate grace, which reached its zenith in a perfectly noble production—namely, his famous fresco painting of Aurora and Phœbus with the Horæ, in the Pal. Rospigliosi in Rome—but which gradually in other works fell into a shallow empty ideal type and into exaggerated tenderness of form, and, finally, even led to a decrease of his formerly fresh and soft colouring.

Lifelike, faithful to nature, and especially distinguished by a strong brilliant colouring, which is only sometimes too heavy in the shadows of the flesh, is Guercino, whose real name was Francesco Barbieri (1590-1666). He, too, appears stronger in his earlier works, and only at a later period falls into a similar effeminacy of style. Among his most important works is the fresco painting of the Aurora, in the Villa Ludovisi in Rome; also the dying Dido, in the Palazzo Spada in the same city; several large pictures in the Pinakothek at Bologna, and many others in the galleries on either side of the Alps. Far more superficial and shallow in his conceptions is Giov. Lanfranco;

while, on the other hand, the charming though limited Sassoferrato, whose real name was Giov. Battista Salvi (1605-1685),
reaches an expression of depth of feeling in his numerous devotional pictures. We have yet to mention Cristofano Allori
(1577-1621) as one of the noblest and most able masters of his
time, whose principal work, the splendid Judith with the Head of
Holofernes, is in the Pitti Gallery in Florence. Lastly, Carlo
Dolci (1616-1686) belongs to this list of artists. Though often
falling into affected sweetness and sentimentality, he is sometimes charming from his purer feeling, and is always attractive
from the soft bloom of his colouring.

Fig. 390. Magdalene from the Pal. Colonna. Rome.

Stronger and more regardless appear the characteristics of
the naturalists of the period, who, in striving after passionate expression, make use of the forms of lower nature, and proceed in
these with the same violence as they deport themselves in life
generally. Persecution and intrigue, poison and the dagger, are
the prevailing power with many of these artists, and which not
rarely afforded them assistance in their ambitious emulation with
other art associates. The head of this style is Michael Angelo

Amerighi, surnamed Caravaggio from his birthplace (1569 1609), in every respect a genuine son of the age, wild and passionate in life like his paintings. When he paints sacred incidents, as in the frescoes from the history of S. Matthew, in S. Luigi de' Francesi in Rome, or as in the great altar-piece of the Entombment of Christ, in the Vatican, he transports the events throughout to the lowest sphere of life. He depicts wild, ugly, and even impudent and common figures, but they are endowed with mighty life, and in the expression of their feelings are never, it is true, noble, but often thrillingly truthful and overpoweringly tragical.

Fig. 391   False Players.   By Caravaggio.

The figures are, moreover, executed in bold strong colouring, and the sudden glaring lights which are gloomily thrown across cause the forms to stand out in dark strong shadows. Most successful are the pictures in which he relinquishes the pretension of sacred incidents, and represents the vagabond rabble of that wild age with daring figures and criminal actions; thus, for instance, the famous and oft-repeated 'False Players' (there is a copy in the Dresden Gallery, and another in the Palazzo Sciarra in Rome), the Foretelling Gypsy, and others of a similar kind.

The volcanic soil of Naples next became the principal seat

of this school, the most extreme and regardless representative of which was the Spaniard Giuseppe Ribera, surnamed Spagnoletto (1593–1656). In his earlier pictures, as well as in his masterly Descent from the Cross, in the sacristy of S. Martino at Naples, he is more moderate; but in his numerous later works he does homage to the powerful representation of the passionate and the terrible, and his martyr scenes become horrible execution scenes. Great boldness of execution, and a masterly chiaro oscuro, impart an almost demon-like tone to his pictures.

Among the followers of this style, who, however, but rarely erred into such extremes, there was, besides Salvator Rosa, with whom we shall subsequently again meet among the landscape painters, an able Sicilian painter named Pietro Novelli, known under the name Monrealese; also the Netherland painter Gerard Honthorst, who bears the surname of Gherardo dalle Notti, from his predilection for effects of light by night; also the distinguished battle painter Michael Angelo Cerquozzi, and the French painter Jacques Courtois (or Cortese), also named Bourguignon; and the highly gifted Luca Giordano, notorious, however, for his furiously rapid painting (1632–1705), who from this peculiarity received the surname of 'Fa presto,' and ruined his splendid talent by superficial execution.

b. *Spanish Painting.*[1]

Spain, the principal home of restored Catholicism, the cradle of Loyola and the Inquisition, the focus of a religious enthusiasm which was combined with the passionate sensuality of the South, witnessed at this epoch the brilliant prime of its painting. So deeply was art here linked with ecclesiastical life, that it experienced no disadvantageous effect from the disorder of the state and the impoverishment of the land. In its works, the ecclesiastical element predominated far more than in those of the contemporaneous art of Italy; but here also it was that new and mighty increase of religious feeling, produced by the opposition

[1] *Denkm. d. Kunst.* Pl. 97.

of Protestantism, which impelled painting to the utmost power of expression. The most sincere monkish asceticism, the tenderest devotion, the earth-forgetting rapture, and the most ardent fanaticism—all these are in no other epoch so powerfully portrayed by art as in the Spanish painting of the seventeenth century. That here also, in a southern excitable people, strict adherence to nature formed the starting-point, may readily be conceived; that, moreover, as in the Italian art of this period, but still more exclusively and predominantly, colour should constitute the fundamental element of this art, designed as it was for effective portrayal, is also a natural result. This tendency, however, was not merely promoted by the study of Titian and of the great Flemish painters Rubens and Van Dyck, but it was increased by a fine perception, innate in the Spaniard, of the effects of colour under the influence of a richly gradated aerial perspective. In the development of this capacity Spanish painting reached its highest triumph, and held an equal rank with the kindred art of poetry, which at this time also reached its prime in Spain.

The greatest importance was now concentrated in the school of Seville, the earlier able beginnings of which we have already considered (vol. ii. p. 364). In Francisco Pacheco (1571–1654) there is still a remnant left of the former style; Juan de las Roélas (1558–1625), however, transplanted the beauty of Venetian colouring to Spanish soil, and found an effective coadjutor in Francisco de Herrera, the elder (1576–1656), who was distinguished by the free and bold execution of his strong colouring. Roélas' pupil, Francisco Zurbaran (1598–1662), next exhibits importance. His works, which are conspicuous for deep religious expression, produce strong effect from their excellent and natural colouring: sacred rapture, contrition, and enthusiastic ardour prevail in all his paintings. St. Thomas Aquinas, in the gallery at Seville, may be mentioned as one of his principal works. Alonso Cano (1601–1667), also distinguished as an architect and sculptor, occupies an independent position: his representations, which are for the most part ecclesiastical, exhibit a stronger plastic form and sharper outline.

One of the principal masters of this school is Don Diego Velazquez de Silva (1599–1660), who passed from the monkish restrictions of most Spanish painters to a freer view and to more extensive and versatile employment of his rich talent.[1] He began with a vigorous adherence to nature, which, in several masterly genre pictures in the Museum at Madrid, and in the Duke of Wellington's Gallery, appears at first hard, but soon after exhibits itself in noble and purified grace. Many journeys to Italy, where he cultivated his style into great nobleness and just beauty, were decisive for his art. But it was of still greater importance that he was appointed court painter to Philip IV., and henceforth was especially employed as a portrait painter. His portraits are incomparably powerful and lifelike, from their grandeur of conception, free and noble bearing, beautiful arrangement, and masterly, bold, and broad treatment of colour. Among his most distinguished works of this kind are Philip IV., life-size, on horseback, in the Uffizi at Florence, a highly effective and imposing picture, and splendid in colouring; also the half-length figure of Pope Innocent X. in the Pal. Doria in Rome, and several of the most excellent in the gallery at Madrid, among them another equestrian portrait of Philip IV., a portrait of the Infanta Margaretha, formed into a too idyllic and graceful genre scene; and the Surrender of Breda, a group of excellent portraits combined into an historical scene. In the Belvedere at Vienna, besides many able portraits of princes, there is a grand and masterly family portrait, representing the wife of the master surrounded by her children, and himself in the background. That Velazquez, however, was also a master in other styles, is evidenced by his excellent landscapes, genre pictures, and many religious compositions, among them the effective Crowning of the Madonna, in the Museum at Madrid.

The other principal master of the Seville school, Bartolomé

---

[1] Velazquez and his works, &c. William Stirling.

Esteban Murillo (1618–1682), stands free above the limited views of most Spanish painters, and surpasses both Velazquez and all others of his countrymen in versatility and depth. In his numerous religious pictures, the national mode of conception is raised to a height of passionate ardour streaming from his innermost soul, which can express both tender feeling and strong enthusiasm. But he also knew how to depict reality with incomparable freshness and power, both in the coarse humorous genre picture and in the fine and lifelike portrait. He also

Fig. 392. Female Portrait. By Velazquez.

brought the colouring and the soft chiaro oscuro, as well as the most delicate gradations of aerial perspective, to unsurpassed perfection. It is, moreover, characteristic of Murillo that he started with the powerful delineation of lower life. Some pictures of this kind, for instance, in the Pinakothek at Munich, which represent peasants, ragged street boys, and others, lounging idly, stealing, and playing cards, are depicted with incomparable observation of nature, and powerful colouring. In many of his religious representations we see the effect of this style of conception, especially in his Madonnas; such, for instance, as those in the Dresden Gallery, the Pitti Gallery at Florence, and others, where the mother, seated quietly with the Child, is only rendered divine by the halo, and in other things does not pass beyond the sphere of homely womanliness.

It was not till he depicted the Madonna herself in enthusiastic rapture, in those wonderful pictures in which she is represented borne upwards on clouds, bathed in celestial light, and

Fig. 393.　Murillo's St. John.　Museum at Madrid.

surrounded by vast drapery, her longing glance seeking to precede her ascent heavenwards, that Murillo reaches an expression of religious enthusiasm, more ardent and entrancing than painting has ever produced. The conception in these pictures—one of the most famous of which is in the Louvre—shows him most nearly allied to Correggio; but the enthusiasm of the Spaniard, although expressed by similar means, is far more noble, pure, and heavenly. His numerous pictures, in which he has depicted the raptures and visions of various saints, all breathe the same tone of fervent devotion; but here also he passes beyond the limited expression of monkish fanatical excitement, and reaches a nobler expression of feeling, enchanting from its naïveté and truth. One of his most extolled works is the Vision of S. Antonius of Padua, in the cathedral of Seville, a similar conception of which is to be seen in the Berlin Museum. Other excellent works of this kind are in the Museum at Madrid. Lastly, there are also some masterly portraits by him, especially the splendidly painted likeness of a Cardinal in the Museum at Berlin.

The school of Madrid, which is more productive in portrait painting, owing to the presence of the Court, is distinguished by many able masters, who likewise reached a fine perfection of colouring, and among whom we must mention Antonio Pereda (1590–1669), and especially Juan Careño de Miranda (1614–1685). Velazquez exercised a decided influence upon these and other masters. A less independent adoption of former styles is exhibited, on the contrary, in Claudio Coello, who lived till the year 1693. Lastly, we must mention Francisco Ribalta (1551–1628) as head of the school of Valencia: he cultivated his art in Italy, especially studying the works of Fra Sebastiano del Piombo, and occasionally he combines grand outline with warm and harmonious colouring. In the eighteenth century, painting languished also in Spain, and was kept miserably alive by a studied imitation of earlier masters.

c. *Historical Painting in the Netherlands.*

The painting of this epoch displayed in the Netherlands greater richness and variety than even in Italy and Spain. Not merely was a similar contrast formed between the school of Brabant and that of Holland as between the Eclectics and the Naturalists of Italy, but this was preeminently the soil on which new and fruitful subjects of representation were opened to art. As the common basis, however, of all these different styles, we can trace a fresh and genuinely national mode of feeling, which gives an original colouring to the conception, the treatment of the forms, and the technical execution.

The school of Brabant[1] adhered more to tradition, for this portion of the land, in spite of the heavy struggles of the sixteenth century, could as little extricate itself from Spanish rule as from Catholicism. It is therefore the third great school of

Fig. 394. Rubens' Raising of Lazarus.

this epoch which drew its ecclesiastical inspirations from revived Catholicism ; but at the same time it yielded to an adherence to nature, in its mode of representation, with the same ease as the Italians and Spaniards had done. The principal master of this school, and its founder, is *Peter Paul Rubens*, who lived from 1577 to 1640, and is one of the most brilliant,

[1] *Denkm. d. Kunst.* Pl. 95.

most gifted, and most versatile masters in the history of art.
From his teacher, Octavius van Veen, he could only receive that
mannered imitation of the Italians, which for almost half a century had supplanted the true national art of the Netherlands.
But in his twenty-third year, the young Rubens went himself
to Italy, where, during a residence of seven years, by the study
of Titian and Veronese, he gained a basis for his representations corresponding with the impulse of his time. In his earlier
pictures, especially those executed in Italy, we find evident
trace of the great Venetian masters. Soon, however, his own
powerful artist nature extricated itself independently, and now
produced a style in which it could express itself freely and
vigorously.

Passionate emotion, bold action, and deep and strong feeling,
are the elements of his art. Out of love for these, he called into
existence a race of beings who, by their frequently superabundant physical power, show themselves equal to every impulse.
If the existence of the forms created by Venetian masters rests
on the highest and noblest capacity for enjoyment, in Rubens'
characters the requirements of action and vigorous life appear as
the root of their being. His men breathe forth a free heroic
power fettered by no impediments; they are, indeed, without the
purer form of the Italian eclectics, but this is compensated by
their inexhaustible life. His compositions are not strictly balanced, but there is a harmony in them of mighty passionately
excited characters, such as no other artist has produced. If we
compare Rubens in this respect with Michael Angelo, we soon
see that in Rubens' figures a coarser materiality prevails, borrowed direct from life, and that the passionate effect flows less
from depth of thought than from the energy of the sensual nature. This is also in keeping with the magic power of his
brilliant colouring, which is executed with bold and broad touches,
and is combined with a perhaps unexampled facility in creation
and an astonishing power of production. For the study of his
technical skill, the numerous original coloured sketches of many
of his works are of especial value. Whole series of these gifted

sketches are in the Pinakothek at Munich and in the Hermitage at St. Petersburg.

A number of large paintings, rich in figures, among which are works of colossal dimension, meet us in the churches and galleries of his native country, and in almost all the galleries of Europe. The most able of these are the works executed shortly after his return from Italy. Subsequently, owing to his numerous orders, the execution was more hurried, and the help of his numerous pupils became necessary; but even then—and in pictures in which there is a somewhat exaggerated fulness, heaviness, and coarseness, and a tendency to low characterisation—the eminent lifelike power bursts forth atoningly in its indestructible majesty through all these imperfections.

From the countless number of his works we will only mention some of the most important. His altar pictures treat the most various subjects of sacred history, and for the most part depict scenes of passionate dramatic excitement. This is the case, for instance, in the two paintings in Antwerp Cathedral, the Raising of the Cross, and the Descent from the Cross, and in many excellent works in the academy there; for instance, the Incredulity of St. Thomas, one of the noblest of his early works; St. Theresa, a painting likewise distinguished for its delicacy and nobleness of feeling; the powerful picture of our Saviour crucified between Two Malefactors; the pathetic lamentation over the dead Christ; a charming Holy Family; an exaggerated picture of St. Francis of Assisi, in comparison with which Domenichino's famous picture appears dignified and classical; and, lastly, the splendid scene of the Adoration of the Kings, a picture full of boldness and action. There is a painting of the same subject in the gallery at Brussels, displaying more depth of feeling and nobleness of expression. In the gallery at Madrid, there is one of the master's most powerful creations, the Miracle of the Brazen Serpent; also, a splendid picture of the Adoration of the Kings. In the gallery of the Belvedere in Vienna, there is an Ascension of the Virgin, surrounded by charming bands of angels. There is also St. Ambrosius, forbidding the Emperor

Theodosius to enter the Church, an altar-piece of grand composition and excellent execution. The same collection also contains one of the master's most perfect creations, painted in 1610, soon after his return from Italy—an altar-piece with folding panels, in the centre the enthroned Virgin, offering an ecclesiastical garment to St. Ildefonso, and on the panels, Archduke Albert and his consort. There are also in the same place the two large altar-pieces containing lifelike representations of the miracles of Francis Zavier and Ignatius Loyola. In the Pinakothek at Munich there is a colossal picture of the Last Judgment, certainly a masterly work as regards arrangement and distribution, and in striking power of effect of light, but unpleasing from its multitude of voluptuous female figures. There is also a grand dramatic composition of the combat between St. Michael and the Dragon. In St. Peter's at Cologne there is the repulsive but masterly painting of the Sufferings of St. Peter, and many others. There are also numerous mythological representations, full of heroic boldness and sensual power—such as the Battle of the Amazons, in the Pinakothek at Munich; the splendid Garden of Love, in the gallery at Madrid (there is a copy in the Dresden Gallery); the poetical and highly coloured Feast of Venus at Cythera, in the gallery of the Belvedere at Vienna; a series of similar pictures in the Hermitage at St. Petersburg. Among others, the Liberation of Andromeda, the River-god Tigris, and, especially remarkable as a powerful expression of Bacchantal revelry, a drunken Silenus with Satyrs. The same subject is depicted also in a coarse picture in the Pinakothek at Munich, where there is also the Rape of the Daughters of Leucippus, a picture full of dramatic action. In the gallery at Blenheim, there is a splendid Bacchanal, as well as the Rape of Proserpine; the latter again occurs in the gallery at Madrid.

Rubens is also great in representations from profane history, especially in dramatic scenes; among the principal works of this kind, are the six large pictures of the history of Decius in the Lichtenstein Gallery in Vienna. Roman history is here handled in the same gifted and bold manner as Shakespeare conceives it in his Roman plays. Even the allegorical representations, wrung from him by the taste of the age, he filled with a grand air of reality; as, for example, the twenty-one paintings in the Louvre, which depict the history of Maria de' Medici. There are also some able genre paintings by this inexhaustible master, such as the Peasants' Dance, in the Louvre, wildly agitated animal pieces, grand landscapes, and lifelike portraits; as, for example, many excellent ones in the Dresden Gallery; and, lastly, some fresh and naïve representations of child-life. (Fig. 395.) Rubens was, besides, active as an architect; and with all

Fig. 395. Children Scene. By Rubens. Berlin Gallery.

these artistic productions he was a man of great and noble life, expert in intercourse with princes and diplomatists, and was even himself entrusted repeatedly with political missions to foreign courts. Thus in him, more than in any other master of his time, were combined all the richness and splendour of the life of that brilliant epoch.

Among his pupils, Anton van Dyck (1599–1641) occupies the first place. At first he cultivated his master's forcible style, which he occasionally carried to excess, as is evidenced by a Christ crowned with Thorns, in the Berlin Gallery. But after journeys to Italy, and direct study from Venetian paintings, his style passed into a more just and noble beauty, a striking proof of which is given by a picture in the same gallery, the Mourning over the Body of Christ. A more refined and nervous sensibility led him by preference in his religious paintings to treat such representations of deep trouble of mind ; and, instead of the passionate desire for action of Rubens' figures, his are distinguished by an elegiac expression of sorrow, verging on the tearful and sentimental. Thus he has most frequently depicted the dead Christ on the Cross, or, after being taken down from the cross, surrounded by His mourning followers.

Van Dyck reached his highest importance as a portrait painter, and he stands forth as one of the first masters of this branch of art. First in Italy, and then at the court of Charles I. of England, he had constant opportunity of immortalising the princes, prelates, and brilliant aristocracy of his time. All these pictures are distinguished by a truly noble conception, by wonderful delicacy of psychological representation, as well as by the charm of an incomparably distinct and soft colouring. Among the most famous of these works, we may mention the imposing equestrian portrait of the Emperor Charles V. in the Tribuna of the Uffizi at Florence ; that of Thomas Carignan, in the gallery at Turin ; of General Moncada, in the Louvre ; of Marchese Brignole, in the palace of this family at Genoa ; and of a Colonna, in the palace of the same name at Rome ;—also the masterly portrait of King Charles I. of England, in the Louvre (and in other places) ; the Children of Charles I., in the galleries of Windsor, Turin, and Dresden ; Prince Thomas of Carignan and the Infanta Eugenia of Spain, in the Berlin Museum ; Cardinal Bentivoglio, in the Pal. Pitti in Florence, and countless other excellent works.

The other numerous pupils of Rubens adhered to his coarser

and stronger style, which they often adopted successfully, but not without heaviness and rudeness. The most talented of these is Jacob Jordaens, who executed many able and powerful genre scenes.

The school of Holland[1] took an essentially different course. A new and fresh political life had here developed itself on a thoroughly civil basis, and political as well as religious liberty was guaranteed by a solid and vigorous existence. As eccle-

Fig. 396. The Children of Charles I. in the Dresden Gallery. By Van Dyck.

siastical tradition had been repressed by the strong Protestantism of the land, art saw itself thrown at first upon the faithful portrayal of reality, which it brought to great perfection, especially in portrait painting. It is not the poetic breath of aristocratic delicacy, as in Van Dyck, nor the agitated life and power of Rubens, but a sober spirit of order and distinctness, a feeling of civil opulence and self-consciousness, which is expressed in the excellent portraits of these Dutch masters. Among the most

[1] *Denkm. d. Kunst.* Pl. 96.

excellent of them are Franz Hals (1584–1666), and, above all, the justly famed Bartholomäus van der Helst (1613–1670), whose principal works are, the Banquet of the Amsterdam Citizens on the Celebration of the Peace of Westphalia, in the Museum at Amsterdam, and the Judges of the Prizes of the Rifle Band of Amsterdam, in the Louvre.

The same starting-point was taken by the principal master of the Dutch school, Rembrandt van Ryn (1606–1669). There are many portraits belonging to his earlier life, in which, with superior talent, he devoted himself to the simple representation of nature. Thus, for instance, there is the famous picture in the Hague Museum, executed in the year 1632, of the anatomist Tulp dissecting a body before his auditors; and many portraits in the gallery at Cassel, especially that of the arithmetician Copenel, and the burgomaster Sixt, executed in the year 1639. Subsequently, he was no longer satisfied with this calm objective mode of representation; a deep, inwardly suppressed, passionate flame urged him to a new style of conception, in which the figures themselves only tended to solve problems of the boldest character; a wonderful perfection of chiaro oscuro, a daring play with fantastic and even glaring effects of light, distinguish his later works. This tendency is, as it were, the expression of a violent protestation against all noble form and cheerful life in the light of day. A masterpiece of this kind is the famous 'Vigil,' in the Museum at Amsterdam (1642), which represents the procession of the rifle band in a night illumination by no means corresponding with the subject and the design. Even when he paints sacred histories, he chooses by preference the figures of common life; and he carries this out in his rare mythological pictures with wanton irony, as in the Rape of Ganymede, in the Dresden Gallery. But, in spite of this want of nobler form and higher expression, his paintings entrance the spectator by their singular charm, by the constraining force of a mind stirred up in its very depths, and by a mysterious poetic power.

Rembrandt executed, by preference, Old-Testament subjects,

which were, in general, more suitable to the Puritan taste of the period, and in which he could satisfy, by Oriental costume and strong characterisation, the fantastic taste which formed an essential element in his art. As specimens of this, we may mention the representation of the family of Tobias with the Angel, in the Louvre; the Sacrifice of Abraham, in the Hermitage at St. Petersburg, and many other pictures of marvellously

Fig. 397. Rape of Ganymede. By Rembrandt.

enchanting effect. There is also a grand painting in the Museum at Berlin—Moses dashing to Pieces the Tables of the Law. In the same place there is also a powerful representation of Samson threatening his father-in-law (1637)—a picture which exhibits the artist at the utmost height of his power. The life of Samson inspired the master to many of his important representations.

The gallery at Cassel possesses a picture belonging to the year 1636, which depicts with terrible truth the blinding of the hero. The same dreadful incident forms the subject of a painting in the Schönborn Gallery in Vienna.   A remarkable picture, on the other hand, in the Dresden Gallery, executed in the year 1638, possesses a perfectly magic and poetic power of attraction :

Fig. 398.   The Raising of Lazarus.   By Rembrandt.

it is there designated as the Banquet of Ahasuerus, but it is more rightly Samson among the Philistines.

In order justly to estimate his representations from the New Testament, we must study closely the numerous compositions which he executed in excellent etchings.   It is true that in these masterly works he indulges predominantly that delight in the mysterious charms of the chiaro oscuro, which no other artist

has displayed so much as he, that he gives way to this occasionally
too exclusively, and brings out the moment of the incident, with
all its effect, at the expense of worthy characterisation and noble
arrangement.   Thus, for example, in the famous Descent from
the Cross (there are paintings of it in the Pinakothek at Munich,
and in the Museum at St. Petersburg), the emphasis is prepon-
deratingly placed on the external event with its realistic consequences.   But in many etchings, as in the Raising of Lazarus
and several others, the figure of Christ appears full of dignity,
and stands out all the more nobly from the fantastic figures
surrounding Him, which often verge on coarse and low life.
Here, also, considerable effect is obtained by peculiar arrangement and light.   One of the most attractive pictures of this
kind is Christ as the Friend of Children, in the Schönborn
Gallery in Vienna, recently placed in the London National
Gallery.

In his later portraits, the master aims still more decidedly at
representing his figures bathed in light; but this light does not
recall the rosy glow of day, but a yellow artificial lamp light.   At
the same time, he throws all the charm of chiaro oscuro even
into the massive parts in shadow, and sketches his forms with
ever broader and bolder touches.   Only in his latest works is
this distinct colouring lost in gloomy and sometimes even dirty
brown and grey.   Lastly, we must not forget that we owe to
Rembrandt many landscapes of grand boldness.   (Galleries of
Cassel, Dresden, Munich, and Brunswick.)

Among Rembrandt's pupils and imitators, this play with
effects of light and finely executed chiaro oscuro gains a more
and more superficial character.   Yet we must mention, as gifted
followers of his style, Gerbrand van den Eeckhout, who
approaches him most nearly; Ferdinand Bol, who is often
charming and attractive; the more temperate Govart Flinck;
J. Lievensz, distinguished for his portraits and landscapes; and
Salomon Koning, remarkable for his technical skill.

d. *German, French, and English Painting.*

In Germany,[1] painting had lost, towards the end of the sixteenth century, every trace of national tradition, and had fallen into a mannered imitation of the Italians. This tendency was most moderately expressed in the artists, who, like Johann Rottenhammer of Munich (1564–1622), followed the Venetians. It was, on the other hand, repulsively exhibited in those who bungled after Michael Angelo with lamentable mediocrity. In the course of the seventeenth century, the art rose to somewhat greater life in artists such as Joachim von Sandrart of Frankfort, Carl Screta of Prague, Johann Kupetzky of Hungary; and it produced in Baltasar Denner (1685–1749) a gifted and wonderful portrayer of nature. Nevertheless, these were only isolated efforts, which here and there arose, without national basis, and without common traditionary rules. In the eighteenth century likewise, various estimable artists appeared; among others, the skilful and fertile eclectic Christian Dietrich (1712–1774), and the painters Tischbein, the elder, and Bernhard Rode, both of whom were formed in the French school. A new return to ideal conception, brought about by Winckelmann's influence, was introduced by Rafael Mengs (1728–1779); yet this tendency remained too deeply fettered by academical externals to be able thoroughly to reform and revive the German art. Among the portrait painters of this time, we must mention, besides Anton Graff, the attractive Angelica Kauffmann (1742–1808). The first true regenerators of German art we shall consider later.

French painting,[2] also, during this whole period, adhered predominantly to the eclectic character, and lacked, just as much as the German, a national basis. Still, several distinguished artists appeared, who in many of their works have obtained an importance beyond their age. Foremost among these, we may place Nicolas Poussin (1594–1665), who in his historical com-

---

[1] *Denkm. d. Kunst.* Pl. 99.   [2] Ibid. Pl. 98.

positions (Fig. 399) adopted that antique style, which certainly is based on a grand conception, and is combined with a noble sense of the beautiful and of purity of form, but which, in a similar manner as the French tragedy of the period, betrays a certain ostentatious coldness of reflection. A similar style is exhibited in Philippe Champaigne, who was especially distinguished as a portrait painter. How much this tendency corresponded with the French character at that period, may be perceived from the fact that Simon Vouet (1582–1641), a master who imitated Caravaggio and the Venetians, remained

Fig. 399. Moses at the Spring. By Nicolas Poussin.

isolated in his more vigorous adherence to nature, although many of the most famous artists of France emanated from his school. Among these was Eustache le Sueur (1617–1655), remarkable for greater fervour of feeling, especially in his scenes of monastic life; also the excellent portrait painter Pierre Mignard, and Charles Lebrun, the court-painter of Louis XIV. (1619–1690), who with great gifts carried the art into false theatrical pathos, and by his universal influence brought about the decline of painting. In the eighteenth century, this inwardly hollow and outwardly coquettish style reached its height in François Boucher, the 'painter of the Graces;' and in portraiture alone do we still find a master of importance, such as Hyacinthe Rigaud, whose clever portraits belong to the best productions of the age.

England,[1] which had never before possessed a school of painting of her own, and whose powerful aristocracy required portraiture alone, a requirement which she had, however, satisfied through the great masters, such as Holbein, and subsequently Van Dyck, possessed, in the seventeenth century, a school of portrait painters, who followed the style of the last-named master. Among these, a foreigner named Peter Lely, rightly P. van der Faes of Soest in Westphalia (1618–1680), was the most distinguished. After him came the likewise renowned Gottfried Kneller of Lübeck (1648–1723), whose numerous works, however, incline for the most part to theatrical mannerism. In the eighteenth century the degenerated style of French painting, it is true, here also gained the ascendancy, as is especially evidenced in the paintings of the historical painter James Thornhill (1676–1734); but in the latter part of the century, England was also the first country which freed itself from this levelling art despotism, and attempted to treat national subjects in an independent manner. The grand undertaking of a simple private man, John Boydell, to illustrate the poems of the greatest dramatists of modern time by the best artists of that day in England, and to gather these together in the splendid work of the ' Shakspeare Gallery,' gave the first impetus to this arousing of the national art spirit. At the same time, Joshua Reynolds (1723–1792) laid the foundation of that brilliant study of colour, which has become the main merit of the modern English school; and Benjamin West (1734–1820) gave a new and fresh impulse to historical painting by his lifelike and clever battle-pieces.

e. *Northern Genre Painting.*[2]

If the strongly awakened delight in the delineation of perfect reality among the Eycks and their pupils had burst asunder the

---

[1] *Denkm. d. Kunst.* Pl. 98. [2] Ibid. Pl. 100.

fetters of strict religious painting, and had transported the sacred figures into the life of the time, it was a necessary result that, in an epoch of strict natural representation, actual daily life in its simple state, without the pretext of sacred history, should acquire in itself considerable importance. Everywhere, in Italy as in Spain, we have found numerous instances of these genre representations, only that there the figures for the most part preserved the large dimensions of historical painting.

The Netherland masters were the first who entered in detail into the delineation of matters of daily life, and were the true founders and perfectors of modern genre painting. Protestantism, which here more than elsewhere disdained the traditional ecclesiastical subjects, or gave them a genre-like colouring as in Rembrandt, essentially contributed to the advance of this branch of painting; and if, on the one side, it was a sober sensible taste which favoured the portrayal of the circumstances of ordinary life, on the other hand, the comfortable ease, which marks the domestic existence of the Germanic nations, possesses a charming touch of poetry, which introduced into these portrayals, in spite of their adherence to nature, an ideal and artistic element. Indeed, in so far as these delineations regardlessly portrayed the natural or unfettered circles of human society, or the life in higher spheres refined by cultivation and manners, they were designated as lower or higher genre. Both styles stood in the same proportion to each other, as the portraits of the coarse solid Dutch masters did to the fine aristocratic portraits of Van Dyck. In the one, the solid character of a bourgeois race was expressed openly, freely, and forcibly; in the other, the fine and complicated life of feeling, of aristocratic and cultivated characters, is veiled under the polished surface of noble reserve.

Even before the end of the sixteenth century, Peter Breughel, the elder, surnamed the ' Bauernbreughel ' (peasant Breughel), depicted peasant life, in all its rudeness and awkwardness, with great effect and coarse humour. In his son, Peter Breughel, the younger, surnamed the ' Höllenbreughel,' the fantastic tendency of the age burst forth powerfully, and led him, like Hieronymus Bosch, to depict various sorts of devilish tricks, goblin stories and the like, which he did with great effect, increased by the introduction of nocturnal illumination. A similar style was exhibited also by the elder David Teniers, who, with this aim in view, gladly undertook the representation of the Temptation of S. Antony.

With such models before him, David Teniers, the younger, the son of the former Tenier (1610–1694), began, in the seventeenth century, the true and mature development of the lower genre style. Trained in Rubens' school, he adopted the great

Fig. 400. Genre Picture. By Teniers. Madrid Gallery.

excellences of this master as a painter, and applied them to the delineation of various scenes of peasant life and doings. He appears most attractive in those pictures in which he introduces smaller groups at play, drinking, or other similar situations. In his more extensive representations of peasant weddings, with dancing, carousing, fighting, and similar pastimes, he repeats himself, indeed, constantly in characters and ideas, though, from masterly arrangement of light, powerful colouring, and skilful employment of chiaro oscuro, he invests these works with an unsurpassably picturesque general effect.

He is most clever in other paintings, in which he admits a touch of fancy; but he deals with it in a delightfully playful manner, and with wanton humour. This is the case especially in his representations of the Temptation of S. Antony; a very favourite subject at this time in the Netherlands, affording, as it did, excellent opportunity for the display of fantastic apparitions. The best picture of this kind is in the Museum at Berlin. Lastly, still more bold and ironical is his humour in other representations, in which apes seriously imitate the doings of men, and pass their time, in ludicrous earnestness, with music and the pleasures of the table. The numerous works by this master are everywhere to be met with in the galleries, and are readily recognised from their bright fresh colouring, clever bold manner of handling the pencil, and masterly reproduction of even the most subordinate things—vessels, implements, and such like.

Less full of action, and rather exhibiting the more quiet condition of awkward ease, is the peasant life depicted by a German artist, Adrian van Ostade of Lübeck (1610–1685), who, however, in his artistic culture belongs to the Dutch school. His paintings do not breathe forth the bold humour and fresh life of Teniers' pictures; but they are attractive from their careful execution, warm and powerful colouring, and excellent chiaro oscuro. No less distinguished is his brother Isaak van Ostade, who especially delighted in depicting peasant life in the open air, in front of taverns and inns. More like Teniers in the representation of wild joviality and active life, but far richer and more varied in invention, is Adrian Brouwer (1608–1641), of whom it is said that he wholly fell into dissolute tavern life. He studied it, indeed, with the greatest fidelity and thoroughness; for more than any other he was able to watch it in its comic, awkward, and even violent scenes, in card playing, wild carousing, and coarse brawls, and to depict them with bold brush.

Lastly, we must mention in this list Jan Steen of Leyden

(about 1626–1679), of whom it is said that, from delight in tavern life, he even himself kept a wine house. Among all the portrayers of lower genre scenes he is the cleverest and the boldest. Not unfrequently, by his fine gift of observation, he imparts to these scenes a dramatic effect, while he depicts with lifelike power a series of events standing in relation to each other. He combines a romance-like interest with his representations, and by this means he often raises them, in spite of the low state of things which they depict, into a poetic sphere.

Essentially different from these masters is Peter van Laar (1613–1674), who studied in Italy, and effectively treated scenes of low Italian life in the manner of the Italian naturalistic school. The Italians gave him the surname ' Bamboccio,' and from this the whole race of lower genre painters received the name of the ' Bambocciades.' Lastly, the wild soldier life of the period received its artistic representation in the paintings of Jan le Ducq (1638–1695), who had had opportunity as an officer to observe it attentively. Somewhat later, Philip Rugendas flourished in Germany (1666–1742), and also produced able works in this branch of art.

The foremost position in higher genre painting is occupied by Gerhard Terburg (1608–1681), one of the most distinguished masters. He depicts the higher classes of his time in all their rich and stately pomp, in graceful elegance, and yet with dignified demeanour. It is a matter of course that the utmost technical skill should exist in the representation of the costly costume, the brilliant material, the heavy gorgeous satin, and the sparkling jewellery. That a poetic charm should be imparted by the aid of chiaro oscuro to the interior of the dwelling rooms and splendid apartments of the time is the common merit of the most able masters of this branch of art; but that the scenes represented should possess, besides this, an interesting romance-like character, exciting the imagination of the spectator to amplify the facts intimated, this is a special excellence, which imparts an attractive charm to the pictures of this master.

No less important is Gerhard Dow (1613–1680), who received in Rembrandt's school the inclination to an unsurpassable perfection of chiaro oscuro, thus giving his masterly works an expression of agreeable ease. He is not so clever and interesting in portrayal as Terburg ; he does not understand how to give his pictures that deeper relation to a romance-like story ; and he therefore aims less at representations of the higher classes. On the other hand, he depicts with pleasing warmth easy bourgeois domestic life, and spreads over it a charming peacefulness, arising from the careful execution of his small cabinet pieces, to which he often gives peculiar effect from a striking introduction of light.

Fig. 401. Genre Picture. By G. Dow. Belvedere at Vienna.

Many other artists of this favourite style followed these two masters, without, however, presenting it in a new aspect, or advancing it further. Far rather, with all their excellence, they cultivated technical skill at the expense of intellectual purport, and the elaborate representation of fine stuffs became imperceptibly the principal matter, while with Terburg and Dow it had served an intellectual or pleasing end. Among the most excellent of these artists we may mention Gabriel Metzu (1615 until after 1667), who seems fully equal to those two masters in his earlier works, and at any rate is the most elegant of all—but he subsequently falls into a cold leaden colouring ; also the extremely prolific pupil of Dow, Franz van Mieris (1635–1681), who is highly elegant, but yet superficial, and his son, Wilhelm van Mieris ; also the excellent and occasionally wholly unconstrained Caspar Netscher of Heidelberg (1639–1684), and Gottfried Schalcken, a pupil of Gerhard Dow, who is especially masterly in effects of light.

These works at last subside into ivory-like smoothness in the works of Adrian van der Werff, who in the same manner delights also in treating historical, and especially mythological, subjects. More simple and agreeably attractive, and thus forming a pleasing contrast to this style, are the works of Peter van Hooghe (about 1628 until after 1671), who, in his cheerful and sunny pictures, loves to represent the interior of comfortable dwellings and the peaceful condition of their inhabitants. The Dresden Gallery is rich in paintings by this master. The last-named painter is frequently confused with an artist less known, but most excellent, Jan van der Meer of Delft, born in 1632, who in his well-executed and harmonious pictures depicts quiet groups of few figures, as in many able paintings in the galleries of Dresden and Brunswick, and is masterly in the representation of street scenes, as is evidenced by a view of his native city in the Hague Museum. Trained also like him in the school of Rembrandt, Nicolaus Maes, born in Dortdrecht in 1632, has produced works of equal excellence and similar style. The galleries of London, Amsterdam, and St. Petersburg possess works of this rare and excellent master.

While in Italy and Spain, genre painting approaches more nearly to historical painting, and therefore has been before alluded to, we must in the next place mention France, who produced in Jacques Callot (1594–1635) a highly original genre painter. Although little known by pictures, and of no great importance as a painter, he has in his numerous engravings treated the most various subjects with a keenness of observation, a richness of invention, and a freedom of humour, such as no other master has done before or after him. He has depicted the wild military life of that time in a series of sheets, which are known as ' Misères et Malheurs de la Guerre,' and which are justly admired for the cleverness with which they are portrayed. There are also many humorous and fantastic masquerades by him, festive pageants, and mummeries of all kinds, as well as various other productions full of sparkling humour.

The subsequent genre painting of France took a wholly

different course. Antoine Wateau (1684–1721) represents, with extraordinary skill and accuracy, the noble French society of his day, especially in their affected pastoral plays and Arcadian idylls; while Chardin (1699–1779) and Greuze (1726–1805) preserve a peculiar style—the one in his pleasing family scenes, and the other by similar representations, already verging on the sentimental.

In the eighteenth century, England produced a genre painter of the first rank in William Hogarth (1697–1764), who, with cutting satire and bitter irony, depicted the reverse side of human circumstances, and lashed with keen raillery the falsity latent beneath the outward gloss of fashionable life, and its follies and vices. With cleverness and life he depicted such scenes, as, for example, his 'Marriage à la Mode,' and a similar execution distinguishes his numerous etchings. In his style he exhibits great mental affinity with the novels of his contemporary Fielding, and with the later masters of English novel-writing, Dickens and Thackeray.

f. *Landscape, Animal Painting, Flower Painting, and Still Life.*[1]

So long as the plastic art made man the subject of its representations, it acquired a distinct spiritual purport. It was otherwise when the painter sought artistically to conceive inorganic and vegetable nature. If he would here introduce a spiritual element, he could do this so far as he could insert it in his material, or could trace in it the working of the soul of nature. Landscape backgrounds had been extensively employed by the Eycks, and also by the Italian painters of the time in their pictures. But then the surroundings of nature, great as was the love with which they were executed, had no importance in themselves; and although the taste of modern times turned to them with love, yet the sacred figures which formed the central point of the representation, served, as it were, as an excuse for the

[1] *Denkm. d. Kunst.* Pl. 101.

landscape. The more freely and universally, however, that the modern spirit of art pervaded the whole world of creation, all the less could it be deprived of a sphere which, especially among the Germanic nations in the North, lay ready for representation from their innate love of landscape nature. Thus landscape painting soon extricated itself from ecclesiastical tradition, retaining indeed at first a remembrance of its origin in accessories of sacred or mythological figures, but speedily casting aside even these last reminiscences of its period of constraint, and developing into perfect independence.

The essence of landscape painting is, however, not the slavish transcript of a distinct locality. It consists rather in the free artistic combination of different aspects of the life of nature into a unity, in which the feeling of harmony and organisation seizes the spectator with the power of a peculiar state of feeling. To compose in the spirit of nature, to create in her own spirit a free poem which wafts to us a presentiment of the life within, this is the task of the landscape painter. As, however, the landscape of the North, especially of Holland and the Lowlands of Northern Germany, is diametrically distinguished in its character from that of the South, this distinction is faithfully reflected in the two principal schools which represent landscape painting. Southern landscape, with its grand and beautifully curved mountain outlines, has a predominantly plastic character; northern landscape seeks to compensate, by the graceful play of varied foliage, by charm of light, and by the lively motion of masses of clouds, for the want of mighty contour. Hence northern landscape is predominantly picturesque.

IN ITALY

the delight in rich landscape backgrounds was awakened even among the masters of the fifteenth century. The Florentine wall paintings of the Sistine Chapel, the frescoes of Benozzo Gozzoli in the Campo Santo at Pisa, the paintings in the cloisters of S. Severino in Naples, afford an abundance of examples. In the sixteenth century, the preponderating plastic character of the masterworks of Raphael and Michael Angelo repressed the landscape element in the Roman school, although Raphael, in many of his most attractive Holy Families, knew how to introduce it with poetic feeling. It found, however, true acceptance among the Venetians, where for the first time it was employed by Titian and Giorgione in a grand style, to give characterisation to historical representations. These afforded suggestion to Annibale Caracci, whom we have already noticed as the father of independent landscape painting. He established the principles which henceforth mark the character of Italian landscape—the bold free motion of the lines, the mighty masses, the plastic distinctness, which convey to the mind a calm elevated feeling. This style was continued by Caracci's successors, and found its representative in the elegantly idyllic Albani, and still more exclusively in Francesco Grimaldi (1606-1680), the true landscape painter of the school.

Great influence on the development of Italian landscape painting, and even upon Annibale Caracci, was exercised by the important Netherland master, Paul Bril (1554-1626), who worked in Rome with his elder and no less distinguished brother Matthäus. He introduced into Italian landscape painting the northern taste for the more tender element of effects of light and atmosphere, combined with which the simple noble plastic style of the southern forms of nature acquires a fresh poetic charm and a more lively character. There are some excellent works by him in the Pitti Gallery in Florence ; others are to be found in the Louvre and in the Dresden Gallery.

There are also several French masters who raised Italian landscape painting to great importance. The first of these is Nicolas Poussin (1594-1665), who was also active as an historical painter. He may, indeed, be designated as the creator of heroic landscape painting, so called, not merely on account of the accessories, which are chiefly taken from heroic myths, but also from their serious and grandly solemn character. The finer play of light and atmosphere is here but little introduced, the colouring has indeed rather a cold and even coarse character; but the mighty masses of foliage, the free outline of the mountains, the rich antique groups of buildings, give these works the stamp of sublime seriousness.

A still higher stage of importance was reached by Poussin's brother-in-law, Caspar Dughet (1613–1675), who also adopted the name Poussin, and painted on the same principles. Gifted with similar talent for noble conception and grand composition, he added to this the freest treatment of atmospheric play and the boldest delineation of its varied motion, and frequently attained to great effect by the sappy freshness of his foliage, his fine gradated perspective, and his careful development of the middle distance. The Doria Gallery in Rome is rich in works by this master; but those executed in oil have suffered much from the darkening of the foliage. The numerous landscapes with incidents from the sacred legends, which adorn the church of S. Martino ai Monti in Rome, are also by him.

Far more profoundly than these and all other masters, did Claude Gelée, surnamed Claude Lorraine (1600–1682), penetrate into the secrets of nature, and by the enchanting play of sunlight, the freshness of his dewy foregrounds, and the charm of his atmospheric distances, he obtained a tone of feeling which influences the mind like an eternal Sabbath rest. In his works there is all the splendour, light, untroubled brightness, and harmony of the first morning of creation in Paradise. His masses of foliage have a glorious richness and freshness, and even in the deepest shadows are interwoven with a golden glimmer of light. But they serve only as a mighty framework, for, more freely than with other masters, the eye wanders through a rich foreground into the far distance, the utmost limits of which fade away in golden mist. The earlier of his numerous works have a warmer tone, while the later appear somewhat colder, although no less fine and clear. There are pictures by him in all the large galleries, especially in the Doria and Sciarra Galleries in Rome, in the Louvre, in the Hermitage at St. Petersburg, and in the London and Dresden Galleries. Yet all that bears his name is by no means genuine; for even during the life of the master his style was imitated, and many spurious works were sold under his name. This fact caused him to prepare sketches of all his paintings, and to gather them together in a book which he called 'Liber Veritatis' (the book of truth). It is now in the possession of the Duke of Devonshire, and a fac-simile has been published.[1]

Among Claude's imitators, his pupil Hermann Swanefeld, a Netherlander, entered most faithfully into his master's manner,

Fig. 402. Landscape. By Claude Lorraine.

as is proved especially in some excellent etched landscapes. Another Netherlander, Johann Both, is distinguished for his grandly conceived and well-executed landscapes in the character of the South. Similar in style, though less important and constantly falling into outward decorative effect, are the numerous works of Adam Pynacker and many other Netherland painters who followed the model of the great master. We must, how-

[1] E. Earlom, *Liber Veritatis*, or a collection of 200 prints, after the original designs of Claude Lorraine, &c. London, 1774.

ever, not conceal the fact that this ideal style of landscape most readily degenerated into mere decoration, since it generalised the forms of nature, and in the effort after beautiful composition frequently lost sight of the characteristic importance of the separate parts. Among those who adapted the same style to the representation of northern nature, Hermann Zachtleven deserves to be mentioned.

Salvator Rosa (1615–1673) was of great and independent importance both as a genre painter and a portrait painter. In many pictures he appears, it is true, dependent on Claude; but in others he exhibits a bold and passionate conception of mighty scenes of nature, of dreadful wildernesses and deserts, into which he delighted in introducing bandits and other gloomy figures. He depicts with vigorous power the unfettered rage of the elements, the fury of the breakers of a stormy sea, and the gloom of steep rocky clefts. Able pictures of this kind are to be found in the Louvre, in the Colonna Gallery in Rome, and in the Berlin Museum.

In the eighteenth century, the French master, Joseph Vernet (1714–1789), adhered to this ideal style of landscape, and showed masterly power, especially in the representation of wild sea storms. At the same time, England possesses in Thomas Gainsborough a painter who knew how to combine the fresh and varied aspect of the landscape nature of his country with the stricter principle of idealistic conception.

IN THE NETHERLANDS

Joachim Patenier and Herri de Bles had, as early as the sixteenth century, laid the foundation of an independent cultivation of landscape painting. In them and in succeeding masters, the gay variety of nature predominates, so that a fantastic rather than a poetic effect is produced. This was the case especially with Johann Breughel (1569–1625), the son of the elder Peter, known under the surname of the 'Sammt- or Blumenbreughel' (Velvet or Flower-breughel). In representations of Paradise, he sought for the most part to introduce all forms of flowers, trees, and plants, in combination with all sorts of animals. Fantastic diversity prevailed, and art was yet unable by limitation and choice of material to produce a specially poetic effect. A similar style is evidenced also in Roland Savery (1576–1639), only that with him occasionally a more serious and measured tone finds expression. A kindred effort is perceived also in the pictures of his contemporary David Vinckebooms. On the other hand, Jodocus de Momper exhibits the preponderance of fantastic caprice.

It was Rubens first who carried landscape painting also by his thorough artistic power to that pitch of importance, in which, like some free afterbirth of nature, a feeling of foreboding is awakened in the spectator, and then dies away. The same mighty power which prevails in his historical pictures raises also his landscape representations to transporting effect. Two of the finest are in the Pitti Gallery in Florence, both of them specimens, moreover, of the versatility of his conception—for in the one he introduces a bold southern rocky shore with temples and palaces, and with Odysseus and Nausicaa as accessories, quite in the heroic style ; and in the other he depicts a homely Netherland landscape with peasant accessories, but rendered no less poetic by splendid distribution of light and lifelike freshness. Similar in style is the hay-harvest, in the Pinakothek at Munich ; and lifelike and effective is the view of the Escurial in the Dresden Gallery. Other landscapes by this master are in the Louvre, and in the collection at Windsor.

The Dutch school adopted a peculiar course of development. As far removed from idealistic conception as from general poetic intention, its masters strove solely to give a simple and faithful representation of the nature of their country, while at the same time they set out with the most careful observation of the detail. Just as their genre painters clearly and exactly portrayed human life in all its reality, so their landscape painters sought with fidelity and zeal to express the life of nature. They entered into the finest detail, depicted the growth of plants and trees, the formation of the soil, the play of the atmosphere and light, with the utmost truth, without at the same time leaning capriciously to any one side. But while they apparently strive after detail, they penetrate so deeply into the laws of nature, and mirror them in such an harmonious manner, that their representations thus acquire the charm of genuine poetic feeling.

Among the earlier masters, the first place is due to the simple and feeling Johann van Goyen (1596–1656). His excellent pupil, also, Adrian van der Kabel, and the lifelike Jan Wynants, are known by many attractive works. Landscape painting next made great advance in Rembrandt, and gained an increase of poetic value in a strong subjective feeling, which is expressed in the play of the atmosphere and in the prevalence of a bold chiaro oscuro. This element appears in masterly perfection in Artus van der Neer (1619–1683), who executed his landscape compositions in the dim twilight of the wood, in the silver beams of the moon, or in the more effective glow of a nocturnal conflagration. Pleasing homelike representations of cheerful forest life are afforded by Anton Waterloo (1618–1660), whose clever etchings express a charming tone of feeling.

Netherland landscape painting reaches its highest poetical expression in the works of the great master, Jacob Ruysdael (1625–1681). He adhered to the simple scenery which the nature of his home afforded—indeed, he represented this with rare fidelity and exactness even to its very details; but by the movement of the clouds, by light and shade, and by a masterly chiaro oscuro, he gave the utmost expression to his landscapes. He delighted in depicting forest solitudes or remote deserted premises, and to such scenes he was able to impart all the melancholy charm of utter seclusion. Sometimes there is a touch of almost passionate feeling in his pictures. We can see the storm wind shaking the lofty oaks, and the wild stream rushing foaming over the rocks. Grey ruins look down dreamily from woody heights upon this restless life of nature, or a churchyard with half-sunken moss-grown tombstones renders still more striking the contrast with the luxuriously green forest. The Dresden Gallery possesses a great treasure in the most valuable pictures of this kind ; among others ' the Chase,' ' the Monastery,' and ' the Jews' Cemetery' (Fig. 403), and many others.   Ruysdael has repeatedly exhibited the same masterly power in sea pieces, among which we must mention a large and well-executed representation of a lively naval scene in the Berlin Museum.

Less important and somewhat more superficial and powerless, though still attractive from their plain and distinct conception,

Fig. 403. Landscape. By Jacob Ruysdael.

are the canal pictures of Salomon Ruysdael, an elder brother of Jacob. Minderhout Hobbema has, on the other hand, justly obtained greater fame, although he also does not equal Jacob Ruysdael in power and depth of poetic feeling.   By an unsurpassable delicacy of characterisation, especially in the foliage, and by his cheerful sunny foregrounds, he gives his paintings the charm of peaceful idylls.   There are excellent works by him in the

English galleries, in the Belvedere in Vienna, and in the Berlin Museum.

A special place is occupied in this series of Netherland masters by Aldert van Everdingen, who lived between 1621–1675, and who took the material for his pictures chiefly from the mountainous regions of Norway. His compositions have, therefore, a wilder and grander character, bolder lines, and a more heroic style. Steep clefts, over which mountain streams rush foaming, gloomy pine forests, over the tops of which the clouds sweep along, these are his favourite subjects. There are many works by him in the Pinakothek at Munich, and in the galleries of Dresden, Vienna, and Berlin. He was undoubtedly Ruysdael's forerunner and unmistakable model.

After landscape painting, sea pieces were cultivated with zeal in Holland, as was natural to a people who owed their existence, power, and prosperity to the sea. Among the important painters of naval pieces are Jan van de Capelle, whose fine and clear pictures, principally devoted to the representation of the calm sea, are almost entirely to be found in England; Bonaventura Peters (1614–1653), who displays a preference for the agitated sea, and depicts it with poetic power, but for the most part in a mannered style (there are some pictures by him in the Belvedere in Vienna); and his brother, Jan Peters (1625–1677), who produced similar works; also the excellent and versatile Simon de Vlieger, many beautiful pictures by whom are in the galleries of Amsterdam, Dresden, and Munich; the no less important Ludolf Backhuysen (1631–1709); and, lastly, the most distinguished of all, Willem van de Velde, the younger (1633–1707), who represented first in Holland the naval victories of his countrymen over the English, and afterwards in England, the victories of the English over the Dutch, and who not merely depicted the sea in the play of lightly agitated waves, but especially amid the excitement of the elements, in the fury of the tempest, and the breaking of the billows.

We must also here mention the architectural painters, among them especially Peter Neefs, the elder, and H. van Steenwyk,

E E 2

the younger, both of some repute on account of their finely executed perspective.   J. van der Heyden produced able works in
town views.   But we must especially mention here two Italians,
the Venetian Antonio Canale and his pupil Bernardo Belotto,
surnamed Canaletto (–1780), both, especially the former, distinguished for his faithful representation of the streets, squares, and
canals of Venice, with their palaces and the lively bustle of city
life.

In many masters the effort to increase the charm of landscape painting by the addition of accessories of various kinds,
led to a fresh extension of the sphere of representation, and
indeed to a complete blending of genre and landscape.   This is
the case in the distinguished and numerous works of Philip
Wouwerman (1620–1668), who, with keen observation, rich
variety, and solid and delicate execution, depicted the upper
classes of his time in the merry tumult of the chase or engaged
in military adventures.   The Dresden Gallery contains about
sixty of these pictures.   They are also not unfrequently met
with elsewhere.   On the other hand, the Netherlander Johann
Miel and the German Joh. Lingelbach introduced scenes of
Italian life into their landscape pictures.

Other masters indulged in compositions of an idyllic character, in which the Italian style of landscape generally forms
the basis, and to this is added corresponding accessories of shepherds with their different flocks.   This is the case, for instance,
with Karl Dujardin and Nicolaus Berchem, also with Joh.
Heinr. Roos, and his son, Philip Roos, known under the name
of Rosa di Tivoli.   In contrast to these, Paul Potter (1625–
1654) gives simple representations of northern pastoral life,
in the midst of an unpretending home landscape ; but he displays
in them a truth and variety of life, which raises his works into
unsurpassable masterpieces of their kind.   One of his most famous
pictures is in the gallery of the Hermitage at St. Petersburg.   The
Berlin Museum possesses a valuable store of clever sketches and
studies by this distinguished master.   On the other hand, the
versatile Albert Cuyp (1606 until after 1672) lays the principle

stress on the landscape element in his pictures, which are distinguished by true observation of nature and by fine effect of light and atmosphere, making it harmonise with the most varied animal life.

Animal painting next aimed directly at the delineation of animal life in its details. Rubens had already given many admirable representations from the animal world of vast hunting scenes and combats. He was followed, between 1579 and 1657, by the gifted Franz Snyders, and somewhat later by the no less important Johann Fyt (1625–1700). We must also here mention Karl Rutharts, and the excellent painter of birds, Johann Weenix. The life of the poultry yard was chosen by Melchior Hondekoeter as a favourite subject for his paintings. The German, Peter Caulitz, was skilled in the same branch; while Joh. Elias Ridinger (1695–1767) has produced many excellent hunting pieces, more as engravings than paintings.

In flower painting, also, the Dutch arrived at independent perfection, which maintained its attractive freshness until the close of this period. The careful representation, the tasteful arrangement, the bloom of the colouring, and the perfect harmony of the whole effect, give these works an imperishable charm. Johann Breughel, the 'Blumen- or Sammt-Breughel,' had been the first to begin this style of art. He was followed by his pupils Daniel Seghers and the excellent and poetic Joh. David de Heem (1600–1674), and subsequently by the talented Rachel Ruysch (1604–1705), and the brilliant Johann van Huysum, whose works extend till 1749.

Lastly, we have still to consider the so-called 'still-life pictures,' which with judicious choice and tasteful arrangement display the elements of a *déjeuner* grouped on an elegant table —the golden wine sparkles in the wine cup, the juicy fruits appear enticingly side by side with the daintiest productions of the sea; and even over these lifeless things art spreads a gleam of poetry by clever treatment, and by the charm of colour and chiaro oscuro. The most excellent masters in this branch of art are Wilhelm van Aelst, Adriaenssen, Peter Nason, and many others.

Thus art passed in the Netherlands through the whole sphere of existence, and, having left ecclesiastical courts, became a free citizen of the world, and a true adherent to nature ; and, while she deemed nothing too insignificant and unimportant, and regarded all existing things with loving mind, it was granted to her to discover everywhere the true spark of life, and even to clothe the most transient things with the eternal robe of beauty.

IF, as a conclusion to our history of art, we endeavour to give a few remarks upon the art of the present day, we must bear in mind beforehand that the moment has not yet arrived for a definitive historical survey. It is true, the artistic development of our own day has passed through more than half a century with enduring power and varied effort, and has produced a world of creations of every kind as evidences of its activity; but this movement has not yet reached its aim, it is yet striving onwards with unwearied effort, and hence forbids a final verdict. Yet by the light of history, and by the standard she has afforded us, we can examine the course already passed over by the art of the present day, and can assure ourselves of the results obtained.[1]

A just estimate of the art of the present day is, however, rendered difficult from the fact that we stand in a transition period full of sharp contrasts, which can only produce a truly vigorous future by strife and contest; and, moreover, that we participate too personally with our feelings in the course of development, and thus lose the repose and freedom of reflection. The great revolutions which convulsed Europe towards the close of the last century, and remodelled her condition, were accompanied by similar events in the sphere of art. But in its new career, art is still exposed to various fluctuations, which likewise impede a calm survey. How many and what manifold

---

[1] See *Denkm. d. Kunst.* Vol. II. Pl. 102–136. Cf. also the lucid and comprehensive remarks of Anton Springer, *Die bildenden Künste in der Gegenwart.* Leipzig, 1857. Also the description of German art in vols. iv. and v. of E. Förster's *Deutsche Kunstgeschichte.* Leipzig. 1860.

influences does the art of our own day experience from the
position which our age occupies historically and critically with
regard to the past! Our historical feeling, but recently fully
awakened, makes us strive after a universal examination of past
forms of culture, and arouses our regard for them. While, however, that rich life of past ages is open to us, it finds its way into
the ideas and even into the feeling of the present. But while
many important and indispensable stimulants are thus obtained,
many errors necessarily also result from it, and thus it is too
difficult to decide the limits of legitimate influence. In general,
however, under the influence of this historical bias, the reflecting
judgment is less continuously called forth than ever before, and
the calm sway of the creative fancy is constantly affected. Added
to this, the independence of the individual increases, he feels
himself perfectly free with regard to tradition, and judges for
himself how far the wings of his own power may carry him.

But in positive merit, also, our age affords many important
new elements to artistic creation. Deepened historical feeling
has given us an historical painting in the true sense of the word,
which conceives its mission more distinctly than it ever before
had done, and which strives to mirror the sway of spiritual
powers in the display of temporal appearances. At the same
time, the eye is rendered more acute to the state of things
around us, and the sphere of representation is enlarged and
enriched on all sides equally, as the active contemplation of
nature raises the landscape painter to a new point of view, from
whence he gains a deeper conception of the essence of nature,
and by the most faithful characterisation of the separate forms,
and by the most exact delineation of all that marks the special
physiognomy of the landscape, arrives at new results. With all
these eagerly pursued tendencies, we cannot, however, fail to perceive that they rest on a narrow basis and on a dangerous soil,
and that their spiritual value is diminished by preponderating
realistic effort, and that the harmony of the whole is coun-
teracted by the emphasising of the separate parts.

On the other hand, the art of the present day has partially

regained that one great excellence of an inward healthiness of practice, in that it is not merely, as was the case for the most part in the last century, an article of luxury for the noble, and an exclusive enjoyment for the more highly cultivated, but a living language for the whole people, an expression of their opinions, ideas, and interests. Closely connected with this is the fact that a serious monumental art has again arisen, the basis of which is newly revived architecture. The separate arts had also, it is true, separate from each other, that independent existence, which modern development has awarded to them as their just due ever since the sixteenth century. But they no longer persist exclusively in this isolation; they have again united for great and public objects, so that sculpture and painting have devoted themselves to the noble service of architecture, and have created, in common with architecture, works of true monumental importance and imperishable worth. Thus the arts have been again engaged in that noblest task, that of giving expression to the public life of the people, in that they have imparted a higher stamp to their common necessities, have veiled their religious views in the garment of beauty, have immortalised their historical remembrances, and have revealed the national mind itself in an ideal and reflected image.

The interest which different nations take in the development of the art of the present day is of characteristic importance. Foremost stands Germany, from whence the reorganisation of art, rich as it is in future promise, emanated. Even in the last century the basis for this was laid, for while everywhere some artists sought to free themselves from the prevailing mannerism by conscientious devotion to nature, the path of true freedom was only opened by the influence of Winckelmann, who led the world to the true understanding of the master-works of classic antiquity, and again discovered the long-buried spring from which art was again to pour forth health and youthful vigour. Next to the Germans, the French grasped the antique with similar enthusiasm, in order again to bring back art to seriousness and depth, to moderation and to beauty. Painters and

sculptors emulated each other, and gave an exclusively antique
stamp to the first epoch of this newly revived art. But to
reach a truly vital and independent stage of development, art
required a new impulse, a national basis. This important qualification for existence was only granted her when the nations,
oppressed by the Napoleonic rule, began to be conscious
of their own power, and to shake off the yoke of foreign
dominion. Since the liberation war, there has been again in
Germany, as in France, a national art, which conceives and
fashions its special tasks in its own distinct style. Belgium and
Holland have also possessed since that period a revived culture
of national art; and England has displayed, more than in former
centuries, the stirrings of an independent artistic power, which
has arrived at able results in many branches of art. The South,
on the other hand, is strikingly behind other lands in artistic
production. Neither in the Pyrenean peninsula nor in the
Italian have any important works been recently produced, and
it is only from the incomparable treasures of past epochs that
Italy still ever exercises—though no longer so absolutely as
before—considerable influence over the artistic culture of the
present day.

ARCHITECTURE.

The researches in Greece and the conscientious exhibition
of her monuments, which took place in the latter part of the last
century by Stuart and Revett, was an event for the history of
architecture. Hitherto, the antique style had been only known
in its coarser metamorphosis, as it had been handled by the
Romans. Now for the first time antique architecture revealed
in truth its incomparable and simple beauty; now for the first
time they began to understand its law, and to feel the rare
harmony of its lines. But it needed a master of rare endowments to transfer into actual life the splendid newly gained
ideas. Karl Friedrich Schinkel (1781–1841), an artist such as
architecture had not seen for centuries, was the genius who
accomplished this mission. His noble mind conceived the

forms of Greek architecture, not as isolated parts, but as living members of an organised whole, the laws of which he was able to fathom, and in the spirit of which he composed new and grand creations. His principal works, the theatre, the museum, and the new guardhouse at Berlin, are affected by the requirements of modern life, but are conceived and executed in the true spirit of Hellenic art. But with these results, great as they were, the aspiring mind of the master was not contented. He penetrated the whole range of architectural development; and while he impressed everything with the classic standard of ancient art in its simple proportions and beauty, the available excellences of the various epochs lay open to him for application. This is most brilliantly exhibited in his designs for the Orianda. But while this grand work was denied execution, in many other creations, especially in the architectural school at Berlin, he laid the foundation for a prosperous development of architecture, by returning to the healthy laws of his native brick building, and combining with it the nobleness of antique forms and the results of later systems of construction. Schinkel's architectural laws were carried on with vigour, after the death of the great master, by his most important pupils, Persius, Soller, Stüler, Strack, to whom we may add Hitzig and Knoblauch in private buildings; and excellent works have been produced by this school, especially as regards fineness of detail and ornament.

Less consistent, less spirited, but highly successful in other ways, was the architectural activity displayed at the same time in Munich under King Ludwig's rare love of art. Scarcely ever had any ruler promoted art so judiciously, so thoroughly, and so comprehensively as this monarch. While the greater number of other princes and Mecænas employed art only as the sport of their whims, for the satisfying of their private desires, the lasting fame is due to King Ludwig of having justly conceived the monumental and national importance of art. While he combined all arts in the production of grand tasks, he knit together for lively action that bond of hearty fellowship which had so long been severed. Architecture stood once more as the central

point, and the other arts vied with each other in youthful
emulation for service and assistance. Almost forsaken branches
of art, such as fresco and glass painting, were revived or newly
discovered. Others, hitherto scantily pursued, such as sculpture
in bronze, rose into active cultivation, and were followed by a
revival of the works of artistic handicraft. Among the Munich
architects, Leo von Klenze predominantly represented the
antique and the style derived from it. Although far removed
from Schinkel's grandeur, purity, and genius (who, however,
was not without some influence over him), and although his
compositions exhibit more of a conventional style, still in the
Glyptothek, the Pinakothek, the Ruhmeshalle at Munich, the
Walhalla at Ratisbon, and the Befreiungshalle at Kelheim,
he produced works of imposing design and true monumental
bearing.

In contrast to him, we must mention Friedrich von Gärtner
as the representative of the Romanticist style.   This style, which
has also played so important a part in the modern literature of
Germany, was first awakened by the liberation war in Germany,
and was greatly furthered by the increase of national feeling.
As, in literary matters, they dived deep into the national poems
of the German middle ages, so, in art, they turned with eagerness
to the study of the great monuments of those epochs.   Gärtner
cultivated the Romanesque style, which he exhibited grandly,
though without fineness of feeling in detail, in a series of works,
such as the Ludwigskirche, the Library, the University, the
Feldhernhalle, and others.   The Basilica, built by Ziebland, also
bears the Romanesque character; while Ohlmüller's Church, in
the Au suburb,[1] successfully followed an elegant Gothic style.
Still, in Munich the Romanesque style essentially prevailed, as
is evidenced in the railway station built by Bürklein,[2] and many
other buildings.   On the other hand, at a more recent period,
during the reign of King Max II., a mixed style has predominated in the buildings in the Maximilian Street (National

---

[1] *Denkm. d. Kunst.* Pl. 57. Fig. 6. Pl. 62. Fig. 2.   [2] Ibid. Fig. 5.

Museum, Government Buildings, Atheneum), combining, with less success, heterogeneous forms without blending them into a complete whole. The Romanesque style was transferred from Munich to other places, especially to Hanover, where it has, however, been recently supplanted, under Haase, by a strictly Gothic tendency—for instance, in the Erlöserkirche, the Marienburg, and others.

The same Romanticist tendency has been recently adopted with considerable results in Vienna, where the imposing buildings of the arsenal and the Altlerchenfelderkirche exhibit the Romanesque style, and the Votivkirche the Gothic. On the other hand, the classic-minded Hansen represents a purified Byzantine style combined with a noble Renaissance, modified by the study of Greek art (designs for the Herrenhause, Todesko Palace, Evangelical Gymnasium, and others); while most of the leading architects there delight in a motley eclecticism, and Fr. Schmidt alone adheres exclusively to a strictly Gothic tendency. In Carlsruhe, Eisenlohr has given himself up to preponderating Romanesque influences, though combined with great delicacy and genius, as is evidenced in the buildings of the Baden Railway, which have been designed by him. Hübsch, on the other hand, whose works are likewise in Carlsruhe, exhibits an independent style, in which the Romanticist tendency is somewhat modified—for instance, in his numerous buildings there, the school of art, the theatre, the orangery, the Trink-halle at Baden, and the church at Bulach.

In Dresden, the Renaissance has for a long period almost exclusively prevailed; in recent times it has been employed by the highly-gifted Semper in many works of importance, and has been carried to a higher stage by the influence of Greek art. The Theatre and Museum at Dresden are able evidences of this effort; the central building of the Polytechnic at Zurich is still more free and grand; and this is also the case in the designs for an opera house for Rio de Janeiro and for Munich. In Stuttgart, also, Renaissance architecture has been successfully adopted in many buildings by Leins, especially in the villa of the Crown

Prince, the present king. There are other no less able works there by Egle.

In France, classic and Romanticist tendencies stand in more violent contrast than elsewhere. The classic style, with its able representatives Percier and Fontaine, is more extensive and enduring in its influence. In the first Napoleonic era, it was the splendid forms of Roman architecture which gave suitable expression to the modern Cæsarian empire. Chalgrin's Arc de l'Étoile, and Vignon's Madeleine in Paris, are among the most splendid monuments of that day. A strong reaction has, on the other hand, been brought about by the Romanticists, among whom are the brilliant names of Lassus and Viollet-le-duc. They inscribe on their banners the Gothic style of the thirteenth century, and seek to adapt the forms of the time of Louis the Saint to the life of the present day. A rich work of this style is the church Ste. Clotilde, built after the design of the German architect Gau. Nevertheless, these Romanticist efforts of modern Gothic art are met with no less energy and artistic power by those adherents of the classic style, who strive after the noble simplicity of Greek forms, and thus in ecclesiastical works occasionally combine a remembrance of the early Christian designs. This has been done by Hittorf in his splendid church of S. Vincent de Paul. In secular buildings, the magnificent and decorative French Renaissance of the sixteenth century is employed, which is equal to the Gothic in picturesque charm, and is superior to it in plastic richness of detail. The grand building of the Hôtel de Ville, and recently the splendid completion of the Louvre, are the principal works of this style. More nobleness and moderation are exhibited by Duban in his École des beaux Arts, one of the most attractive and best works of modern Parisian architecture. We must here also mention Labrouste with his strictly classic library of S. Geneviève, and Normand with his villa of Prince Napoleon in the Champs Élysées, which is rich and tasteful in the Pompeian style.

England, grand as are her architectural undertakings on all sides, has no great importance in the artistic cultivation of architecture. While at the commencement of the century a stricter, and at the same time a sober, classic style was adopted there also, an example of which we may adduce in Robert Smirke's Covent Garden Theatre, architectural works subsequently returned to the ancient models. In secular buildings, such as palaces, they contented themselves with the designs of Palladio and Vignola, thus ignoring half a century of modern development. In ecclesiastical buildings, such as schools and churches, and in fortress-like designs, the late Gothic style of the country was chiefly employed, in the adoption of which Pugin was essentially influential, and which occasionally, as in the Houses of Parliament by Barry, rivalled in luxuriant splendour the richest monuments of the sixteenth century. Next to him, Scott and Street, and recently Waterhouse, have been distinguished by an able understanding of form. The most original and valuable of the later productions of English architecture are the numerous large and small country residences, in which a free picturesque element is successfully introduced.

In all other lands, these modern movements have not been able to supplant the Renaissance system, with its traditions of five centuries. So far, therefore, as we can survey the architectural works of the present time, they remain strictly within the limits of forms historically received. Freer or more fettered, bolder or tamer, skilful or unskilful, conceived with life and independent feeling or in thoughtless imitation, they ever seek to satisfy us with traditionary forms. An historical feeling is predominantly stamped on the architecture of our age. Yet this is the only way by which architecture can reach that point at which the present age can unerringly give perfect expression to its own innermost nature and to its own needs.

SCULPTURE.

From the affected sweetness into which the plastic art of the eighteenth century had fallen, Antonio Canova was the first who led the way to purer classic feeling (1757–1822). In the representation of female beauty especially he attained to a pleasing grace, which is, however, diminished by a touch of the former mannerism, and by an elegant smoothness. He succeeded less in the sublime dignity of monumental compositions; and in heroic subjects, such as the Two Gladiators and Perseus, in the Vatican Collection, he falls completely into a theatrical style. His influence on his contemporaries was most extensive, and few plastic artists of his epoch were unaffected by it. The purest of these is Johann Heinrich Dannecker of Stuttgart (1758–1841), who displayed a purer grace, especially in female figures, such as the famous Ariadne, in the possession of Herr Bethmann, at Frankfort, and who was also distinguished in his portraits by a delicate feeling for nature and noble characterisation. This is evidenced in the colossal bust of Schiller, in the Stuttgart Museum. Among the French, Chaudet (1763–1810) especially represents the stricter antique style, though with a certain conventional mannerism. At the same time, the Englishman, John Flaxman (1755–1826), applied himself to the simple conception of the antique, as is evidenced in numerous ideal works, monuments, and sketches from Homer and Dante. The famous Swedish sculptor Sergell, also (1736–1813), who likewise received his artistic culture in Rome, is among the earliest revivors of the classical ideal style, the laws of which have been followed out still further by his countrymen Byström (born 1783) and Fogelberg.

More profoundly than all these masters did the Dane, Bertel Thorwaldsen (1770–1844), enter into the spirit and beauty of classic art, and with inexhaustibly rich fancy and with the noblest sense of form produced a number of works, conceived with as much purity and chasteness of Greek feeling as the architectural works of Schinkel. In his famous frieze of the March of Alexander, in the Villa Sommariva, on the Lake Como, the true Greek relief style is revived in all its strength and purity; in numerous statues, groups, and smaller reliefs, he produces with skilful variety and naïveté the materials of the ancient mythology; and even Christian subjects receive new dignity and beauty in the plastic works for the Frauenkirche in Copenhagen.

While thus, with manifold activity, the vast kingdom of idealistic sculpture was enriched, Johann Gottfried Schadow, of Berlin (1764–1850), applied himself with energy to a more realistic style, striving predominantly after lifelike conception and exact characterisation of individual figures. His monument of the Count von der Mark, in the church of St. Dorothy, at Berlin; the statues of Ziethen and of Prince Leopold of Dessau, in the Wilhelmsplatz, in the same city; the statue of Frederic the Great, at Stettin (perhaps less so the monument of Blücher at Rostock and of Luther at Wittenberg), and many others, are a lively protest against the mannerism of the style hitherto prevalent, and opened anew to plastic art a sphere which had been wholly closed to her for two centuries.

By these works a path has been opened to modern sculpture by which she has recently arrived at grand results, and which secures to her a varied and glorious sphere of action, so long as she adheres to the principles obtained, and advances with a due estimation of her object. Although the world of ideal forms can never again attain to that importance for us which it had among the Greeks, yet natural life increasingly offers subjects full of beauty and naïveté, which afford the plastic art rich incitement to ideal creations; and in the chaste grace, in the pure nobleness of the antique conception, there lies an imperishable charm, which addresses itself to all human feeling, and pledges to all works emanating from a similar spirit the lively sympathy of those who love to refresh themselves in the simple beauty of nature. Hence the ideal style of Hellenic art, such as the present age has acknowledged in its purity and has appropriated anew, will ever remain an inalienable and precious possession to modern plastic art.

But still more originally, still more nationally, does the other fountain gush forth from which modern sculpture draws its subjects. The old tendency of the Germanic mind to the exact characterisation of each separate existence, which almost exclusively marked the plastic art of the fifteenth century, has asserted itself with fresh might, and has received powerful allies in the awakened historical mind and in increased national feeling.

The newly revived historical consciousness of nations demands at the present day the glorification, in all the truth of reality, of its heroes, of the defenders of its freedom, of the representatives of its ideas, and of combatants in battles of the sword as well as of opinion. Plastic art, therefore, must enter into the entire characteristic appearance of the individual, must discover the working of the individual mind as it is expressed in the natural figure, in the physiognomy and even in the externals of bearing and attire, and must even give expression to the mysterious life of the soul, so far as is within the limits of plastic art. While the study of the works of the fifteenth century exercise important influence upon this style, the influence of antique conceptions, on the other hand, must not here also be too lightly estimated, as, without the feeling of beauty obtained by this, a degenerated and exaggerated adherence to nature would ensue.

The first rank among the German schools of sculpture in the present day belongs to that of Berlin. While Friedrich Tieck here, in a series of valuable works, adhered to the antique conception, the style which Schadow had introduced reached a noble and just expression under the steady and influential labours of Christian Rauch (1777–1857). This master occupies an important position, not so much from his wealth of creative ideas as by his fine feeling of nature, and his pure taste for a truly plastic style, and an unsurpassable care in execution. His importance, however, does not merely rest in his numerous works, but also in the influence which he has exercised upon a large circle of gifted scholars. While in ideal works, as in the Victory, and many excellent representations in relief, he displays a truly classic beauty, his statues of Prince Blücher, of Generals Bülow and Scharnhorst, his colossal equestrian statue of Frederic the Great, at Berlin, and many others, exhibit an extreme delicacy of characterisation and a lifelike exactness of conception. Many able pupils have risen in his atelier to independent importance and free masterly power, and by able works, comprising a number of grand public tasks, form the choice of the present Berlin school. Among the ablest of these masters are, Friedrich Drake, whose reliefs on the statue of Friedrich Wilhelm III., in the Zoological Gardens at Berlin, are full of naïve grace; Schievelbein, who displays a richness of fancy, especially in his relief compositions; Bläser, who executed the most effective of the marble groups on the Castle Bridge; A. Fischer; and in animal sculpture A. Kiss, Th. Kalide, and W. Wolff. Among the younger sculptors, we may also especially mention Reinhold Begas, who executed the Schiller monument for Berlin and several ideal groups.

Ernst Rietschel (1804-1861) undoubtedly occupies one of the first places among the sculptors of this century in variety of endowments, delicacy of form, and depth of feeling. In Rauch's school he acquired the tendency to true and characteristic representation of life and faithful care of execution, and his double monument of Schiller and Göthe at Weimar, and, still more pure and successful, that of Lessing in Brunswick, and that of Luther, designed for Worms, are striking specimens of this style. In the group of Mary with the Body of Christ, executed for the Friedenskirche at Potsdam, he has produced a work full of thrilling expression and deep religious feeling; while the numerous reliefs for the pediment of the Opera House at Berlin, and the Theatre and Museum at Dresden, exhibit him in a no less valuable and important aspect in the field of ideal subjects. At Dresden, we must also mention Ernst Hähnel, whose compositions (Theatre and Museum at Dresden) for the most part belong to the antique style, but who has produced works of delicate characterisation in monumental statues—as, for instance, in that of Beethoven at Bonn, the Emperor Charles IV. at Prague, and in the statues executed for the Dresden Museum, among them the splendid Raphael.

In Munich, the richly gifted Ludwig Schwanthaler (1802-1848) was the principal representative of a more romantic style, which opened to modern plastic art a new field of fresh ideas. Gifted with almost inexhaustible imagination, this master in his

short life executed a number of extensive works, furnishing most
of the buildings erected under King Ludwig with their plastic
ornament. While these works are distinguished for prolific
invention and happy decorative feeling, the artist, impelled as
he was to unceasing production and impeded by physical weakness, could not give his independent monumental creations that
perfect finish of form which is essentially necessary to plastic
works. Yet in these works, also, we cannot fail to perceive a
grand monumental conception, as is especially evidenced in the
colossal statue of Bavaria at Munich. A numerous school has
emanated from the atelier of this master. The more gifted
artists, such as Schaller, Widmann, Brugger, and Zumbusch,
well known by his model for the monument to King Max II,
have successfully introduced a more careful finish into Munich
plastic art. Schwanthaler's influence was recently transported
to Vienna, where Fernkorn, one of his pupils, executed many
monumental works, especially an equestrian statue of the Archduke Charles.

In France, plastic art speedily sought to free itself from the
strict sway of the antique, and predominantly strove after lifelike effect and expression, and even after a one-sided adherence
to nature. While individual artists, such as Bosio, Rude, and
Duret, adhered to a nobler and moderate style, P. J. David
of Angers (1793–1856) despised all stricter plastic laws, and
abandoned himself to a vigorous adherence to nature, which,
although combined with great talent and skill in conception, falls
into styleless exaggeration in monumental works. His numerous portrait busts are extremely clever and lifelike. Among
the artists who render predominant homage to the representation of sensual beauty, the Genevese James Pradier (1792–1852)
occupies the first place. Among animal sculptors, the gifted
Barye holds the first rank. Belgian sculpture follows for the
most part a similar style with that of France.

An important central point to modern plastic art is occupied
by Rome with her numerous ateliers, her ancient marble works,
and her mighty treasures of antique works of art. Canova and

Thorwaldsen had here their ateliers, which for many decades were the famous nurseries of modern plastic art. That the antique conception, the ideal style, here exclusively prevailed, lies in the nature of the matter. Only where the life of a modern state and people is in free action are tasks afforded to plastic art, based on the characteristic representation of important individuals and on the lifelike delineation of historical events. Roman plastic art follows predominantly ideal and poetic impulses, and only in funeral monuments and other memorials of private memory does the tendency to individual characterisation likewise appear. Hence, in spite of all differences of the nations which are represented there, a certain common similarity belongs to the Roman schools. Among the Italians, who constantly lapse into effeminacy of conception, and a refined or theatrical manner, Pietro· Tenerani, a pupil of Canova and Thorwaldsen, free from such errors, stands in the first rank as the representative of a noble and classic style. Similar and no less attractive in manner were the works of the Englishman John Gibson. Among the numerous plastic artists whom England has also recently produced, the tendency to the genre style and to the graceful manner of Canova is most popular. We may mention the thoughtful Macdowell, Sir Richard Westmacott, well known by many public monuments, and R. J. Wyatt, who has executed some pleasing works after subjects from the antique myths. We may also here add North America, which in Randolph Rogers, Miss Hosmer, and the gifted but somewhat too picturesque Palmer, possesses able sculptors. Among the German sculptors in Rome, Martin Wagner, who died in 1860, is distinguished by his powerful style; and among those still living, Carl Steinhäuser is remarkable for his noble sense of form and depth of feeling. Lastly, Holland possesses in Matthias Kessels, formed in Thorwaldsen's school (1784–1830), an able plastic artist of a similar style.

PAINTING.

Although painting is far more removed from the classic style of conception than sculpture is, yet here also we find a return to antique art. Asmus Carstens (1754–1798) gave significant expression to this new tendency in his simple and noble paintings and drawings, and the masters who succeeded him, Eberhard Wächter and Gottlieb Schick, followed with eagerness in his direction. In France, at the same time, J. L. David (1748–1825) introduced into painting the strict antique conception, though it was not maintained by him with the same purity, and degenerated either into insipidity or theatrical effect. Among the pupils of David, who obtained extensive influence in the development of French art, Ingres (1781–1867) adhered most decidedly to the strictly classic mode of expression.[1] Moderate in his powers of invention, more intelligent than imaginative, this principal representative of idealism starts with perfect representation of form, for which, following Raphael and the antique, he strives to find the noblest expression. This he has most successfully achieved in single ideal figures, especially nude female figures, such as ' the Fountain,' which no other modern painter has created with so much purity and beauty. Among his portraits, also, many are distinguished by nobleness of conception, perfection of form, and even by considerable effect of colour. On the other hand, in his compositions from classic antiquity (Apotheosis of Homer in the Luxemburg, Œdipus and the Sphinx, Stratonice, Jupiter and Thesis, in the Museum at Aix), that cold external character prevails, into which the French fell in contrast to the antique. In his ecclesiastical pictures (the Martyrdom of S. Symphosion, in the Cathedral at Autun, Christ among the Scribes, in the Museum at Montauban, Christ giving the Keys to Peter, in the Luxemburg, Oath of Louis XIII., in the Cathedral at Montauban) he obtains, under the influence of Raphael, that effect which a

[1] See the second volume of A. Gösling's *Geschichte der Malerei.* Leipzig, 1867.

constant seriousness, and an unlimited devotion to the noble and the sublime, may produce even without considerable imagination.

But a truly lifelike advance of painting was not lastingly to be obtained from the antique sphere of ideas and the classic conception of form. This most modern of the fine arts needed, above all, a new purport and a national sustenance. This was afforded, above all, in Germany by the rise of the national feeling which so gloriously burst forth in the war of liberation. The influential efforts of the Romanticists, which proceeded from it, communicated this new impulse to painting also, opened the eye to the importance of the national life, and revealed a rich Past, which was displayed with incomparable splendour in the beautifying light of poetry. Full of these youthful and enthusiastic ideas, some gifted artists met together in Rome at the period of this important revolution, and by common study sought to advance each other mutually on the same basis. These were Peter Cornelius of Düsseldorf, Friedrich Overbeck of Lübeck, Philipp Veit of Frankfort, and Wilhelm Schadow of Berlin. United by the same national views, they studied the great frescoes of the brilliant epoch of Italian art which render so convincingly apparent the importance of a serious monumental painting. The opportunity for the realisation of their efforts was afforded in 1816, when the Prussian Consul Bartholdi had the History of Joseph represented in fresco paintings in his house on Monte Pincio. A short time after there followed a second cycle of frescoes from Dante's 'Divina Commedia,' Ariosto's 'Orlando Furioso,' and Tasso's 'Gerusalemme Liberata,' which were executed in the Villa Massimi by Schnorr, Veit, Koch, Overbeck, and Führich. With these two important creations, among which there are some of imperishable value, the history of modern German art begins. Painting here again reached a deeper power of thought, a stricter form, and a monumental importance. Soon after, by the return of the different masters to Germany, the germs of this new life were transplanted to the soil of the Fatherland, where they were to bloom in the most manifold form. Only one of the party, Overbeck, remained in Rome, renouncing his country and his faith, henceforth in his artistic style wholly alienated from modern efforts. As this artist forms a strange anachronism in the artistic life of the present, we will consider him and his followers separately.

Friedrich Overbeck (born 1789) ever stands, as the founder of this style, foremost in able productions. His world is that of the exclusively mediæval church, and his feeling is that of a newly revived Fra Giovanni da Fiesole. Whatever steps beyond the views of the fourteenth century, either in truthful characterisation or completeness of form, he discards as heresy. Many of his works express undeniably a true feeling and hearty religion. This is the case with Christ's Entry into Jerusalem, and in the Entombment, which is in the Marienkirche at Lübeck. It is also evidenced in the profoundly conceived sketches from the Life of Christ. In other works, such as the Triumph of Religion, in the Städel Museum at Frankfort, the reflective tendency appears exhibited with too much design to have a pure effect. Among the other representatives of this style, who are designated ' Nazarenes,' Philipp Veit and Eduard Steinle, in Frankfort, are the most conspicuous.

Other artists, who are predominantly engaged in religious painting, endeavour to combine with it the results of a freer conception of nature and a finished technical skill; thus, for instance, Joseph Führich and Kuppelwieser, in Vienna, who executed some of the frescoes in the Altlerchenfelderkirche in that city; also Heinrich Hess and Schraudolph, in Munich—the former well known by his frescoes in the basilica and in the court chapel, and the latter by the decoration of Spires Cathedral. Lastly, we must here also mention the Düsseldorf painter Ernst Deger, who, in conjunction with many other artists, executed the beautifully conceived and ably finished frescoes in the Apollinariskirche at Remagen. Ecclesiastical painting has altogether, since the last ten years, considerably increased in Germany both in extent and importance. In the mass of these productions, however, the works which evidence independent conception and lifelike feeling form only a small portion.

Advancing with grand freedom, Peter v. Cornelius has become one of the profoundest and mightiest masters of German art (1783-1867). Even before he came to Rome he had, in the choice of his subject and in the form of representation, both in his compositions upon Göthe's 'Faust' and the 'Nibelungen Lied,' again touched a truly national keynote, and had shown himself a true follower of that genuine German art which rose to such richness and splendour in Albert Dürer. When, after a long residence in Rome, in the year 1820, he was called to Düsseldorf as director of the Academy, and in 1825 was appointed by King Ludwig to be the head of his Munich Academy, and was entrusted with the execution of the most important tasks, a new era in the history of art began in Germany. In the extensive frescoes of the Glyptothek he glorified the antique world of gods and heroes, and created with mighty touch a race of figures in whom all the beauty and sublimity, and also all the passions of the human heart, find an overpowering expression. In the Loggie of the Pinakothek he depicted with lifelike grace and naïveté the history of the Christian art, exhibiting excellent architectural construction and cleverness of arrangement. Next in the extensive cycle of paintings in the Ludwigskirche, he designed with profound thought and grand execution a delineation of the Christian ideas, from the Creation of the World to the Last Judgment—a work which, in power of thought, dignity, and inexhaustible richness, would alone make him one of the first masters of Christian art. But the creative power of the master was not yet ended. After the accession of Friedrich Wilhelm IV., he received a call to Berlin, in order to adorn the new royal sepulchre with frescoes ; and now, in his more advanced age, he began that mighty cycle of compositions upon the Campo Santo, in which he again represented, in works full of imperishable freshness, profound wisdom, sublime beauty, and overwhelming power of expression, the Redemption from Sin by the Life and Sufferings of Christ, the Work of the Church on Earth, the End of all Things, the Perishing of the Body, and the Resurrection to eternal Life. Although in Cornelius's works he has latterly never reached that perfection of form to which he attained in the Hall of the Gods in the Glyptothek; although, not without reason, he has been reproached for hardness and even faults of drawing; though, lastly, true painting and command of colour lie· beyond his reach—yet these deficiencies so lightly counterbalance his positive merits that they in no wise lessen them.

The thoughtful ideal art of this master, thus exhibited in grand monumental tasks, first gave the Munich school a tendency to important works, to the cultivation of the taste for linear beauty, architectural rhythm, and strong development of form. By a series of significant tasks, King Ludwig knew how to give definite aims to this effort, and to open an extensive sphere of action. Besides the before-mentioned cycle of paintings of a religious purport, which Heinrich Hess executed in the basilica and in the court chapel, Julius Schnorr painted in the halls of the palace the History of Charlemagne and Frederic Barbarossa, and the heroic legends of the Nibelungen, in a number of large pictures full of bold life and romanticist feeling. In other halls, the king had a series of scenes painted from the works of the great German poets; and even landscape painting was employed for large public objects in the paintings which Rottmann executed in the arcades of the court garden. At the same time, glass painting was revived and gained an opportunity for important display in the lately built church of the Au suburb, and in the restoration of the mediæval cathedral. We must here also mention the highly gifted Alfred Rethel, who died young, and who, first trained at Düsseldorf and subsequently at Frankfort, possesses most inner affinity with Cornelius, as is evidenced in his grandly composed works from the Life of Charlemagne, in the town hall at Aix-la-Chapelle, and in his no less important drawings from the March of Hannibal.

Among Cornelius's pupils there is only one who knew how to give his ideal style a new and independent impress. We allude to Wilhelm von Kaulbach, born at Arolsen in 1805, and who was first trained at Düsseldorf, and subsequently at Munich under Cornelius's direction. The most brilliant and distinguishing trait in this master is his gift of satire, which he employed with great humour in his compositions for Reineke Fuchs. Among the great symbolically historical compositions which he designed for the new Museum at Berlin, the Battle of the Huns stands foremost in poetic value, in lifelike beauty, and distinct unity of composition; the Building of the Tower of Babel is rich in strong characterisation and beauty; the Reformation ex- hibits an effectively grouped assembly of important personages. Among his separate figures, Tradition and History are distin- guished by grandeur of expression and nobleness of style. In the other pictures—for instance, the Golden Age of Greece, the Destruction of Jerusalem, and the Crusaders—the master has given himself up too much to the play of his ingenious fancy, and to the capricious mingling of historical, symbolical, legendary, and natural elements, and thus has endangered the strict unity, and gradually levelled his power of characterisation into conven- tional generalities. His compositions, too, of Shakspeare's and Göthe's female figures betray too little serious and profound understanding of the poet's mind, and exhibit too much an in- clination to coquettish pleasing and theatrical arrangement, for them to produce a pure effect. Later works, such as the colossal painting of the Battle at Salamis, for the Maximilianeum at Munich (coloured sketches of it are in the Stuttgart Gallery) exhibit unmistakably, like all preceding works, the wonderfully light and flowing figures of the richly gifted master, but at the same time his previous striking inclination to outward effect.

Among other Munich artists is Genelli, born in Berlin in 1803, the representative of a strictly classic style, which he evi- denced in drawings full of poetic power and often charming linear beauty, though combined with many conventional peculi- arities. On the other hand, Moritz v. Schwindt, born in Vienna in 1804, and likewise distinguished more for his gifted designs than for his paintings, adheres to a romanticist style, which is rendered most evident in his compositions upon the fable of the Seven Ravens—a work full of noble grace and true German feeling. Among his larger works we must mention the frescoes of the Wartburg, especially the scenes from the life of St. Elizabeth and the works of Mercy, as well as his recent compositions from Mozart's Zauberflöte for the Opera House at Vienna. Genre painting has also been variously fostered in the battle pieces of Albrecht Adam, Peter Hess, and Dietrich Monten, in Kirner's and Bürkel's fresh delineations of Bavarian life, as well as by many other able artists. L. v. Hagn and Ramberg appear as excellent representatives of the Rococo period ; and among animal painters Fr. Voltz must be mentioned on account of his delicate delineations of pastoral life. On the other hand, the works of Ferdinand and Karl Piloty betray a somewhat too superficial imitation of the French realists.

A second nursery of German painting arose in Düsseldorf, where the academy, since the year 1826, rose to new importance under Wilhelm Schadow. While the Munich school developed in its monumental works a high ideal style, in which profound thought, architectural arrangement, linear beauty, and strict drawing predominated, Düsseldorf art saw itself especially limited to oil painting, aimed rather at tenderness and feeling, and sought to increase this by a loving and careful study of nature and delicate perfection of colour. While Munich painting had a plastic character, a musical tone might be traced in the Düsseldorf works. Although this effort, owing to the political stagnation of the period in the limited circles of a central provincial town, erred into the soft and sentimental, just as Munich art had occasionally fallen into external effect, yet we must not judge this with one-sided severity, as it was just the enthusiastic acknowledgment which the Düsseldorf pictures at that time received, which irrefutably proves its important position in the history of the development of modern art. The passive dreamy feeling which prevails in the most famous pictures of this school, in the Mourning Kings by C. F. Lessing, the Sorrowing Jews by Eduard Bendemann, the Two Leonoras by Karl Sohn,

the Sons of Edward by Theodor Hildebrandt, and the Fisher-
man by Julius Hübner, was a natural efflux of the state of things
at that period; but the noble feeling, the loving devotion to
nature, the striking beauty of a colouring full of depth and
tenderness, are the imperishable merits of this school. At the
same time, they first applied themselves to a pleasing representation of the simple circumstances of actual life, and produced a
fresh revival of genre painting, in which Adolph Schrödter is
conspicuous for his solid humour, Jacob Becker for his thrilling
representation of village stories, Karl Hübner for effective
scenes from social circumstances and conflicts, Rudolph Jordan
and Henry Ritter for their fresh delineations of North German
fishing life, the Norwegian Tidemand for poetic and profoundly
felt scenes from the popular life of his native country, and Hasen-
clever for his humorous conception of armed citizen life. In the
later generation, Ludwig Knaus has shown himself one of the
most important delineators of the inner life, both in tragic conflicts and in the sunny brightness of mirthful feeling, by his incomparably finely felt and masterly genre pictures. The excellent Vautier is allied to him in fineness of conception. Incidents
of an agitating kind, such as occur in the tumult of battle, are
depicted by Bleibtreu and Camphausen with great artistic skill.

The transition to a freer conception of historical life, to the
striking delineation of great epochs and events, is made by Karl
Lessing, in his pictures from the Hussite war and the period of
the Reformation. Recently, however, Em. Leutze, in his bold
representation of Washington's Passage across the Delaware,
has furnished an historical picture, which, in force of expression,
is among the most important productions of this kind.

In Berlin, painting was conceived in a similar manner as in
Düsseldorf, and took a similar inclination to the genre and
romanticist style, without, however, arriving at the same important and extensive results. No opportunity was afforded this
art for public monumental works. It saw itself, as in Düsseldorf, limited to panel painting; but although there was no lack of
ably endowed artists, their efforts were isolated, and there was

no union among them, as at Düsseldorf, in one common direction. While Karl Wilhelm Kolbe (1781–1853) drew his subjects from the romanticist sphere, Wilhelm Wach (1787–1845) was especially active in religious historical painting, Von Klöber dwelt most willingly in the bright regions of classic mythology, and Karl Begas (1794–1855) wandered with versatile talent among the most different fields of art. Fr. Krüger must also be mentioned as a portrait painter and an excellent horse painter; and Eduard Magnus (born 1799) belongs to the most distinguished portrait painters of modern time, from his clever conception, noble arrangement, and atmospheric clearness of colouring. Among the historical painters of this school, Karl Schorn (1802–1850) stands foremost, from his great talent for powerful compositions, and his thrilling expression. Clever and lifelike, though often falling into coarse realistic hardness, Adolph Menzel depicted the life and times of Frederic the Great; while Julius Schrader gives his historical representations the charm of a powerful and brilliant colouring. Among the numerous genre painters, Eduard Meyerheim is attractive from his feeling and delicately executed delineations of the family life of the lower classes. Mention must also be made of E. Kretzschmer with his humorous scenes, Karl Becker with his picturesque works, Hosemann with his coarsely humorous delineations of vulgar life, and Cretius with his elegant and admirable representations of national Italian life.

In Vienna, also, painting was impelled to a similar course for want of larger monumental tasks. The most talented of the artists there have produced many charming works in fresh and lifelike genre pictures. In this branch of art, passing direct from the conventional style of the past century, Peter Krafft (1780–1856) led the way, and was followed by F. Waldmüller with his charming delineations of Austrian life, and Jos. Danhauser with his characteristic and often touching genre representations. In historical painting, Karl Rahl in his too short life (1812–1865) stands forth as one of the most gifted in his powerful conception, ideal feeling, and able colouring. In the sketches for the

Armoury of the Arsenal, and the Todesco Palace at Vienna, for the portico of the University at Athens, and other works, he has shown himself as a master of grandly designed and nobly finished frescoes.

An important share in the rise of German art has been taken by landscape painting. The increasing lifelike adherence to nature tends everywhere to the furtherance of this branch of art, so that all gradations of landscape are represented from the strictly ideal landscape composition to the mere view. At the same time, from increased intercourse with the world, the landscape painter's range of view extends over all quarters of the globe, and is enriched with an immeasurable abundance of new forms, new impressions, and effects. The revivor of modern landscape painting, Joseph Anton Koch (1768–1839), returned to ideal composition, such as Poussin had cultivated, and combined with it faithful characterisation, simple truth, and depth of feeling. This idealistic conception, based as it is upon poetic feeling, and which seeks to produce effect by grand arrangement, noble flow of lines, and harmony of design, has been only exceptionally represented among modern artists. Karl Rottmann (1798–1850), in his delineations of Italian and Greek landscapes, knew how to sustain this poetic element in the grandest manner, and to impart to his pictures the stamp of historic feeling by noble flow of lines, and by characteristic effects of light and atmosphere. With no less talent Friedrich Preller, in Weimar, in his compositions upon the Odyssey, exhibits this ideal character of landscape in rich variety, with-gifted imagination, and with true poetic power. In a similar manner, J. W. Schirmer, formerly at Düsseldorf, and subsequently at Karlsruhe (†1863), designed a series of biblical compositions; while Wilhelm Schirmer of Berlin, in his atmospheric delineations of the South, added the charm of magic effects of light to the simple beauty of lines. On the other hand, the early deceased Karl Blechen, at Berlin, knew how with peculiar power to give a poetic character to the grave northern landscape, but at the same time to depict with delicate feeling the beauty of the South.

That which distinguishes these masters of ideal landscape from those of the seventeenth century, is the greater exactness of detail and the more defined emphasising of the characteristic varieties of the forms of nature. Other masters place greater weight upon the latter, without, however, sacrificing in consequence the poetic feeling of the whole. Among these, Karl Friedrich Lessing, whom we have already mentioned as an historical painter, holds the first rank, from his acute observance of nature, depth of feeling, and touching truth in the delineation of natural life. The Alpine landscapes of the two Munich artists, Christian Morgenstern and Heinrich Heinlein, are also distinguished by poetic power. Among Düsseldorf artists, Weber occupies a similar position in his feeling wooded landscapes, and Oswald Achenbach in his noble Italian pictures; while the greater number of the rest, especially Andreas Achenbach, and the Norwegians Gude and Leu, with brilliant and masterly power, render homage to the realistic style. This style, especially in the further development of modern landscape, has drawn around it such a vast amount of talent, that we cannot give especial mention to the different artists.

French painting,[1] which began with the severely classic style of David, experienced later than the German that reaction to the Romanticist tendency, which was to become so full of importance in the development of modern art. If modern art never here reached that depth of thought which it did in Germany, the reason for this lay in the great diversity of the French character, which is distinguished by a tendency to the external conception of life and to the strong delineation of reality. The first powerful impulse to art was given by Géricault (1791–1824) in his Destruction of the Medusa, now in the Louvre, a work of thrilling power; Jean Victor Schnetz, born 1787, with his biblical, romantic, and historical representations; Carl Steuben, born in Mannheim in 1791, with his numerous large historical and battle pieces; and the Dutchman Ary

[1] Cf. J. Meyer's able work, *Gesch. d. mod. Französ. Malerei* seit 1789. Leipzig, 1866.

Scheffer (1795–1863), with his elegiac scenes from the Bible and from the poets, especially Göthe's 'Faust,' and his delineations from the Greek struggles for liberty, are the most distinguished representatives of the Romanticist style, in the cultivation of which the influence of German ideas, especially German poetry, is unmistakably apparent. More strongly, however, is this new striving against the usual classic style evidenced in Eugène Delacroix (1799–1863), who at the same time as a brilliant colourist declared war against the strict study of form cultivated by masters trained in the antique school. In his thrilling and powerful picture, Dante and Virgil in the Bark of Phlegyas (1822), he boldly trod in the steps of Géricault; and in works such as the Massacre of Chios, the Murder of the Bishop of Liége, from Walter Scott's 'Quintin Durward,' and the Shipwrecked, from Byron's 'Don Juan,' he gave powerful expression to the passionate and the terrible, as among the Romanticists of the same period in French literature, especially Victor Hugo. In monumental works (Chambre des Députés, dome of the Luxemburg, Apollo Gallery of the Louvre, and the church of S. Sulpice), with all his grand and bold style, the want of a stricter feeling for linear drawing is apparent. While Hippolyte Flandrin (1815–1864) exhibits great independent importance in his peculiarly noble and beautiful frescoès in S. Germain des Prés, S. Vincent de Paul, and S. Severin, the greater number of French artists incline to strong realism, to a fresh and often bold delineation of reality, and to a bold and touching representation of historical events. All of them possess more or less, as a distinguishing characteristic, a warm and lifelike colouring, the art of producing which has for the last ten years exercised increasing influence also on the German schools.

Foremost, we may mention Horace Vernet (1798–1863), with his charming delineations of African contests (Smalah, and other important works, at Versailles), his numerous smaller and larger scenes from military life and from history, and his animal contests, full of passionate action ; Paul Delaroche (1797–1856), with his historical pictures, which are distinguished by psychological acuteness and clever characterisation (Mazarin, Richelieu, Execution of Jane Grey, Cromwell by the Coffin of Charles I., Napoleon at Fontainebleau, Marie Antoinette's Condemnation, as well as a fresco painting in the École des beaux Arts); and Leopold Robert (1797–1835), with his delineations of Italian national life, rising as they do to the highest point of historical conception. As brilliant colourists, we may distinguish Robert Fleury, who represents particularly the agitated life of the middle ages, especially the shadow side of its Jewish persecutions, popular insurrections, and other bloody outrages; Léon Cogniet, who combines with effective colouring a striving after the expression of deeply excited feeling; and Decamps (1803–1860), who chiefly produced Eastern scenes with striking effects of light and contour. Among the numerous genre painters, we may mention the humorous François Biard and the elegant Meissonnier, incomparable in his own style. Winterhalter, born in Baden, enjoys a widespread reputation as an elegant portrait painter.

The new Empire has not exercised a favourable influence on the development of the arts. Outward splendour, increased technical skill, and extreme realism, combined with inward emptiness, poverty of idea, and want of feeling, distinguish the latest phase. Gérome, with his sad delineations of the shadow side of human life (gladiators in the circus, scenes of Turkish brutality, and the like), occasionally, as in Phryne before the Judges, readily falling into a sort of voluptuousness, cannot, with all the masterly technical power of his neat and somewhat too dainty pictures, create more than cold admiration. Only in genre pictures from modern history is he more attractive. Cabanel seeks in vain to conceal frivolity of feeling under an antique mask (Venus Anadyomene, nymph and fawn). Landelle, also, is not free from this danger, but he is excellent in delineations of national life in the South. Hébert is distinguished by his melancholy tone, Bonnat by the deep colouring of his Italian scenes, Fromentin by his lifelike delineations of the East. Modern battle pieces are produced with more or less success by Pils, Yvon, Armand-Dumaresq, and Protais. Comte shows himself an able colourist in his historical genre pictures. All these and many other artists are, however, surpassed by two painters of peasant life, in whom depth of feeling, truth of expression, unvarnished naturalness, and broad free handling, combine in producing an effect of rare power. These are, Jules Breton, who depicts with unsurpassable truth country people at field-work (weeding, gleaning, girls with turkeys, return from the field), or church festivals, such as processions with the crucifix and the blessing of the harvest, and who, with great simplicity of conception, evidences great feeling for the beautiful; and François Millet, who is devoid of this feeling for grace, but compensates for it by almost religious seriousness and unassuming chasteness.

In the delineation of nature, French art seems to find a revival, and this is evidenced in landscape painting. Few artists follow that ideal style, which seeks landscape beauty in the plastic flow of lines, to the same extent as Paul Flandin, Hippolyte Lanoue, Louis Français, and, above all, Corot, have done in their atmospheric pictures. The greater number disdain that richer form of the lines, and expend all their power on the reproduction of effects of light and atmosphere in the simplest scenery and the most homely and commonplace reality. But in this style such masters as Daubigny, Théodore Rousseau, who died in 1867, and Jules Dupré, have reached a depth of effect which, proceeding as it does from the unvarnished representation of simple nature, produces a highly poetic feeling. Animal painting is also worthily represented by Troyon, one of the greatest masters of this style, and likewise by Brascassat and Rosa Bonheur. Among the representatives of one-sided realism, we must, lastly, mention Courbet, who produces charming things in landscape representations. In conclusion, mention must also be made of the excellent illustrator Gustav Doré, whose best works are in fantastic and landscape subjects (Dante's 'Inferno' and 'Don Quixote'); but who, on the contrary, in his ideal representations, such as biblical or legendary scenes, appears meagre and styleless to an insufferable extent.

Switzerland also possesses, in the Genevese Calame a landscape painter who depicts with masterly power the grand Alpine nature of his native country, in Böcklin of Basle a delineator of southern nature, distinguished for poetry and splendid tone of colouring, in Alfred de Meuron an excellent master of Swiss landscape, and in Rudolph Koller of Zurich one of the most gifted portrayers of animal life, which he represents in various manners with acute characterisation and powerful truth to nature.

Recently, two of the principal old schools of painting, after having long languished in the fetters of a lifeless mannerism and subsequently in those of a pseudo-classic style, have risen to fresh life by the help of a careful study of nature, aided by the modern French school. The first of these is Italy, where the late great transformations seem to have rendered historical feeling more acute, so that a number of artists delight in taking their subjects from the history of their country. We may mention the talented Ussi of Florence, the Venetians Zona, Molmenti, and Gianetti, also Puccinelli, Focosi, and the Neapolitan Morelli. These all possess great taste for colour to a greater or lesser extent. On the other hand, Hayez chooses subjects of a higher ecclesiastical or historical purport.

A similar revival is also exhibited in Spain, where we may mention Rosalez, Antonio Gisbert, and Edvardo Cano of Seville in historical painting, Escosura and Luis Ruiperez in genre painting, as well as the excellent masters of architectural interiors, Palmaroli and Gonzalva.

In Belgium, modern realism has almost exclusively prevailed, and has even exercised an important influence on German painting, since the year 1843, when Louis Gallait's Abdication of Charles V., and E. de Biefve's Compromise of the Netherland Nobles, made such a great noise in Germany. In these pictures there appeared that full power of reality, that constraining force of an historical incident represented with lifelike truth, combined with a richness of characterisation and a boldness and brilliancy of colouring, which seemed to have vanished since the great masters of the seventeenth century. Modern historical painting indisputably received a considerable impulse from these remarkable pictures; although only one of these artists, Louis Gallait, could subsequently maintain the reputation he had won, and could establish it still more securely. Among his works, we may mention the Brussels' Citizens before the Corpses of Egmont and Horn, Egmont's last Moments, and Jeanne la Folle by the Corpse of her Husband. Next to these masters, Wappers, in his works, the Burgermeister van der Werff, Parting of Charles I. from his Children, and others; and Nicaise de Keyser, in his works, Battle of Worringen, Battle of Courtray, the Emperor Max in the Memling Workshop, Justus Lipsius before the Archduke Albert, and the Giaour, may be mentioned as representatives of the same style. Foremost among the Belgian genre painters are Leys in Antwerp, with his masterly and faithful delineations from the national life of the fifteenth and sixteenth centuries, especially of the Reformers; Alfred Stevens, with his elegant pictures of modern society; and Willems, with his representations in the costume of the seventeenth century. Foremost among the landscape painters are Fourmois, De Knyff, and Lamorinière; and among animal painters Eugen Verboekhoven in Brussels. On the other hand, in Holland there is principally a tendency to landscape and cattle pieces, in which we may trace a healthy adherence to the old school of the land. Among the artists here we may mention B. C. Koekkoek, with his fresh landscapes; De Haas, with his natural animal pieces; Roelofs, Gabriel, and Maeten, with their feeling landscapes; and Kuytenbrower, with his hunting pieces. Israels is distinguished for genre paintings full of harmony and able effect of colour, and Alma Tadema is especially worthy of note from his pictures from classic and even Oriental antiquity. .

England also, in recent times, has experienced a brilliant advance in painting. Yet painting here, more than in any other country, bears the character of a local and separate art, though without arriving in consequence at any inward harmony. Grand historical painting and monumental composition here find no culture. All the more richly are genre painting, landscape painting, portraits, and animal pieces cultivated. In her excellent water-colour painting, England has reached unsurpassable perfection. If among the great number of artistic powers here at work we would distinguish the most important in the principal styles, we must mention Sir Charles Eastlake, trained after the master-works of the Italian schools, especially the Venetian; the gifted portrayer of the English and Scotch national life, David Wilkie (1785–1841); the humorist Leslie; the landscape painter Turner (1780–1851), famous for his brilliant effects of light, though at length falling into a want of form, and subsequently degenerating into fantastic impossibilities; and the versatile Landseer, who as animal painter stands unequalled in clever observation, delicate characterisation, and unsurpassable life. Throughout English painting, the inclination to their own country, the delineation of their own people, and of all peculiar to their own land, is a trait all the more remarkable from the fact that they are without doubt more fond of travelling than any nation in Europe; while among the French, who travel only exceptionally, painting seeks its subjects in all regions of the world. Among the other numerous artists of England, we must yet mention W. Mulready, with his vigorously conceived pictures of boy life; W. P. Frith, who takes his subjects from the poems of Shakspeare, Goldsmith, and Molière; Fr. Stone and Cattermole, who principally represent scenes from novels; Thomas Faed, with his freshly painted genre scenes; A. Elmore and Ph. Calderon, who take their subjects from history, though rather in the tone and character of genre painting; E. Nicol, who possesses a power of characterisation that reminds us of Dickens; and John Philips, who has recently died, and whose works are distinguished for strong realistic colouring. Among the great number of landscape painters who attain to pure poetic feeling from fidelity of delineation and delicacy of effect, though for the most part without any ideal tendency, we have yet to name Cl.

Stanfield, remarkable for his masterly treatment of aerial perspective; H. MacCulloch and P. Graham, principally known for their representations of Scotch scenes. Formal landscape painting, on the other hand, has no distinguished representative in England.

Whatever able artists have appeared in Denmark, evidence rather the influence of the German schools than an independent national stamp. Elizabeth Jerichau is distinguished for her able male figures, which are executed with realistic power; Extner and Gertner for their fresh genre pictures; Soerensen and Melbye produce excellent sea pieces; and Rump and Kjeldruss landscapes. Scandinavia also belongs to the offshoots from the German schools, in which we have already mentioned her principal masters, Tidemand, Gude, and Leu. We must here add, above all, Fagerlin, with his humorously painted village stories; Jernberg, with his representations of national life; Höchert, with his well-conceived scenes from Lapland; and, lastly, among numerous landscape painters, Knuth Baade, Morton Müller, Eckersberg, and Nielson.

In Russia, also, we find no independent original art, though she possesses some distinguished artists. We may mention Peroff, who has been called the Turghenieff of painting from his masterly genre paintings from Russian life; also Rizzoni, Mestschersky, and Koscheleff, who likewise produce fresh representations from national life; while Kotzebue is distinguished for his excellent battle pieces, and Aiwasowsky for his brilliant naval pieces. Lastly, North America is beginning to take an active part in the art movement, although here also there is a leaning towards the German schools. We have already spoken of Leutze among the Düsseldorf artists. We may add to him Winslow Homer and Thomson, and among the numerous landscape painters, Bierstadt, Whittridge, Colman, and Gifford.

We must not conclude this brief sketch of the art movement of the present day, without mentioning an important branch of artistic production, which furnishes a pleasing evidence that interest in works of art is becoming gradually the common possession of the whole people. The branch to which we allude is that of multiplying works of art, a branch which in no former epoch exhibited even an approach to the same activity. Not merely are copperplate and steel engraving executed by able masters, not merely has the long-neglected woodcut again risen to honour, to which we owe works such as Ludwig Richter's lifelike and feeling representations of German national and family life, and the great Bible work of Julius Schnorr, but a new invention, that of lithography, is extending wider and wider in various kinds; and, lastly, the daguerreotype, photography, and stereoscope add new and unimagined results to these rich means of multiplying art.

All this points to the fact that a lively feeling, and a fresh participation in artistic works, extend over ever-widening circles. The more, however, that a truly healthy advance of art rests on its nationality, the more must it keep its ideal pure and true. The dangers of external effect, over-adherence to nature and emptiness, lie so fatally near the art of the present day, above all, to that of painting, from the fact that the characteristic of the age is predominantly realistic. Hence it must guard its heritage of the ideal, must truly, faithfully, and profoundly adhere to life, but in its productions it must seek not to grasp the dazzling clothing of this life, but its imperishable intrinsic value. This is its task, its vocation, and the condition of its living duration.

INDEX OF ARTISTS.

A

Abel, Gregor, ii. 317
— Peter, ii. 317
Achenbach, Andreas, ii. 448
— Oswald, ii. 448
Adam, Albrecht, ii. 444
Adriaenssen, ii. 422
Aelst, Willem van, ii. 422
Aëtion, i. 199
Agasias, i. 245
Agatharcus, i. 196
Ageladas, i. 147, 152
Agesandrus, i. 185
Agoracritus, i. 159
Aiwasowsky, ii. 455
Alamano, Giov., ii. 96
Albani, Francesco, ii. 381, 412
Alberti, Leo Batt., ii. 117
Albertinelli, Mariotto, ii. 240
Alcamenes, i. 158
Aldighiero, da Zevio, ii. 96
Alessi, Galeazzo, ii. 132
Algardi, Alessandro, ii. 371
Allegri, Antonio, ii. 267
Allori, Cristofano, ii. 382
Altdorfer, Albrecht, ii. 364
Alunno, Nicolo, ii. 182
Amberger, Christoph, ii. 316, 355
Amerighi, Michelangelo, ii. 383
Ammanati, Bartolommeo, ii. 210
Angelico, Fra Giov., ii. 93
Anthemius, i. 297
Antiphilus, i. 199
Antonello da Messina, ii. 175
Apelles, i. 198
Apollodorus, A., i. 234
— i. 196
Apollonius of Athens, i. 245
— von Tralles, i. 187
Aretino, Spinello, ii. 89
Aristocles von Athen, i. 145
— von Sicyon, i. 147
Aristonidas, i. 185
Arler, Peter, ii. 29
Arnolfo di Cambio, ii. 47
Arras, Matthias von, ii. 29

Athenodorus, i. 186
Austen, William, ii. 321
Avanzo, Jac. d', ii. 96

B

Baade, ii. 455
Backhuisen, Ludolf, ii. 419
Bagnacavallo, ii. 266
Baker, Jan de, ii. 320
Bandinelli, Baccio, ii. 210
Barbarelli, Giorgio, ii. 275
Barbieri, Francesco, ii. 381
Barisanus von Trani, i. 459
Baroccio, Federigo, ii. 274
Barozzio, Giacomo, ii. 131
Barry, ii. 431
Bartollomeo, Fra, ii. 237
Barye, ii. 436
Bassano, Jacopo, ii. 293
Bathykles, i. 143
Bazzi, Gian Antonio, ii. 224
Beccafumi, ii. 225
Becker, Jacob, ii. 445
— Karl, ii. 446
Beer, Georg, ii. 141
Begarelli, Antonio, ii. 205
Begas, Karl, ii. 446
— Reinhold, ii. 435
Beham, Barthol., ii. 364
— Hans Sebald, ii. 364
Bellini, Giovanni, ii. 176, 178
— Gentile, ii. 180
Belotto, Bernardo, ii. 420
Beltraffio, ii. 222
Bendemann, ii. 444
Berchem, Nicolaus, ii. 420
Bernini, Lorenzo, ii. 130, 134, 367
Bernward, i. 440
Berruguete, Alonso de, ii. 321, 368
Biard, ii. 450
Biefve, de, ii. 452
Bierstadt, ii. 455
Bläser, ii. 435
Blechen, ii. 447
Bleibtreu, ii. 445
Bles, Herri de, ii. 341, 415
Böcklin, ii. 452

Bol, Ferdinand, ii. 400
Bologna, Giovanni da, ii. 210
Bonannus, i. 406
Bonheur, Rosa, ii. 451
Bonifazio, ii. 286
Bonnat, ii. 450
Bonneuil, Etienne de, ii. 44
Bontemps, Pierre, ii. 319
Bonvicino, Alessandro, ii. 286
Bordone, Paris, ii. 288
Borgognone, Ambrogio, ii. 119, 176
Borromini, Francesco, ii. 135
Bosch, Hieronymus, ii. 341
Bosio, ii. 436
Both, Johann, ii. 414
Botticelli, Sandro, ii. 162
Boucher, François, ii. 402
Bourd, John, ii. 321
Bourguignon, ii. 384
— ii. 120, 124
Boydell, ii. 403
Bramante, ii. 176
Bramantino, ii. 176
Brascassat, ii. 451
Bregno, Antonio, ii. 155
— Lorenzo, ii. 155
Breton, ii. 451
Breughel, Johann, ii. 415, 421
— Peter, the elder, ii. 404
— Peter, the younger, ii. 404
Bril, Mathäus, ii. 412
— Paul, ii. 412
Briosco, il, ii. 128, 206
Bronzino, Angiolo, ii. 237
Brouwer, Adrian, ii. 406
Brüggemann, Hans, ii. 299
Brugger, ii. 436
Brunellesco, Filippo, ii. 113, 151
Brunsberg, Heinrich, ii. 35
Bruyn, Bartholomäus de, ii. 342
Bryaxis, i. 182
Bürkel, ii. 444
Bürklein, ii. 428
Buonaccorsi, ii. 266
Buonarroti, ii. 128, 129, 196, 227
Buono, Bartolommeo, ii. 154
Burgkmair, Hans, ii. 345

Busketus, i. 405
Byström, ii. 432

C

Cabanel, ii. 450
Calame, ii. 452
Calamis, i. 151
Caldara, ii. 266
Calderow, ii. 454
Caliari, Paolo, ii. 290
Callicrates, i. 122
Callimachus, i. 170
Callon, i. 147
Callot, Jacques, ii. 409
Cambiaso, Luca, ii. 266
Campagna, Girolamo, ii. 209
Campagnola, Domenico, ii. 286
Campaña, Pedro, ii. 368
Campen, Jacob van, ii. 139
Camphausen, ii. 445
Campi, ii. 377
Canachos, i. 147
Canale, Antonio, ii. 420
Canaletto, Bernardo, ii. 420
Candido, ii. 374
Cano, Alonso, ii. 385
— Edoardo, ii. 452
Canova, ii. 431
Capelle, Johann van de, ii. 419
Caracci, Agostino, ii. 378
— Annibale, ii. 378
— Lodovico, ii. 377
Caravaggio, Michelangelo da, ii. 383
— Polidoro da, ii. 266
Carotto, Francesco, ii. 226
Carpaccio, Vittore, ii. 181
Carstens, ii. 438
Carucci, Jacopo, ii. 236
Cattermole, ii. 434
Caulitz, Peter, ii. 421
Cellini, Benvenuto, ii. 204
Cerquozzi, Michelangelo, ii. 384
Chalgrin, ii. 430
Champaigne, Philippe, ii. 402
Chardin, ii. 410
Chares, i. 185
Chaudet, ii. 432
Christoph, Meister, ii. 303
Christophsen, Peter, ii. 332
Ciccione, Andrea, ii. 157
Cimabue, Giovanni, i. 464
Cione, Andrea di, ii. 85, 89
Civitali, Matteo, ii. 152
Claux Sluter, ii. 65
Cleanthes, i. 194
Cleomenenes, i. 244
Clouet, François, ii. 367
Coello, Alonzo Sanchez, ii. 368
— Claudio, ii. 389
Cogniet, ii. 450
Colantonio del Fiore, ii. 98

Colin, Alexander, ii. 317
Colman, ii. 455
Colotes, i. 159
Comte, ii. 451
Conegliano, Cima da, ii. 181
Contucci, Andrea, ii. 194
Cornelius, ii. 439, 442
Corot, ii. 451
Correggio, ii. 267
Cosmata, i. 404
Costa, Lorenzo, ii. 188
Couci, Robert de, ii. 18
Courbet, ii. 451
Courtois, Jacques, ii. 384
Cousin, Jean, ii. 320
Coxcie, Michael, ii. 338
Cranach, Lucas, ii. 364
Credi, Lorenzo di, ii. 170, 553
Cresilas, i. 170
Cretius, ii. 446
Critios, i. 147
Cronaca, Simone, ii. 116
Cullock, ii. 455
Cuyp, Albert, ii. 420

D

Daedalos, i. 141
Danhauser, ii. 446
Dannecker, ii. 432
Daubigny, ii. 451
David, d'Angers, ii. 436
— Gerhard, ii. 337
— J. L., ii. 438
Decamps, ii. 450
Deger, Ernst, ii. 440
Delacroix, ii. 449
Delaroche, ii. 449
Delorme, Philibert, ii. 137
Demetrius, i. 171
Denner, Baltasar, ii. 401
Deutsch, Niclas, ii. 355
Dichter, Michael, ii. 308
Dietrich, Christian, ii. 401
Diogenes, i. 245
Dioscorides, i. 258
Diotisalvi, i. 405
Dipoenus, i. 143
Dolci, Carlo, ii. 382
Domenichino, ii. 379
Donatello, ii. 149
Donner, Rafael, ii. 371
Doré, ii. 451
Dossi, Dosso, ii. 267
Dow, Gerhard, ii. 408
Drake, ii. 435
Duban, ii. 430
Duccio, di Buoninsegna, i. 465
Ducq, Jean le, ii. 407
Dughet, Caspar, ii. 413
Dujardin, Karl, ii. 420
Dumaresq, ii. 451
Dupré, ii. 451
Duquesnoy, ii. 372
Dürer, Albrecht, ii. 324, 356
Duret, ii. 436
Dyck, Anton van, ii. 395

E

Eastlake, ii. 454
Eckersberg, ii. 455
Ecphantos, i. 195
Eeckhout, Gerbr. van den, ii. 400
Egl, Andreas, ii. 29
Egle, ii. 430
Eisenlohr, ii. 429
Elmore, ii. 454
Engelbrechtsen, Cornelius, ii. 341
Escosura, ii. 452
Eumaros, i. 195
Eupompos, i. 198
Everdingen, ii. 419
Extner, ii. 455
Eyck,, Hubert van, ii. 322, 326
— Johann van, ii. 329
— Lambert van, ii. 332
— Margarethe van, ii. 332

F

Fabius Pictor, i. 259
Fabriano, Gentile da, ii. 96
Faed, ii. 454
Faes, Peter van der, ii. 403
Fagerlin, ii. 455
Falconetto, ii. 128
Fernkorn, ii. 436
Ferrari, Gaudenzio, ii. 222
— Francesco, Bianchi, ii. 267
Fiammingo, ii. 372
Fiesole, Fra Giovanni da, ii. 93
— Mino da, ii. 153
Filarete, Antonio, ii. 120, 151
Filipepi, Sandro, ii. 162
Fiore, Colantonio del, ii. 98
Fischer, von Erlach, ii. 143
Fischer, A., ii. 435
Flandrin, Hippolyt, ii. 449
— Paul, ii. 451
Flaxman, ii. 432
Fleury, ii. 450
Flinck, Govart, ii. 400
Floris, Franz, ii. 339
Focosi, ii. 452
Fogelberg, ii. 432
Fontaine, ii. 430
Forli, Melozzo da, ii. 175, 270
Fossano, Ambrogio, ii. 176
Fouquet, Jean, ii. 367
Fourmois, ii. 453
Français, ii. 451
Francesca, Pier della, ii. 170
Francia, Francesco, ii. 187
— Giacomo, ii. 189
— Giulio, ii. 189
Franciabigio, Marcantonio, ii. 244
Frith, ii. 454
Fromentin, ii. 450
Führich, ii. 439, 440
Fyt, Johann, ii. 421

G

Gabriel, ii. 453
Gaddi, Taddeo, ii. 89 •
Gadier, Pierre, ii. 137
Gainsborough, Thomas, ii. 415
Gallait, ii. 452
Garofalo, Benvenuto, ii. 267
Gärtner, Friedr. von, ii. 428
Gau, ii. 430
Geertgen von St. Jans, ii. 339
Gelée, Claude, ii. 413
Genelli, ii. 443
Gent, Justus van, ii. 332
Gerhard, i. 441
Gerhard von Harlem, ii. 339
Géricault, ii. 448
Gérôme, ii. 450
Gertner, ii. 423, 455
Ghiberti, Lorenzo, ii. 145
Ghirlandajo, Domenico, ii. 166
— Ridolfo, ii. 244
Gianetti, ii. 452
Gibson, ii. 437
Gifford, ii. 455
Giocondo, Fra, ii. 121
Giordano, Luca, ii. 384
Giorgione, ii. 275
Giotto, ii. 47, 84, 87
Girardon, François, ii. 372
Girolamo da Trevigi, ii. 140
Gisbert, ii. 452
Glycon, i. 244
Gmünd, Heinrich von, ii. 48
Godl, Melchior, ii. 316
— Stephan, ii. 317
Goes, Hugo van der, ii. 331, 332
Gonzalva, ii. 452
Goujon, Jean, ii. 319
Goyen, Joh. van, ii. 417
Gozzoli, Benozzo, ii. 165
Graff, Anton, ii. 401
Graham, ii. 455
Greuze, ii. 410
Grimaldi, Francesco, ii. 412
Grünewald, Matthias, ii. 364
Gude, ii. 448, 455
Guercino, ii. 381

H

Haas, de, ii. 453
Haase, ii. 429
Hagn, L. von, ii. 444
Hähnel, ii. 435
Hals, Franz, ii. 397
Hansen, ii. 429
Harlem, Gerhard van, ii. 339
Hayez, ii. 452
Hébert, ii. 450
Heem, David de, ii. 421
Hegias, i. 147
Heinlein, ii. 448
Heinrich von Gmünd, ii. 48

Helst, Bartholom. van der, ii. 397
Herlen, Friedrich, ii. 343
Hermogenes, i. 132
Herrad von Landsberg, i. 451
Herrera, Francisco de, ii. 385
Hess, Heinrich, ii. 440
— Peter, ii. 444
Heyden, J. van der, ii. 420
Hildebrandt, Theodor, ii. 445
Hiram, i. 64
Hittorf, ii. 430
Hitzig, ii. 427
Hobbema, Minderhout, ii. 418
Höckert, ii. 455
Hogarth, William, ii. 410
Holbein, Hans, the elder, ii. 348
— the younger, ii. 346
— Sigmund, ii. 346
Holzschuher, Eucharius, ii. 143
Homer, ii. 455
Hondekoeter, Melchior, ii. 421
Honthorst, Gerhard, ii. 384
Hooghe, Peter van, ii. 409
Hosemann, ii. 446
Hosmer, ii. 437
Houdon, ii. 372
Hübner, Julius, ii. 445
— Karl, ii. 445
Hübsch, ii. 429
Hültz, Johann, ii. 29
Huysum, Joh. van, ii. 421

J

Jacob, Meister, ii. 46
Jacobus, Friar, i. 463
Jerichau, ii. 455
Jernberg, ii. 455
Ictinus, i. 122, 128, 174
Ingres, ii. 438
Joanez, Vicente, ii. 368
Johann von Köln, ii. 52
John of Padua, ii. 140
Jones, Inigo, ii. 141
Jordaens, Jacob, ii. 396
Jordan, Rudolph, ii. 445
Isidorus, i. 297
Israel von Mekenem, ii. 342
Israels, ii. 453
Juste, Jean, ii. 318

K

Kabel, Adrian van der, ii. 417
Kalide, ii. 435
Kauffmann, Angelica, ii. 401
Kaulbach, Wilh., ii. 443
Kessels, ii. 437
Keyser, de, ii. 453
Kirner, ii. 444
Kiss, ii. 435
Kjeldruss, ii. 455
Klenze, Leo von, ii. 428
Klöber, A. von, ii. 446
Knaus, Ludwig, ii. 445

Kneller, Gottfried, ii. 403
Knobelsdorff, G. von, ii. 143
Knoblauch, ii. 427
Knyff, de, ii. 453
Koch, ii. 439, 447
Koekkoek, ii. 453
Köln, Joh. von, ii. 52
Kolbe, ii. 446
Koller, Rud., ii. 452
Koning, Salomon, ii. 400
Koscheleff, ii. 455
Kotzebue, ii. 455 •
Krafft, Adam, ii. 305
— Peter, ii. 446
Kretzschmer, E., ii. 446
Krüger, ii. 446
Kulmbach, Hans von, ii. 363
Kundze, ii. 77
Kupetzky, Joh., ii. 401
Kuppelwieser, ii. 440
Kuytenbrower, ii. 453

L

Laar, Peter van, ii. 407
Labrouste, ii. 430
Lala, i. 259
Lambespring, Barth., ii. 321
Lamorinière, ii. 453
Landelle, ii. 450
Landseer, ii. 454
Lanfranco, Giovanni, ii. 381
Lanfrancus, i. 413
Lanoue, ii. 451
Lassus, ii. 430
Laurana, Luciano, ii. 121
Lazzari, Donato, ii. 124
Lebrun, Charles, ii. 402
Legros, ii. 372
Leins, ii. 429
Lely, Peter, ii. 403
Lendenstrauch, Hans, ii. 317
Leochares, i. 133, 182
Leopardo, Alessandro, ii. 152, 156
Lerch, Niclas, ii. 308
Lescot, Pierre, ii. 137
Leslie, ii. 454
Lessing, ii. 444, 445, 448
Leu, ii. 448, 455
Leutze, ii. 445, 455
Leyden, Lucas van, ii. 341
Leys, ii. 453
Lievensz, ii. 400
Lingelbach, Johann, ii. 420
Lionardo da Vinci, ii. 193, 212
Lippi, Fra Filippo, ii. 161
— Filippino, ii. 160, 163
Lochner, Stephan, ii. 81
Löffler, Gregor, ii. 316
Lombard, Lambert, ii. 339
Lombardo, Alfonso, ii. 205
— Antonio, ii. 155
— Pietro, ii. 118, 155
— Tullio, ii. 155
Lorenzo, Bernardo di, ii. 118

Lorrain, Claude, ii. 413
Lotto, Lorenzo, ii. 286
Ludius, i. 259
Luini, Bernardino, ii. 221
Lunghi, Martino, ii. 134
Lysippus, i. 182

M

Mabuse, Johann, ii. 338
Macdowell, ii. 437
Maderno, Carlo, ii. 130
— Stefano, ii. 370
Maes, ii. 409
Maeten, ii. 453
Magnus, Eduard, ii. 446
Majano, Benedetto da, ii. 116, 152
— Giuliano da, ii. 118
Maitani, Lorenzo, ii. 47
Malvito, Tommaso, ii. 158
Mantegna, Andrea, ii. 172
Manuel, Niclas, ii. 355
Martino, Simone di, ii. 93
— Pietro di, ii. 118
Masaccio, ii. 159
Masolino, ii. 159
Mazzoni, Guido, ii. 157
Mazzuola, Francesco, ii. 274
Meer, Jan van der, ii. 409
Meeren, Gerhard van der, ii. 332
Meissonnier, ii. 450
Melanthios, i. 198
Melbye, ii. 455
Melozzo da Forli, ii. 175
Melzi, Francesco, ii. 222
Memling, Hans, ii. 334
Memmi, Lippo, ii. 93
Mengs, Rafael, ii. 401
Menzel, Adolph, ii. 446
Messina, Antonello da, ii. 178
Messys, Quintin, ii. 337
Mestschersky, ii. 455
Metzu, Gabriel, ii. 408
Meuron, ii. 452
Meyerheim, Eduard, ii. 446
Michelangelo, ii. 128, 129, 196, 227
Michelozzi, ii. 115
Micon, i. 195
Miel, Johann, ii. 420
Mieris, Franz van, ii. 408
— Wilhelm van, ii. 408
Mignard, Pierre, ii. 402
Millet, ii. 451
Miranda, Juan Careño de, ii. 389
Mnesikles, i. 123
Molmenti, ii. 452
Momper, Jodocus de, ii. 416
Monrealese, ii. 384
Monten, ii. 444
Montereau, Peter of, ii. 20
Montorsoli, ii. 210
Morales, Luis, ii. 368
Morelli, ii. 452
Moretto, ii. 286
Morgenstern, ii. 448

Moro, Antonio, ii. 339
Moroni, Giov. Batt., ii. 288
Moser, Lucas, ii. 298, 343
Müller, Morton, ii. 455
Mulready, ii. 454
Murillo, ii. 387
Myron, i. 147, 151, 171

N

Nason, Peter, ii. 422
Naukydes, i. 172
Navarrete, ii. 368
Neefs, Peter, ii. 419
Neer, Artus van der, ii. 417
Nehring, ii. 143
Nepveu, Pierre, ii. 137
Netscher, Caspar, ii. 408
Niccolo di Pietro, ii. 89
Nicol, ii. 454
Nicolaus von Verdun, i. 448
Nielsen, ii. 455
Normand, ii. 430
Novelli, Pietro, ii. 384
Novius, Plautius, i. 214

O

Oggione, Marco d', ii. 222
Ohlmüller, ii. 428
Onatas, i. 147
Orcagna, Andrea, ii. 85, 89
— Bernardo, ii. 92
Orley, Bernardin van, ii. 338
Ostade, Adrian van, ii. 406
— Isaak van, ii. 406
Ouwater, Albert van, ii. 329
Overbeck, ii. 439

P

Pacchia, Girol. del., ii. 225
Pacheco, Francisco, ii. 385
Pacher, Michael, ii. 299, 355
Pachiarotto, ii. 225
Pacuvius, i. 259
Paeonius, i. 159
Palladio, Andrea, ii. 131
Palma Vecchio, ii. 277
Palmaroli, ii. 452
Palmer, ii. 437
Pamphilos, i. 198
Panaenus, i. 155
Parmigianino, ii. 274
Parrhasios, i. 197
Patenier, Joachim, ii. 341, 415
Patras, Lambert, i. 441
Pausanias, i. 198
Pencz, Georg, ii. 363
Penni, Franc., ii. 266
Pennone, Rocco, ii. 132
Percier, ii. 430
Pereda, Antonio, ii. 389
Perez, Pedro, ii. 52
Pericoli, Niccolo, ii. 204
Peroff, ii. 455

Persius, ii. 427
Perugino, Pietro, ii. 170, 182
Peruzzi, Baldass, ii. 125, 226
Peters, Bonaventura, ii. 419
— Johann, ii. 419
Phidias, i. 147, 152
Philips, ii. 454
Piazza, Calisto, ii. 286
Pietro, Niccolo di, ii. 89
Pigalle, J. Bapt., ii. 372
Pilgram, Meister, ii. 305
Pilon, Germain, ii. 319
Piloty, Carl, ii. 444
— Ferdinand, ii. 444
Pils, ii. 451
Pintelli, Baccio, ii. 121
Pinturicchio, ii. 185
Piombo, del, ii. 234, 277
Pippi, Giulio, ii. 265
Piræcus, i. 199
Pisano, Andrea, ii. 84
— Giovanni, ii. 47, 82
— Nicola, i. 459
Pollajuolo, Antonio, ii. 151, 170
Polydoros, i. 186
Polygnotus, i. 195
Polycletus, i. 171
Ponce, Ponzio, ii. 320
Ponte, Jacopo da, ii. 293
Pordenone, ii. 288
Porta, Baccio della, ii. 237
— Guglielmo dela, ii. 210
Potter, Paul, ii. 420
Pourbus, Franz, ii. 339
Poussin, Caspar, ii. 413
— Nicolaus, ii. 401, 412
Pradier, ii. 436
Praxiteles, i. 177
Preller, ii. 447
Prieur, Barthélemy, ii. 320
Primaticcio, Franc., ii. 266
Procaccini, ii. 377
Protais, ii. 451
Protogenes, i. 199
Puccinelli, ii. 452
Pugin, ii. 431
Pujet, Pierre, ii. 371
Puligo, Domenico, ii. 244
Puntormo, ii. 236, 244
Pynacker, Adam, ii. 414
Pyrgoteles, i. 191
Pythagoras, i. 151
Pytheos, i. 131

Q

Quellinus, Arthur, ii. 373
Quercia, Jacopo della, ii. 145

R

Rahl, ii. 446
Raibolini, Francesco, ii. 187
Rainaldus, ii. 405
Ramberg, ii. 444

Ramenghi, Bartolommeo, ii. 266
Raphael, ii. 126, 169, 244
Rauch, ii. 434
Regillo, ii. 288
Rembrandt, ii. 397, 417
Reni, Guido, ii. 381
Rethel, ii. 442
Reynolds, Joshua, ii. 403
Rhoecus, i. 120, 143
Ribalta, Francisco, ii. 389
Ribera, Giuseppe, ii. 384
Ricciarelli, ii. 236
Riccio, Andrea, ii. 128, 206
Richier, ii. 319
Richter, Ludwig, ii. 456
Ridinger, ii. 421
Riemenschneider, Tilman, ii. 398
Rietschel, ii. 435
Rigaud, Hyacinthe, ii. 403
Ritter, Henry, ii. 445
Rizzo, Antonio, ii. 119, 155
Rizzoni, ii. 455
Robbia, Luca della, ii. 115, 147
Robert, Leop., ii. 450
Robusti, Jacopo, ii. 289
Rode, Bernhard, ii. 401
Roélas, Juan de las, ii. 385
Roelofs, ii. 453
Rogers, ii. 437
Romano, Giulio, ii. 127, 253, 255
Roos, Joh., Heinr., ii. 420
— Philipp, ii. 420
Rosa, Salvator, ii. 384, 415
Rosalez, ii. 452
Rösch, Jacob, ii. 299
Roselli, Cosimo, ii. 165
Rosellini, Antonio, ii. 151
Rossetti, Biagio, ii. 121
Rossi, Francesco, de', ii. 237
— Rosso di, ii. 244
Rottenhammer, Johann, ii. 401
Rottmann, ii. 442, 447
Rousseau, ii. 451
Roussel, Frémin, ii. 320
Roux, Roullant de, ii. 318
Rovezzano, Benedetto da, ii. 322
Rubens, ii. 139, 390, 416
Rude, ii. 436
Rugendas, Philipp, ii. 407
Ruiperez, ii. 452
Rumanino, Girolamo, ii. 286
Rump, ii. 455
Ruysdael, Jacob, ii. 417
— Solomon, ii. 418
Rustici, Francesco, ii. 184
Rutharts, Carl, ii. 421
Ruysch, Rachel, ii. 421

S

Sabbatini, Andrea, ii. 266
Salaino, Andrea, ii. 222

Salvi, Giov. Battista, ii. 382
Salviati, Francesco, ii. 237
Sandrart, Joachim von, ii. 401
Sangallo, Antonio da, ii. 127
— Giuliano da, ii. 116
Sanmicheli, ii. 128
Sansovino, Andrea, ii. 194
— Jacopo, ii. 127, 206
Santi, Giovanni, ii. 187
— Rafael, ii. 126, 196, 244
Sarto, Andrea del, ii. 187
Sassoferrato, ii. 379
Savery, Roland, ii. 416
Savoldo, Girol., ii. 286
Scalza, Lodovico, ii. 317
Scamozzi, ii. 128
Schadow, Joh. Gottfried, ii. 433
— Wilhelm, ii. 439, 444
Schaffner, Martin, ii. 344
Schalcken, Gottfried, ii. 408
Schaller, ii. 436
Scheffer, Ary, ii. 449
Schick, ii. 438
Schievelbein, ii. 435
Schinkel, ii. 426
Schirmer, J. W., ii. 447
— Wilhelm, ii. 447
Schlüter, Andreas, ii. 143, 374
Schmidt, Fr., ii. 429
Schnez, ii. 448
Schnorr, ii. 439, 442, 456
Schongauer, Schön, Martin, ii. 343
Schonhofer, Sebald, ii. 64
Schoreel, Jan van, ii. 338
Schorn, Carl, ii. 446
Schrader, Julius, ii. 446
Schraudolph, ii. 440
Schrödter, ii. 445
Schwanthaler, ii. 435
Schwindt, Moritz v., ii. 443
Scott, ii. 431
Screta, Karl, ii. 401
Sebastiano, Fra, ii. 234
Seghers, Daniel, ii. 421
Semper, ii. 429
Sergell, ii. 432
Sesslschreiber, Gilg, ii. 316
Sesto, Cesare da, ii. 222
Signorelli, Luca, ii. 168
Siloë, Gil de, ii. 321
Simone di Martino, ii. 93
Sinan, i. 352
Scopas, i. 129, 133
Skyllis, i. 143
Sluter, Claux, ii. 65
Smirke, Robert, ii. 431
Snyders, Franz, ii. 421
Soddoma, ii. 224
Soerensen, ii. 455
Sohn, ii. 444
Solario, Andrea, ii. 223
— Antonio, ii. 189
Soller, ii. 427
Sosus, i. 200
Spagna, Giovanni lo, ii. 186

Spagnoletto, ii. 384
Spinello Aretino, ii. 89
Squarcione, Francesco, ii. 171
Stanfield, ii. 455
Steen, Jan, ii. 406
Steenwyk, H. van, ii. 419
Steinbach, Erwin von, ii. 28
Steinhäuser, ii. 437
Steinle, ii. 440
Steuben, ii. 448
Stevens, ii. 453
Stevyns, Thomas, ii. 321
Stone, ii. 454
Stoss, Veit, ii. 300, 310
Strack, ii. 427
Street, ii. 431
Stuerbout, Dirk, ii. 339
Stüler, ii. 427
Suardi, Bartolommeo, ii. 176
Sueur, Eustache le, ii. 402
Sunder, Lucas, ii. 365
Sustermann, Lambert, ii. 339
Swanefeld, Hermann, ii. 414
Syrlin, Jörg, the elder, ii. 301
— the younger, ii. 301

T

Tadema, ii. 453
Tafi, Andrea, i. 464
Tatti, Jacopo, ii. 127, 206
Tauriscus, i. 187
Telephanes, i. 194
Tenerani, ii. 437
Teniers, David, the elder, ii. 405
— the younger, ii. 405
Terburg, Gerhard, ii. 407
Theoderich von Prag, ii. 77
Theodoros, i. 120, 143
Theon, i. 199
Thomson, ii. 455
Thornhill, James, ii. 403
Thorpe, John, ii. 141
Thorwaldsen, ii. 432
Tidemand, ii. 445, 455
Tieck, Friedrich, ii. 434
Timanthes, i. 197
Timomachus, i. 200
Timotheus, i. 182
Tintoretto, ii. 289
Tischbein, ii. 401
Tisio, Benvenuto, ii. 267
Tiziano, ii. 277
Torell, Wilhelm, ii. 68
Torrigiano, Pietro, ii. 140, 321
Torriti, Jacobus, i. 463
Tribolo, ii. 204
Trinqueau, Pierre, ii. 137
Troyon, ii. 451
Trupin, Jean, ii. 318
Turner, ii. 454

U

Uccello, Paolo, ii. 159
Udine, Giov. da, ii. 255
Ussi, ii. 452

V

Vaga, Perino del, ii. 266
Vanucci, Pietro, ii. 182
Vargas, Luis de, ii. 364
Vasari, Giorgio, ii. 131, 237
Vautier, ii. 445
Vecellio, Tiziano, ii. 277
Veen, Octavius van, ii. 339
Veit, ii. 439
Velazquez, ii. 386
Velde, Willem van der, ii. 419
Venius, Otto, ii. 339
Venusti, Marcello, ii. 236
Verboeckhoven, ii. 453
Vernet, Horace, ii. 449
— Joseph, ii. 415
Verocchio, Andrea, ii. 152, 170
Veronese, Paolo, ii. 290
Vignola, ii. 131
Vignon, ii. 430
Vincenzi, Antonio, ii. 48
Vinci, Lionardo da, ii. 193, 212
Vinckebooms, David, ii. 416
Viollet-le-Duc, ii. 430
Vischer, Hermann, the elder, ii. 309
— — the younger, ii. 315
— Johann, ii. 315
— Peter, ii. 309
Vite, Timoteo della, ii. 266
Vitruvius, ii. 229

Vivarini, Antonio, ii. 96
— Bartolommeo, ii. 176
— Luigi, ii. 176
Vlieger, Simon de, ii. 419
Volterra, Daniele da, ii. 236
Voltz, Friedrich, ii. 444
Vouet, Simon, ii. 402
Vriendt, de, ii. 339
Vries, Adrian de, ii. 374

W

Wach, ii. 446
Wächter, ii. 438
Wagner, Martin, ii. 437
Waldmüller, ii. 446
Wappers, ii. 453
Wateau, Antoine, ii. 410
Waterhouse, ii. 431
Waterloo, Anton, ii. 417
Weber, ii. 448
Weenix, Johann, ii. 421
Wenzla, ii. 33
Werff, Adrian van der, ii. 409
Werner von Tegernsee, i. 452
West, Benjamin, ii. 403
Westmacott, ii. 437
Weyden, Rogier van der, the elder, ii. 333
— the younger, ii. 337
Whittridge, ii. 455
Widemann, ii. 436
Wilhelm von Innsbruck, i. 406

Wilhelm von Köln, ii. 80
— — Sens, ii. 38
Wilkie, ii. 454
Willems, ii. 453
Winterhalter, ii. 450
Witte, Peter de, ii. 374
Wohlgemuth, Michael, ii. 300, 355
Wolff, W., ii. 435
Wolvinus, i. 329
Wouwerman, Philipp, ii. 420
Wren, Christopher, ii. 141
Wurmser, Nicolaus, ii. 77
Wurzelbauer, Benedict, ii. 374
Wyatt, ii. 437
Wynants, Jan, ii. 417

Y

Yvon, ii. 451

Z

Zachtleven, Hermann, ii. 415
Zampieri, Domenico, ii. 379
Zeitblom, Barthol., ii. 344
Zeuxis, i. 196
Zevio, Aldighiero da, ii. 96
Ziebland, ii. 428
Zona, ii. 452
Zuccaro, Federigo, ii. 237
— Taddeo, ii. 237
Zumbusch, ii. 436
Zurbaran, Francisco, ii. 385

INDEX OF PLACES.

A

ABU (MOUNT)
Pagoda, i. 83
ABURY
Celtic Monument, i. 2
ADRIANOPLE
Mosque of Selim, i. 251
ÆGINA
Temple of Athene, i. 121, 147
AGRA
Mosques, i. 354
Mausoleum, i. 354
AGRIGENTUM
Temple, i. 118
Tomb of Theron, i. 131
AIX
Cathedral, ii. 367
Museum, ii. 438
AIX-LA-CHAPELLE
Minster, i. 303, 396 ; ii. 363
Town Hall, ii. 442
In the possession of Herr Suermondt, ii. 331
AIZANI
Temple of Jupiter, i. 132
AJUNTA
Caves, i. 86
ALA WERDI
Church, i. 356
ALBY
Cathedral, ii. 22
ALCANTARA
Bridge, i. 236
ALLAHABAD
Columns, i. 77
ALTENSTADT
Michaelskirche, i. 395
AMALFI
Cathedral, i. 410, 458
AMIENS
Cathedral, ii. 18, 59, 318
AMPHISSA
Gate, i. 100
AMSTERDAM
Town Hall, ii. 139, 373
Museum, ii. 397, 409, 419

ANGOULÊME
Cathedral, i. 419, 446
ANI
Cathedral, i. 356
ANTIPHELLUS
Tombs, i. 70
ANTWERP
Cathedral, ii. 23, 392
S. Charles, ii. 139
Academy, ii. 178, 331, 389
Town Hall, ii. 139
ANURAJAPURA
Thuparamaya-Dagop, i. 78
AOSTA
Triumphal Arch, i. 229
APHRODISIAS
Temple of Aphrodite, i. 132
AQUILEJA
Baptistry, i. 459
ARENDSEE
Monastery Church, i. 402
AREZZO
Cathedral, ii. 82
S. Francesco, ii. 170
ARGOS
Cyclopean Walls, i. 100
ARLES
S. Trophime, i. 417, 446
ARUNDEL CASTLE
Gallery, ii. 349
ARVAD
Phœnician Remains, i. 63
ASCHAFFENBURG
Collegiate Church, ii. 314, 315
ASSISI
S. Francesco, ii. 46, 89
ASSOS
Temple Remains, i. 120, 143
ATHENS
Old Parthenon, i. 119
Erechtheion, i. 125, 169
Temple of Nice, i. 122, 179
Parthenon, i. 122, 161

Propylæa, i. 123
Acropolis, i. 127
Temple of Ilissus, i. 122
Temple of Theseus, i. 122, 160
Temple of Jupiter, i. 119, 237
Monument of Lysicrates, i. 130, 179
Monument of Thrasyllus, i. 130
Tower of the Wind, i. 130
Arch of Hadrian, i. 236
Museum, i. 145, 159
AUGSBURG
Fountain, ii. 374
Cathedral, i. 385, 440
Museum, ii. 345, 347
Maximil.-Mus., ii. 304
AUTUN
Porte d'Arroux, i. 241
Cathedral, i. 419 ; ii. 438
AUXERRE
Cathedral, ii. 21
AVANTIPUR
Temple, i. 88
AVIGNON
Cathedral, i. 416
AZAY-LE-RIDEAU
Chateau, ii. 137

B

BADEN
Trinkhalle, ii. 429
BADENWEILER
Baths, i. 242
BALBEK
Roman Remains, i. 242
BAMBERG
Cathedral, i. 395, 440, 445 ; ii. 61, 307, 310
Upper Parish Church, ii. 301
Library, i. 450
BAMIYAN
Rock Reliefs, i. 84
BAQUZA
Basilica, i. 292

BARCELONA
  Cathedral, ii. 54
  S. Maria del Mar, ii. 54
  S. Pablo, i. 431
BARI
  Cathedral, i. 410
BAR LE DUC
  S. Etienne, ii. 319
BARNAK
  Church, ii. 321
BASEL
  Minster, i. 395; ii. 443, 446
  Museum, ii. 347, 350, 352, 355
BASSÆ
  Temple of Apollo, i. 128, 174
BATALHA
  Monastery Church, ii. 54
BAUG
  Caves, i. 79, 86
BEAUNE
  Hospital, ii. 333
BEAUVAIS
  Cathedral, ii. 19
BEDJAPUR
  Buildings, i. 355
BEHIOH
  Basilica, i. 292
BENEVENTUM
  Triumphal Arch, i. 236
BENI-HASSAN
  Tombs, i. 20, 36
BERGAMO
  Cathedral, ii. 286
  S. Bartolommeo, ii. 286
  S. Bernardino, ii. 286
  S. Spirito, ii. 286
BERLIN
  Cathedral, ii. 315
  Church of S. Dorothy, ii. 433
  Architectural School, ii. 427
  Royal Castle, ii. 143, 234, 374
  New Guard-house, ii. 427
  Opera House, ii. 435
  Theatre, ii. 427
  Arsenal, ii. 143, 374
  Statues, ii. 434
  Friedrich's Monument, ii. 434
  Statue of Fr. Wilhelms III., ii. 435
  Monument of the Great Elector, ii. 374
  Castle Bridge, ii. 435
  Wilhelmsplatz, ii. 433
  Library, i. 452
  Museum, i. 146, 214, 312; ii. 162, 170, 174, 176, 178, 179, 181, 187, 189, 206, 236, 240, 244, 247, 255, 273, 285, 288, 312, 314, 328, 332, 333, 337,

338, 340, 344, 352, 381, 389, 395, 398, 406, 415, 418, 419, 420, 427
  New Museum, i. 312; ii. 443
BESANÇON
  Cathedral, ii. 240
BETHLEHEM
  Church of the Virgin, i. 293
BEVERLEY
  Minster, ii. 40
BHILSA
  Topes, i. 79
BISUTUN
  Rock Reliefs, i. 61
BITETTO
  Cathedral, i. 410
BITONTO
  Cathedral, i. 410
BLAUBEUREN
  Monastery Church, ii. 298, 302, 344
BLENHEIM
  Residence, ii. 249, 393
BLOIS
  Chateau, ii. 137
BOGHAZ-KOEI
  Rock Reliefs, i. 72
BOLOGNA
  S. Cecilia, ii. 188
  S. Domenico, i. 462; ii. 198, 205
  S. Giacomo Maggiore, i. 188
  S. Maria della Vita, ii. 205
  S. Michele in Bosco, ii. 378
  S. Petronio, ii. 48, 145, 189, 204, 205
  S. Pietro, ii. 205
  Loggia de' Mercanti, ii. 50
  Pal. Bevilacqua, ii. 121
  Pal. Fava, ii. 121
  Pal. Gualandi, ii. 121
  Fountain, ii. 210
  Museum, i. 213
  Pinakothek, ii. 188, 189, 261, 378, 381
BONN
  Münster, i. 392
  Monument to Beethoven, ii. 435
BOPPARD
  Carmelite Church, ii. 308
BORGO S. SEPOLCRO
  Church, ii. 170
BORGUND
  Church, ii. 428
BORO BUDOR
  Temple, i. 89
BOURGES
  Cathedral, i. 447; ii. 18, 73, 319
  House of Jacques Cœur, ii. 22

BRANDENBURG
  Cathedral, i. 402
  Katharinenkirche, ii. 35
BRAUWEILER
  Chapter Hall, i. 457
  Monastery Church, ii. 71
BREISACH
  Minster, ii. 298
BRESCIA
  Old Cathedral, ii. 286
  S. Clemente, ii. 287
  S. Maria de' Miracoli, ii. 121
  S. Nazaro e Celso, ii. 287
  Pal. Communale, ii. 121
BRESLAU
  Cathedral, ii. 35, 310
  Elisabethkirche, ii. 35
  Kreuzkirche, ii. 68
BRIEG
  Piastenschloss, ii. 141
BROU
  Church, ii. 318
BRUGES
  Frauenkirche, ii. 198, 320
  Jakobskirche, ii. 320
  Johannes-Hospital, ii. 335
  Halle, ii. 25
  Palace of Justice, ii. 320
  Town Hall, ii. 25
  Academy, ii. 331, 332, 337
BRUNSWICK
  Cathedral, i. 394, 457
  Town Hall, ii. 35
  Lessing Monument, ii. 430
  Museum, ii. 400, 409
BRUSSELS
  Cathedral, ii. 23
  Town Hall, ii. 26
  Museum, ii. 321, 340, 392
BULACH
  Church, ii. 429
BURGOS
  Cathedral, ii. 51

C

CAEN
  S. Etienne, i. 421
  S. Pierre, ii. 136
  S. Trinité, i. 421
CAGLI
  Church of the Dominicans, ii. 187
CAHORS
  Cathedral, i. 419
CAIRO
  Mausoleums, i. 341
  Mosque Amru, i. 340
  Mosque Barkauk, i. 341
  Mosque Hassan, i. 341
  Mosque Ibn Tulun, i. 340
  Mosque el Moyed, i. 341
CALCAR
  Church, ii. 299, 342
CAMBRIDGE
  Fitzwilliam-Mus., ii. 284

CANTERBURY
  Cathedral, i.425; ii. 39, 68
CAPRAROLA
  Castle, ii. 131
CARLSRUHE
  Kunsthalle, ii. 182, 429
  Theatre, ii. 429
  Orangery, ii. 429
CASSEL
  Library, ii. 75
  Gallery, ii. 397, 399, 400
CASTELFRANCO
  Parish Church, ii. 275
CASTELLACCIO
  Tomb Façades, i. 208
CASTIGLIONE
  Church, ii. 159
  ˙Baptistry, ii. 159
CEFALÙ
  Cathedral, i. 409
CERE
  Etruscan Tombs, i. 208
CEYLON
  Ruanvelli-Dagop, i. 78
CHAMBORD
  Château, ii. 137
CHANDRAVATI
  Pagodas, i. 83
CHAQQA
  Basilica, i. 291
CHARTRES
  Cathedral, i. 447 ; ii. 18,
    39, 73, 318
CHATSWORTH
  Residence, ii. 331
CHEMNITZ
  Monastery Church, ii. 33
CHENONCEAUX
  Château, ii. 137
CHILLAMBRUM
  Pagoda, i. 82
CHIUSI
  Etruscan Wall Paintings,
    i. 213
CHUR
  Cathedral, ii. 299
CLAUSEN
  Church, ii. 299
CLERMONT
  N. Dame du Port, i.
    418
CLERMONT-FERRAND
  Cathedral, ii, 21
CLUNY
  Abbey Church, i. 418
COLBERG
  Marienkirche, ii. 35, 71
COLMAR
  Church of St. Martin, ii.
    343
  Museum, ii. 343
COLOGNE
  Cathedral, i. 448 ; ii. 13,
    27, 63, 68, 71, 73, 81,
    373
  Church of the Apostles, i.
    390
  ˙Maria im Cap'tol, i. 390

COLOGNE
  St. Geréon, i. 390
  St. Martin, i. 390
  St. Peter's, ii. 393
  Town Hall, ii. 141
COMBURG
  Abbey Church, i. 442
COMO
  Cathedral, ii. 157
COMO, LAKE
  Villa Sommariva, ii. 432
CONQUES
  Church, i. 446
CONSTANCE
  Cathedral, i, 385
CONSTANTINOPLE
  Church of the Virgin Mary,
    i. 301
  St. Sergius and Bacchus,
    i. 296
  S. Sophia, i. 297, 322,
    328, 351
  Obelisk of Theodosius, i.
    306
  Mosque of Soliman, i. 351
  Tomb of Soliman, i. 352
COPENHAGEN
  Frauenkirche, ii. 432
CORDOVA
  Mosque, i. 343
CORINTH
  Temple Remains, i. 119
CORNETO
  Etruscan Tombs, i. 208
CORTONA
  Churches, ii. 170
CUSSA
  City Walls, i. 209
CRACOW
  Frauenkirche, ii. 300
  Cathedral, ii. 315
CREGLINGEN
  Pilgrims' Church, ii. 298
CYPRUS
  Phœnician Remains, i. 63

D

DAMASCUS
  Mosque, i. 339
DANTZIG
  Marienkirche, ii. 35, 335
  Artushof, ii. 36
DARMSTADT
  Museum, i. 263
  In Possession of the Prin-
    cess Elizabeth, ii. 348
DEIR ABU FÂNEH
  Basilica, i. 291
DEIR SETA
  Basilica, i. 292
DELHI
  Mausoleum, i. 354
  Columns, i. 77
DELPHI
  Temple of Apollo. i. 119
DENDERAH
  Temple, i. 28

DENIS, ST.
  Church, ii. 17, 67, 319
DERRI
  Rocky Tombs, i. 27
DEUZ
  Church, i. 448
DIJON
  Carthusian House, ii. 65,
    318
  Museum, ii. 66, 318
DJEBEL-RIHA
  Early Christian Monu-
    ments, i. 292
DOBBERAN
  Cistercian Church, ii. 35
DOGAN-LU
  Tomb of Midas, i. 69
DORTMUND
  Church of St. Peter's, ii.
    299
DRESDEN
  Museum, i. 150, 250 ; ii.
    188, 244, 255, 261, 265,
    266, 268, 271, 273, 276,
    277, 278, 281, 284, 292,
    331, 348, 352, 383, 388,
    393, 394, 395, 397, 399,
    400, 409, 412, 413, 416,
    417, 419, 420, 429, 435
  Renaissance Buildings, ii.
    143
  Theatre, ii. 429, 435
DRONTHEIM
  Cathedral, i. ·426 ; ii. 44

E

EDFU
  Temple, i. 28
EL BARAH
  Basilica, i. 292
ELEPHANTA
  Cave, i. 80, 86
ELEPHANTINE
  Temple, i. 27
ELEUSIS
  Temple of Demeter, i. 128
  Propylæa, i. 129
ELLORA
  Caves, i. 80, 86
ELLWANGEN
  Monastery Church, i. 395
ELTHAM
  Palace, ii. 44
EPHESUS
  Temple of Artemis, i. 120
ERFURT
  Cathedral, ii. 314
ESCURIAL
  Monastery, ii. 139
ESNEH
  Temple, i. 28
ESRA
  S. Georg, i. 291
ESSEN
  Monastery Church, i. 442,
    448

ESSLINGEN
Dionysiuskirche, ii. 73
Frauenkirche, ii. 32, 64,
303
ETSCHMIAZIN
Monastery Church, i. 356
EXETER
Cathedral, ii. 41, 44
Chapter House, ii. 44
EXTERNSTONE
Stone Reliefs, i. 443

F

FAURNDAU
Church, i. 385
FERRARA
Cathedral, ii. 205
Pal. de' Diamanti, ii. 121
Pal. Scrofa, ii. 121
FIESOLE
Badia, ii. 115
FLIESSEM
Rom. Villa, i. 242
FLORENCE
Cathedral, ii. 47, 84, 113,
146, 148, 149, 204, 207,
210
Clock Tower, ii. 47, 84
S. Ambrogio, ii. 165
S. Annunziata, ii. 118,
242, 244
S. Apostoli, ii. 148
Badia, ii. 164
Baptisterium, i. 407 ; ii.
84, 145, 150, 194
S. Croce, ii. 89, 115, 152
Innocenti, ii. 115, 148
S. Lorenzo, ii. 114, 129,
150, 202, 203
S. Marco, ii. 95, 208, 239
S. Maria del Carmine, ii.
89, 159, 163
S. Maria Novella, i. 465 ;
ii. 89, 95, 117, 151, 152,
159, 163, 167
S. Maria Nuova, ii. 238,
240, 333
S. Miniato, i. 407 ; ii. 151
S. Onofrio, ii. 186
Or S. Micchele, ii. 85,
145, 150, 152
S. Salvi, ii. 242
Comp. dello Scalzo, ii.
242, 244
S. Spirito, ii. 115, 194
S. Trinità, ii. 167
Academy, i. 465 ; ii. 94,
96, 168, 204, 214, 238
Pal. Pitti, ii. 115, 184,
186, 214, 227, 236, 239,
242, 248, 250, 258, 259,
261, 262, 276, 285, 382,
388, 395, 412, 416
Uffizi, i. 180, 210 ; ii. 131,
145, 147, 149, 150, 162,

FLORENCE
170, 190, 202, 204, 207,
210, 214, 226, 236, 237,
238, 239, 240, 243, 244,
249, 262, 269, 284, 285,
360, 386, 395
Bargello, ii. 50
Loggia de' Lanzi, ii. 50,
86, 150, 205, 210
Pal. Vecchio, ii. 50, 199,
211, 217, 228
Piazza del Granduca, ii.
210
Pal. Buonarroti, ii. 198
Pal. Gondi, ii. 116
Pal. Pandolfini, ii. 126
Pal. Riccardi, ii. 115
Pal. Rucellai, ii. 117
Pal. Strozzi, ii. 116
FONTAINEBLEAU
Château, ii. 137, 319
FRANKFORT A. M.
Städel Museum, ii. 236,
287, 331, 332, 334, 345,
367, 440
In possession of Hrn.
Bethmann, ii. 432
In possession of Hrn.
Brentano, ii. 367
FREIBERG
Cathedral, i. 444 ; ii. 303,
317, 374
FREIBURG
Minster, ii. 28, 62, 73,
347
FREISING
Cathedral, i. 395
Palace, ii. 143
FÜNFKIRCHEN
Cathedral, i. 387

G

GALLEN, S.
Library, i. 304, 327
GEBWEILER
Church, i. 396
GELATHI
Church, i. 356
GELNHAUSEN
Parish Church, i. 392
GENEVA
Cathedral, ii. 22
GENOA
Cathedral, ii. 152, 194
S. Maria da Carignano,
ii. 133, 368
S. Stefano, ii. 265
Pal. Ducale, ii. 132
Pal. Brignole, ii. 395
Pal. Andrea Doria, ii.
266
Pal. Sauli, ii. 132
Pal. Spinola, ii. 132
Pal. of the University, ii.
135

GENOA
Gallery of Marchese d
Negro, i. 182
GERNRODE
Monastery Church, i. 380
GERONA
Cathedral, ii. 54
GHENT
S. Bavo, ii. 328, 332
Town Hall, ii. 139
GIACOMO, S.
Church, ii. 187
GILLES, S.
Church, i. 417
GIMIGNANO, S.
S. Agostino, ii. 166
GIRSCHEH
Tombs, i. 27
GIZEH
Pyramids, i. 18
Sphinx Colossus, i. 18
Tombs, i. 19
GLOUCESTER
Cathedral, i. 425 ; ii. 66
GMÜND (SCHWÄB)
Cross Church, ii. 65, 298
GNESEN
Cathedral, i. 441
GÖRLITZ
Peter-Paulskirche, ii. 33
GORKUM
Church, ii. 72
GOZZO
Phœnician Remains, i. 63
GRANADA
Alhambra, i. 346, 351
Generalife, i. 350
GRANDSON
Church, i. 419
GREIFSWALD
Marienkirche, ii. 299
GRÖNINGEN
Church, i. 443
GROTTA FERRATA
Church, ii. 379
GUADALAXARA
Pal. del Infantado, ii. 139
GUATUSCO
Teocalli, i. 4
GURK
Cathedral, i. 387

H

HAGENAU
St. Georg, i. 385
HAGUE
Museum, ii. 397
HALBERSTADT
Cathedral, ii. 29
Liebfrauenkirche, i. 444
HALICARNASSUS
Mausoleum, i. 132, 177
HALLE
Market Church, ii. 33
Ulrichskirche, ii. 300

HAMPTON COURT
Palace, ii. 175
HANOVER
Erlöserkirche, ii. 429
Town Hall, ii. 36
New Buildings, ii. 429
In possession of IIm. Fr.
Hahn, i. 312
HÂSS
Basilica, i. 292
HATTON LE CHÂTEL
Church, ii. 319
HAVELBERG
Cathedral, ii. 35
HECHINGEN
Church, ii. 315
HEIDELBERG
Church of the Holy Ghost,
ii. 304
Château, ii. 141
HEIDINGSFELD
Church, ii. 307
HEILBRONN
Kilianskirche, ii. 298
HEILIGENKREUZ
Abbey Church, i. 397
HEISTERBACH
Abbey Church, i. 391
HELIOPOLIS (EGYPTIAN)
Obelisk, i. 20
HELIOPOLIS (SYRIAN)
Roman Buildings, i. 242
HERCULANEUM
Ancient, i. 251
HERFORD
Minster, i. 394
HERSFELD
Monastery Church, i. 385
HILDESHEIM
Cathedral, i. 365, 440,
442, 444, 448
S. Godehard, i. 365
S. Michael, i. 384, 444,
457
HILLAH
Remains, i. 40
HIRSCHAU
Church, i. 385
HITTERDAL
Church, i. 428

J

JAK, ST.
Church, i. 399
JERICHO
Monastery Church, i. 211
JERUSALEM
Tombs, i. 65, 133
Temple Walls, i. 65
Church of Holy Sepul-
chre, i. 293
Aksa-Mosque, i. 339
Sachra-Mosque, i. 296
IGEL
Tomb of the Secundines,
i. 242

INNSBRUCK
Church, ii. 316
IPSAMBUL
Tombs, i. 27
JUGGERNAUT
Pagoda, i. 82

K

KALAT SEMA'N
Basilica, i. 292
Church of St. Simon Sty-
lites, i. 292
KARLI
Cave, i. 79
KARLSBURG
Cathedral, i. 399
KARLSTEIN
Fortress, ii. 36, 72
KARNAK
Temple, i. 23
Temple of Chensu, i. 23
KATHMANDU
Temple, i. 88
KEHLHEIM
Befreiungshalle, ii. 428
KHERBET-HASS
Basilica, i. 292
KHORSABAD
Palace Ruins, i. 48
KINGSTON LACY
Palace, ii. 276
KIRCHLINDE
Church, ii. 299
KLOSTER-NEUBURG
Church, i. 448
KÖNIGSFELDEN
Monastery Church, ii. 74
KÖNIGSLUTTER
Abbey Church, ii. 395
KOMMODU
Temple, i. 90
KUJJUNDSCHIK
Palace Ruins, i. 48
KURNA
Temple, i. 26
KUTTENBERG
Buildings, ii. 35
KYANEÄ-JAGHU
Monuments, i. 71

L

LAACH
Abbey Church, i. 389
LANDSHUT
Martinskirche, ii. 35
Palace, ii. 143
Trausnitz, ii. 143
LAON
Cathedral, ii. 18
LAUSANNE
Cathedral, ii. 22
LAVENHAM
Church, ii. 43

LEON
Cathedral, ii. 53, 74
S. Isidoro, i. 430
LERIDA
Cathedral, i. 431
LEYDEN
Museum, i. 210
Town Hall, ii. 341
LICHFIELD
Cathedral, ii. 41
LIÉGE
S. Barthélemy, i. 441
S. Jacques, ii. 139
LILIENFELD
Abbey Church, i. 398
LIMBURG (A. D. HARDT)
Monastery Church, i. 385
LIMBURG (A. D. LAHN)
Cathedral, i. 392
LIMOGES
Cathedral, ii. 21
LIMYRA
Rock Façade, i. 71
LINCOLN
Cathedral, ii. 41, 66
LONDON
St. Paul's, ii. 141
Temple Church, ii. 66
Westminster Abbey, ii.
39, 43, 68, 140, 322
Brit. Museum, ii. 48, 71,
146, 163, 164, 182, 258,
270, 271, 347
National Gallery, ii. 90,
159, 162, 165, 166, 170,
174, 178, 184, 218, 219,
249, 255, 273, 282, 331,
342, 400, 409, 413, 419
Bridgewater Gallery, ii.
259, 283
Kensington Palace, ii. 236
Lambeth Palace, ii. 352
Covent Garden Theatre,
ii. 431
Houses of Parliament, ii.
431
Whitehall, 141
In possession of Mr. La-
bouchère, ii. 234
In possession of the Duke
of Wellington, ii. 386
LORETO
Casa Santa, ii. 196, 204
LORSCH
Portico, i. 305
LOUVAIN
St. Peter, ii. 339
Town Hall, ii. 26
LÜBECK
Cathedral, ii. 68, 336
Marienkirche, ii. 34, 440
LUCCA
Cathedral, i. 460; ii. 145,
152, 240
S. Frediano, i. 406; ii.
145
S. Micchele, i. 406
S. Romano, ii. 240

LUGANO
  Church of the Franciscans, ii. 221
LUKSOR
  Temple, i. 26
LUND
  Cathedral, i. 426
LYON
  Cathedral, ii. 21

M

MADRID
  Royal Museum, ii. 259, 260, 262, 283, 284, 286, 327, 363, 386, 389, 392, 393
MAGDEBURG
  Cathedral, ii. 26, 309
  Market-place, ii. 62
MAGNESIA
  Temple of Artemis, i. 132
MAHAMALAIPUR
  Pagoda, i. 82, 85
MAIDBRUNN
  Church, ii. 307
MAINZ
  Cathedral, i. 387; ii. 68, 304, 308, 373
MALTA
  Phœnician Remains, i. 63
MANS, LE
  Cathedral, i. 447; ii. 21, 73
MANTUA
  Castello di Corte, ii. 173
  Pal. de Te, ii. 127, 266
  Ducal Palace, ii. 266
MARBURG
  Elisabethkirche, ii. 27, 68
MARIENBURG
  Château, ii. 37
MARIENWERDER
  Cathedral, ii. 71
MARTAND
  Temple, i. 88
MAURSMÜNSTER
  Church, i. 397
MECCA
  Kaaba, i. 339
MEDINET-HABU
  Temple, i. 26
MEILLANT
  Château, ii. 22
MEISSEN
  Cathedral, ii. 31, 365
  Albrechtsburg, ii. 36
MELFORD
  Church, ii. 43
MEMPHIS
  Pyramid, i. 16
  Tombs, i. 16
MERDASHT
  Royal Tombs, i. 58
  Palace Ruins, i. 55
MEROË
  Pyramids, i. 28
MERSEBURG
  Cathedral, ii. 33

METHLER
  Church, i. 394, 457
MILAN
  Cathedral, ii. 48
  S. Ambrogio, i. 310, 324, 326, 414, 450
  S. Lorenzo, i. 303
  S. Maria delle Grazie, ii. 120, 222, 281
  Refectory, ii. 214
  S. M. di S. Satiro, ii. 120
  S. Maurizio, ii. 221
  S. Simpliciano, ii. 176
  Ambrosian Library, i. 326; ii. 214, 221
  Gallery of the Brera, ii. 96, 176, 182, 188, 215, 221, 222, 223, 224
  Ospedale Grande, ii. 120
MILETUS
  Temple of Apollo, i. 132
MINDEN
  Cathedral, ii. 31
MIRAFLORES
  Carthusian House, ii. 321
MODENA
  Cathedral, i. 413
  S. Domenico, ii. 206
  S. Francesco, ii. 206
  S. Giovanni decollato, ii. 157
  S. Maria pomposa, ii. 205
  S. Pietro, ii. 206
MOLFETTA
  Cathedral, i. 410
MONREALE
  Monastery Church, i. 409, 459, 463
MONTAUBAN
  Cathedral, ii. 438
  Museum, ii. 438
MONTE CASINO
  Cathedral, i. 458
MONTE FALCO
  Church, ii. 166
MONTE OLIVETO
  Monastery Church, ii. 169, 224
MOSKAU
  Church Wasili-Blagennoi, i. 358
MOSUL
  Ruins, i. 41
MUGEIR
  Ruins, i. 41
MÜHLHAUSEN (ON THE NECKAR) Vituskapelle, ii. 71, 77
MÜHLHAUSEN (in Thüringen)
  Marienkirche, ii. 31
MUNICH
  Aukirche, ii. 428, 442
  Basilica, ii. 428, 440
  Frauenkirche, ii. 35, 304, Court Chapel, ii. 440
  Ludwigskirche, ii. 428, 441

MUNICH
  Library, i. 450; ii. 74, 363, 428
  Glyptothek i. 144, 148; ii. 428, 441
  Pinakothek, i. 180; ii. 188, 249, 258, 264, 283, 333, 334, 335, 340, 341, 448, 347, 362, 387, 341, 345, 400, 416, 419, 292, 393
  Athenäum, ii. 429
  Gallery, i. 270
  Railway Station, ii. 428
  Feldherrnhalle, ii. 428
  National Museum, ii. 428
  Hofgarten Arcade, ii. 442
  Propyläa, ii. 421
  Government Buildings, ii. 429
  Renaissance Buildings, ii. 143
  Palace, ii. 374, 437
  Ruhmeshalle, ii. 421
  Bavaria, ii. 436
  University, ii. 428
MÜNSTER
  Cathedral, i. 393
  Lambertikirche, ii. 31
  Liebfrauenkirche, ii. 31
  Town Hall, ii. 35
  Private Buildings, ii. 35
MURBACH
  Abbey Church, i. 396
MURGHAB
  Tomb of Cyrus, i. 54
MYCENÆ
  Cyclopean Walls, i. 100
  Lion's Gate, i. 101, 141
  Treasure House of Atreus, i. 101
MYRA
  Tombs, i. 70, 71, 72

N

NANKING
  Porcelain Tower, i. 91
NAPLES
  Cathedral, ii. 156
  S. Chiara, ii. 86
  S. Domen Maggiore, ii. 190
  S. Giov. a Carbonara, ii. 86, 157
  S. Maria Incoronata, ii. 97
  S. Martino, ii. 384
  Monte Oliveto, ii. 152, 157
  S. Severino, ii. 190
  Catacombs, i. 276, 278
  Royal Palace, ii. 248
  Porta Capuana, ii. 118
  Triumphal Arch of K. Alfons, ii. 118
  Museum, i. 150, 199, 244, 90, 236, 27
NARBONNE
  Cathedral, ii. 21
NAUMBURG
  Cathedral, i. 394; ii. 62

NEMEA
Temple of Jupiter, i. 129
NENNIG
Rom. Villa, i. 242
Mosaics, i. 263
NEU DELHI
Buildings, i. 354
NIMRUD
Palace Ruins, i. 48
NISMES
Amphitheatre, i. 242
Temple, i. 237
NORCHIA
Tomb Façades, i. 207
NORWICH
Cathedral, i. 425
NOWGOROD
Cathedral, i. 441
NUREMBERG
Ægidienkirche, ii. 315
Frauenkirche, ii. 32, 64, 78
Church of St. Laurence, ii. 32, 63, 78, 300, 306, 374
Marthakirche, ii. 73
Church of S. Sebald, ii. 65, 79, 301, 305, 310
Stations, ii. 305
School of Art, ii. 314
Nassau House, ii. 36
Town Hall, ii. 143
Public Scales, ii. 306
Fountain of S. Laurence, ii. 371
Beautiful Fountains, ii. 64
In possession of Hrn. Holzschuher, ii. 359
NYMPHENBURG
Château, ii. 143

O

OFFENBACH
Castle, ii. 141
OLD CAIRO
Nile-Measurer, i. 340
OLYMPIA
Temple of Jupiter, i. 128, 175
OPPENHEIM
Church of S. Catharine, ii. 28, 73
ORANGE
Theatre, i. 242
Triumphal Arch, i. 241
ORLÉANSVILLE
Basilica, i. 290
ORVIETO
Cathedral, ii. 47, 83, 95, 168
OSNABRÜCK
Cathedral, i. 393, 441, 448
OTTMARSHEIM
Church, i. 396

OUDENARDE
Town Hall, ii. 26
OXFORD
Church of S. Mary's, ii. 43

P

PADERBORN
Cathedral, i. 394
PADUA
S. Antonio, ii. 96, 150, 155, 206, 209, 248
Capella, S. Giorgio, ii. 96
Church of the Eremitani, ii. 172
S. Giustina, ii. 128
S. Maria dell' Arena, ii. 87
Scuola del Carmine, ii. 279
Scuola del Santo, ii. 279
Pal. del Consiglio, ii. 121
Pal. Giustiniani, ii. 128
City Gates, ii. 128
PÆSTUM
Temple of Demeter, i. 131
Temple of Poseidon, i. 118
PALERMO
Cathedral, i. 410, 464
Martorana, i. 462
Palace Chapel, i. 408, 463
Kuba, i. 337
Zisa, i. 336
Museum, i. 144, 150 ; ii. 178
PALMA
Cathedral, ii. 54
PALMYRA
Roman Buildings, i. 242
PAPANTLA
Teocalli, i. 4
PARENZO
Cathedral, i. 464
PARIS
Notre.Dame, ii. 18, 58
Ste. Chapelle, ii. 20, 61, 73
S. Germaine des Près, ii. 449
Ste. Clotilde, ii. 436
S. Eustache, ii. 136
Ste. Madeleine, ii. 430
S. Séverin, ii. 449
S. Sulpice, ii. 449
S. Vincent de Paul, ii. 430, 449
Invalides, Les, ii. 137
Pantheon, ii. 137
Arc de l'Étoile, ii. 430
Chambre des Députés, ii. 449
École des beaux Arts, ii. 425, 430, 450
Maison du Pr. Napoléon, ii. 430
Hôtel de Cluny, i. 312, 438

PARIS
Hôtel de Ville, ii. 135, 430
Tuileries, ii. 137
Château, Madrid, ii. 137
Maison de François I., ii. 137
Library, i. 326, 327 ; ii. 74, 75, 332
Louvre, i. 29, 48, 63, 143, 145, 150, 164, 168, 175, 245, 247, 248, 258, 270; ii. 94, 164, 166, 174, 175, 178, 206, 217, 218, 219, 224, 240, 243, 249, 258, 259, 261, 264, 271, 273, 279, 281, 285, 293, 319, 320, 331, 352, 380, 388, 394, 395, 397, 398, 412, 415, 416, 430, 448, 449
Luxemburg, ii. 438, 449
Musée Napol. III., ii. 219
In possession of M. O. Mündler, ii. 97
PARMA
Cathedral, i. 415 ; ii. 270
Baptistry, i. 464
S. Giovanni, ii. 269
S. Paolo, ii. 269
Museum, ii. 271
PASARGADÆ
Monuments, i. 54
PAULINZELLE
Monastery Church, i. 384
PAVIA
Certosa, ii. 49, 119, 157, 176, 224
S. Micchele, i. 414
PAYACH
Temple, i. 88
PAYERNE
Church, i. 419
PEGU
Temple, i. 90
PERIGUEUX
S. Front, i. 419
PERSEPOLIS
Palace Ruins, i. 55, 59
PERUGIA
Cathedral, ii. 169
S. Agostino, ii. 185
S. Domenico, ii. 84
S. Francesco del Monte, ii. 184
S. Maria Nuova, ii. 182
S. Severo, ii. 249
Academy, ii. 186
Fountains, i. 462
Collegio del Cambio, ii. 184
Pal. Connestabile, ii. 248
PETERBOROUGH
Cathedral, i. 424
PETERSBURG
Imperial Collection of Antiques, i. 192
Hermitage, i. 265, 269,

PETERSBURG
i. 271; ii. 217, 259, 392, 393, 398, 400, 409, 413, 420
PETRA
Roman Remains, i. 242
PFAFFENHEIM
Church, i. 397
PHELLUS
Monuments, i. 70
PHIGALIA
Gate, i. 100
Temple of Apollo, i. 128
PHILÆ
Temple, i. 28
PIENZA
Renaissance Palaces, ii. 116
PISA
Cathedral, i. 405
Baptistry, i. 405, 460
Bell Tower, i. 406
Camposanto, ii. 47, 89, 91, 165
S. Francesco, ii. 89
PISTOJA
S. Andrea, ii. 83
Hospital, ii. 148
POLA
Temple, i. 229
POMPEII
Buildings, i. 230, 259, 261
POPULONIA
Walls, i. 209
POTSDAM
Friedenskirche, ii. 435
Palace, ii. 143
New Palace, ii. 143
Sanssouci, ii. 143
PRAGUE
Cathedral, i. 439, 442; ii. 29, 72
Wenzels Kapelle, ii. 72
Stift Strahof, ii. 360
Belvedere, ii. 141
Palaces, ii. 143
Gallery, ii. 77
Library of Prince Lobkowitz, ii. 76
Monument of Charles IV., ii. 435
PRATO
Cathedral, ii. 161
PRENZLAU
Marienkirche, ii. 35
PRIENE
Temple of Athene, i. 131
PTERIUM
Rock Reliefs, i. 72

Q

QUALB-LUZÉ
Basilica, i. 291
QUEDLINBURG
Church, i. 383, 437

R

RAMERSDORF
Chapel, ii. 71
RANGUN
Temple, i. 90
RATISBON
Cathedral, ii. 29, 73, 313
S. Emmeran, i. 386
S. Jakob, i. 386
Obermünster, i. 386
Stephanskapelle, i. 386
Walhalla, ii. 428
RATZEBURG
Cathedral, i. 402
RAVELLO
Cathedral, i. 410, 459
RAVENNA
S. Apollinare in Classe, i. 287, 323
S. Apollinare Nuovo, i. 322
S. Giovanni in Fonte, i. 317
S. Maria della Rotonda, i. 288
SS. Nazario e Celso, i. 3
S. Vitale, i. 296, 321
REMAGEN
Apollinariskirche, ii. 440
REUTLINGEN
Marienkirche, ii. 303
RHAMNUS
Temple of Nemesis, i. 128
RHEIMS
Cathedral, ii. 18, 59
S. Remy, ii. 18, 73
RIMINI
Triumphal Arch, i. 229
S. Francesco, ii. 118
RÖMHILD
Church, ii. 315
ROESKILDE
Cathedral, i. 426
ROME
Basilica of Constantine, i. 239
Basilica Julia, i. 226
Basilica Ulpia, i. 234
Arch of Constantine, i. 235, 253, 256
Arch of Goldschmiede, i. 238
Arch of Sept. Severus, i. 238, 256
Arch of Titus, i. 233, 253
Carcer Mamertinus, i. 209
Cloaca Maxima, i. 209
Colosseum, i. 233
Dioskuri of Monte Cavallo, i. 248
Forum of Augustus, i. 226
Forum of Nerva, i. 234
Forum of Trajan, i. 234

ROME
Tomb of Cäcilia Metella, i. 225
Tomb of Constantia, i. 241, 285, 317
Arch of Janus, i. 240
Statue of Augustus, i. 250
Mausoleum of Augustus, i. 229
Mausoleum of Hadrian, i. 236
Pantheon, i. 227
Porta Maggiore, i. 230
Porticus of Octavia, i. 228
Pyramid of Cestius, i. 229
Statue of M. Aurel., i. 251
Column of M. Aurel., i. 238, 256
Column of Trajan, i. 234, 253
Aurelian's Temple of the Sun, i. 238
Tabularium, i. 225
Temple of Antoninus, i. 238
Temple of Castor and Pollux, i. 230
Temple of Fortuna Virilis, i. 225
Temple of Mars Ultor, i. 226
Temple of Saturnus, i. 240
Temple of Venus and Roma, i. 236
Temple of Vespasian, i. 233
Temple of Vesta, i. 238
Temple Remains of Dogana, i. 238
Theatre of Marcellus, i. 228
Baths of Caracalla, i. 238
Baths of Diocletian, i. 239
Baths of Titus, i. 233
Tullianum, i. 209
Via Appia, i. 224
Aqueduct of Claudius, i. 234
Catacombs, i. 276, 278, 313
S. Agnese Fuori, i. 285, 324
S. Agnese (Piazza Navona) ii. 135
S. Agostino, ii. 196, 206
S. Apostoli, ii. 175
S. Andrea della Valle, ii. 379
S. Cecilia, ii. 370
S. Clemente, i. 285, 414; ii. 159
S. Cosma e Damiano, i. 318
S. Costanza, i. 285, 317
S. Crisogono, i. 404
S. Croce in Gerusalemme, ii. 185

ROME
. S. Ponziano, Katakomben, i. 314
Kirche del Gesù, ii. 131, 372
S. Giovanni in Laterano, i. 404, 463
Baptisterium desLaterans, i. 286
S. Lorenzo Fuori, i. 278, 285
S. Luigi de' Francesi, ii. 379, 383
S. Maria degli Angeli, ii. 372
S. Maria dell' Anima, ii. 265
S. Maria in Araceli, i. 404; ii. 185
S. M. in Cosmedin, i. 404
S. M. di Loreto, ii. 373
S. M. Maggiore, i. 285, 463
S. M. Minerva, ii. 164, 201
S. M. della Pace, ii. 236, 255
S. M. del Popolo, ii. 153, 185, 194, 196, 256
S. M. in Trastevere, i. 404, 463
S. M. della Vittoria, ii. 368
S. Martino ai Monti, i, 404 ; ii. 413
S. Nereo ed Achilleo, i. 404
S. Onofrio, ii. 185, 214
S. Paolo Fuori, i. 283,285, 317, 458
S. Pietro in Vaticano, i. 285 ; ii. 129, 151, 153, 198, 210, 265, 371
S. Pietro in Vincoli, i. 285 ; ii. 199
S. Prassede, i. 285, 324
S. Pudenziana, i. 404
S. Sabina, i. 285
Church of Sapienza, . ii. 135
Capitoline Museum, i. 200
Scala Santa, i. 324
S. Stefano Rotondo, i. 285
S. Teodoro, i. 324
Church Trinità de' Monti, ii. 236
SS. Vincenzo ed Anastasio, i. 404
Capitol, i. 210; ii. 129
Lateran, i. 184, 306
Quirinal, ii. 175
Vatican, i. 210 ; ii. 124, 134, 163, 165, 167, 168, 175, 182, 228, 234, 245, 246, 248, 250, 254, 255, 260, 262, 268, 371, 380, 381, 383, 432

ROME
Pal. Barberini, ii. 134, 264
Casa Bartholdi, ii. 134
Pal. Borghese, ii. 378, 380
Pal. della Cancelleria, ii. 124
Pal. Colonna, ii. 395, 415
Pal. Dor a, ii. 386, 413
Pal. Farnese, i. 171 ; ii. 127, 378
Pal. Giraud, ii. 124
Pal. Massimi, i. 151 ; ii. 126
Pal. Rospigliosi, ii. 381
Pal. Sc arra, ii. 220, 263, 277, 383, 413
Pal. Spada, ii. 220, 381
Pal di Venez a, ii. 118
Villa Albani, ii. 266
Villa Borghese, i. 263 ; ii. 273
Villa Farnesina, ii. 125, 224, 256
Villa Papst Julius III., ii. 131
Villa Lante, ii. 265
Villa Ludovisi, i. 172, 177, 189 ; ii. 381
Villa Madama, ii. 127, 265
. Villa Massimi, ii. 439
Museo Kircheriano, i. 214
Porta Pia, ii. 129
ROSHFIM
Church, i. 396
ROSTOCK
Marienkirche, ii. 35
Monument of Blücher, ii. 433
ROTHENBURG
. Jakobskirche, ii. 298
ROUEN
Cathedral, ii. 20, 73, 318
S. Maclou, ii. 22
S. Ouen, ii. 22
Palais de Justice, ii. 22
RUEIHA
Basilica, i. 292
RUVO
Cathedral, i. 410

S

SADREE
Pagodas, i. 83
SALAMANCA
Cathedral, i. 430
SALERNO
Cathedral, i. 410, 458
SALISBURY
Cathedral, ii. 39
Stonehenge, i. 1
SALONA
Palace of Diocletian, i. 239

SALSETTE
Caves, i. 79
SALZBURG
St. Peter, i. 387
SAMOS
Temple of Hera, i. 120
SANCHI
Topes, i. 79, 84
SANTIAGO DE COMPOSTELLA
Cathedral, i. 429
SARDES
Tomb Mounds, i. 68
SARDINIA
Nuraghen, i. 207
SARONNO
Church, ii. 222, 223
S. SAVIN
Church, i. 454
SCHAFFHAUSEN
Minster, i. 385
SCHLEISSHEIM
Castle, ii. 143
SCHLESWIG
Cathedral, ii. 299
SCHLETTSTADT
Fideskirche, i. 397
SCHNEEBERG
Church, ii. 365
SCHÖNGRABERN
Church, i. 446
SCHWARZACH
Church, i. 385
SCHWARZRHEINDORF
Church, i. 371, 389, 455
SCHWERIN
Cathedral, ii. 35 68
Castle, ii. 141
SCHWERTE
Church, ii. 299
SECCAU
Cathedral, i. 387
SECUNDRA
Mausoleum, i. 354
SEGESTA
Temple, i. 118
SEGOVIA
S. Millan, i. 430
SELINUNT
Temple Remains, i. 117
Metope Reliefs, i. 144, 150
SESSA
Cathedral, i. 410
SEVILLA
Giralda, i. 345
Cathedral, ii. 54, 364, 389
Museum, ii. 385
SIENA
Cathedral, i. 465 ; ii. 47, 150, 185
S. Agostino, ii. 226
S. Bernardino, ii. 225
S. Cater na, ii. 226
S. Domenico, ii. 226
S. Francesco, ii. 226
S. Giovanni, ii. 146
S. Spirito, ii. 226

SIENA
  Piazza del Campo, ii. 145
  Pal. Buonsignori, ii. 50
  Pal. Pubblico, ii. 50, 93, 226
  Renaissance Pal., ii. 166
  Academy, ii. 93
SION
  N.-Dame de Velère, i. 419
SIPYLUS
  Niobe Relief, i. 142
SMYRNA
  Tomb of Tantalus, i. 67
SOEST
  Cathedral, i. 393
  Wiesenkirche, ii. 31
  Thomaskirche, ii. 71
  Nicolaikapelle, i. 457
  Solothurn, ii. 349
SPALATO
  Palace of Diocletian, i. 239
SPELLO
  Cathedral, ii. 185
SPIRES
  Cathedral, i. 387 ; ii. 440
SPOLETO
  Cathedral, ii. 187
  Pal. Pubblico, ii. 186
STARGARD
  Marienkirche, ii. 35
STENDAL
  Cathedral, ii. 35
  Marienkirche, ii. 35
  Gate, ii. 36
STETTIN
  Theatre Square, ii. 432
STRALSUND
  Marienkirche, ii. 35
  Nikolaikirche, ii. 68
STRASSBURG
  Minster, i. 397 ; ii. 28, 62, 73, 303
  Stephanskirche, i. 397
  Thomaskirche, ii. 369
  Library, i. 451
STUTTGART
  Leonhardskirche, ii. 303
  Stiftskirche, ii. 303, 374
  Library, i. 451 ; ii. 75
  Museum, ii. 427, 443
  Gallery, ii. 344
  Old Palace, ii. 141
  New Pleasure House, i. 141
  Royal Villa, ii. 430
  Polytechnic, ii. 432
  Buildings, ii. 424
SUSA
  Arch, i. 229

T

TABRIZ
  Mosque, i. 352
TADMOR
  Roman Buildings, i. 242

TAFKA
  Basilica, i. 290
TAKT-I-SULEIMAN
  Ruins, i. 53
TANGERMÜNDE
  Town Hall, i. 36
TARQUINII
  Etruscan Tombs, i. 208, 213
TARRAGONA
  Cathedral, i. 431
TEFACED
  Basilica, i. 291
TEGEA
  Temple of Athene, i. 129
TEHUANTEPEC
  Teocalli, i. 4
TELMISSUS
  Monuments, i. 70, 71
TEOS
  Temple of Bacchus, i. 132
THANN
  Church, ii. 65
THEBEN (EGYPTIAN)
  Temple Ruins, i. 24, &c.
  Royal Tombs, i. 26, 33
TIAGUANACO
  Colossal Head, i. 6
TIEFENBRONN
  Church, ii. 298, 343
TIND
  Church, i. 428
TIRYNS
  Cyclopean Walls, i. 100
TISCHNOWITZ
  Monastery Church, i. 399
TIVOLI
  Temple of Vesta, i. 225
  Villa of Hadrian, i. 236
TODI
  Walls, i. 209
TOLEDO
  Cathedral, ii. 52, 74, 139, 321
  S. Joh. Bapt., ii. 321
TORO
  Monastery Church, i. 430
TOULOUSE
  S. Sernin, i. 417
TOURNAY
  Monuments, ii. 65
TOURNUS
  S. Phillibert, ii. 72
TOURS
  Cathedral, ii. 21, 73, 319
TRANI
  Cathedral, i. 410, 459
TREBITSCH
  Abbey Church, i. 398
TREVISO
  Monte di Pietà, ii. 276
TRIBSEES
  Church, ii. 70
TREVES
  Ampitheatre, i. 242
  Basilica, i. 242
  Imp. Palace, i. 242
  Porta nigra, i. 237

TREVES
  Cathedral, i. 303, 385 ; ii. 308
  Liebfrauenkirche, ii. 27
TROJA
  Cathedral, i. 410
TROYES
  Cathedral, ii. 22
  S. Urbain, ii. 22
TÜBINGEN
  Monastery Church, ii. 374
TUDELA
  Cathedral, i. 431
TURIN
  Palazzo delle Torri, i. 303
  Gallery, ii. 223, 335, 391, 395
TURMANIN
  Basilica, i. 292

U

UEJÜK
  Portal, i. 72
ULM
  Minster, ii. 29, 298, 301, 302, 303
  Market, ii. 301, 303
UPSALA
  Cathedral, ii. 44
URACH
  Church, ii. 303
  Castle, ii. 143
  Market, ii. 303
URBINO
  Cathedral, ii. 170
  S. Agata, ii. 332
  Ducal Palace, ii. 121
URNES
  Church, i. 428
UTRECHT
  Cathedral, ii. 23
UXMAL
  Mexican Monuments, i. 5

V

VAGHARSCHABAD
  Church, i. 356
VALENCIA
  Cathedral, ii. 53
VARALLO
  Minoritenkirche, ii. 222
VEJI
  Etrusc. Wall Paintings, i. 213
VENICE
  S. Marco, i. 329, 411, 458, 462 ; ii. 156, 208
  Campanile, ii. 209
  Abazzia, ii. 154
  S. Giorgio Magg., ii. 132
  S. Giov. Crisostomo, ii. 155, 179, 236
  S. Giov. e Paolo, ii. 152, 154, 155, 156, 280
  S. Giuliano, ii. 209

VENICE
Jesuit Church, ii. 281
S. Maria Formosa, ii. 277
S. Maria de' Frari, ii. 154, 155, 177, 179, 281
S. Maria della Salute, ii. 290
Kirche del Redentore, ii. 132
S. Salvatore, ii. 180, 209, 282
S. Sebastiano, ii. 291
S. Zaccharia, ii. 179
Scuola di S. Marco, ii. 119, 154, 155
Scuola di S. Rocco, ii. 119, 290
Academy, ii. 132, 178, 179, 180, 181, 276, 279, 282, 290, 293
Doge's Palace, ii. 50, 119, 154, 209, 290, 293
Library di S. Murco, ii. 127
Fabbriche Nuove, ii. 128
Procurazie Nuove, ii. 128
Zecca, ii. 128
Cà Doro, ii. 50
Pal. Corner, ii. 128
Pal. Foscari, ii. 50
Pal. Grimani, ii. 128
Pal. Manfrin, ii. 279
Pal. Pesaro, ii. 135
Pal. Pisani, ii. 50
Pal. Vendramin Colergi, ii. 118
VERCELLI
S. Cristoforo, ii. 223
S. Paolo, ii. 223
VERONA
S. Fermo, ii. 226
Mad. di Campagna, ii. 128
S. Zeno, i. 414, 457; ii. 174
Pal. del Consiglio, ii. 121
Pal. Bevilacqua, ii. 128
Pal. Canossa, ii. 128
Pal. Pompei, ii. 128
Gates, ii. 128
VERSAILLES
Palace, ii. 449
VERUELA
Abbey Church, i. 431
VÉZELAY
Church, i. 446
VICENZA
Basilica, ii. 132
Palace, ii. 132
Teatro Olimpico, ii. 132
VIENNA
St. Stephen's, i. 397; ii. 32, 303, 308

VIENNA
Altlerchenfelder Church, ii. 429, 440
Karl Borromäuskirche, ii. 143
Michaelskirche, i. 397
Votivkirche, ii. 429
Ambraser Gallery, ii. 205, 353
Gallery of Antiques, i. 192, 258
Belvedere, ii. 77, 178, 240, 249, 260, 262, 273, 277, 281, 283, 288, 331, 339, 341, 353, 360, 363, 367, 386, 392, 393, 419
Arsenal, ii. 429, 447
Evangel. Gymnas., ii. 424
Todesco Palace, ii. 424, 442
Renaissance Buildings, ii. 143
Monument of Archduke Charles, ii. 436
Fountain, ii. 374
Gallery Lichtenstein, ii. 393
Gallery Schönborn, ii. 399, 400
VILLENEUVE
Hospital, ii. 367
VOLKACH
Wallfahrtskapelle, ii. 306
VOLTERRA
City Gate, i. 209
VREDEN
Parish Church, ii. 299
VULCI
Cucumella, i. 207
Etruscan Tombs, i. 207

W
WARTBURG
Castle, ii. 444
WARWICK
Church, ii. 321
WECHSELBURG
Church, i. 444
WEIMAR
Church, ii. 365
Grand Ducal Gallery, ii. 215
Schiller and Göthe's Monument, ii. 435
In possession of Hrn. Schuchardt, ii. 362
WEISSENBACH
Church, ii. 299
WELLS
Cathedral, ii. 37, 40, 66
WERNIGERODE
Town Hall, ii. 36

WERTHEIM
Church, ii. 308
WIENHAUSEN
Monastery Church, ii. 71
WINCHESTER
Cathedral, i. 425
WINDSOR
Castle, ii. 205, 338, 352, 395, 416
WISMAR
Marienkirche, ii. 35
Fürstenhof, ii. 141
WITTENBERG
Castle Church, ii. 314, 315
Church, ii. 309, 365
Market, ii. 433
WOLFGANG, ST.
Monastery Church, ii. 299, 355
WORCESTER
Cathedral, i. 425; ii. 37, 40
WORMS
Cathedral, i. 389
WÜRZBURG
Cathedral, i. 385; ii. 308, 373
Frauenkirche, ii. 306
Neumünsterkirche, ii. 306
Château, ii. 143
WURKA
Ruins, i. 41

X
XANTEN
Monastery Church, ii. 299, 342
XANTHOS
Monuments, i. 70
Tomb of Harpagos, i. 71
XOCHICALCO
Teocalli, i. 4

Y
YORK
Cathedral, ii. 41, 74
YPERN
Hall, ii. 24

Z
ZAMORA
Cathedral, i. 430
Magdalen Church, i. 430
ZÜRICH
Minster, i. 396
Cloisters, i. 396
Polytechnic, ii. 429
ZWETL
Abbey Church, i. 398
ZWICKAU
Marienkirche, ii. 300, 356

LONDON : PRINTED BY
SPOTTISWOODE AND CO., NEW-STREET SQUARE
AND PARLIAMENT STREET